Pushkin's Button

Pushkin's Button

Serena Vitale

TRANSLATED FROM THE ITALIAN
BY ANN GOLDSTEIN AND JON ROTHSCHILD

FOURTH ESTATE • *London*

First published in Great Britain in 1999 by
Fourth Estate Limited
6 Salem Road
London W2 4BU

First published in 1995 by Adelphi edizioni s.p.a. Milano,
Italy as *Il bottone di Puškin*

1 3 5 7 9 10 8 6 4 2

A catalogue record for this book is available from the
British Library.

ISBN 1-85702-884-8

Typeset by Rowland Phototypesetting Ltd,
Bury St Edmunds, Suffolk
Printed in Great Britain by
Clays Ltd, St Ives plc, Bungay, Suffolk

Acknowledgments

Baron Claude de Heeckeren, who died in 1996, allowed me to study his family archive. I am infinitely grateful to his memory for the trust he generously accorded me, for the hospitality and friendship he showed me, for the extraordinary stories he shared with me, and for the support that he and his wife, Janine, gave my research. Even more, I thank them both for their trust, their friendship, their extraordinary stories.

I want to express my gratitude to Baron and Baroness von Poschinger-Bray, who welcomed me to Irlbach Castle, facilitating my work in every way, and to the Count and Countess de Nicolay, who welcomed me to Malesherbes Castle, permitting me to study a part of the rich archive preserved there.

With their kindness, availability, and knowledge, the director and the entire staff of the RGADA in Moscow were immensely helpful to me.

In deciphering the hard-to-read parts of certain manuscripts I made use of instruments kindly put at my disposal by the Manuscript Section of the Bibliothèque Nationale in Paris and by the Polizia Scientifica of Milan, to whom my thanks are due.

To Sergio Ferrero, the first loving, attentive reader of the book, I owe a lot.

Luciano Foà and Roberto Calasso gave me invaluable advice.

For the English-language edition, my thanks to Elisabeth Sifton for the generous attention she devoted to this book; to Ann Goldstein and to Jon Rothschild for their fine work on the translation; to Clarence Brown for his wise counsel; and to Nina Khrushcheva for her invaluable help. I should add that for this edition, I have used Vladimir Nabokov's translation of *Eugene Onegin* for all passages quoted from that poem.

Serena Vitale

Contents

Author's Note

Russian names of French and German descent (especially those from the Baltic nobility) are given in their original spelling (except in cases in which there is no source – including Pushkin's own writings in French). In the text as in the Index, however, the patronymics of these persons have been preserved as they appear in Russian sources (in order to facilitate the recognition of family relations). In aristocratic names of German origin the particle "von," which had fallen into disuse among the Russified nobility, has been dropped except where it appears in the signature of a person who is quoted.

All dates (except those of the deaths of Catherine Goncharova and Georges d'Anthès, those on pages 9–11, and those indicated as "new style") are given according to the Julian calendar, which Russia abolished after the October Revolution and which was twelve days behind the Gregorian calendar used in the West.

The date of a letter is given in brackets when it does not appear in the original; the place is not given when sender and addressee are both in Petersburg.

All words and phrases in quotation marks are quotations; the sources can be found in the Notes at the end of the book.

All the poems and prose fragments that appear without attribution in Chapter 6, "Pushkin's Button," are from Pushkin.

To avoid misunderstanding and confusion in a very tangled

matter, Georges d'Anthès is referred to as "Georges d'Anthès" throughout, even after he officially became "Georges de Heeckeren" and signed himself thus, and was often so called by others and so referred to in official documents, letters, etc. To be precise: from May 1836 until his death, Georges d'Anthès took for his cognomen "de Heeckeren"; later, some of his descendants chose to call themselves "de Heeckeren-d'Anthès."

The critic: investigator and lover . . .
— Marina Tsvetayeva

I am one of those students of Pushkin who believe that his family tragedy should not be discussed. Surely by making it taboo we would be fulfilling the poet's wishes. And if despite what I've said I nevertheless take on the subject, it's only because so many truly outrageous lies have been written about it, and readers are so willing to believe the first thing they come across . . . If, thanks to a long series of documents that have come to light, these lies can now be destroyed, it is our duty to destroy them.
— Anna Akhmatova

Dispatches from St. Petersburg

... Russia has just lost its greatest man of literature, Mr. Alexandre Pouschkin, the most famous Poet it has ever had. He died at the age of thirty-seven, at the apex of his career, after being gravely wounded in a duel. The details of this catastrophe, unfortunately provoked by the dead man himself with a blindness and a kind of frenetic hatred well worthy of his Moorish origins, have for days been the sole talk of the town here in the capital. His opponent in the duel was his own brother-in-law, Mr. Georges de Heeckeren, French by birth and adopted son of Baron Heeckeren, the Dutch ambassador. The younger Mr. Heeckeren, formerly known as d'Antès, was an officer in the *"chevaliers gardes"* and had recently married Mrs. Pouschkin's sister. . . .

> *Maximilian von Lerchenfeld-Köfering,*
> *ambassador of the Kingdom of Bavaria*
> *January 29, 1837*

... A young Frenchman, Mr. Dantès, last year formally and legally adopted as son and heir by Baron Heeckeren, the Dutch ambassador, was joined in matrimony to Mrs. Puschkin's sister just a few days ago. Mrs. Puschkin, a woman of remarkable beauty, is the wife of the writer Mr. Puschkin, who has won well-deserved fame in Russian literature, mainly as the author of works in verse. . . . A boundlessly jealous man of a most violent character, he was driven to madness at the suspicion of a secret understanding between his wife and brother-in-law, and vented his rage in a letter whose crudely offensive language made a duel inevitable. . . .

> *Otto von Blome,*
> *ambassador of the Kingdom of Denmark*
> *January 30, 1837*

. . . This duel is considered a public catastrophe by all classes, especially the middle class, both because Mr. Pouchkine's poetry was so popular and because national sensibilities have been stung by the circumstance that a Frenchman, an officer in government service, has robbed Russia of its best poet. It was, moreover, barely two weeks ago that the officer in question was wedded to Pouchkine's wife's sister, who lived in the home of the deceased, and it is said that the officer contracted the matrimonial bond precisely so as to avert suspicion and to lend legitimacy to his frequent visits to the Pouchkine house. Duels are quite rare here, and Russian law stipulates the death penalty for participants. . . .

> *George Wilding di Butera e Radoli,*
> *ambassador of the Kingdom of Naples and the Two Sicilies*
> *February 2, 1837*

. . . Mr. Pouchkinn had a young and beautiful wife who had already given him four children; irritation with Mr. Danthées, who pursued this young woman with his attentions, led to the challenge that proved fatal to Mr. Pouchkinn. He lived for thirty-six hours after being mortally wounded. In this circumstance the Emperor has exhibited the great magnanimity of which His entire character bears the stamp. Very late in the evening His Majesty learned that Mr. Pouchkinn had fought a duel and that his condition was desperate. He deigned to write a few words telling him he had pardoned him, urging him to fulfill his duties as a Christian, and easing his final moments by assuring him that his wife and little children would be properly cared for. . . .

> *Karl Ludwig von Ficquelmont,*
> *ambassador of the Kingdom of Austria*
> *February 2, 1837*

... It is said that nearly fifty thousand people of all classes visited Mr. Pouschkine's funeral chamber before his remains were conveyed to the Chapel, and many corporations asked to be allowed to act as pallbearers for the deceased; there was even talk of unharnessing the horses from the funeral carriage and having it be drawn by the people; the outpouring of display and acclaim on the occasion of the death of a man noted for his ostentatious atheism eventually reached such a pitch that the authorities, fearing a disturbance of public order, suddenly decided to change the place of the funeral service (which initially was to be held in the Cathedral of St. Isaac at the Admiralty) and moved the body there by night. ...

August von Liebermann,
ambassador of the Kingdom of Prussia
February 2, 1837

... Funeral rites for Mr. Pouchkin were celebrated in the most sumptuous yet moving fashion. All the heads of the foreign missions attended, with the exception of Lord Durham and Prince Souzzo, who were ill; Baron Heeckeren, who was not invited; and Mr. Liebermann, who declined to attend because he had been told that the aforesaid poet had been suspected of liberalism in his youth, a youth which, like that of many geniuses of his race, was indeed tempestuous. ...

Karl August von Lütɜerode,
ambassador of the Kingdom of Saxony
February 6, 1837

... The elder Baron Heeckeren has written to his court asking to resign from the ambassadorial post he holds here. It is not yet known what punishment will be meted out to his son, who, as a Russian officer, is awaiting a court-martial, but it is expected that he will be allowed to leave after being discharged from the regimental ranks, in particular since the insults addressed to him by his brother-in-law made a duel to the death inevitable. ...

Gustaf af Nordin,
secretary to the
Embassy of the Kingdom of Sweden and Norway
February 6, 1837

. . . The Emperor has extended his generosity of heart to the deceased Mr. Pouschkinn's widow and children. He has granted pensions of 6,000 rubles to the former and 1,500 rubles to each of the latter. . . . But to these acts of generosity on the Emperor's part must be added another, earlier one: before the writer's death, His Imperial Majesty, aware of the man's character and ideas, instructed a friend to burn all writings that might be harmful to him. . . .

Luigi Simonetti,
ambassador of the Kingdom of Sardinia and Piedmont
February 9, 1837

. . . His Majesty the Emperor has just commuted the death sentence issued by a court-martial in accordance with Russian law against young Baron Heeckeren, who instead is to be banished from the Empire, and yesterday morning the baron was escorted to the border and thereby expelled from the Russian Army. In this gesture one must yet again take note of the mercy and gracious kindness of His Imperial Majesty; up to now all Russian officers punished for dueling have been demoted to the rank of private. . . .

Christian von Hohenlohe-Kirchberg,
ambassador of the Kingdom of Baden-Württemberg
March 20, 1837

. . . The insinuation which is directed against the Dutch minister with regard to the letter written by Pouschkin is very clearly to be understood and is not very complimentary to His Excellency. He has left this Court on leave of absence, applied for in consequence of this unfortunate transaction, and was refused an audience of His Imperial Majesty, but was presented with a snuffbox. . . .

John George Lambton, Earl of Durham,
ambassador of the Kingdom of Great Britain
April 22, 1837

2

The Chouan

"Baron d'Anthès – may his name be triply cursed." So wrote Nikolai Mikhailovich Smirnov in 1842, five years after Pushkin's death. Smirnov more than got his wish: the name was cursed a thousand times, becoming synonymous with iniquity and deicide. Placed forever on the Index, it appears in indexes as "D'Anthès, Baron Georges Charles . . . murderer of Pushkin, adopted son of L. Heeckeren" – as though "murderer" were a profession or title, an eternal freeze-frame of the moment when its owner earned Russia's curse, a lasting snapshot of the shooting: Chernaya Rechka (Black Creek), dull light of the late northern sun, an arm outstretched, a man collapsing in the snow.

The bait with which death lured Pushkin to its dark world was a handsome young man, merry and genial, expansive and carefree, true champion of the game of life. Tall, well built, with wavy blond hair, a mustache, delicate features, blue eyes, Georges d'Anthès left a trail of broken hearts in Petersburg. Everyone liked him, and he was welcome everywhere. At receptions he was the life of the party, doting on Petersburg's most renowned beauties, entertaining young soldiers with barracks tales and off-color jokes, taking care to amuse *mamans* and *tantes* with just the right polite chatter, treating dignitaries, state officials, diplomats, high-ranking officers, and members of the imperial family with due respect while never losing his innate joviality. But his real triumphs began with the opening notes of a polonaise. He threw himself into dancing with fervor, with a kind of inspired elation; he was never one of those frigid dandies lazily shuffling their feet as though mired in a tedious chore. His every muscle would tense, the sound of his heels rang loud and clear on the parquet floor, his legs hovered gracefully in the entrechats. Nor was he one of those "ultrafashionable" types who came late and left before the mazurka – the climax of the dancing, magic moment of amorous trysts; this was a man who left the ballroom – hot, red-faced, and exhausted – only after the cotillion, and even then with the energy for one last witticism, one last penetrating glance, the kind of glance that set fans fluttering and filled red morocco diaries with breathless entries of pounding hearts and fainting spells recorded at dawn's first light.

A highly sought-after escort, he was careful to please all the ladies: never one to ask only the richest or most beautiful girls to dance, he was only too happy to take an ardent spin clasping in his expert arms the elderly wife of some heroic veteran. He knew how to charm and be charmed. A tenacious and zealous flirt, he preferred targeting married women, especially married women of broad-minded morals, for with them he could be more suggestive and impassioned, resorting to the more daring in his inexhaustible arsenal of gallantries without eliciting storms of modesty. He never seemed sad or melancholy. Other young men his age thought him an insolent, amusing rogue. He would make funny faces, leap onto tables and sofas, cling to ladies' necks and pretend to whimper. He laughed at himself and at others, and made people laugh till they doubled over in tears. In the choicest Petersburg society he staked out a solid position: pleasant ornament at any party, amiable ladies' man, waggish jester, but above all impeccable, inexhaustible dancer.

Some looked askance at a certain presumptuous arrogance

in his manner, others at his penchant for boasting of successes with women. One observer who saw him in action at a ball called him a "stableboy," but most people liked him like that, and no one feared a congenial youth whose glories faded after the ball was over – however long and exhausting the balls may have been in the Petersburg of the 1830s. During the time he served in the Horse Guards of Her Majesty, Empress of All the Russias, he was cited forty-four times for lateness, unexcused absences, and other breaches of discipline: he summoned his troops too loudly, slumped lazily in the saddle before ordering at-ease, lit up cigars or got into carriages at the end of drills and parades without waiting for higher-ranking officers to leave, on bivouacs strolled out onto the path outside the camp in his dressing gown, his greatcoat draped over his shoulders. His superiors punished him with extra shifts of guard duty, but his fellow soldiers were beguiled and amused by his nonchalance – so French, so Parisian – in sharp contrast to the rigid militarism prevailing in the Russian armed forces.

His merry disposition, loose tongue, and ready wit won him much forgiveness. Grand Duke Mikhail Pavlovich, a great fan of jokes and wit, loved his company. Pushkin himself laughed mightily when d'Anthès, seeing him enter a salon with his wife, Natalie, and the two inevitable sisters-in-law, Catherine and Alexandrine, called him *"Pasha à trois queues,"* meaning "Pasha with three pigtails," except that the word for "pigtail" also denotes another, less mentionable appendage. "D'Anthès," Count Apraksin once teased him, "I hear you do well with the ladies," to which the guardsman replied, "Get married, Count, and I'll prove it to you." All this in French, of course. One day General Gruenewaldt invited him to dine with three other officers on guard duty. The orderly was serving the first course when the oil lamp hanging from the ceiling crashed onto the table, splattering food and diners with an oily spray, ruining the evening. On the way out, d'Anthès immortalized the event: *"Grünwald nous fait manger*

de la vache enragée assaisonnée d'huile de lampe."* The crack
was duly reported to the general, who stopped inviting officers
on guard duty to dinner, but it also made the rounds of the
barracks of Shpalernaya Street and soon ricocheted into the
salons, thereby consolidating the fame of "that young, handsome, insolent d'Anthès."

He was born on February 5, 1812, in Colmar, Alsace, where
his family owned a house; their regular residence was an
estate in Soultz, acquired around 1720 by Jean Henri d'Anthès,
Georges's great-great-grandfather. Originally from Wein-
heim, in the Palatinate, Jean Henri moved to Alsace to take
charge of property he inherited from his father: blast furnaces
in Belfort and silver mines in Giromagny; later he managed
a foundry in Oberbrück and established a bayonet factory in
Klingenthal. An able and enterprising man, Jean Henri
d'Anthès eventually acquired the Blotzheim estate and castle,
as well as the Brinkheim estate and lands previously owned
by the Függers; in Burgundy he held the Longepierre, Ville-
comte, and Vernot domains. In December 1731, two years
before his death, letters from the crown granted him the title of
baron. His son, Jean Philippe, and later his nephew, Georges
Charles, made good use of the family patrimony, consolidating
their social position by marrying into families of the French
and German nobility.

A decline in the fortunes of the d'Anthès line began with
the whirlwind of 1789. The property of Georges Charles, who
fled France, was confiscated; his son Joseph Conrad, convicted
of membership in the detachments that tried to help King

---

* "Gruenewaldt had us eat rabid cow with lamp-oil seasoning" – an
untranslatable play on words, since "to eat rabid cow" was an idiom
meaning "to go hungry." But neither the officers of the Guard nor the
denizens of Petersburg salons would have required any translation. French
was the prime language of Russian high society, and d'Anthès had learned
at most the few Russian phrases needed to pass orders on to his men and
to respond to his superiors.

Louis XVI flee to Varennes in June 1791, took refuge with a German uncle, Baron von Reuttner. Father and son returned to Soultz on the tenth of Prairial of the Year V in the revolutionary calendar, and Georges Charles was amnestied for the crime of emigration. The family properties were restored on the sixteenth of Brumaire of the Year X. In 1806 Joseph Conrad married Maria Anne Luise von Hatzfeldt, a noblewoman from Mainz. The Restoration brought peace and prosperity to the d'Anthès family. Already a member of the General Council of the Upper Rhine, Joseph Conrad also held a seat in the Chamber of Deputies from 1823 to 1828. "He never took the floor, participating in deliberations only to move for their closure, whence his nickname, Baron of Closure." After the revolution of 1830 he withdrew to private life on his estate in Soultz, deeply embittered by the new political upheaval.

The events of July 1830 also indelibly stamped the life of Georges d'Anthès, Joseph Conrad's third child and first son. In 1829, having graduated from the Lycée Bourbon in Paris, young Georges enrolled in the Saint-Cyr military academy; the following year, along with others loyal to King Charles X, he took to the streets in support of the sovereign deposed in the July Revolution. When their efforts failed, he made no secret of his hostility to the "bourgeois king" Louis-Philippe and was accordingly forced out of Saint-Cyr. Back in Soultz he found himself unable to adjust to provincial life or the family atmosphere. Baron Joseph Conrad – swindled by dishonest stewards and advisers who took advantage of his lack of common sense, compelled to provide refuge for a tribe of relatives reduced to near poverty by the July monarchy – was dejected and depressed. In 1832, the year of his mother's premature death, Georges d'Anthès also lost all hope for his country's future: he was among the followers of the Duchess de Berry who tried in vain to foment an armed uprising in the Vendée. He now found both Soultz and France wholly unendurable and decided to pursue his military career in a foreign army.

At first he tried Prussia, where family connections assured him the favor of Prince Wilhelm, but the rank he was offered, noncommissioned officer, failed to satisfy his ambitions – he was, after all, the former cadet of a renowned military academy. The heir to the Prussian throne then suggested that d'Anthès seek his fortune in Russia, where Wilhelm's brother-in-law, Tsar Nicholas I, would certainly welcome a French legitimist with open arms. On September 24, 1833, Count von Gerlach provided Georges d'Anthès with a letter of recommendation signed by Prince Wilhelm of Prussia and addressed to Major General Adlerberg, a high official in the Russian Ministry of War. With that letter and a modest nest egg in hand, the young man set out for faraway, immense, unknown Russia. At least he had a few relatives on his mother's side there: Count and Countess Nesselrode and Count and Countess Musin-Pushkin. The Musin-Pushkins, like Pushkin himself, were descendants of Radsha, who lived in Kiev in the twelfth century and was a subject of Vsyevolod II. Through them Georges d'Anthès was very distantly related to the poet Alexander Sergeevich Pushkin.

On his way through Germany he suffered constipation; confident in his hardy constitution, he paid little attention at first, but the illness soon worsened, an acute inflammation leaving him bedridden in a godforsaken little town in the provinces. The days passed slowly for a lonely traveler lost in a foreign land, confined to his sickbed and watching anxiously as his meager resources dwindled rapidly and omens of death loomed. He had no one to help him, and d'Anthès began to lose faith in his lucky star. Then suddenly an uncommon commotion was heard in the modest inn. A clatter of carriages, a clamor of voices; the owner himself was roused, the servants bustled about. . . . It turned out to be the convoy of Baron Heeckeren, ambassador of Holland, on his way back to his mission at the Russian court. A broken carriage had forced him to make a long stopover. During dinner the loquacious innkeeper sought to distract and console his gloomy and irritated guest by contrasting his misfortune to others', and happened to mention the serious illness of the lonely young Frenchman already confined under his roof for some time. The baron, curious, hoping to vanquish his boredom, decided to have a look, and it was there, at the sickbed, that they first met. D'Anthès later maintained that compassion soared so powerfully in the old man's heart at the sight of his desperate condition and his face so ravaged by suffering that from that moment on he refused to leave his side, affording him care so attentive as to be worthy of the most tender mother. When his carriage was repaired, the ambassador would not even think of leaving. Instead, he waited patiently until d'Anthès was strong enough to continue his journey and, on learning where he was headed, proposed that the young man join his party and enter Petersburg under his aegis. One may well imagine with what joy that offer was received!

A provincial German inn, a traveler at death's door, a convoy forced to make an unwanted stop, a sudden uproar, the din of excited voices reaching the patient's ear through the fog of his delirium . . . the vexed new arrival forced into an unwelcome change of plans, boredom, a talkative innkeeper, a stairway, a door, a young stranger, his handsome face twisted by suffering, body racked by tremors, vacant eyes peering at the dark shadows hovering at his bedside. Tender care, a slow reawakening to the world, gratitude to the man who snatched him from death's jaws, short walks together near the inn, and then to the forest on the outskirts of the godforsaken little town, long talks, confessions, plans . . .

How much credence can we place in this tale of Fate's kindly and tempestuous intervention, this touching, romantic crossing of paths in the shadow of illness and death? Caution would seem indicated, for we have here a version of events presented in a long account published early in the twentieth century by Alexandra Petrovna Arapova, daughter of Push-kin's widow and her second husband. Arapova was recounting events in the remote past, which she knew of only indirectly or from sources of dubious objectivity. And most of all she was writing – her impassioned pen dripping with ill-concealed rancor against Pushkin, her ink tinged with a dime novel's lurid hues – to defend the memory of her dead mother (whom Russia never forgave for the death of its greatest poet) against "unfair and often insulting judgments." We may therefore doubt much in her story, including that first meeting between Georges d'Anthès and Jacob van Heeckeren.

We don't know for sure when d'Anthès first set foot on Russian soil. Arapova says he arrived on October 8, 1833. On that day, according to the *St. Petersburg News*, the steamer *Nicholas I* docked at Kronstadt, after a 78-hour voyage, "with forty-two passengers aboard, among them the Royal Dutch ambassador, Baron Heeckeren." If d'Anthès was really one of those forty-two passengers, then the claim of serious illness and slow recovery smacks of exaggeration, since he was still in Berlin on September 24 and would have boarded the *Nicholas I* in Lübeck on October 5. This is only the first knot in the tangle of inconsistencies, contradictions, half-truths, and occasional outright lies that must be unraveled by anyone looking into Pushkin's death or its distant origins.

An old registry preserved in an archive in Nantes tells us that only on November 2, 1833, did Georges Charles d'Anthès, "landowner, twenty-two years old, born in Colmar (Upper Rhine)," notify the French Embassy in Petersburg of his arrival in Russia. He was staying at the English Hotel on Galernaya Street (Jail Street – Fate's clairvoyant choice), third floor, apartment No. 11.

Louis Metman, Georges d'Anthès's grandson, writes: "The interest shown in various ways by Tsar Nicholas, his family ties in Germany and Russia . . . an appearance that portraits of the time suggest was quite attractive soon afforded the young officer a prominent place in the salons of Petersburg. He had the good fortune to encounter Baron Heeckeren-

Beverweerd, the King of Holland's ambassador to the Russian emperor, and the baron, attracted by his intelligence and amiability, took an interest in Georges d'Anthès and began corresponding regularly with his father."

In other words, Metman suggests that the young Frenchman met the Dutch ambassador only after he arrived in Petersburg and had already won the blessings of the Tsar and the sympathy of the salons. Whom to believe? All we know for sure is that on December 9, 1833, Joseph Conrad d'Anthès replied as follows to a letter from Jacob van Heeckeren: "I cannot adequately express my gratitude for all Your kindness to my son, and I hope he will prove worthy of it. Your Excellency's letter has set my mind at ease, for I cannot deny that I was concerned about his fate. His naïveté and heedlessness, I feared, might have caused him to fall in with people who might harm him, but thanks to Your kindness and Your taking him under Your protection and treating him as a friend, I am reassured. I hope his examination goes well."

Konstantin Karlovich Danzas, a friend of Pushkin's, recalled:

Among other letters of recommendation, d'Anthès had one addressed to Countess Ficquelmont, who enjoyed the special favor of the now deceased Empress. To this lady d'Anthès owed the beginning of his success in Russia. During one of her soirées she presented him to the Empress, and d'Anthès was lucky enough to attract His Majesty's attention as well. . . . Ladurnère, the famous painter of battle scenes, was living in Petersburg at the time. . . . The late sovereign would sometimes visit his studio at the Hermitage, and during one of these visits, noticing a few sketches of King Louis Philippe on the artist's easel [a later source indicates they were caricatures], he asked Ladurnère, "Is this your work, by any chance?" to which Ladurnère replied, "No, Sire, a compatriot of mine, a legitimist like me, Mr. d'Anthès." "Ah, d'Anthès," said the sovereign. "I've heard of him, the Empress has spoken of him." He then expressed a desire to meet him, at which point Ladurnère had d'Anthès come out from behind the screen where he'd hidden upon the sovereign's arrival. The Tsar spoke to him kindly, and d'Anthès took the opportunity to ask him point blank for permission to enter Russian military service. The sovereign gave his consent.

Once again it would be nice to believe in Fate's benign intervention, but Countess Dolly Ficquelmont, wife of the Austrian ambassador in Petersburg, gave no receptions or balls graced by the presence of Their Imperial Majesties before January 1834. She led a quiet life even in normal times, and the winter season had not yet opened when she went into mourning at the premature death of her beloved cousin Adèle Stakelberg in early November 1833; a heaven-sent burn on her foot also afforded her a perfect excuse to continue to shield her grieving heart from social events. Thus the introduction to the Empress recalled by Danzas could have occurred only after d'Anthès was already preparing for the regimental entrance examination. Someone must be making a mistake, or forgetting something, or mixing something up, and the truth is now shrouded in the smudged and swollen contours of legend. In every variant, however, a glittering aura of stardust seems to shine upon Georges d'Anthès, ever favored by the warm breath of fair winds. Truly a boy born lucky.

Unlike his young protégé, Baron Jacob Derk Anne Borchard van Heeckeren-Beverweerd, posted to Petersburg in 1823 as chargé d'affaires and later as ambassador of the Low Countries, was not universally appreciated; many feared his bilious tongue and devious, scheming nature. Dolly Ficquelmont had only recently settled in Russia when she wrote of him: "Here he is considered a spy for Nesselrode [the Russian Foreign Minister], a conjecture that gives the clearest idea of his personality and character." And after coming to know him better: "I cannot help admitting to myself that he is nasty, at least in speech, but I wish and hope that what is said about him in society is unfair . . . although I consider him a man dangerous to society, I am flattered to have him in my salon."

Countess Ficquelmont's portrait of Heeckeren is the most compassionate one bequeathed to us by any Russian. After Pushkin's death a ring of loathing and contempt was forged around the Dutch ambassador: "that old snake," "a sly man, more calculating than depraved," "an evil, selfish man prepared to use any means to achieve his ends . . . Known to all Petersburg as a gossip, he had already set many people to fighting and was despised by all those who grasped his true nature," "an old scoundrel, always with a smile on his face, wise-cracking, sticking his nose into everything," "an extraordinarily amoral man," "famous for his depravity, surrounding himself with shamelessly dissolute young men enamored of amorous gossip and many other intrigues of that type."

A receding hairline, elongated face, inscrutable pale eyes, Greek profile, sensual lips, thick beard, narrow shoulders, slim build. No wife, no known relations with women. Distinguished, impeccable manners, highly elegant and cultured, a lover of music and good books. His house on the Nevsky Prospect — "a tiny miniature, but a jewel of elegance" — was filled with paintings by noted artists, sculptures, antique furniture, silver, bronzes, crystal, tapestries. He was highly prized at salons: "He told the most amusing stories, and a hearty laugh was had by all." He frequented the flower of the Petersburg aristocracy. Polished and shrewd, as attentive to history's great events as he was to the softest salon whispers, he sought out the most varied and confidential sources, soaked up everything his big, floppy ears could take in, and wrote it all up in reports to The Hague. He had an elastic idea of truth, and nothing he said "was ever assumed to contain even the slightest touch of sincerity." Though he was only just short of forty-three in October 1833, everyone recalls him as "old." Pushkin himself once threatened, "With the son it's all over. Now bring me the old man."

One way or another, somewhere in Europe, on a day we do not know, this caustic and hardly tenderhearted man made his "providential" entry into the life of Georges d'Anthès, the French *"bon enfant"* destined to be so lethal for Russia. Heeckeren's most important contribution was his financial aid, since the hundred louis a year sent to d'Anthès by his father could never have covered the huge outfitting expenses required of any member of the prestigious, exclusive *chevaliers gardes*, most of whom were scions of the oldest and wealthiest families of the Russian nobility. In general, d'Anthès could afford no luxury and in the early days of his stay in Petersburg he appeared in public in outdated, inappropriate dress – a long black tailcoat over gray culottes with red piping.

But Lady Luck had powerful accomplices, in the form of letters of recommendation. On January 5, 1834, Count Adlerberg wrote to Georges d'Anthès:

Today General Sukhozanet told me, dear baron, that he intends to give you the examination just after Epiphany, and that he hopes to get you through it in a single morning, provided all the professors are free the same day. The general has assured me that he has already had Mr. Heeckeren ask where you might be found in order to inform you in good time as soon as the great day is set; you would do well to see him and ask for instructions. He has also promised me he won't be nasty, as you people put it, but don't be too sure of that, don't forget to repeat everything you've learned, make sure they see that you're well read. . . .

P.S. The Emperor asked me if you're studying Russian. I thought I'd better say yes. I believe I recommended that you find a Russian-language teacher.

On January 27, 1834, Georges d'Anthès passed the entrance examination. Exempted from the tests in Russian and in military law and regulations, he compensated with wit for the many gaps in his knowledge. It is said that when he was asked what river ran through Madrid, he admitted he didn't know, but wrested a smile from the stern-faced committee by adding, "And to think I've watered my horse there!" On February 8 he was named an ensign in the Horse Guards, and six days later he enrolled in the 7th Reserve Squadron.

On January 26, 1834, Pushkin wrote in his diary: "Baron d'Anthès and Marquis Pina, two Chouans, are being taken directly into the Guards as officers. The Guards protest." It could not have been much later that they first met, perhaps when Pushkin, dining with Danzas in a well-known Petersburg restaurant, found himself seated beside the young Frenchman at the table d'hôte. But let us leave them for the moment at Dumé's, in merry and boisterous male company, unaware of the hatred that was later to come, savoring their rare roast beef, truffles, and Strasbourg pâté. Fast-forwarding the tape, let us consider the wretched fate of these two Chouans on Russian soil. The Marquis Pina never made it into the Guards, serving instead in the Zamoshchski Rifle Regiment, from which he was discharged for stealing silverware, while Baron d'Anthès was demoted and banished from Russia for spilling the blood of the country's purest voice, robbing it of its sun.

"The Empress Alexandra Fyodorovna is writing her memoirs. . . . Will they survive to posterity?" Pushkin wondered. In fact, a portion of the memoirs of Friederike Luise Charlotte Wilhelmina of Prussia – duly renamed Alexandra Fyodorovna upon her marriage to Nikolai Pavlovich Romanov on July 1, 1817 – did survive, along with her diaries: tiny notebooks thickly filled with German scrawl, secret refuge of a tender soul immersed in a joyful happiness covered with countless rose-colored veils to shield her from the real world. One of many German empresses to ascend the Romanov throne, she was a beauty whose blond, diaphanous grace Pushkin himself found striking: "I love the Empress to death, even though she's already thirty-five, maybe thirty-six years old." Those who knew her well thought of her as a girl encountering life for the very first time: she had an innocence born of unawareness of evil and "spoke of unhappiness as of a myth."

She liked to be liked and was naïvely flirtatious with men. She adored dancing. She danced into the night, putting her fragile physique to the test, moving splendidly, like an airborne sylph, a creature hovering between earth and sky, a *Tochter der Luft*, a "daughter of air."

To the diaries of the dancing Empress we owe mention of what in all likelihood was the debut of *chevalier garde* Georges d'Anthès in Petersburg high society: "February 28, 1834 . . . At 10:30 we repaired to the Ficquelmonts', where I changed, in Dolly's room, to a white dress with lilies, very beautiful . . . my lilies soon wilted. Danteze* kept staring at me." Was d'Anthès really so bold as to cast longing glances at the Tsarina? And was she, too, bewitched by his lady-killing gaze? Malicious conjecture would be amiss. The truth is that Alexandra Fyodorovna's heart throbbed (chastely and innocently) for another young officer of the Guards. What probably struck her was the admiring wonder, the delighted gleam, of those wide blue eyes as they gazed upon her, on Nicholas I (looking even taller and more impressive in his Austrian Hussars uniform), and on the glittering crowd of guests bedecked with jewels and medals – a whole new world now magnanimously opening its doors to the young foreigner.

The name of Georges d'Anthès, albeit consigned to history by a truly august witness, then drops out of the Petersburg social pages until the winter of 1835–36. Nothing surprising about that. The social lions of the capital saw d'Anthès as no more than a princeling of the cotillions, a likable, jovial French fellow whose friends in high places had gotten him into the Guards. Surprisingly, however, his name is not mentioned by

---

* The German-born Tsarina was not the only one to mangle his name, which was often written "Dantais," "Dantesse," "Dantest." His comrades in the Guards thought it bore a comical resemblance to "dentist." ("He started out a dentist, and now he's a doctor," they said when he was adopted by Heeckeren, whose name sounded vaguely like the Russian *lekar*, "doctor.") "Dantes" finally became the standard spelling in Russian.

the Dutch ambassador's few real friends, such as Otto von Bray-Steinburg, chargé d'affaires at the Bavarian Embassy. Count Otto's letters to his mother, Sophie, in Mitau, often speak of Baron Heeckeren, "a witty and quite amusing man who has been most kind to me," but also "a cold and generally not very nice man, capable, however, of bestowing true favors upon those he takes a liking to." Yet never a word about d'Anthès, though he was a frequent visitor to the elegant private residence adjoining the Dutch Embassy. The Bavarian and Dutch diplomats became a kind of "gang of two," their friendship growing and solidifying to the point that Bray felt great anxiety when Heeckeren fell seriously ill: "I spend as much time as possible with him and bitterly regret my scant capacities in caring for the sick. He is in such a state that he barely notices the presence of his friends." And still no word about d'Anthès, who surely must have spent long and anxious hours at the ambassador's bedside.

On May 19, 1835, Count von Bray informed his mother: "The other day I accompanied Heeckeren to Kronstadt . . . It was with genuine regret that I took my leave of this friend who has done so much to make my stay in this city a pleasure. I will miss him both in daily life and in my affections and will be unable to replace him in either respect. He is going to Baden-Baden. . . . We returned from Kronstadt to Petersburg during a frightful storm, on one of Alexei Bobrinsky's boats, ourselves acting as crew members despite our terrible indisposition." And still no word of d'Anthès, who was aboard the very same boat. Was the French officer's personality so pallid and unworthy of note? Or were the ambassador's closest associates deliberately silent about his young friend? If so, why?

Georges d'Anthès to Jacob van Heeckeren, Petersburg, March 18, 1835: "My dear friend, you cannot imagine the pleasure your letter gave me and how reassuring it was, for truly I was terribly afraid that you would get cramps from being seasick. . . . We were less fortunate in our crossing, for our return was the most ridiculous yet extraordinary thing – surely you recall the terrible storm that was raging as we left you. Well, it only got bigger and better once we got out in the bay. . . . Bray, who made such a fuss on the big ship, couldn't decide which saint to pray to, and immediately treated us to a rehearsal not only of the dinner he had eaten on board but also of whatever else he had ingested in the past week, accompanied by oaths in all languages and sighs in every key."

Paris, early summer of 1989, 152 winters and 153 springs since Georges d'Anthès mortally wounded Pushkin. The attic of an apartment in the sixteenth arrondissement, a worn gray suitcase, old business papers belonging to the apartment's distinguished elderly owner, photographs, postcards, prints, personal letters. Then all at once what you dream of yet dare not hope for: a bundle of old letters, from another era, another world.

Buried – or hidden? – for more than a century and a half in the private files of the Heeckeren family, the letters that Georges d'Anthès wrote to Jacob van Heeckeren beginning in May 1835 are a virtually miraculous discovery for anyone investigating the events that led to Pushkin's last duel. A gift from the winged herald of the gods suddenly gives voice – as well as thoughts and feelings – to a man who, for the Russian part of his very long life, left no legacy but a few witticisms and a terrible burden of guilt. Legend obliges: one last stroke of stagecraft in the case of Georges d'Anthès. One last stroke of luck? It is hard to say which.

3

Those Fateful Flannel Undershirts

D'Anthès to Heeckeren, Petersburg, May 18, 1835: The void left by your absence is indescribable. I can compare it only to that which you must feel, because even though you sometimes grumbled when you greeted me (I speak, of course, of times when you were in a great hurry), I knew nevertheless that you were happy to chat with me a bit, and that our seeing each other at any moment of the day became a need for you as for me. I came to Russia expecting to find only strangers: and so you have been providential for me! Thus it is not correct when you call yourself a friend, because a friend would not have done all you have done for me without even knowing me; in the end you have spoiled me, I became used to it, as one does become so easily used to happiness, and with all this an indulgence I would never have found in my own father; well, suddenly surrounded as I am with people envious and jealous of my position, just imagine whether I don't feel the difference and whether every hour of the day doesn't bring home to me that you are no longer here. . . . Adieu, my dear friend. Take care of yourself, and enjoy yourself somewhat more. . . .

A warning before continuing: even with an indulgent translation – the addition of a comma or a period, a repair of the sequence of tenses, a correction of outlandish grammatical error – the letters of Georges d'Anthès still demand a magnanimous and active reader, a reader-editor willing to overlook mistakes and to lend order to a style that shows scant familiarity with the rules of syntax, indeed with the written word in general. Louis Metman said of his grandfather: "Neither in his youth nor as an adult did he display any real interest in literature. No one in the family recalls ever having seen him read a literary work in all his long life."

In late May Baron Heeckeren arrived in Baden-Baden to take the waters, as Dr. Zadler had urged after a bout of cholera that nearly sent him to his Maker, but also to meet Joseph Conrad d'Anthès, who was visiting the spa city with Alphonse, his other son. Heeckeren wanted to talk to Joseph Conrad about an idea he had been toying with fondly for some time: giving Georges the Heeckeren name and making him heir to his property. But it would not be easy for a man of the most ancient Dutch nobility to adopt a Frenchman on active duty in the Russian Imperial Guard, a twenty-three-year-old nobleman whose real father was alive and kicking. Well aware of the obstacles, Heeckeren was determined to bring all his diplomatic and conversational skills to bear in skirting or surmounting them. He knew he could count on the goodwill of his King, whom he had long served so loyally, defending the rights of little Holland at one of Europe's most powerful courts, but the first step was to win the consent of Georges's natural father. He began by discreetly sounding him out.

Perhaps it was in daylight, as they strolled along Baden-Baden's shaded lanes, or maybe after an evening game of whist, but at some point he told Joseph Conrad of the terrible illness he had just endured and of the anguish and sense of futility that assails a man without offspring when death stalks him. Perhaps he confessed his deep yearning for a family: his own had never forgiven him his conversion to Catholicism and ever since had treated him coldly or with outright hostility. Perhaps he described the worrisome life of a boy alone in a frozen foreign land, a boy harried by envy and prey to the many temptations of his own lively and impetuous character.

One way or another, he succeeded not only in winning Joseph Conrad's confidence but in touching his heart. Confirmation of this came at the end of June, in a letter from Georges: "My poor father is enchanted and writes me that it is impossible to feel more affection than that which you feel for me, that my portrait never leaves you for a single instant, thank you, a thousand thanks, my dear." Jacob van Heeckeren promised his future – what shall we call him? – co-father that he would visit him in Soultz as soon as his recovery was complete.

On May 21 Georges d'Anthès set out for Pavlovsk, twenty-five versts from the capital, where the Horse Guards held their regular summer bivouac. Here he lived a grueling, grinding life, billeted in the fetid common room of a log hut shared with several peasants. Only with the greatest effort did he manage to find a quiet corner where he could snatch time to write to his faraway friend: "Drill after drill, maneuvers and maneuvers, and on top of it all this frightful weather, never the same for two days running, sometimes stifling heat, other times so cold you don't know what to do." The weeks he had spent in the Vendée seemed like a pleasant holiday compared to this. Russia was ruled by an inflexible soldier who loved to demonstrate – to his subjects, the world, and himself – the power and iron discipline of his armed forces. There were only two bright spots in this debilitating chore: the splendid parties in honor of illustrious visitors like Frederick, Prince of the Low Countries; "and the Empress continues to be good to me, for never are three officers of the regiment invited without my being among them."

When the Guards finally left Pavlovsk for their quarters at Novaya Derevnya, Georges d'Anthès threw himself into the intense social whirl of "the Islands," the web of islets by which Petersburg extends into the Gulf of Finland, an archipelago of grassland, woods, and gardens furrowed by countless streams, brooks, and canals, studded with ponds and lakes. For slightly more than a decade the Islands had been a fashionable vacation spot for the Petersburg aristocracy, with richly appointed dachas, a theater where a French company performed, and even a spa (the water was imported, of course; the Empress's favorite came from Ems) boasting a sumptuous reception hall. Apart from the balls, not a day passed without *parties de plaisir*, picnics, boat rides, and horseback riding. Three Amazons – the Goncharov sisters – were the talk of the Islands that season for the skill and elegance with which they handled the thoroughbreds of the acclaimed stables of Polotnyany Zavod. The youngest and most beautiful of the sisters was married to Pushkin. They were spending the summer in Chernaya Rechka, near Novaya Derevnya, and our French officer seemed to become even wittier and more gallant in their company. With the nightmare of maneuvers finally at an end, that second Russian summer would have been a delight in all respects were it not for the annoying stomach pains that had plagued him for some months. "But in any case don't worry," he reassured Heeckeren. "When you return to Petersburg I'll be in fine enough form to clasp you in my arms so tight you'll cry out."

Pushkin to Alexander Khristoforovich Benckendorff, Petersburg, July 26, 1835: It pains me, Count, at a time when I am already receiving one unexpected favor, to have to ask for two others, but I have decided to resort in all sincerity to the man who has deigned to be so providential to me. Of the 60,000 rubles I owe, half are debts of honor. To settle them I am forced to borrow from usurers, which will compound my problems or oblige me to appeal yet again to the Emperor's generosity. I therefore beseech His Majesty to do me an immense favor: first by making it possible for me to repay the 30,000 rubles: second by deigning to allow me to consider this sum a loan, accordingly suspending payment of my remuneration until such time as the debt is liquidated.

Commending myself to your indulgence, it is my honor to declare myself, with the deepest respect and most heartfelt gratitude . . .

Heeckeren continued to demonstrate his affection for d'Anthès
with offers of money, which were steadily rejected with a
courtesy and frugality surprising in a man whose real father
accused him of being a spendthrift. "My dear friend," d'Anthès
wrote, "you always worry needlessly about my well-being,
before leaving you gave me the wherewithal to manage
honorably and comfortably. . . . If I ask for nothing, it's
because I need nothing. . . . I am still far from buried and we
shall have all the time to spend together the money you are
always offering me so kindheartedly." Despite these reassuring protests, the baron went on sending money and gifts and
paid his protégé's outstanding debts. Apparently bemused and
disturbed by such generosity, d'Anthès twisted his careless,
colloquial French into knots trying to express his gratitude to
the man now striving to satisfy his every need and anticipate
his every desire, a man moving heaven and earth to secure
him a happy future free of the shadow of want, under the
kindly wing of a new and loving father.

That future, sad to say, proved more distant than expected,
for adoption by persons under fifty was forbidden by Dutch
law. "I have no need of papers and documents and assur-
ances," d'Anthès wrote when he learned of this unforeseen
obstacle. "I have your friendship, which will surely endure,
I hope, until you reach fifty, and that is better than all the
papers in the world." Comforted by his ward's affectionate
words, the ambassador battled on, casting about for any possible way out of the lamentable bureaucratic impasse. And he
continued to spin his plans even when Georges, concerned
about the baron's health, affably asked him to desist: "When
the doctors had you leave Petersburg it was not only for the
change of air but also to take you away from business and
to put your mind at rest. . . . Take good care of yourself and
there will always be more than enough left for us to go and
live our lives where the climate is more favorable and be
assured that we will be happy anywhere." Heeckeren was
making efforts to acquire an estate near Freiburg where he

could settle down for good someday; he had often thought of leaving Russia and its impossible climate; the rumor in Petersburg was that he had his eye on the legation in Vienna. The usually judicious d'Anthès, sworn enemy of daydreams and castles in the air, seems to have let himself be carried away by his benefactor's enthusiasm: "As you say, we shall be, so to speak, *en famille*: since you are now part of it. . . . My father has a large estate three hours from Freiburg, on the banks of the Rhine, so it may not be impossible to find property bordering on his. I assure you it is a splendid idea, and since you are now fond of my brother as well, we'll be able to marry and live almost all together and have you at our disposal."

Georges d'Anthès had a delicate constitution. And the northern summer was deceptive. At night the Islands were mired in a dampness that cut to the bone; nasty winds blew salt-sodden air through cracks in the log huts of Novaya Derevnya; sudden downpours turned the fragrant paradise into a swamp; all at once it seemed like autumn. One night in late August the *chevalier garde* left the ballroom of the spa in a sweat after one of his usual bouts of fervent dancing, but this time he was imprudent enough to return home in an open carriage. The next day he couldn't get out of bed: difficulty in breathing, tremors, a burning sensation in the head and chest; Dr. Zadler was summoned and diagnosed pleurisy. D'Anthès cautiously reported his illness to Heeckeren; the anxious ambassador replied with a flood of advice and instructions, concrete proof of his paternal solicitude.

Pushkin to his wife, Natalya Nikolaevna [Mikhailovskoe, September 21, 1835]: You can't imagine how vividly the imagination works when you're alone in a room or walking in the woods, with no one to stop you from thinking, thinking until your head spins. What do I think about? Just this: what are we going to live on? My father won't leave me any property: he's already squandered half of what he had; your people are one step from ruin. The Tsar won't let me be a country squire or a journalist. God knows I can't write books for money. We have not one cent of guaranteed income, but about 30,000 rubles of guaranteed expenses. Everything depends on me and your aunt. But neither of us will live forever. God only knows where all this will lead. In the meantime I'm sad. Kiss me, perhaps it will pass. How stupid of me, your lips can't stretch over four hundred versts. . . .

According to Louis Metman, "The Dutch ambassador's affectionate devotion and prudent counsel inevitably had a salutary influence on the ardent character of a twenty-three-year-old youth who in a glittering social setting had to control the urges of his impulsive nature." But d'Anthès's letters give a different impression. In them the youth seems the more prudent and reasonable of the two. In August 1835, when the ambassador heard that cholera was raging in Italy, he considered changing his plans and returning to Russia sooner than expected. But Georges dissuaded him: "You know how happy I'd be to see you, but just yesterday I talked to Zadler. . . . He told me that in no circumstances should you return before a year is up if you want to be completely cured, and he added that the Russian climate would kill you; so think whether I would let you come back after hearing such a secret. . . . Go spend the winter in Vienna or Paris and you'll be back among us in fine form in the spring."

Georges was always the one giving lectures about moderation and common sense: "When you* tell me you couldn't survive if anything happened to me, do you think by any

---

* After many letters and some hesitation, d'Anthès began addressing Heeckeren with the familiar *tu* instead of the formal *vous*: "My dear, you really are a child, how can you insist that I call you *tu*, as if that word could give more value to the thought, as if saying I love you [*vous*] were less sincere than saying I love you [*tu*]. Besides which, you see, it would be a habit I'd have to break in public, where you hold a position that does not permit a youth like me to be so informal."

chance that the idea hasn't ever occurred to me? But I'm much more reasonable than you, because I never stop there but banish these thoughts like horrible nightmares; after all, what would become of our lives if while we're truly happy we amused ourselves letting our imaginations run wild and worried about the calamities that might befall us? Life would become a constant torture."

Far from being cheered by Georges's wisdom, as a real father would have been, the baron took offense. There were times when he would have preferred more impulsiveness and less discretion, and times when, racked by uncertainty about his future son's real feelings, an anxiety, a vague unease, may be glimpsed in his veiled reproofs and bitter allusions. When yet another difficulty in the increasingly complicated business of the adoption arose, for instance, he chided Georges for not being sufficiently dismayed, and the young man had to mollify him: "I'm sure you will soon receive a letter that will make us both happy. I say us both because in your letter you talk as though I were happy about what's been happening." The ambassador complained that his protégé expressed his feelings for him in halfhearted, empty phrases, accusing him of epistolary laziness. Georges claimed it wasn't his fault: "Sometimes my letters are so short that I'm truly ashamed to send them, so I wait till I have some gossip about the fine inhabitants of Petersburg to amuse you a bit."

Gossip was d'Anthès's way of trying to make up for the lack of ardor that troubled Heeckeren. He recounted an incident that occurred at the wedding of their friend Marchenko. When the priest prompted him with the ritual formula "*moi, Jean, l'épouseur,*" the Jean in question, proud of his title of gentleman of the bedchamber, got ahead of the officiant: "*moi, Gentilhomme de la Chambre.*" All Petersburg had a good laugh at Jean's expense. He told him of the latest scandal in the lives of their theater friends: after discovering that Evdokya Istomina, the most famous Russian ballerina, had cheated on him with a visiting Parisian staying with his colleague La Ferrière, the actor Paul Mignet slapped the proprietor of the house where the infidelity had been consummated; the whimsical La Ferrière retorted by announcing that he would continue to perform only if the offender publicly declared that he had never laid a finger on him, and an absurd document to that effect was distributed throughout the city along with the programs for the French Theater. He told him what was going on in the "diplomatic family": Count von Lerchenfeld, tightfisted ambassador of the Kingdom of Bavaria, had showed up at a picnic with nothing but leftover roast beef, a crust of bread, and a little mustard; Count von Bray was head over heels in love with one of the Empress's ladies-in-waiting but was being kept on a short leash by his lover, Josephine Ermolova, who in the summer of 1835 had presented her lawful husband with a fine-looking bastard child. He told him of the antics of his colleagues in the Guards: some wiseacres in a box at the Alexandrinsky Theater had thrown a most intimate masculine undergarment filled with confetti at an actress whose performance they found wanting – "and the Emperor recalled what he'd had us told before we left: that if the slightest nonsense occurred, he would see to it that the guilty parties were transferred to the Army: surely I would not like to be in their shoes, since the poor devils' careers will now be ruined on account of a few pranks that weren't even funny or clever, nor was the game worth the candle." It does make you wonder. Whatever became of Georges d'Anthès's famous merriment, daring, and carefree lightheartedness?

"Blazing young colt of the icy steppes." Thus did one poet, perhaps Maffei, sing of Julie Samouloff, a Russian noblewoman who settled in Milan in 1824. Yulya Pavlovna Samoylovna made her debut in Milanese high society on January 30, 1828, at a memorial ball hosted by Count Giuseppe Batthyáni. She soon became famous as the "Russian lady of Milan," legendary for her stormy love affairs, extravagance, generosity

to the poor, and the pomp of her unforgettable parties, which
made the Navigli canals, modest enough substitutes for the
Neva, sparkle through the night with song and light. Her
every visit back to Russia stirred one or another scandal.
D'Anthès wrote to Heeckeren in August 1835: "I keep forgetting to give you details of Julie's stay in Petersburg. . . . To
start with, the house looked like a barracks, since all the
officers of the regiment spent the evening there, you can
imagine doing what; yet morality was always preserved,
because well-informed people insist that she has cancer of the
uterus." Julie Samoylovna threw herself a big birthday party
on the Slavyanka estate:

I wasn't there, but incredible things are being said that I know
aren't true. For example that she had peasant women climb greased
poles and every time they fell there were endless cries of joy, and
also that she had the peasant women run horse races, that the
women sat astride without saddles, in short, all sorts of jokes of
this type, and the most unfortunate thing is that Alexander Trubetskoy broke an arm on his way home. . . . The Emperor found out
about all these rumors and about Alexander's broken arm, and at
the Demidovs' ball the next day he was furious and, addressing
our general in front of forty people said: "So the officers of your
regiment will persist in this foolishness and will not be satisfied
until I transfer half a dozen of them to the Army, and as for that
woman," speaking of Julie, "she'll behave herself only when I have
the police throw her out." . . . I'm sorry for that, because Julie is
a very good person, and even if I didn't visit her home I did see
her often; I must tell you I thought it better not to visit her because
the Emperor had so explicitly condemned the people who intimately
frequented her home.

The more we hear of d'Anthès's own voice, the more does
the image of dissolute, arrogant adventurer bequeathed to us
by so many witnesses seem to fade before our eyes. Were
they blind? Lying? Or were there two d'Anthèses, one public,

the other revealed only to the man to whom he owed everything, the man without whom, as he said, he "was nothing"? And was this second, secret d'Anthès bonded to that man by something more than mere esteem and gratitude? Alexander Trubetskoy, the *chevalier garde* who broke his arm on the way home from the rustic orgy at Slavyanka, had no doubt on this score: "He got up to all sorts of pranks, innocent and typical of the young, except for one, which we found out about only much later. How shall I put it? He was Heeckeren's lover, or Heeckeren was his. . . . Homosexuality was quite widespread in high society at the time. Judging by the fact that d'Anthès was constantly chasing women, one must suppose that he played only a passive role in the relationship with Heeckeren."

Among his contemporaries and comrades in the Russian armed forces, with their unruly ways and reckless, dissolute lives, Georges d'Anthès stands out like an albino fly. It was still summer when he wrote to the ambassador: "New adventures in the regiment. A few days ago Sergei Trubetskoy and several other buddies of mine, after a more than lavish dinner in a restaurant outside town, started smashing in the fronts of all the houses along the road on their way home. You can imagine the stir it caused the next day." Later he informed Heeckeren of the consequences of the stunt: "The storm has burst. Trubetskoy, Gervet, and Cherkassky have been transferred to the Army. . . . You can see that you have to stay calm if you want to stroll along the Prospect and get a little fresh air, and winding up in the hoosegow doesn't take much, since times are definitely hard, very hard in fact, and you need a lot of caution and prudence if you want to paddle your own boat without bumping into anyone."

A most cautious helmsman guiding his own little craft through the swell of Russian waters, a cool head among the reckless, a moderate in the midst of excess, a spectator detached and uninvolved, d'Anthès sounds like a near relative of Hermann, the protagonist of Pushkin's *The Queen of Spades*, written in 1833. Hermann attends endless games of faro every night but never plays; sober, self-controlled, lacking his companions' largesse in ways and means, determined never to sacrifice the necessary in a dubious quest for the superfluous, he lives by the watchword "frugality, moderation, hard work." But he has "the profile of Napoleon and the soul of Mephistopheles." Disturbed to learn that a certain countess has an infallible formula for winning at the game, he becomes obsessed with her marvelous secret and tries to wheedle it out of her at any price. In the end it is revealed to him by the ghost of the aged countess, whose death he has caused: "Three, seven, ace" – and Hermann begins to play for the first time; he is on his way to winning fabulous sums when a decrepit, peevish queen of spades winks at him from the third card, causing him to lose his riches and his mind in a single stroke.

Grinning through the gloom of his gloomiest story, Pushkin settled accounts with Mephistophelean Romantics once and for all and declared open war on Napoleon's scions, once again armed to the teeth and marching on Russia's distant expanses. From the pinnacle of his eighteenth-century prose – polished, spare, inimical to psychology – he condemned Balzac's *marivaudage* and Stendhal's "certain deceitful declamations." Granted, this was a matter of style, but not of style alone: Pushkin scorned and secretly feared the Rastignacs and Sorels as relentless fanatics driven by a mania for conquest, inflexible and methodical artisans of their own destinies.

Literature anticipates – doesn't follow, doesn't imitate – life. Georges d'Anthès – tenacious careerist, polished and frugal, ever careful to make no false moves, supremely clever broker of his capital of good looks and good humor, "a practical man who came to Russia to get ahead" – was to lose everything he had amassed so patiently and laboriously when he yielded to the charms of the superfluous, in the guise of an enchanting queen of hearts. And literature corrects life too: with *The Queen of Spades* Pushkin had already routed d'Anthès and other heroes of his Balzacian stripe. But not for good and all. New "d'Anthèses" — more intelligent, cultured, and dedicated, poorer in cash but rich in ideas, Russified now, Raskolnikovs now — would return to Petersburg to kill again.

Pushkin to his wife [Trigorskoe, September 25, 1835]: . . . Are you well, my darling? and what are my little babies up to? What of our home, how are you managing it? Just think, so far I haven't written a line — and all because I'm worried. At Mikhailovskoe I found everything just as it was, except that my nurse is gone, and while I was away a family of small pines sprouted near the old pines I knew so well, and it makes me angry to look at them just as it sometimes makes me angry to look at the young *chevaliers gardes* at balls at which I no longer dance. But what can you do: everything around me tells me I'm getting old, sometimes even in plain Russian. Yesterday, for instance, I ran into a peasant woman I know and couldn't help saying that she'd changed. To which she replied, "But you, too, good sir, have gotten old, and ugly to boot." Well, I can join my pure-hearted deceased nurse in saying, Handsome I never was, but I was once young. None of this matters, though. All that matters is that you take no notice of what I myself notice too much, dear one. What are you doing in my absence, my beauty?

D'Anthès to Heeckeren, October 18, 1835: Before bringing you up-to-date on the gossip and news of Petersburg, I shall begin by telling you about myself and my health, which in my opinion is not what it should be. I lost so much weight since that cold I caught at the spa that I was beginning to worry, so I called for the doctor, who assured me that I have never been so well and that this state of debility is quite natural after a pleurisy, that it is the result of taking so much blood from me; nevertheless, he instructed me to wrap myself with flannel, for he maintains that I am highly susceptible to colds and this is the only way to prevent them; I frankly confess that this latter remedy is beyond my financial means, and

I have no notion how to go about procuring these undershirts, which are too expensive, especially inasmuch as I would have to wear them all the time. I would therefore need many.

In October Baron Heeckeren went to Soultz, where he had already paid a brief visit early in August. Welcomed with grateful joy and overwhelmed with kindness, he seemed happy with the warm reception and savored the simple pleasures of country life. He also took the opportunity of his long stay in Alsace to lend some order to the chaotic finances of Papa d'Anthès, who by now had blind faith in him. He assessed the estate, calculated income and outgo, pored over old records, consulted lawyers and notaries, negotiated with debtors and creditors, had a dishonest steward fired, advised spending cuts, suggested profitable improvements in the use of vineyards and grain fields. He stayed with the d'Anthès family longer than planned, arriving in Paris only toward the middle of December. It was from there, on December 24, that he informed Georges that the adoption request had finally been granted. The news elicited elated thanks: "I love you more than all my family put together, I can't any longer put off confessing it."

"No one here can remember a winter this harsh since 1812, the season so fatal to the French armies," the Prince of Butera wrote in January 1836. Delayed by snow and ice, the new French ambassador spent no less than forty-three days making his way to Petersburg (arriving – irony of history – just as Te Deums of thanksgiving commemorating the victory over Napoleon were being celebrated in all the churches). We may be sure that our *chevalier garde* from Colmar, sensitive to the damp and the wind as he was, would not have survived that terrible Russian winter had not Baron Heeckeren come to his rescue with the money for those precious flannel undershirts, as well as permission to use his elegant carriage and his diplomat's warm fur coat. But not even the astute, farsighted Dutch ambassador could have guessed what ruin and havoc his munificent attentions would engender.

D'Anthès had not been slow to learn that in Russia, "far to the north as it is, the blood runs hot." Indeed, incredible and outrageous things were wont to happen in that boundless, savage land:

I almost forgot to tell you what everyone in Petersburg has been talking about for the past few days, a truly frightful thing, and if you deigned to confide news of it to any of my compatriots, they could make a good novel of it; here's the story: in the environs of Novgorod is a convent of women, one of whom is known through-out the land for her beauty. An officer of the dragoons fell hopelessly in love with her and pursued her for an entire year, after which time she finally consented to receive him, provided he came to the convent on foot and accompanied by no one. That day he left his home around midnight and repaired to the designated site, where he found the nun in question, who without a word escorted him into the convent. Arriving in her cell, he found an excellent dinner with all sorts of wines, and after the dinner tried to take advantage of the tête-à-tête and began to regale her with great declarations of love; she, after listening with the greatest sangfroid, asked what proof he would give of his love, and he promised everything he could think of, including that if she consented he would carry her off and marry her. She kept saying it wasn't enough, and the officer, at his wit's end, finally told her he would do anything she asked; after making him swear to this, she took him by the hand, led him to a cupboard, pointed to a sack, and told him that if he would only carry it to the river, upon his return she would deny him nothing; the officer agreed, she led him out of the convent, but before he had gone two hundred paces he felt ill and fell. Luckily one of his comrades, who had followed him from afar when he saw him go out and had waited for him near the convent, ran quickly to him, but it was too late: the wretched woman had poisoned him, and he survived only long enough to relate the events; when the police opened the sack they found half the body of a horribly mutilated monk.

The things now happening right before d'Anthès's eyes – vacant, inexpressive, glassy blue – reminded him of stories recounted in books he'd only heard about: "That poor devil Platonov has been in a lamentable state for three weeks, so in love with Princess B. that he has locked himself in his home and won't see anyone, not even his own relatives. . . . He refuses to talk to his brother or sister. He claims he's very ill; such behavior in an intelligent boy is quite amazing, for he's in love the way they say it is for heroes in a novel. Them I understand very well, because you have to make up something to fill the pages, but it's as strange as can be for a man with any common sense; I hope he soon puts an end to all this foolishness and comes back to us, for I miss him very much." The cautious and sensible d'Anthès never guessed that he was himself about to enter the eccentric fraternity of "poor devils" who fall madly in love like the heroes in novels – in this case a novel quite as taxing and with an ending quite as bloody as any being written in his beloved and distant France.

In late December Georges d'Anthès was finally able to inform Jacob van Heeckeren of his complete recovery: "Now, thank God, I no longer suffer at all. True, I am enveloped in flannel like a woman rising from her bed after childbirth, but this has the twofold advantage of keeping me warm and filling out my clothes, which hang on me like sacks since I've grown so incredibly thin. Herewith I offer you an account of how I live: I eat at home every day, my manservant has made an agreement with Panin's cook to provide me with very good and copious lunches and dinners for six rubles a day, and I'm convinced that the lack of variety in the cooking is doing me much good, because my stomach pains have almost completely disappeared."

But he didn't tell his faraway friend everything. He never

mentioned his increasingly frequent evening outings and was silent about his new acquaintances: Pyotr Valuev, the fiancé of Marya Vyazemskaya; Alexander and Andrei Karamzin; Klementy and Arkady Rosset – all young friends of Pushkin. Through them d'Anthès entered the poet's circle.*

At noon on January 1, 1836, a long cortege followed the Tsar and his family to the church in the Winter Palace for the solemn New Year's Mass. An hour later Tsarina Alexandra Fyodorovna, attended by Litta, the grand chamberlain, and Vorontsov-Dashkov, the chief of protocol, received the congratulations of the guests, in strict hierarchical order: ladies of state, of the court, and of the city; members of the Council of State; senators, generals, and aides-de-camp; first and second ranks of the court, and so on. As a gentleman of the bedchamber and Class IX official, Pushkin was among the last to wish the sovereign a happy new year. Later that same day Tsar Nicholas I was to celebrate the tenth anniversary of his accession with a masked ball to which thirty-five thousand people representing all the classes of Russia had been invited. At six in the evening huge throngs began pouring into the Winter Palace: the White, Gilded, and Concert Rooms; the Rotunda; the Marble, Field Marshal's, and St. George's Rooms; the Portrait Gallery, the Hermitage, and the Hermitage Theater. At nine, accompanied by the heir to the throne and other members of the imperial family, Nicholas I and his consort entered the Gilded Room and inaugurated the dancing with a polonaise. Two hours later, 485 lucky guests dined in

---

* From an unpublished letter that Marya Petrovna Vyazemskaya wrote to her mother on December 16, 1835, we discover that at the end of 1835 d'Anthès also saw the Pushkins at the homes of mutual friends. The young Princess Vyazemskaya wrote: "On Saturday I was also at Nadinka Salagoub's, who had made me promise to come see her that morning. Returning home I found a great crowd: the Pushkins and d'Anthès, later Scalon and Walouieff came. At eleven the last two left us to go with Papa to Joukowsky's. D'Anthès finally went away and the evening ended with the four of us. . . ."

the Hermitage Theater. The others were offered buffets with drinks to slake their thirst. It was nearly midnight when Alexandra Fyodorovna, once again in the family way, claimed to feel slightly faint; the imperial couple quickly retired, declaring the party at an end. Natalya Nikolaevna Pushkina did not pass unnoticed even in the enormous crowd at the Winter Palace. She, too, was pregnant, five months along, but none the worse for it; in fact, she seemed to get more beautiful with each pregnancy. Georges d'Anthès never took his eyes off her, even in the enormous crowd at the Winter Palace.

Sometime around January 10, 1836, Pushkin wrote to Nashchokin: "My family is proliferating, growing, clamoring around me. I now believe there is no reason to begrudge life or to fear old age." At first he had written: "or to fear death," but the ever vigilant demon of self-censorship stayed his hand, and the poet crossed out the word that had slithered in among the others, betraying the gloomy thoughts then stalking him. He continued with his joyful hymn to wedded bliss: "The bachelor is a man of boredom, infuriated at seeing new, young generations; only a father can gaze without envy at the young people around him. It follows that I did well to marry."

It was known in literary circles and among Pushkin's close friends that the poet was about to publish a literary quarterly "like the English *Quarterly Review.*" D'Anthès had learned a little Russian and was now hazarding clumsy puns in that intractable language. He knew, for example, that *kvartalny nadziratel* meant "neighborhood police commissioner," and one day (at the Karamzins', at the Vyazemskys'?) he said to Pushkin, "Why not call your magazine *Kvartalny Nadziratel?*" The poet replied with a forced smile, almost a grimace. The play on words, *kvartalny* ("neighborhood") and *yezhekvartalny* ("quarterly"), struck him as both crude and ambiguous. Was the Frenchman mocking the local gendarme, Natalya Nikolaevna's eager Cerberus?

D'Anthès to Heeckeren, Petersburg, January 20, 1836: My dearest
friend, I feel truly guilty for not having replied immediately to the
two lovely and amusing letters you wrote me, but you see, my life
for the past two weeks has consisted of nights of dancing, mornings
of riding, and afternoon naps, and at least as much of the same lies
ahead, and the worst of it is that I'm madly in love! Yes, madly,
because I don't know where to turn, I won't tell you who she is,
since a letter can go astray, but try to remember the most delicious
creature of Petersburg and you'll know her name, and what is most
painful about this situation is that she loves me, too, and we can't
see each other, which has been impossible so far because her husband
is a man of revolting jealousy. I confide all this to you, my dearest,
as to my best friend, because I know you will share my pain, but
in God's name don't say a word to anyone and don't ask anything
about who it is I'm courting, you would unwittingly ruin her and
I would be inconsolable, because, you see, I would do anything in
the world for her just to please her, since the life I've been leading
has been a constant torture for some time now: to be in love and
to be able to say so only between *ritournelles* of the quadrille is a
terrible thing; perhaps I'm wrong to confide all these things to you,
and you might consider them folly, but my heart is so swollen and
full that I need to let it out a little. I am sure you will forgive me
this madness, for I agree that's what it is, but I find it impossible
to think reasonably, no matter how much I need to, since this love
is poisoning my life; but be assured I am cautious, so cautious that
up to now the secret is hers and mine alone. . . . I repeat: not a
word to Bray, because he writes to Petersburg, and the merest
word from him to his ex-Wife and we would both be ruined!
Because God only knows what might happen, and so, my dear
friend, I count the days to your return, and these four months will
seem like centuries to me, because anyone in my situation absolutely
needs someone he loves to whom he can open his heart and seek
encouragement. That's why I look so miserable, since never in my
life have I been better physically, but my head is in such turmoil
that I can't get a moment's peace night or day, which is what gives
me this sick sad look. . . . The only gift I'd like you to bring me

from Paris is some gloves and socks of *filoselle,* it is a fabric made of silk and wool, a very warm and pleasant material which I don't think costs much, or if it does, let's pretend I never mentioned it. As to cloth, I think there's no point: my overcoat will last until we go to France together, and for the uniform the difference would be so slight it's not worth the trouble. . . . Adieu, my dear friend, indulge me in my new passion, because I love you, too, from the bottom of my heart.

Jacob van Heeckeren had never been jealous of Georges d'Anthès. If anything, it was the younger man who sometimes felt suspicious misgivings: "The papers say the cholera is almost completely over with in Italy, maybe you'll go there, a place where eyes are very big and dark, and you have a soft heart." Nor had Heeckeren ever objected to his ward's affairs: women "scratched each other's eyes out for him," and the passionate *chevalier garde* always took maximum erotic advantage of his charm; it seemed only natural, in the order of things. The ambassador had raised no objection to d'Anthès's long relationship with a certain married woman – the "Wife," in their private lexicon. And when in November 1835 Georges informed him that he was about to leave his lover, he was not surprised: he knew that d'Anthès was an insatiable, fickle philanderer. Far from hiding anything from him, the young man enjoyed boasting of his conquests, past and present: "Tell Alphonse to point my latest passion out to you, and you can let me know if I've got good taste and whether with a girl like this it isn't easy to forget the commandment that one should deal only with married women." Baron Heeckeren was already scouting the Russian, French, and German nobility for a suitable match for Georges, a girl with a good name and substantial fortune, so that someday the *chevalier garde* and the old ambassador could retire from their military and diplomatic careers and spend the rest of their days together, *"en famille,* so to speak."

When he received d'Anthès's breathless confession, Heeckeren assumed it was just another brushfire doomed to flicker
out in the arms of yet another "Wife." He knew how persistent
his Georges could be and was well aware of the dubious virtue
of the ladies of Petersburg. This latest "madness" would soon
collapse into a banal adulterous affair, the kind of thing that
satisfies a young man's senses and that high society is generally
content to wink at or close both eyes to. Except this time the
restless officer, who generally sought his prey in the wings
of theaters, had set his sights far higher, targeting one of
Petersburg's most beautiful women, a woman to whose charms
not even the Tsar was indifferent.

4

Herring and Caviar

Beauty trailed in her wake like a radiant shadow and walked before her as tenaciously as the inevitable epithets: "lovely wife," "most beautiful wife," "magnificent lady of the house," "the beautiful Natalie," "glorious woman," "most gracious creature." No one called Natalya Nikolaevna Goncharova Pushkina just plain Natalie. Other women seemed to fade in the aura of her charm, and people who had merely heard of her hurried to come near her and stare, trying to find out whether the preeminence accorded her by the salons of Petersburg was real. Was she truly the most beautiful, more beautiful than Elena Zavadovskaya, Nadezhda Sollogub, Sofya Urusova, Emilya Musina-Pushkina, Avrora Schernwall von Vallen? She invariably emerged from the comparison victorious. There wasn't a single young man in Petersburg who didn't secretly pine for her. Her luminous beauty, combined with the magical name she bore, set all heads spinning. Fellows who not only didn't know her personally but had never even seen her from a distance seriously believed themselves in love. Tall, "supple as a palm tree," luxuriant, snow-white décolleté, preposterously narrow waist, slender neck, a sculpted head "like a lily on its stem," her face a perfect oval, a complexion of soft ivory pallor. Delicate features of classical perfection, eyebrows like black velvet, long lashes as dark as her hair, which she wore swept up or falling loose on her neck, "like a fine cameo," with ringlets framing her temples. There was "a vagueness in her gaze," for she had a very slight squint, perhaps the result of a touch of nearsightedness, and limpid eyes of shifting colors – green and gray and chestnut – eyes reminiscent of gooseberries, their tiny imperfection only heightening the enchantment of a face that was all grace and harmony, sublime symphony of shape and form.

"The little Goncharova girl was ravishing in the role of Dido's sister" at the ball organized for the court by Dmitry Vladimirovich Golitsyn, governor-general of Moscow, during the imperial family's visit to the former capital during the Christmas holidays of 1829. The youngest of the Goncharova sisters stepped out of the *tableau vivant* to receive the Tsar's congratulations; on February 18, 1831, the day she married Russia's most famous poet, she appeared yet again in a living canvas as Venus, Psyche, the Madonna, Angel, Muse, Goddess, Euterpe. Any garment that clothed her slender body ("Where does that woman put her food?" envious ladies, among others, often wondered) left an indelible image on the memory of onlookers: "the high-necked black satin dress," "the fur-lined blue velvet cape," "the white dress, round hat, and red shawl draped over her shoulders," "the priestess of the sun costume," "the loose black gown" she wore at home, "the boa" Pushkin caressed at his ill mother's bedside. Even a male observer, the romantic marine painter Ayvazovsky, described her with a wealth of detail worthy of a ladies' fashion magazine: "elegant white dress, black velvet jacket with braided black ribbons, broad-brimmed canary-yellow straw hat. Long white gloves."

The sweetness of her features, the beauty of her shape, and the elegance of her dress erased any other impression in those who knew and regularly visited Natalya Nikolaevna. Few managed to see beyond the wondrous wrapping, and even fewer left any record of her words: "Good Lord, how you bore me with your poetry, Pushkin! . . . Please keep reading . . . while I go take a look at my clothes," "Be my guest, read; I'm not listening." But these are unreliable witnesses, their memories blurred by posthumous rancor. To our ears Natalya Nikolaevna is mute. Every attempt to capture her living voice founders on the plush barrier of silence. Her letters to Pushkin are gone; we don't even know how many there were. Perhaps she destroyed them herself as tokens of a painful past, or perhaps they survive even now, forgotten among other old papers in the family archives of some noble European house. All that remains are echoes and glints in her husband's letters, for Natalie told him of her own and the children's health, kept him informed about the servants (whom she had a hard time managing in the early days of their married life), complained about the eternal lack of money, chatted about weddings and engagements, recounted the latest gossip of the capital, and described parties, balls, and her rivals' gowns and makeup. All this was standard under the epistolary code of her class and time: hers were no different from thousands of other letters from thousands of other young Petersburg women. But no hint of what went on in the depths of her soul, nothing that might tell us what Beauty really thought of the Beast, how Venus really saw Vulcan. Nothing, that is, except jealousy.

Natalie was obsessively suspicious that her husband was unfaithful (not without cause), and Pushkin labored to convince her of his innocence: "I am behaving myself; you have nothing to pout about"; "I am paying no court to young ladies, nor pinching postmasters' wives, nor flirting with Kalmyk girls; a few days ago I even turned down an offer from a Bashkir woman, despite my more than comprehensible traveler's curiosity"; "in Christ's name I swear I am courting neither that Sollogub woman nor Smirnova." Now and then the poet apparently felt his angel's dainty little hand fall heavily on his own person, and he chuckled, seemingly content, when he told friends of the blows. The humiliated love goddess giving vent to her pain and scorn? Or to her whims? Who can say? We know all there is to know about her bewitching body, every detail of her incomparable allure, but all we can do is guess when it comes to what stirred her heart, basing our thoughts on the words of others – those written to her by her husband and those ascribed to her by d'Anthès in his confessions to Heeckeren. Thus fate has left her forever: a voiceless, aphasic icon of beauty.

Sometimes we even wonder whether she had real feelings and emotions other than those so lovingly attributed to her by the two men for whom she became the apple of deadly discord. We have detailed knowledge of only one passion of Natalie's: her love of dancing, which vanquished her innate shyness and acquainted her with the many fleeting pleasures of salon merriment – a kind of gratuitous giddiness that causes one to say countless mindless charming things, a little fever of the brain induced by the music, the lights, the chaos, the crowd, a euphoria that fades at the slightest sign of thought and is doomed by dawn's first light.

But the fateful question is this: why did she finally accept the repeated, anxious, urgent marriage proposals of Pushkin, a poet perennially broke, a heretic and a schemer, a man whose features had been compared to "that very witty and intelligent little animal" indigenous to African lands? He could offer neither riches nor titles nor prospects of ease. Was her mother determined to marry her off to the first suitor to appear on her greedy horizon? Was it Natalie's vanity, her desire to bear a name whose fame had spread to every corner of Russia? Perhaps eagerness to escape her family's gloomy, oppressive Moscow home? Or maybe it was all these things, compounded by a vague feeling akin more to fear than to love. Not fear of winding up a spinster, of course – for she was the most beautiful marriageable girl in Moscow – but awe and terror at something unknown that overwhelmed her and swept her away: fate, power, passion, poetry.

The earliest years of her life had been spent in Moscow, on country estates, and in Polotnyany Zavod, the thriving factory

that once made sails for Peter the Great's fleet and still manufactured Russia's best sailcloth and finest paper. Early in the
nineteenth century the substantial Goncharov fortune was
sapped by forfeitures, mortgages, and the profligate spending
of the family patriarch, an extravagant tyrant who died owing
one and a half million rubles. In 1812 Natalie's grandfather
Afanasy Nikolaevich Goncharov, separated from his mentally
ill wife, returned from a long holiday abroad with a new lover
in tow, one Babette – or "that French laundress," as she was
called in the family's increasingly luxurious home, ever more
riven by discord and squabbles over material issues.

Nikolai, Afanasy Goncharov's only male child, was
abruptly dismissed from the management of the family
business, and in 1815 he moved to Moscow with his wife and
four of his small children. Natalie alone – known as Tasha,
from Natasha, another diminutive of Natalya – the despot's
favorite grandchild, remained at Polotnyany Zavod. But one
day at the age of six or seven the very beautiful Tasha was
brought to Moscow as well. Her sable coat, a gift from her
grandfather, was taken from her upon her arrival; her mother
made muffs out of it. Gone was the life of luxury, with its
privileges and caresses. Gone, too, were Polotnyany Zavod,
the hundreds of servants, the huge grounds, the greenhouses
with peaches and pineapples, the games in the open air, the
horses, the stables, and her superb riding. Instead, she had to
get used to the rigid discipline of the Goncharov household,
ruled by a fickle, autocratic, bitter woman who was often
cruel and surely unhappy. Only rarely did the children see
their father, "a shattered creature" according to his own
description.

Nikolai Afanasyevich Goncharov, his disturbed mind
clouded by alcohol, lived in a wing of the great residence on
Nikitskaya Street to which he'd been confined to keep his
violent rages out of sight. On calmer days the heart-
wrenching, melancholy sounds of his violin could be heard.
His wife went to see him only in the evening, and it was

whispered that at night she was known to visit the rooms of the male servants; by day her sanctimonious soul made amends for her sins by praying in the chapel, dispensing alms, and offering lodging to pilgrims, beggars, and fools in Christ. She exercised her maternal authority with harsh punishments and proscriptions, often accompanied by painful slaps with the back of a hand. She instilled fearful respect, especially in her daughters, who were brought up to be blindly and mutely submissive. Unable to administer properly the inheritance from her mother and the annuity from her father-in-law, she became in time morbidly greedy. She drank. It was mainly to escape her constant complaints, tantrums, and quarrels that Pushkin and Natalie left Moscow for Tsarskoe Selo a few months after their marriage. From there they went on to Petersburg.

Dolly Ficquelmont, October 26, 1831: Our second *grande soirée* went off perfectly last night: there were a lot of people. It was the social debut of Mrs. Pushkin, the poet's wife: she is a great beauty, with something poetic about her entire persona. She has a superb figure, regular features, a gracious mouth, a lovely though timid gaze; something sweet and fine about her face. I don't yet know what her conversation is like; with a hundred and fifty people it is of course impossible to talk, but her husband says she is a woman of spirit. As for him, he ceases to be a poet in her presence; it seemed to me that he felt all the little pricks of excitement and emotion of any husband who hopes to see his wife succeed in society.

In public she spoke rarely, and "women found her a little strange." She was taciturn and bashful in the intervals between dances, her gazelle-like gaze lowered, head slightly bowed, perhaps by the weight of beauty itself. She was more talkative in the intimacy of her own and friends' homes – and then she spoke perhaps too much. It was as if other people's voices echoed off the fragile alabaster of her body, itself seemingly devoid of depth, lacking a sound box of its own. To her friends, sisters, aunt, and husband she reported every gallantry, every compliment from the swarm of admirers who besieged her in the salons. She boasted of her perennial, inevitable social triumphs, and her fatuous twittering melted Pushkin's heart. He was flattered by other men's admiration and homage, but was always on his guard: "I was expecting an outburst from you, since by my calculations you couldn't have received my letter before Sunday, and instead you seem so calm, indulgent, and amusing – a real delight. Which means what? I wouldn't by any chance be wearing horns, would I?" "Thank you for promising not to flirt: even though I gave you permission, it's better if you don't exercise it." "I don't blame you. It's all quite natural: be young, because you are young, and reign because you're wonderful. . . . I hope that you are pure and innocent toward me, and that we will meet again as we parted." Jealous, of course. Yet Pushkin had boundless faith in the virtue of his "cross-eyed Madonna."

He was disturbed more by certain of Natalie's habits than by his fear that she would cheat on him. Magnificent creature that she was – undisputed queen of Petersburg, secret dream of so many men and envy of so many women – there was sometimes something cheap and provincial about her, something that smacked of the little girl from Moscow. He always forgave her, but he scolded her constantly, too, striving to train her. He would tell her that it was vulgar to entice admirers from her friends, to boast of her conquests, to flirt with country gentry, to pay respects to the Mother Superior of Kaluga, to visit merchants' daughters, to crowd into waiting rooms crammed with people seeking favors, to attend fireworks displays with the common people, to frequent second-rate salons, and to dance at the homes of noblewomen of less than sterling reputation. There were times when his wonderful wife reminded him of the sort of women Prince Metternich scornfully called *petites femmes*. Well, she was young, Pushkin thought, and he continued to instruct her gently in the secrets of spiritual elegance and the more exquisite tricks of snobbery. But he could be coarse as well:

You like it when the dogs trail after you like a bitch in heat, raising their tails and sniffing your c . . . . Really something to be glad about! . . . It's easy enough to train rogue bachelors to run after you: all you have to do is make sure everyone knows, "I love it." That's the whole secret of flirting. *As long as there's a trough, the swine will find it.* What's the point of receiving men paying court to you? You never know whom you might run into. You should read A. Izmaylov's fable about Foma and Kuzma. Foma fed Kuzma herring and caviar. Kuzma asked for something to drink, and Foma didn't give him anything. So the scoundrel Kuzma showered him with kicks. From which the poet deduces this moral: Serve no herring, my beauties, unless you're ready with something to drink. . . . Enjoy yourself, little wife of mine, but not too much, and don't forget me. I'm dying to see you with your hair done up *à la* Ninon: you must be bewitching. How is it you never thought of copying that old whore's hairdo before? Tell me how you looked at the balls, which, according to what you write me, must have already begun.

In the next letter he apologized for losing his temper, but still reminded her: "Ninon, the whore whose hairdo you copied . . . used to say, The heart of every man is stamped: 'To the easiest.' . . . Have some regard for me as well. To the inevitable vexations of a man's life do not add family worries, jealousy, etc., etc. – not to mention cheating, on which, by the way, I read an entire essay in Brantôme the other day."

Dolly Ficquelmont, November 12, 1831: Mrs. Pushkin's poetic beauty touches the depths of my heart. There is something so ethereal and stirring about her entire person; this woman will not be happy, of that I am sure. Her brow is marked by pain. For now, the world smiles upon her, she is completely happy, life unfolds splendid and joyous before her; yet her head is bowed and her whole countenance seems to say, "I am suffering." It also must be said: what a harsh fate it is to be a poet's wife, especially a poet like Pushkin.

In Petersburg she was invited to court and admitted to the elite circle summoned to the Anichkov, the private mansion on the Nevsky Prospect where the Empress liked to vent her passion for dancing. In the autumn of 1833, Alexandrine and Catherine Goncharov moved in with Natalie and her husband; and the sisters, too, had to be brought into society, introduced to the marriage mart. Every day saw a ball, a *raout* (a gala reception with no dancing), a play, a concert, or a gathering of friends. Someone complained that Natalya Nikolaevna was never at home in the evenings. Pushkin was uneasy about this lifestyle. Whenever he had to be away from his wife, he entrusted her to the tender tutelage of the elderly Miss Zagryazhskaya, an aunt of Natalie's who was well respected at court and had a seasoned flair for social life. But even so he was anxious:

I don't know why, but I've been afraid for you from the moment I left you. You won't stay home, you'll go to the Winter Palace, and before you know it you'll miscarry on the hundred and fifth step of the grand stairway ... you're probably pregnant, aren't you? If so, you have to take care of yourself in the early days. Don't go horseback riding, find some other way of flirting ... don't forget you have two children, and you lost the third, take care of yourself; be careful, dance with moderation, have fun in small doses ... for the love of God take care of yourself; Woman, says [the abbé] Galiani, is by nature a weak and sickly creature. But what wonderful workers and helpers! You work only with your little feet at dances and help your husbands on the road to bankruptcy.

He himself had first noticed her in Moscow in 1828, at a ball hosted by the dancing master Yogel — and Pushkin's libertine heart thirsted for deliverance, pounding as never before.

"*Tour, battement, jeté, révérence,*" Yogel ordered, and Natalie performed each step impeccably, with gracious, perfect movements, almost mechanically, like a charming automaton.

Sophie Bobrinskaya, September 3, 1832: The wife of Pushkin, the poet, was undoubtedly the most beautiful woman at the party. She looks like a Muse, a Raphael Hour. Vyazemsky said to me: "This Pushkin woman is like a Poem; she makes the other one [Countess Emilya Karlovna Musina-Pushkina] look like a Dictionary."

"I'm not stopping you from flirting," Pushkin wrote, "but I demand that you exhibit coolness, decorum, dignity." Pushkin had been alarmed and distressed by another kind of coolness in the "little Goncharova girl" – a mysterious apathy, a chilly torpor – back in the days when he was still wrestling with the countless practical difficulties standing in the way of their marriage and his own wrenching uncertainties. He had written to his future mother-in-law: "Only persistence and long intimacy could enable me to win your daughter's affection; I can only hope that in time she will come to love me, but I have nothing with which to please her. If she consents to give me her hand, I will see that consent as no more than evidence of her heart's placid indifference." He was more sincere than circumstances or etiquette required. He sensed, he guessed, and his perspicacity was daunting: "As God is my witness, I am ready to die for her love, but the idea of having to die and leave her a sparkling widow free to choose a new husband the very next day – that idea is hell."

Dolly Ficquelmont, September 15, 1832: Mrs. Pushkin, the poet's wife, has been a huge success; one could hardly picture a more beautiful woman, or one with a more poetic air; yet she is not very intelligent and seems to have little imagination.

She was a splendid, bitter enigma wholly innocent of passion – and Pushkin wanted her for himself whatever the cost. A cross and a ring fell and a candle went out during the wedding ceremony. "All the omens are evil!" the superstitious groom exclaimed. But the auguries of gloom were forgotten in his happiness. He became a tender but exacting husband, striving to instill in Natalie the sovereign grace of detachment and self-control, to transform the chill of indifference into deliberate coldness, haughty reserve, a frosty pinnacle out of mortal reach.

He had already succeeded in this once, with Tatiana Larina, whom he encountered, passionate and untamed, in a godforsaken corner of provincial Russia in the second book of *Eugene Onegin* and by the eighth had transformed, Pygmalion-like, into "a faithful reproduction / *du comme il faut.*" Married to an older general she doesn't love, the former country girl and now *grande dame* sweeps through rooms trailed by admiring gazes; she never hurries, never speaks, never looks guests in the eye, doesn't mince, doesn't show off, doesn't boast of success, and doesn't flirt – "none could have found in her / what by the autocratic fashion / in the high London circle / is called 'vulgar.'" This ideal woman mirrors the Muse of Pushkin's maturity: cold, aloof in her unadorned splendor, daughter of the soul's eternal North. But the facile miracles of poetry are not so easily transferable to life. In all good conscience can we blame Natalie, or hate or denounce her, for falling short of such a demanding model, such a drastic poetic of non-being?

Dolly Ficquelmont, November 22, 1832: The most beautiful yesterday was of course the Pushkin woman, whom we call Poetry both because of her husband and because of her heavenly, incomparable beauty. This is a figure one might contemplate for hours on end, as a perfect work of the Creator!

Between mazurkas and cotillions Natalya Nikolaevna led the life of all Russian wives of her class and time: she gave birth to children, supervised the servants, picked out summer dachas, tried on clothes in the ateliers of Madame Sikhler and Monsieur Durier, and wrote to her brother Dmitry to ask for money or "a nice new-style landau" or the paper needed for her husband's publishing efforts. She tried to speed her grandfather's suit against his former steward, made every effort to see that her sisters were married off, did what she could to balance a household budget that was constantly springing leaks, argued about money with publishers and booksellers, and helped Pushkin as best she could. Yet it is hard to picture her in these roles or in this garb – or rather, it can be done, but it feels as if she'd suddenly stepped out of a picture frame or down from a marble pedestal. "Natalya Nikolaevna stood leaning against a column at the entrance waiting for the carriage, while young officers, especially the *chevaliers gardes*, ringed her and showered her with compliments. Not far away, near another column, stood a pensive Alexander Sergeevich, taking no part in the conversation." Like a group sculpture by a minor nineteenth-century artist: fatuous Beauty and mature Reflection. Even after her husband's death, Natalya Nikolaevna failed to escape her statue's fate. In a letter to Sophie Bobrinskaya the Empress lamented the image of this "young woman standing at the tomb like an angel of death, white as marble, blaming herself for the bloody turn of events."

All we have of what Natalie wrote to Pushkin is a brief postscript that she added to a letter from her mother: "Only with great effort have I decided to write to you, *because I have nothing to tell you*, and I sent you some news a few days ago with someone who was passing through. Also, Mama was about to postpone this letter to the next post but was afraid you might worry if you heard nothing from me for some time, so she decided to vanquish the drowsiness and weariness that have taken possession of both of us because we spent the entire day outside. From Mama's letter you will see that we are both well, so I say nothing on that subject. I end my letter with a very tender kiss for you, and I plan to write at greater length at the first opportunity. Adieu, then, be well and don't forget us."

We are reminded of a line Georges d'Anthès wrote to Jacob van Heeckeren: "Tell Papa and my sisters that I'm not writing *because I have nothing to tell them*, that you will tell them everything I could write, which is much better."

The italics are mine, for I believe that the causes of everything that happened lie concealed behind those identical "nothings" – and not only "to tell."

They used to say of Natalya Nikolaevna that hers was an "*âme de dentelles.*" Soul of lace.

When Pushkin died she was the mother of four children and twenty-four years old.

5

The Heights of Zion

On February 1, 1836, Pushkin went to a loan shark called Shishkin and pawned one of Natalya Nikolaevna's shawls — white cashmere, with a wide fringe. He got 1,250 rubles for it.

The carnival of 1836 began ominously. For days a monk had been wandering the capital warning the Orthodox that plague and other horrors would be visited upon them if they abandoned themselves to the usual carousing and debauchery. They didn't listen. On February 2, the first day of the weeklong festivities, the solemn calm and smug neoclassical haughtiness of the City of Peter were shattered by an uproar worthy of Bruegel. Throngs of revelers poured into the streets, slipping and sliding over mounds of ice on the frozen Neva and packing the square at the Admiralty, now transformed into a huge fairground of booths in which illusionists, jugglers, acrobats, animal trainers, actors, and balalaika players performed. But the merrymaking lasted only a few hours, for on that day a horrible disaster plunged the Palmyra of the North into mourning. The magician Lehmann's booth was reduced to ashes in minutes. It was a big tent, held up by resinous poles that became ready fuel for the flames that flared so suddenly. Hundreds of people were burned to death in the terrifying blaze, hundreds more seriously injured. The Tsar himself rushed to the scene and personally helped to man the pumps, exposing his holy person to the flames and scorching his clothes.

At nine that night a messenger from Nicholas I informed the directors of the Assembly of the Nobility that His Majesty could not imagine that anyone could go dancing after such a deadly event. But the ball had already begun and could not be canceled or postponed. An impromptu collection from the guests raised 10,000 rubles for the injured and the families of the dead. Then the dancing began again, though under a pall of gloom. The Admiralty disaster provided a new topic of salon conversation, hitherto dominated by outrage at Pushkin's latest act of bravado: his "Ode on the Convalescence of Lucullus," a cruel lampoon of an imperial minister that widened the already deep gulf dividing him from the powers that be, from bureaucratic Petersburg at its most reactionary, from right-thinking bigots and hypocrites. But weeping and wailing duly vanished from the salons upon the arrival from Moscow of the lovely Alexandra Vasilievna Kireeva, who left everyone breathless and shifted talk back to its usual fatuous track: was she more beautiful than Zavadovskaya, Sollugub, Urusova-Radziwill, Musina-Pushkina, or Schernwall? Could her classic beauty contend with Natalya Nikolaevna Pushkina's romantic allure? Most felt it couldn't, and Petersburg danced on, from early afternoon to dawn, until the *folle journée* of February 9, when the exhausted participants thronged the churches for Lenten services.

Those who saw Pushkin in early February describe his mood as "miserable." He was gloomy, peevish, and irritable, likely to fly into a rage at imagined assaults on his good name and trivial offenses blown out of proportion by his own testiness. In only a few days he came close to duels three times – in words, actions, and thoughts. He was rude to Semyon Khlyustin, a guest who thoughtlessly mentioned the offensive slurs about the poet published in the *Library for Reading*. "I lose my temper when respectable people repeat the idiocies of swine and scoundrels," Pushkin commented, concluding with this menacing phrase: "It's too much! This won't be the end of it." Only delicate mediation by Sergei Sobolevsky (hurriedly summoned as a second) managed to avert the impending clash.

Around the same time Pushkin received a letter from Vladimir Sollogub, a young acquaintance in Tver. In it Sollogub presented his excuses, after a long and inexplicable silence, for the unfortunate misunderstanding that had arisen between the two men some months earlier, but declared that he was at the poet's disposal if need be and would in fact be flattered to be his opponent in a duel. Pushkin curtly rejected "this never requested explanation" and postponed the encounter of honor to the end of March, when he would be passing through Tver. Lastly, on February 5, upon hearing that an individual of dubious reputation was spreading unflattering opinions about him, attributing them to Prince Nikolai Grigorievich Repnin, Pushkin wrote this to Repnin: "As a gentleman and a father, I am duty bound to protect my honor and the name I will bequeath to my children. . . . I beg Your Excellency to be so kind as to inform me what I must do." Prince Repnin's calm reply averted the worst. Debt, exhausting negotiations with the censors, vulgar attacks by newspaper hacks, the storm of condemnation raised by "Lucullus" – not even all this seems adequate to explain such an uncontrollable craving to settle accounts with the entire world.

Pushkin jotted down some figures on the rough draft of his letter to Vladimir Sollogub: 2,500 × 25 + 62,500. This was the 62,500 rubles (2,500 subscriptions at 25 rubles each) he was hoping to raise each year from *The Contemporary*, the review that had finally been passed by the Censorship Committee. He had forgotten to deduct expenses, however, and to make allowances for shifts in public taste.

At the first light of dawn on February 5, the Empress lost the child she was carrying: heedless of the warning signs, she had apparently danced too much. She was therefore unable to attend the first grand ball given in Petersburg by Prince George Wilding di Butera e Radoli, which was held that evening. The Englishman (whose exotic title came courtesy of his first wife, a Sicilian noblewoman who died young) was celebrating not only the birth of the royal prince of the Two Sicilies but also his recent appointment as ambassador from Naples to the Romanov court and his equally recent marriage to Princess Barbara Petrovna Polier, a fabulously wealthy woman already twice a widow. Barbara Polier was born Princess Shakhovskaya, and her family had long opposed this new marriage, a misalliance with a foreigner who would thereby be in a position to deprive Russia of one of its most substantial fortunes.* Hastening to the Buteras' lavish mansion to celebrate the happy ending of this fraught and controversial love affair, long kept secret, Petersburg discovered yet another forbidden idyll to tug at its heartstrings – and here, too, the protagonist was a foreigner named George. A young maid of honor, Marya Mörder, confided her vivid impressions of the evening to her diary:

On the stairway stood rows of servants in magnificent livery. Exotic flowers filled the air with their sweet aroma. Uncommon luxury! Ascending the stairs, we found ourselves in a magnificent garden – before us an enfilade of rooms flooded with flowers and greenery. Through the spacious apartments wafted the intoxicating sounds of an invisible orchestra. Truly an enchanted magic castle. The grand ballroom with its gilded white marble walls was like a temple of fire – it glowed. . . . I noticed d'Anthès in the crowd, but he didn't see me. Maybe he simply had something else on his mind. It seemed to me his eyes looked anxious – his gaze was seeking someone, and after suddenly staring at a door, he disappeared into the adjoin-

---

* If he really was the title- and dowry-hungry adventurer that some suspected, then Prince Butera was an unlucky soul indeed, for he died without issue in 1841, leaving undying pain in his wife's heart and huge Russian properties as big as three or four Sicilies.

ing room. Some moments later he reappeared, now with Mrs. Pushkin on his arm. These words reached my ears: "Leave – do you
really mean it? I don't believe it, that wasn't what you wanted. . . ."
The tone with which these words were spoken left no doubt as to
the truth of my earlier observations: they are madly in love. After
no more than half an hour at the ball, we set out for the door: the
baron was dancing the mazurka with Mrs. Pushkin. How happy
they seemed at that moment!

D'Anthès to Heeckeren, Petersburg, February 14, 1836: The carnival is over, my dear friend, and with it a part of my torment, for
I truly believe I am more at ease when I don't see her every day,
and now everyone else can't come along and take her hand and
hold her by the waist and talk to her as I do – them even better
than me because their conscience is clearer. It sounds stupid to say
it and it even seems it was jealousy – something I would never
have believed – but I was in a constant state of irritation that made
me unhappy. Then the last time I saw her we had an explanation,
which was awful but did me good; this woman, generally assumed
to be of scant intelligence, I don't know if it's love that provides
it, but it would be impossible to put more tact, grace, and intelligence
than she did into this conversation, and it was difficult to endure
because it was a matter of no less than rejecting a man whom she
loves and who adores her, of violating her duties for him: she
painted her situation with such abandon, asked for pity with such
candor that truly I was overwhelmed and utterly at a loss for words
to reply to her; if you knew how she consoled me, for she knew
very well I was bursting and that my condition was frightful, and
when she told me, "I love you as I have never loved, but never
ask me for more than my heart, for the rest does not belong to
me, I can be happy only honoring all my duties, have pity on me
and love me always as you do now, my love will be your reward"
– well, I believe that had I been alone I would have fallen at her feet
to kiss them, and I assure you that my love for her has grown since
then; but it isn't the same anymore, I worship and honor her as one
worships and honors a being to whom one's whole life is devoted.

Forgive me, my dear friend, if I begin my letter by speaking of her, but she and I are a single thing; to speak of her is also to speak of myself, and in all your letters you chide me for not lingering longer on that subject. . . . As I was telling you before, I am much better, and thank God am beginning to breathe again, for my torment was unbearable: to be merry and laugh before everyone, before the people who saw me every day, while death was in my heart, is a horrible condition I would not wish on my cruelest enemy; yet the compensation comes later, because for words like the ones she said to me I believe that I will pass them on to you, for you are the only being who ranks with her in my heart, since when I am not thinking of her, I think of you, but don't be jealous, my dear, and do not abuse my trust: you will be forever, while time will undertake to change her until someday nothing will remind me of her whom I loved so much, while you, my dearest, each day that dawns binds me to you and reminds me that without you I would be no one.

The main characters of *Eugene Onegin*, Pushkin's novel in verse, are the eponymous hero, a young Petersburg dandy precociously jaded and bored with life, and Tatiana Larina, a girl of the minor provincial nobility, a melancholy creature who cherishes romantic tales, a dreamy moonlight lover. Their story is simple. Tatiana is in love with Eugene. She opens her heart, writing to him of her love, but he rejects her: "in vain are your perfections: / I'm not at all worthy of them." Many years later he encounters her again – completely transformed, a bewitching and unapproachable queen of society – and is irresistibly drawn to her. He writes to her of his love, but she rejects him. It is a spare, mirror-image plot, a simple diptych in the middle of which is embedded an absurd and pointless death that tinges the play of mirrors with a mist of sadness: challenged to a duel by Lensky for a slight (albeit cynical) offense, Onegin accepts, and kills his young friend. It all happens with the implacable symmetry and merciless banality of life. Thus do people who may be meant for each other wind up apart, thus does happiness always come at the wrong time, thus does an invisible enemy, a cruel tyrant, maim hearts and cut down lives.

But it is more than an enemy if it affords men an intense yet subtle pleasure – a nostalgia for what might have been but never was – and thereby throbs forever in that secret place in the soul where suffering and warm delight are mingled; and if it affords things the agonizing charm of the unfulfilled – of what has not been marred, impoverished, or damaged by life. And it is more than a tyrant if it often smiles upon and pities its victims, acting as the narrator's merry accomplice, telling him to go ahead and enjoy himself, to use its toys: little wagons filled with figurines in frock coats and crinolines, ringing with laughter and sighs, canticles and madrigals. Pushkin indeed enjoyed himself, shuffling the passengers around in the uproarious omnibus, packing in a huge crowd of friends and rivals, of acquaintances old and new! And by playing this game, by spinning the plots both grievous and lighthearted woven together by his accomplice Chance, he dared to perform an unprecedented experiment: to raise literature to the status of (supreme, imperial) heroine, and to force heroes oozing literature – "parodies" molded of the clay of books well loved and obsolete – to bend to the laws of life.

Georges d'Anthès did not know, could not have known, *Eugene Onegin*. And in dumb amazement he wondered where his beloved had found the grace and intelligence with which she denied him all but her heart. I think I know: in *Onegin*, 8, XLVII: "I love you (why dissimulate?); / but to another I've been given away: / to him I shall be faithful all my life." The sincere and noble words that make Tatiana Larina a lofty symbol of honesty and duty, "apotheosis of the Russian woman,"* came to Natalya Nikolaevna Pushkina's rescue at the most delicate moment of her career as wife, and the whole

* The phrase is Dostoyevsky's, from his essay on *Pushkin* (1880).

story would have had a happy ending, virtue and poetry would
have triumphed, if only . . .

Master of the unspoken, of the fraught cliffhanger, Pushkin
left Tatiana and Eugene at the zenith of pain and beauty.
Down in the valley we wonder: Will they ever meet again?
Will she yield to her unsatisfied yearnings? Will she betray
her husband? Will he blow his brains out? Love another
woman? Will they ever be happy? But life is a greedy publisher, always avid for new chapters of books that sell well,
and all at once it snatched the novel it had momentarily
plagiarized so perfectly out of Pushkin's hands to write a
sequel of its own, in untidy prose, striving to meet the expec-
tations of an audience eager for complex intrigue and powerful
emotions *à la Balzac*.* D'Anthès did not remain immobile,
"as if by thunder struck," but returned, restless, to the charge,
using every trick he could think of to see Natalie again, to
coax out of her the "yes" he craved. Desperate, he sought
counsel and comfort from Heeckeren:

Now I think I love her more than I did two weeks ago! In short,
my dear, it's an obsession that never leaves me, that sleeps and
wakes with me, a frightful torment. I can barely manage to collect
my thoughts to write to you, and yet that is my sole consolation,
for when I speak to you of this my heart seems to lighten. I have
more cause than ever to be happy, because I have succeeded in
penetrating her home, but to see her alone I think is almost impossible, and yet I absolutely must; and no human power will stop me,
for only then will I rediscover life and repose: surely it is madness
to struggle too long against an evil fate, but to withdraw too quickly
is cowardice. In short, my dear, only you can help guide me through
these shoals, so tell me, what must I do? I will follow your views
as those of my best friend, because I would like to be cured by the

---

* Alexei Karamzin to his brother Andrei, January 16, 1837: "And so this
novel *à la Balzac* has ended, to the distress of the gossips of Petersburg."

time of your return so as to have no other thought but the happiness of seeing you and to have pleasure nowhere but at your side alone. I am wrong to give you all these details, I know they will upset you, but I'm being a little selfish because you give me relief. Perhaps you will forgive me for beginning with this when you see that I have saved the good news for last, to take away the bad taste. I have just been made lieutenant. . . . I end my letter, dear friend, convinced that you won't be angry with me for writing so briefly, but you see, nothing comes to mind but her, I could go on about her all night long, but it would bore you.

And once again the Dutch ambassador came to his aid, with affectionate advice and stern reproof, just like a real father worried about his son's future, about his health in body and mind alike, but also with hints that made him sound like a jealous lover: was Georges really sure that this woman was lily-pure?

D'Anthès wore a ring containing a miniature portrait of Henry V, posthumous son of the Duke de Berry, whom French legitimists hoped would succeed to the throne usurped by Louis Philippe. One evening at the Vyazemskys' Pushkin jokingly said that d'Anthès wore an ape's portrait on his finger. The *chevalier garde* raised his hand so everyone could see the ring and replied, "But look, don't these features look like Mr. Pushkin's?"

D'Anthès to Heeckeren, Petersburg, March 6, 1836: My dear friend, I am so late answering you because I've had to read and reread your letter many times. In it I found all you'd promised: encouragement in bearing up in my situation; yes, it's true, man always has enough strength within himself to overcome what he truly wishes to overcome, and God is my witness that since I received your letter I have decided to sacrifice this woman for you. It is a big decision, but your letter was so good, full of so much truth and such tender friendship that not for a moment did I hesitate, and from that instant I have completely changed my behavior toward her: I have been avoiding her with the same care with which I earlier sought to meet her, I have spoken to her with all the indifference I could summon, but I believe that had I not learned all you wrote to me by heart, I would have lacked the will. . . . Thank God I have gained control of myself, and all that now remains of the unchained passion of which I spoke in all my letters is a placid devotion and admiration for the being who made my heart pound so intensely. Now that it's all over, please allow me to tell you that your missive was too harsh and that you took the matter too tragically; to make me believe and to tell me that you knew you were nothing to me and that my letter was full of threats was too severe a punishment. . . . You were no less harsh in what you said about her, that she had already tried to sacrifice her honor to another before me, because, you see, this is impossible – that there are men who have lost their heads over her I believe, she is beautiful enough for that, but that she heeded them, no: because she has never loved anyone more than me, and in recent times there has been no lack of opportunities for her to have given me everything, and yet, my dear – nothing, never ever! She has been far stronger than I, has asked me more than twenty times to have pity on her and her children and her future, and at those moments she was so beautiful (what woman isn't?) that if she'd wanted to be contradicted she would not have been so fervent, because as I've told you, she was so beautiful she might have been taken for an angel from heaven; there isn't a man in the world who wouldn't have helped her at that moment, so great was the respect she inspired, and thus she remained pure and can walk with her head held high. No other woman would have behaved as she did, certainly there are some whose lips may speak more often of virtue and duty, but of virtue in the heart not a one; I speak to you in this manner not to boast of my sacrifice, on this point I shall be forever in your debt, but to make you see how wrong it can sometimes be to judge by appearances. Another thing: remarkably enough, before I got your letter no one in the world had ever so much as spoken her name to me; then barely as your letter arrived, that very evening I went to the ball at court and the Grand Duke and Heir teased me about her, from which I immediately concluded that people must have noticed something about me, but about her I am sure no one has ever entertained a suspicion, and I love her too much to want to compromise her, and as I said before, it's all over, and I hope that when you return you will find me cured root and branch. . . . Here's another story that's making quite a stir in our regiment. We had to discharge Thiesenhausen, Countess Panina's brother, and Novosiltsev, an officer who'd just joined the regiment. These gentlemen had a kind of corps dinner with some infantry officers, and after getting dead drunk had a fight and exchanged punches. Instead of blowing each other's brains out on the spot, the fine fellows kissed and made up and tried to keep the whole thing quiet. But in the end someone let the cat out of the bag.

Could Pushkin himself have been unaware of what was so obvious to the entire city that it was now being mentioned in diaries and becoming the subject of jocular remarks by members of the imperial family? Clearly not. *"Il l'a troublée,"* he told a friend, referring to d'Anthès and his wife. He saw, he understood. A seasoned veteran of long and valiant service in the troops ranked against husbands – "the sly spouse, / Faublas's disciple of long standing, / and the distrustful old-ster, / and the majestical cornuto, / always pleased with himself, / his dinner, and his wife" – he had opted for the most effective and least ridiculous tactic: to keep a discreet eye on things from a distance, to wait patiently. He was sure it wouldn't go beyond the limit he feared. But deep inside pain gnawed at him.

On March 13 the usurer Sishkin gave him 650 rubles for a Bréguet watch and a silver coffeepot.

There is a sudden, violent rumble that gladdens the hearts of Petersburgers when the river's frozen surface cracks, riven by fissures steadily widening under pressure from the captive water beneath, and gleaming blocks of ice begin their slow, imperceptible journey to the sea, closely followed by icebergs broken loose from Lake Ladoga, whistling and roaring as they collide to form jumbles of bizarre angular sculptures and finally, vanquished, rush to their tumultuous death. Soon the last snow will melt and the wooden sidewalks and paved streets will be covered with brown muck that makes roads slippery and travel difficult for days, but Petersburgers rejoice: spring is on its way. The Neva cracked that year on March 22, a day brightened by the sun's reappearance after three interminable months in hiding. Petersburg streamed to the riverbanks. Georges d'Anthès, too, took advantage of the mild weather to go out and enjoy himself and to recover from his bad luck in love. He began to frequent the home of Prince Alexander Baryatinsky, a lieutenant of the Cuirassiers of the Guard. This congenial and generous young comrade had a very pretty seventeen-year-old sister, Marya, who was to make her social debut that very year. But these diversions turned out to be of little use.

D'Anthès to Heeckeren, Petersburg, March 28, 1836: I wanted to write to you without speaking of her, but I frankly admit that my letter goes nowhere unless I do and so I am forced to offer you an account of my behavior since my last letter: I have done what I promised, refraining from seeing or meeting her, in more than three weeks I have spoken to her four times of absolutely trivial things, and God is my witness I could talk to her for ten hours at a stretch and say only half of what I feel when I see her; I freely admit that the sacrifice I am making for you is immense. I should have to love you as I do to keep my word this way, and I never would have believed I had the heart to live in the same places as a creature beloved as I love her without going to see her even when it is quite possible for me to do so, since, my dear friend, and I cannot hide this from you, I am still madly in love with her; but God Himself has come to my aid: yesterday she lost her mother-in-law,* so that she will have to stay at home for at least a month, and since it will be impossible to see her, I will probably be delivered from this terrible inner struggle – to go to her or not? – which began anew every hour when I was alone, and I confess that lately I've been afraid to stay at home alone and have been out constantly, and if you knew how anxiously I await your return and, far from dreading it, count the days until I will have someone I can love beside me, because my heart is so full and I so need to love and not be alone in the world as I am now that six weeks of waiting will seem like years.

On April 11 Pushkin arrived in the governorate of Pskov to bury his mother in the cemetery of the monastery of Svatye Gory. He liked the earth there, "with no worms, no dampness, no clay," and made an offering to the monastery to reserve himself a grave in its vast, serene spaces. He detested crowded urban cemeteries with tombs wedged in next to one another like greedy guests at a beggars' banquet.

On April 14 K. N. Lebedev, an official in the Ministry of Justice, noted in his diary: "I have received Pushkin's *The Contemporary*. Was it worth waiting three months for this? ... Some little poems, small articles, short short stories, criticism. ... This is not the way to broach the matter: a 'Contemporary' should not be playfully literary or solely literary. Our times are better than this. ... What's the point of this familiar conversational tone? ... And Mr. Gogol's stories: can stories of this kind be published?"

At the end of April d'Anthès wrote to Heeckeren for the last time, telling him of how impatiently he awaited his return – "I count the minutes, yes, the minutes" – and thanking him for his suggested cure for lovesickness: "It was helpful. ... I am beginning to live a little again and I hope that [her] move

---

* The poet's mother, Nadezhda Osipovna Pushkina, died on the morning of March 29, 1836. This would suggest that d'Anthès started the letter on March 28 and finished it two days later.

to the countryside will cure me root and branch, because that way I won't see her for months." Pushkin, too, may have had the cure-all recommended by the ambassador in mind when he wrote to Natalie from Moscow: "And on your own account, my darling, rumors are flying that I do not quite hear in full, since husbands are always the last in town to know about their wives, but it seems that your flirtation and cruelty have driven someone to such despair that he has consoled himself by collecting a harem of girls from the theater school. It's not good, my angel: the finest charm of your sex is modesty."

At 4:17 on the afternoon of May 3, the sun over Petersburg went dark. Dumbstruck, the city looked up. It was "one of the most beautiful eclipses of the century," but the common people read unlucky omens in it.

On May 13 the ambassador from Holland disembarked from the steamer *Alexandra* at Kronstadt, returning to Russia laden with gifts, stories, and love. He also brought papers attesting to his adoption of Georges d'Anthès.

Pushkin to his wife [Moscow, May 18, 1836]: Here in Moscow all is calm, thank God. Kireev's fight with the Yar has aroused much indignation in our haughty local society. Nashchoken defends Kireev with quite simple and sensible arguments: what's the difference if a Hussar lieutenant gets drunk and starts beating an innkeeper, who in turn defends himself? As if any of us ever took it without hitting back, in the days when we used to get into it with the Germans over at the Red Tavern. In my view Kireev's brawl is far more excusable than that glorious dinner of your Petersburg *chevaliers gardes*, or the supposed maturity of those young men who, when someone spits in their eye, wipe it off with a little batiste handkerchief, terrified that they won't be invited back to the Anichkov Palace if the story gets out. Bryullov, who came to call on me, just left. He's setting out for Petersburg – reluctantly, for he fears the climate and the lack of freedom. I tried to comfort and encourage him, but my own heart sinks when I remember that I'm a journalist now. When I was still worth something, I suffered rebukes from the police. . . . What will become of me now? . . . It's the devil's fault I was born in Russia with spirit and talent.

On May 21 Baron Heeckeren in a private audience informed the Tsar that he'd adopted the Horse Guardsman Georges d'Anthès. The next day he wrote to Count Nesselrode, the Russian Foreign Minister, asking him please to see to it that his "son" was referred to as Georges Charles de Heeckeren in all future official documents.

Christian von Hohenlohe-Kirchberg to Count von Beroldingen, St. Petersburg, May 23, 1836: Baron Heeckeren . . . has found that he is being treated differently in society and perhaps also at court, where there has been no great rush to receive him. A somewhat caustic man, the baron has few friends in this capital, which is why, I believe, the old proverb "Those who are absent are always in the wrong" has proved especially apposite in his case. Mr. Heeckeren has recently adopted a young baron, d'Anthès . . . for some years in the Russian Army, to which he was admitted at Baron Heeckeren's request.* This adoption has been the talk of many a St. Petersburg salon and has occasioned remarks scarcely flattering to the Barons Heeckeren.

On May 23 Pushkin's wife gave birth to another little Natalya in a dacha rented for the summer in Kamenny Ostrov. Aunt Zagryazhskaya, fearing the damp with which the whole ground floor was saturated, refused to let the new mother leave her upstairs room until the last days of June.

Although part of the female population of Petersburg suddenly came to see Georges d'Anthès as a respectable catch – partly

---

* And not, therefore, by stepping out from behind a screen at just the right moment. Ambassadors are always master string pullers.

because of his impressive new surname, but mainly because of the yearly stipend of 80,000 rubles his new father was reportedly preparing to give him – others took a more jaundiced view of the French *chevalier garde*'s "three countries and two surnames" and the Dutch ambassador's sudden yen for fatherhood. There were rumors that Georges "de Heeckeren" was actually related to the ambassador (possibly a nephew or even his natural son) or was the illegitimate son of the King of Holland or of Charles X of France. Baron Heeckeren himself may have encouraged such gossip so as to justify his action, lending it a romantic halo of mystery. However that may be, the fanciful rumors no doubt proved useful to him at a ticklish moment, and he certainly did nothing to squelch them: volumes could be spoken with a well-timed meaningful silence, an eloquent smile, an inadvertent flicker of his distant gaze.

On the morning of May 23, Heeckeren wrote to Baron Verstolk van Soelen, the Dutch Foreign Minister, to report on his lengthy exchange of views with Count Nesselrode on the ever thorny issue of Belgium, which had seceded from Holland in an armed rebellion six years earlier. He was on the point of concluding his report when he received the official summons to court which he'd been impatiently expecting for some days. He promptly repaired to the Elagin Palace, and upon his return to the Embassy completed his dispatch with a detailed account of the cordial discussion he'd just had with Their Imperial Russian Majesties, a discussion that was to play a significant role in the matter close to our hearts – for the duel and Pushkin's death were to become strangely and quite unexpectedly entangled with the public and private affairs of the Oranges. But everything in its time.

Jacob van Heeckeren to Johan Verstolk van Soelen, St. Petersburg, May 23, 1836: After receiving my respects with his customary benevolence, His Majesty dwelt at length on the family relations of His Royal Highness the Prince of Orange. . . . His Majesty, who quite naturally feels the keenest affection for Their Royal Highnesses, expressed himself frankly on the fickle character of Madame la Princesse* and regretted what he called Monseigneur the Prince of Orange's failure to display greater indulgence toward this regrettable tendency and to make greater efforts to restore good harmony, the absence of which he considers a parlous example for the august children of Their Royal Highnesses and not at all reassuring for the future of the young Princes. . . . Upon departing from this audience, I repaired to the Empress. . . . With no further ado Her Majesty asked me why we maintain such a substantial army and general staff at the borders, adding that such a thing is utterly pointless today, serving only to satisfy the propensities of the Prince of Orange, who, it would seem, dislikes residing in The Hague.

Ah, those quiet, verdant spas nestled in Europe's heartland, with their celebrated waters, their ornate jugs, the fawning welcoming parties and, by the massive wooden counters in spacious reception halls, the silver bells that seem to ring more shrilly and with heightened excitement when "the Russians" come, with their promise of high society and strange goings-on, of big tips for the casino attendants and succulent barbarian blood for eager local mosquitoes! To them our thoughts now gratefully turn, for when Baron Heeckeren returned to Petersburg, thereby severing our only link to the truth (assuming Georges d'Anthès was truthful in his letters), young Andrei Karamzin, menaced by consumption, departed Petersburg for a long stint of cure and study abroad, thus engendering a new flood of letters out of Russia – to Switzerland, Germany, France, and Italy.

On May 28 Princess Catherine Meshcherskaya, née Karamzina, wrote to her brother Andrei: "The Princess of Butera, chatelaine of Pargolovo, gave us permission to have access

---

* Anna Pavlovna, wife of Prince William of Orange, was Tsar Nicholas's sister.

to her elegant residence, and we enjoyed the excellent picnic supper we'd brought with us in a lovely room, sparkling fresh and fragrantly flowered. . . . The Crément and Sillery streamed down the throats of our escorts, all of whom rose from the table merrier and more flushed than when they sat down, especially d'Anthès." On June 5 Sophie Karamzina wrote to her half brother Andrei: "Our sort of life . . . is ever the same, we have people every night, d'Anthès almost every day, tortured by two daily drills (since the Grand Duke insists that the Horse Guards don't know how to ride), but nonetheless gayer and more amusing than ever, somehow even managing to find a way to accompany us on our rides." And on July 8, after the Peterhof party: "I saw nearly all our friends and acquaintances again, among others . . . d'Anthès, whose presence, I admit, gave me much pleasure. The heart, it seems, always gets somewhat used to the people one sees every day. He was casually coming down the stairs when he noticed me, whereupon he leaped down the last few steps and rushed to me flushed with pleasure. . . . We all went to our house for tea as best we could, without cups or chairs for half the company, and at eleven that night we set out, myself on the arm of d'Anthès, who amused me no end with his foolishness, merriment, and even outbursts of feeling (always for the beautiful Natalie), which were also very funny." One is slightly taken aback by this resurrection of the merry and jovial, gallant and comical d'Anthès, this vivacious, exuberant ghost of a man whose own letters to the Dutch ambassador seemed to have buried forever.

The Muse is a clever prima donna, seldom yielding to mortals, carefully timing her forays into the world and savoring their effects in advance. During that summer of 1836 – cold and rainy as usual, yet another clumsy caricature of a southern winter – she visited Pushkin with a persistence long denied him, as if deliberately muddying the waters for future biographers. In what was to be the last summer of his life, the Poet experienced a fresh surge of creativity, like a dying man whose cheeks suddenly bloom with a ruddy glow and whose breathing becomes free and easy with a mysterious influx of vital forces just before the end. So Pushkin, perhaps driven by a vague foreboding, hastened to deliver his swan song, the ultimate evidence of his immortal genius.

Or to be more down to earth about it: at Kamenny Ostrov – where he completed *The Captain's Daughter*, continued his historical research, and wrote a dozen or so articles for *The Contemporary* – he also returned to poetry. Between June and August he composed a brief lyric cycle of depth and mystery: polished sepulchral reveries, spare meditations on biblical themes, painful spiritual exercises, and of course "Exegi Monumentum" and "From Pindemonte," both essential in any anthology. The time had come for his soul to repent, and he heeded Ephraim the Syrian's Lenten prayer:

> . . . *Lord of my days! save my soul from the heavy spirit of sloth,*
> *of that hidden viper ambition.*
> *and of idle, empty talk.*
> *But grant that I may see my sins, O Lord,*
> *let me not condemn my brother*
> *and may the spirit of love and humility, of patience and pure*
> *   chastity revive in my heart. . . .*

Of another lyric, never completed, we have only the first stanza:

> *In vain I flee toward the distant heights of Zion*
> *closely pursued by ravenous sin.*
> *So the lion, nostrils to the dry sand,*
> *greedily follows the deer's fragrant flight.*

It is impossible to say what these verses or the whole cycle would have looked like in their final form had fate granted Pushkin more time. It is impossible to say that the Kamenny

Ostrov cycle, proud testament and humble act of contrition, sprang from the private anguish that afflicted him in those days. But it is hard to shake the image of a nimble deer relentlessly pursued in its race toward peaks now well beyond its reach.

Alexander Vasilievich Trubetskoy was an old man when ten copies of his *Account of the Relations of Pushkin and d'Anthès* were published, virtually underground. The slim pamphlet, written from memory, reads in part:

Novaya Derevnya was a fashionable place in those days. We were lodged in the isbas [log huts], and the squadrons' drills were held in a field now covered with little dachas and gardens of the 1st and 2nd Line. . . . D'Anthès visited the Pushkins often. He courted Natasha as he did all beautiful women (and a beautiful woman she was), but never "besieged" her, as we used to say then, with any particular insistence. The many little notes delivered by Liza (the Pushkins' maid) were meaningless: they were customary in our day. Pushkin was well aware that d'Anthès was not besieging his wife and he was not at all jealous, but as he himself used to say, he found d'Anthès *disagreeable* because of his somewhat impudent manner and his tongue, less discreet than Pushkin felt was proper with ladies. With all due respect for Pushkin's great talent, it must be admitted that his personality was unbearable. It was as if he constantly feared being disrespected, not being rendered sufficient homage; we revered his muse, naturally, but he maintained that we failed to venerate him enough. D'Anthès's manner quite simply irritated him, and he expressed the desire to dispense with his visits more than once. In this Natalie did not oppose him. Perhaps she even agreed with her husband, but utterly silly as she was, she could never bring herself to end her innocent encounters with d'Anthès. Perhaps she was flattered that the splendid *chevalier garde* was ever at her feet. . . . Had Natalie not been so monumentally stupid and d'Anthès so spoiled, the whole thing would have come to nothing, since at least at that time there really had been nothing

– a clasp of hands, an embrace, a kiss, but no more, and such things
were common in our day.

Painful as it is to admit, d'Anthès's old friend and comrade-in-
arms is not entirely wrong – despite the mistakes of date and
place in which his *Account* abounds (his memory being quite
unreliable by then), despite some outright lies (God knows that
d'Anthès did "besiege" Natalya Nikolaevna in the summer of
1836), despite his evident ill will toward Pushkin. But what
we seek in Trubetskoy's story is not truth but merely the
stench of blatancy and barracks lewdness that now enveloped
Pushkin (however rich and elegant the Guards' barracks may
have been), as if drawing it upon ourselves so as to purify
the air around him in a kind of belated homage.

G. and N. are in love. N. renounces G., sacrificing him for
P. while continuing to flirt with him. G. renounces N., sacrificing her for H. while continuing to be consumed with love
for her. P. and H. are both racked by jealousy on account of
N. but strive to hide it. Meanwhile, two female supporting
actors are waiting in the wings, eager for their chance to
capture audience attention in what looks more and more like
a farce at the Petersburg French Theater. The two additional
players are Catherine and Alexandrine Goncharova – Koko
and Azinka to family and friends. Both slender, with olive
complexions and dark hair and eyes, Natalie's sisters resembled
her, but it was as if nature distributed similar material differently and more haphazardly, with no touch of the miraculous.
The bewitching vagueness of Natalie's gaze became a more
pronounced squint in Alexandrine, and where Natalie was tall
and wasp-waisted, Catherine, a few pounds lighter and a few
inches taller, had been called "a broomstick." The constant
visual contrast to Petersburg's most beautiful woman did her
older sisters no good, thinning out the ranks of potential
suitors. Catherine was frivolous and not especially intelligent;
the more astute Alexandrine had a cantankerous, introverted

character inclined to melancholy. At this particular time something bound Alexandrine and Pushkin that was stronger than mere affection between in-laws, more intimate – even illicit, some thought. But all witnesses agree that Catherine was in love with Georges d'Anthès. For some time he'd been pretending to be madly in love with her as well – perhaps to facilitate his visits to his real beloved's household as the welcome suitor of a marriageable girl past her prime, perhaps to allay Pushkin's suspicions or to undermine Natalie's chaste fortitude by making her jealous, or perhaps simply out of inveterate habit. Little by little Koko's heart yielded to a tender emotion that seemed to sweeten her sad impending status as an old maid. If only to be close to the object of her impossible love, Catherine Goncharova became a go-between for Natalie and d'Anthès.

When he wasn't writing, Pushkin was always on edge: he couldn't stay still for more than a few minutes, shuddered if an object fell, became irritated if the children made noise, and opened the mail with anxious agitation. At night he was stalked by insomnia and its menacing cohort of ghostly creditors: the wood seller Obermann, the wine merchant Raoult, the tailor Rutch, the coachman Savalev, the grocer Dmitriev, the bookseller Bellizard, the pharmacist Bruns, the cabinet-maker Gambs. His rash and rosy dreams of lush profits from *The Contemporary* failed to pan out: the journal attracted little more than a quarter of the anticipated 2,500 subscribers, generating barely enough money to pay for paper, typesetting, and contributors – except that Pushkin had already long since spent it. He was dejected and depressed. "I'm not popular anymore," he bitterly admitted to Loeve-Veimars, a French man of letters who visited him at Kamenny Ostrov that summer. Once more he wished he could withdraw at least temporarily to his mother's estate of Mikhailovskoe, where he'd spent two years of enforced isolation and which he dreamed of as a last-ditch refuge of peace and security now that Petersburg had begun to smell more and more like a latrine. But his countless commitments as historian and "journalist" made it impossible, quite apart from the greedy insistence of Nikolai Pavlishchev, his sister Olga's husband, that Mikhailovskoe be put up for sale. Besides, Natalie wouldn't hear of moving to the country.

Shortly after noon on July 31 the Goncharova sisters took a carriage to Krasnoe Selo, where the Horse Guards were celebrating the end of maneuvers. They arrived at four and joined three lady friends and other high-ranking guests in partaking of the excellent meal provided by the Guards. They were just about to enjoy a fireworks display when a violent downpour drove them into the quarters of Captain Petrovo-Solovovo. Informed of their presence, the Empress invited them to an impromptu ball in her tent, but the ladies, inhibited by their traveling clothes, reluctantly declined, instead spending the evening at the windows of the isba, listening to the *chevaliers gardes'* band. It was probably here that Georges d'Anthès and Natalie Pushkina managed to snatch a few minutes alone together for the first time in more than three months.

The fireworks were postponed until August 1, when the much-missed Guards, albeit exhausted after their maneuvers, at last became available again for dances on the Islands. August was a whirlwind of parties as usual, and as Danzas later recalled, "All at once, after a couple of balls at the spa where Mrs. Pushkin and Baron d'Anthès were present, the word in Petersburg was that d'Anthès was courting Pushkin's wife." All at once? The whole town already knew all about it: don't forget Marya Mörder, the girl with a thousand eyes and ears. Something new must have piqued the gossipy interest of the Islands' denizens, fueling rumors now tinged with indignation. Most likely that something was the behavior of Georges d'Anthès, for it was during that late summer that the young Frenchman, suddenly casting caution to the winds and abandoning

decorum and propriety, showered Natalya Nikolaevna Pushkina, "before the eyes of the entire social world, with gestures
of admiration impermissible when addressed to a married
woman." He continued courting Catherine but paled at the
sight of Natalie, constantly sought her company, invited her
to dance or to go for walks in the open air, devoured her
with his eyes whenever he was unable to be near her, seized
any pretext to talk to mutual friends and acquaintances about
her. The Empress herself disapprovingly noted his "too
unconstrained manner" and told Countess Sophie Bobrinskaya
that she feared that association with his bold friend might
have a bad influence on Alexander Trubetskoy, the *chevalier
garde* for whom her own heart had a weakness. Once again
it is hard to recognize the trepid lover who was telling his
protector just a few months ago: "Not a word to Bray . . .
the slightest hint from him would ruin us both . . . Be assured
I've been careful . . . I love her too much to compromise
her." Did d'Anthès no longer fear the world's censure? Had
he come to believe that with his new rank, new name, and
new wealth he could get away with anything? Was Natalie's
reputation no longer of concern to him? Had he ceased to
respect and worship her like an angel from heaven? Or did he
hope that flaunting his passion for Petersburg's most beautiful
woman would squelch poisonous comments about his recent
adoption and his relations with Baron Heeckeren? Perhaps
his thoughtless behavior was simply the inevitable result of a
love too long suppressed, a love whose smoldering ashes flared
with reborn force one summer night, as raindrops streamed
down an isba's windows to the strains of distant, joyous music.
Only one thing is certain: Natalie alone could have called a
halt to his "abnormally flagrant" advances. And she did not.

On August 8 Pushkin got 7,000 rubles from Sishkin for the
silverware Sobolevsky had left at his disposal before setting
out on a long journey.

*

Whispers, gossip, music, the pain and passion of love, all vanished from the Islands in September. The court left Elagin on September 7; the Guards returned to their Shpalernaya Street barracks on September 11. On September 12 the Pushkins, accompanied by Alexandrine and Catherine, went back to Petersburg, moving into a new apartment on the Moyka Canal owned by Princess Sofya Grigorievna Volkonskaya. Only the Karamzins remained out of town for some time, in Tsarskoe Selo. On September 17 Sophie celebrated her name day:

The dinner was excellent; as guests we had Pushkin, his wife, and the other Goncharov sisters (all three dazzling in their elegance, their beauty, and their incredible waists), my brothers, d'Anthès, A. Golitsyn, Arkady and Karl Rosset . . . Scalon, Sergei Meshchersky, Paul and Nadine Vyazemsky . . . Zhukovsky. As you can well imagine, you were not forgotten when it came time to toast everyone's health. In such good company the after-dinner hour seemed short indeed: at nine the neighbors arrived. . . . So it was that we were able to put together a real ball, a very merry one judging by everyone's expressions, except for Alexander Pushkin, who is ever sad, dreamy, and sullen. I found his anxiety contagious. His wandering eyes, fierce and remote, alighted with worrisome attention only on his wife and d'Anthès, who persists in his earlier farce, clinging to Catherine Goncharova while casting distant glances at Natalie, with whom he nevertheless wound up dancing the mazurka, and it was painful to see Pushkin, brooding, pale, and menacing, framed in the doorway opposite. Lord, how stupid this is! When Countess Stroganova arrived, I asked him to chat with her. Blushing (the countess, you know, is one of his devoted flirtations), he started in her direction, but suddenly stopped and crossly turned away. "What is it?" "No, I'm not going; that count's over there."* "What count?" "D'Anthès, or what's his other name, Heeckeren."

* Pushkin knew very well that d'Anthès was by birth and adoption a baron, but count was a title even obscure Russian subjects could readily acquire by performing favors of various sorts, not always noble.

From a twentieth-century point of view Sophie Karamzina's thoughtlessness seems deplorable. *"Que c'est bête!"* she exclaims, referring to something that rouses our anger, pity, or dismay. But we are far from the broad moral standards of a time and a world in which the love affairs of married women caused little outrage, in which love notes, "hand-holding, kisses, and embraces" between a lady and her paramour (possibly even more than one) were written off as routine – provided they remained within the bounds of propriety in public. Modern puritans that we are, we forget that Pushkin was a man of the eighteenth century, in the bedroom as elsewhere. We therefore scowl at the notion that this great man so soon to die his martyr's death had a secret relation with his sister-in-law Alexandrine. We strive to still the strident little voice inside us that asks, So why shouldn't his wife have her fun with someone else? And we try to find excuses for him: perhaps it wasn't a lascivious relationship after all, perhaps it was no more than the sort of complicity that binds unhappy souls, the intimacy of understanding, trust, and empathy with others' pain. And last of all we wonder why Pushkin – while not necessarily going to the feudal lengths of his paternal grandfather, who had his sons' French tutor hanged on suspicion of having had an affair with his wife and kept the poor woman under lock and key for the rest of her life – did not at least raise his voice to Natalie or scold her more than he did. Well, perhaps he did, in the privacy of their own home. But he wanted the public and even his closest friends to see only nonchalance and scorn, which was all a swaggering ladies' man, an ill-bred wooer of Natalya Nikolaevna, deserved. She was not just Caesar's wife but *Pushkin's*. He bided his time, waiting for Natalie's wounded heart to heal, ready to act at the right moment, when whatever he did would not rebound against him by revealing that his trust in his beautiful young wife was not limitless after all. He bided his time, virtually provoking Fate in his secret desire to prove that he was unique and different even as a husband, immune to the risks of a man with a wife too young and beautiful. He bided his time – and he watched. But try as he might, he could not keep others from noticing his look of worry, disappointment, anger.

On September 19 he borrowed 10,000 rubles from the loan shark Yurev, undertaking to repay him with interest by February 1, 1837.

Sometime between October 6 and 8 Prince Ivan Gagarin, having returned from Moscow, brought Pushkin a copy of Pyotr Chaadaev's "Philosophical Letter," published a few days earlier in *The Telescope*. Pushkin had already seen the French first draft, but he now carefully reread the work of this friend from whom he had learned crucial life lessons in his youth:

There is something that goes beyond futility in our best minds. In the absence of connections and coherence, even the best ideas are sterile flashes ossifying in our brains. It is man's nature to lose his way when he finds no means of linking himself to what came before him and will come after him. All solidity and certainty eludes him. Unguided by any feeling of permanence, he loses his way in the world. Such lost souls exist in all countries; among us it is a common trait. . . . Some foreigners have counted as a virtue that variety of heedless boldness found mainly in the nation's lower classes; but having been able to observe only isolated manifestations of the national character, they have been unable to assess the whole. They fail to see that the very principle that sometimes makes us so bold always makes us incapable of depth or perseverance. They fail to see that what makes us so indifferent to life's whims makes us equally indifferent to every good and evil, every truth and lie.

Pushkin thought long and hard about that passage.

On the night of October 16 a powerful northwest wind raised the level of the Neva six feet eight inches. The next evening mournful cannon fire was heard: nerve-racking alarms warning Petersburgers of imminent danger and uncontrollable threat. But the water sank back to safe levels, and life returned to normal.

Sophie Karamzin to her half brother Andrei, Petersburg, October 18, 1836: "We have resumed our city habits and our evenings, in which from the very first day the usual places were taken by Natalie Pushkina and d'Anthès, Catherine Goncharova flanked by Alexander and Alexandrine by Arkady, and toward midnight also Vyazemsky.... Everything as before ..."

Tsar Nicholas I, too, carefully read the "Letter" that made Russia shudder with patriotic horror. Chaadaev: "We alone in the world have brought the world nothing and taught it nothing; we have not contributed a single idea to the mass of human ideas.... Not a single useful thought has sprouted in our country's barren soil; not a single great truth has emerged from our ambit.... Something in our blood repulses all true progress. In the end we have lived and now live solely to serve as some inscrutable great lesson for the distant generations that will grasp it; today, whatever anyone might say, we are a void in the intellectual firmament."

On October 22 Nicholas I added in his own hand a brief comment to a report from Minister Uvarov: "Having read the article, I find its content to be a hodgepodge of arrant nonsense worthy of a lunatic: this we shall ascertain without fail, but that is no excuse for the review's editor or for the censor. See to the immediate closure of the review." On that same day Count Benckendorff wrote to the governor-general of Moscow ordering that a medical expert visit Chaadaev every morning and that he be kept from "exposing himself to the season's damp, cold climate." The state's official lunatic was being placed under house arrest.

· 6 ·

Pushkin's Button

In winter, in his last years, he would stroll along the Nevsky Prospect in a slightly shabby top hat and a long *bekesh*, similarly timeworn. Since he was the darling of the Muses and the poet favored by the gods, lingering, curious glances pursued him. The more attentive onlookers noted with surprise that in the back, where thick folds of material were gathered at the waist, Pushkin's *bekesh* was missing a button.

MINI-DICTIONARY

Almaviva: a man's cloak, also called "Spanish mantle," named after the count in *The Marriage of Figaro*.

Bekesh, or *bekesha:* a man's winter overcoat, trimmed and lined with fur, named for the sixteenth-century Hungarian nobleman Gáspár Békéš, valiant martial chieftain and famous dandy.

Caftan: a man's long overcoat, from the sumptuous gem-studded, brocade *pardessus* of the boyars to the rough canvas worn by peasants and merchants. With the reforms of Peter the Great in the eighteenth century, the term was also used for the top half of a European-style suit.

Kamerger: from the German *Kammerherr*, chamberlain. The chamberlain's dress uniform included a gold key hanging from a blue ribbon.

Kamerjunker: from the German *Kammerjunker,* gentleman of the chamber, the rank immediately below that of *kamerger.*

Lineika: a four-wheeled carriage with seats for six or more, resembling a wide sofa with a canopy, called a *break* in English.

Okazia: from the French *occasion,* an unofficial courier; someone who happens to be making a trip and to whom letters and packages are entrusted.

Salop: from the French *salope,* a warm, loose-fitting woman's coat.

Even as a courtier, Pushkin appeared at society receptions in middle-class evening dress: double-breasted waistcoat, loosely knotted wide silk tie under a floppy unstarched collar. On December 16, 1834, he finally wore his kamerjunker's tailcoat to the Anichkov Palace, but on his head an inappropriate, flamboyant, feathered tricorne. Count Alexei Bobrinsky immediately sent for the round hat required by protocol, but it was so old and soaked with pomade that its mere touch stained Pushkin's gloves a sticky, dubious yellow. For that evening at least, Tsar Nicholas nevertheless seemed satisfied. He was ever attentive to the poet's dress and had taken umbrage more than once: *"Il aurait pu se donner la peine d'aller mettre un frac."** He had Count Benckendorff chide Pushkin – "His Majesty has been so kind as to observe that you wore civilian dress to the French ambassador's ball when all the other guests were in uniform" – and jokingly shared his displeasure with Natalya Nikolaevna: *"Est-ce à propos des bottes ou des boutons que votre mari n'est pas venu dernièrement?"*†

In the thirties a rich American came to Petersburg with his beautiful daughter. . . . He wore an American naval uniform to special official events, and when people chatted with him, they politely spoke of

---

* "He could have at least taken the trouble to put on a tailcoat."
† "Is it on account of boots or buttons that your husband hasn't been seen lately?" But "on account of boots" is also an idiomatic expression meaning "for a trifle" or "for a trivial reason."

the sea, the U.S. fleet, and so on. But he seemed loath to respond, and his replies were evasive. Finally the American, fed up with all the maritime nonsense, said to someone, "Why do you keep asking me about all this seafaring? It's none of my concern, I'm not in the Navy." "Then why are you wearing that uniform?" "Simple. I was told you can't get by in Petersburg without a uniform, so while I was getting ready to come to Russia I had this one made just in case. When it seems right, I show it off." (Vyazemsky)

Even Pushkin's characters were scolded for their style of dress and invited to change their clothes: "He told me jokingly," one acquaintance noted, "how his *Count Nulin* was censored. Apparently it was considered undignified for His Highness to be seen in his dressing gown. When the author asked what he should put on him, they suggested a tailcoat. The girl's blouse was also seen as indecorous; they asked him to give her at least a salop." The censors didn't miss a thing. "Several indecent expressions" were expunged from Gogol's "The Coach," which appeared in the first issue of *The Contemporary*, for example: "The officers' top buttons were undone."

Yusupov asked that Solntsev be granted the title of kamerger. In Petersburg it was felt that in view of his civilian status, kamerjunker would be good enough. But apart from the fact that he was already of rather advanced age, Solntsev was a man of such massive height and girth that the youthful title of kamerjunker was utterly inappropriate to his face and bulk.... Prince Yusupov nominated him again on the basis of his physical merits, and this time the proposal was accepted. Solntsev finally got his key. The whole incident could hardly have failed to attract the notice of a chronicler like Neelov, who wrote this quatrain for his *Muscovite Bulletin*: "Some advance their careers / through grandfathers, fathers, and lovers, / others through beautiful, willing wives, / he alone gets ahead ... with his belly." (Vyazemsky)

Pushkin was named a kamerjunker on New Year's Eve of 1834, and when he heard the news during a reception at the home of Count Alexei Fyodorovich Orlov, he reacted with a terrifying burst of rage, foaming at the mouth and uttering words so violent that someone hurriedly led him into Orlov's private study in an effort to squelch the scandal. He was convinced that he'd been given that title, normally reserved for "snot-nosed eighteen-year-olds" just beginning their careers at court, because "the court wishes to see Natalya Nikolaevna dancing at the Anichkov." Everyone in Petersburg agreed. His closest friends had to soothe him, quell his rages. Alexandra Osipovna and Nikolai Mikhailovich Smirnov patiently explained that the Tsar's intent in naming him a kamerjunker was not to humiliate him but on the contrary to offer yet another token of his benevolence, that there was no dishonor in the sovereign's wish to have Russia's greatest poet and his wife at court, and that no other title could be conferred upon a Class IX civil servant.

The obligation to don a kamerjunker's uniform – actually, three uniforms: the dress green and golds, the everyday uniform, and the tailcoat of special cut – was the most insidious, perverse snare that destiny could have cast in Pushkin's path; the green and gold threads may as well have been spun by the Fates themselves. He said he didn't have the money for the outfits, and the Smirnovs bought him the dress uniform: originally ordered by young Prince Wittgenstein, who had in the meantime been sworn into military service before wearing it even once, it had been left hanging fresh and useless in a tailor's shop. But Pushkin sneaked out of town, feigned illness, pleaded serious family problems – anything to avoid appearing in public in that hated "striped caftan."* And he endured condemnation and rebuke when unmasked, caught *flagrante delicto* in flagrant lies.

---

* "Stripes" was his word for the gold chevrons that adorned each chest button of the ordinary uniform.

One day during dinner at his house, the blind [Pyotr Stepanovich] Molchanov heard his little grandson crying and the boy's mother scolding him at the far end of the table. He asked what was the matter. "He's having a tantrum," the mother replied, "because he doesn't want to sit where he's supposed to. He wants his old place back." "What do you expect?" Molchanov said. "Everyone in Russia wails about the same thing, so why shouldn't he? Let him sit where he likes." (Vyazemsky)

Pushkin was even more vulnerable to hostility and malicious gossip in his new clothes, his new dark green cloth. His enemies accused him of toadyism and servility, of having bartered his conscience for a minor position in the court's glittering ambit. Vicious lampoons of the new kamerjunker, ex-champion of freedom, began to circulate in Petersburg.

"Here in Asia you're better off using an okazia when you write," Pushkin had written to Vyazemsky on December 20, 1823.

In 1833 Alexander Yakovlevich Bulgakov was frankly delighted when he was named director of the Moscow postal service. He swam among letters like a sturgeon in the Oka, for correspondence was his natural element and his vocation. It also became his secret vice. A large part of everything written in Russia now had to pass through his hands, and he found himself unable to resist the ignoble temptation to peek at the missives in his charge. He would read them, indeed delight in them, and then hurry to inform friends and acquaintances about engagements and weddings, quarrels and cuckolding, divorces and duels, illness and death, wills and lawsuits. Not an especially abject man, Bulgakov was simply a virtuoso practitioner of an activity widespread in Tsar Nicholas's Russia: espionage by interception of correspondence. He was the archetypal society reporter, and it was to him that the former capital turned for news of Petersburg and the provinces. The obliging director's tidbits, always the most up-to-date available, would then spread rapidly in new letters and confidential conversations, eventually bouncing back to Petersburg and the provinces in more flavorful and spicy form. But Bulgakov was also a loyal servant of the state. Every so often he would catch a whiff of subversion or free thought in the words of others, and he would then snatch up his pen and draft detailed reports for the Third Section. Thus did the lucky man reconcile passion and duty.

He had a weakness for literature and salivated at the private correspondence of famous writers. The chance capture of one of their letters drove his busybody soul to an ecstasy of ineffable delight. He was slow to open such letters, like a seasoned lover postponing the instant of climax as long as possible. One evening in April 1834 he went home with a letter from Pushkin to his wife, unable to believe his good fortune. He knew from mutual acquaintances in Petersburg that Natalya Nikolaevna had gone to stay with her family in the country to recover from a miscarriage, the consequence of an overly strenuous season of balls — or, some spiteful gossips claimed, of a beating from her husband. Hoping to come upon some juicy details of this ugly tale, he was disappointed but indignant when he read this instead:

I'm saying I'm ill and I'm afraid to meet the Tsar. I'm going to stay home for all the festivities.* I have no intention of offering the heir good wishes and congratulations; his reign lies in the future, and I probably won't live to see it. Of tsars I have seen three: the first ordered my nurse to take off my cap and scolded her on my account, the second didn't like me, and the third, who has so kindly named me a page of the chamber on the threshold of old age, I have no wish to exchange for a fourth. Best leave well enough alone. We shall see how little Alexander gets along with his imperial

---

* Marking the coming of age of Alexander Nikolaevich, the Tsar's first-born and heir to the throne.

namesake; I have had some friction with mine. God preserve him from following in my path, writing poetry and quarreling with tsars! With verses he will not surpass his father, and reason avails not against force.

Defamation of the throne! Jacobin speechifying! Bulgakov filed a report with Count Benckendorff forthwith, appending a copy of the outrageous letter.

Count Alexander Khristoforovich Benckendorff – head of the Third Section of His Imperial Majesty's chancery, a vast, ubiquitous network of police spies prying into the actions and speech, thoughts and dreams of all Russian subjects – commanded unbounded power second only to the Tsar's. He was the police embodiment of imperial legitimacy, secular arm of the gendarme of Europe as sanctified by the Congress of Vienna.

Bibikov told me of an episode he'd heard from Benckendorff. One day a policeman rushes into his office and hands him a package someone had furtively tossed through the entrance gate. The package has Benckendorff's name on it, so he opens it. Inside he finds a letter for the Tsar marked "Most Urgent." He gets into his carriage and delivers it. The Tsar opens it, and what do you think he finds? An anonymous claim that Muravyev is insane: ". . . and as proof that your secretary of state is truly insane, I enclose one of his works." The Tsar says: "What am I supposed to do with this letter? Send it to Muravyev and ask what he thinks." (Vyazemsky)

Pushkin referred to punch as "Benckendorff" because, he said, it has a "policing, sedative effect that restores order to everything."

Stratford [Lord Canning] came to Russia on the English government's behalf for negotiations on the Greek question. He spent Easter in Moscow. Walking along Podnovinsky Street, he noted that here, contrary to English custom, the police are in plain sight everywhere. "It isn't right," he said. "Some things require a wrapper. Nature, if I am not mistaken, was careful to conceal the circulation of blood from our sight." (Vyazemsky)

Count Benckendorff's exquisite manners were complemented by his sparkling conversation and perfect social aplomb. He was attentive to beautiful women, for whom he felt unchained passion. He was an impeccable dancer. Nothing about him suggested a policeman. History can be amusing at times: the man who supervised thousands of secret agents scattered throughout the Russian Empire to "protect the oppressed, thwart crime, and keep their eyes on those with a criminal bent" was monumentally absentminded and forgetful.

Benckendorff [Count Alexander's father] was very absent-minded. . . . Once, he was at a ball at someone's house. It ended fairly late, and the guests took their leave. Only the master of the house and Benckendorff remained, sitting together. The conversation was not going well: they were both tired and sleepy. . . . A little more time passed, and finally the master of the house asked, "Perhaps your carriage has not arrived yet; would you like me to order them to hitch the horses to mine?" "What do you mean yours? I was about to offer you mine!" . . . He thought he was at his own house and was angry with his guest who lingered so long. (Vyazemsky)

Count Benckendorff's personal secretary, Pavel Ivanovich Miller, was a cultured man who had studied at the Tsarskoe Selo lyceum and worshipped its greatest student, Pushkin. Taking advantage of his boss's absentmindedness, he often raided the file set aside for the most important cases (those requiring the Tsar's personal attention), transferring the many letters from Pushkin that crossed the desks of the Third Section to more innocuous files; later, when time had passed and he was sure Benckendorff had forgotten them, he would steal them outright. His aim was to shield the poet from the overly intrusive attentions of the secret police, but also, I suspect, to acquire holographs that were invaluable – in the sublime, as opposed to commercial, sense of the word. Such was the fate of the poet's intercepted letter to Natalya Nikolaevna, although it was not in Pushkin's own handwriting. Miller realized that it would cause him serious trouble. But this time Bulgakov had pulled out all the stops: other copies of the compromising document were already circulating in Petersburg. The Tsar therefore knew all about it. Vasily Andreevich Zhukovsky, a well-known poet and tutor to the heir to the throne, managed to placate Nicholas I's indignation. "The whole business came to nothing," Pushkin wrote in his diary. "The sovereign was displeased that I failed to express excitement or gratitude about my title of kamerjunker – except that I may be a subject or even a slave, but I will not play lackey or buffoon, even to the King of the heavens. Yet how deeply immoral are our government's methods! The police open letters from a husband to his wife and bring them to the Tsar (a well-bred, upright man), and the Tsar isn't ashamed to admit it. . . . All I can say is, an autocrat's life is not an easy one."

Prince Yusupov tells us that the Empress [Catherine] loved the motto "*Ce n'est pas tout que d'être grand seigneur, il faut encore être poli.*"* (Vyazemsky)

The Tsar's shadow loomed like an intrusive Stone Guest surveying all before him even at the threshold of Pushkin's house and bedroom. Pushkin and Nicholas I had long had a double-edged relationship. In public they chatted cordially, exchanging compliments, witticisms, and opinions on the issues of the day; but all troublesome matters – requests and permissions, entreaties and rejections, reprimands and excuses, manuscripts and harsh censorious glosses – were handled by

* "Being a great lord isn't everything, you also have to be polite."

Benckendorff, or in especially delicate instances by Zhukovsky. This Janus tone – casual and amicable, rigid and
officious – was perfectly suited to an odd couple who were
linked by bonds far more complex than those immortalized
by Russian hagiography and demonology. Nicholas I must
surely have hoped that by magnanimously pardoning Pushkin
in the late summer of 1826 – releasing him from exile and
offering to act as his personal censor and protector – he would
at least partly alter his image as the bloody tyrant who had
sent the Decembrist insurgents of 1825 to Siberia or the gal-
lows. But his generosity and paternal solicitude were not pure
calculated pretense. The new Tsar was also motivated by a
sincere desire to bring the lost sheep back into the fold, to
force this highly talented but impulsive youth, so refractory
to any discipline and so susceptible to pernicious ideas of all
kinds, back to the straight and narrow. An unbending and
effective executor of history's ukases, practical and shrewd,
with the unfailing intuition possessed by some limited minds,
Nicholas I sensed that he and Pushkin would someday stand
face-to-face alone, protagonists of the eternal duel between
power and impotence, heaviness and lightness, the secular
world and the sacred realm of poetry. And he sought at least
to soften the picture's stereotypical hues with the chiaroscuro of
gentilhommerie. Pushkin, too, himself exasperated by the banal
mawkishness of the canvases that would adorn posterity's walls,
ill at ease in the role of slayer of tyrants and coming to prefer
that of astute adviser to the sovereign, felt respect and gratitude
for the man striving so ardently – through military inflexibility,
courage, and a keen sense of honor – to earn a halo of greatness
that had not been his birthright.

On a cold winter day with a biting wind, Alexander Pavlovich
meets Mrs. D. walking along the English Prospect. "How is it
you're not afraid of the cold?" he asks. "And you, Majesty?" "Oh,
that's different: I'm a soldier!" "What, Majesty? I don't understand.
What do you mean you're a soldier?" (Vyazemsky)

To ensure that some of what he had to say would reach Tsar Nicholas's ears, Pushkin resorted to the very instrument that had been used against him: the watchful eye of the postal system. First he warned his wife to be very careful when she wrote to him, since that Moscow scoundrel Bulgakov had no shame about sticking his nose into other people's business or about "pimping for his own daughters." Then, again in letters to Natalie, he launched a lengthy long-distance dialogue with the Tsar: "To live without political freedom is quite easy, to live without the inviolability of the family is impossible: forced labor is far better. I am not writing this for you. . . . I'm not angry at *Him* anymore, because, *toute réflexion faite*, he's not to blame for the filth that surrounds him. And if you live in a cesspool, you get used to shit despite yourself, so the stench doesn't bother you, even if you're a gentleman. Ah, if only I could flee where the air is pure! . . . With your permission, I believe I'll have to resign and, with a sigh of relief, retire the kamerjunker's uniform that has been so pleasantly flattering to my pride and in which I have sadly lacked the time to strut."

In 1812 Count Ostermann said to the Marquis Paulucci, if I am not mistaken, "For you Russia is a uniform: you've put it on, and you'll take it off when the mood strikes you. For me it is my skin." (Vyazemsky)

Pushkin was a man under permanent special surveillance, and the title of gentleman of the chamber brought him a stern new guardian: Count Yuly Litta, grand chamberlain to the court of the Romanovs. When the poet was summoned by the chamberlain on April 15, 1834, he realized straightaway that he was in for yet another scolding: like many a kamerger and kamerjunker, he had failed to show up at the Easter religious services, to the Tsar's disappointment and Count Litta's dismay. The latter shared his keen indignation with Count Kirill Alexandrovich Naryshkin: "After all, there are set rules [*règles*] for kamergers and kamerjunkers." To which Naryshkin, a man known for his sarcasm, replied, "Oh, I thought only ladies of honor had *règles* [periods]." But Pushkin didn't show up for Litta either. Instead, he sent a letter begging off, pleading yet another excuse.

In Moscow one wag translated "*le bien-être générale en Russie*" as "It's good to be a general in Russia." (Vyazemsky)

Pushkin feared ridicule more than cholera, bills, or the devil. He always gave tit for tat, never letting down his guard, returning cracks and insinuations, double meanings and mocking grins. To Grand Duke Mikhail Pavlovich, who congratulated him on his appointment as kamerjunker, he replied, "My humble thanks, Your Highness. Until today everyone laughed at me. You are the first to congratulate me." This sharp riposte, like everything else he ever said, quickly made the rounds of the salons. A sentence beginning "Pushkin said . . ." always promised pungent sarcasm and gleeful venom. Once again he won, albeit by a close score. But he was consumed by bile and impotent rage. In June 1834 he wrote to his wife (though he was talking mainly to himself, acknowledging the rot that was destroying his life): "The dependency of family life makes a man more moral. The dependency we impose on ourselves out of pride or need humiliates us. They now consider me a lackey whom they can treat as they wish. Political disgrace is better than scorn."

He informed the Tsar of his wish to resign, to withdraw to the countryside, also asking for one last gesture of generosity, permission to pursue his research on Peter the Great in the State Archives. Nicholas refused. The Tsar told Zhukovsky, "I stand in no one's way, and I will not stand in his. But if he resigns it's all over between us." To Benckendorff he said, "I forgive him, but summon him and explain to him yet again how completely absurd his behavior is and what the possible consequences are. What can be forgiven a twenty-year-old scatterbrain is unacceptable in a married man of thirty-five with children."

"It's all over between us." It sounds like an angry father or a wounded lover. Poet and Tsar were truly an odd couple, one testier than the other. The sovereign's benevolence, which more than once had taken the form of financial subsidies (though never comparable to the gifts lavished on high-ranking petitioners and schemers, of course; this was, after all, a mere poet), now stymied Pushkin where he might otherwise have been reckless and rash, thus blocking his only route of escape from the huge expenses imposed by Petersburg and the court, from his complete inability to manage time and money, from his debts, and from the tragic ruin of all his naïve dreams of rapid enrichment. Pushkin's gratitude ("I would rather be taken for inconsistent than ungrateful") and his loyalty to his word (back in September 1826 he had promised the new Tsar to end his hostilities with the regime forever) bound him to a perennial cycle: immaturity and rashness, faux pas and violent outbursts of pride, always followed by humiliating apologies and humble acts of contrition.

At a court reception the Empress Catherine circulated among the guests, addressing a cordial word to each. One of them was an old Navy man. "Cold today, don't you think?" the oblivious Empress asked him three times. "No, ma'am, Your Majesty, in fact it's rather hot today," he replied on each occasion. "Well," the sailor finally said to his neighbor, "by now Her Majesty must be convinced I am truly a demon from hell." (Vyazemsky)

Pushkin had jokingly announced a new credo at age thirty: "Now my ideal is a fine wife, / my great desire – a little peace / and a big pot, full of soup." In the autumn of 1830, marooned on a small country estate in Boldino by quarantine zones meant to halt the spread of cholera into southern Russia, isolated from the world, torn between memories and forebodings, he diligently performed the ritual of leave-takings –

parting forever from *Eugene Onegin*, his favorite child, saying farewell to his resounding fame as a national rebel and good-bye to his chaotic, turbulent, dissolute, nomadic, breakneck lifestyle. He took a wife and abandoned the checkered path of endless sedition in favor of smoother, more prosaic routes, countless times more traveled. *"Il n'est pas de bonheur que dans les voies communes,"* he said with a grin, quoting Chateau-briand. "Happiness is found only on well-traveled paths." Yet the shimmering veil of playfulness concealed a confused tangle of apprehension, misgiving, tremors. Behind Pushkin's smile there was weariness: there are times when poets – the chosen, the damned – yearn to wipe away the lofty yet terrifying sign that marks them. There was fear: there are times when poets hear in the most harmless noises of the night – at Boldino the poplars rustled, invisible field mice scurried, the floorboards of the decrepit wooden house creaked, an ancient grandfather clock ticked tediously – the dark stammer of fate, the ominous voice of the owl. And when those times come, they opt (being shrewd, as well) for docile obedience to law and taboo; they declare themselves beaten. No more butting heads with hostile destiny. Pushkin would now settle down, casting off his antique, garish poet's garb and joining the meek, anonymous mass of ordinary mortals. He hastened to inform friends and acquaintances of his metamorphosis: "I am bourgeois, just a Russian petit bourgeois." *"Le fait est que je suis bonhomme et que je ne demande pas mieux que d'engraisser et d'être heureux – l'un est plus facile que l'autre."**

He was ensconced in Tsarskoe Selo with his delicious little wife and had had time to gain only a couple of pounds when he was stricken by the scourge of cholera morbus for the second time. A year earlier, in Boldino, this disease had given him the most productive period of his creative life – along with excruciating anxiety and claustrophobic panic. But now,

---

* "The truth is, I'm just a good fellow who asks nothing better than to get fat and happy, the former being easier than the latter."

maliciously, spitefully, it dashed his hopes for a placid middle-class life in the shadow of his beloved lyceum.

When cholera first appeared in Moscow, one suburban priest – a reasonable man and not at all ignorant, I might add – was heard to say, "Think of it what you will, but in my view this cholera is only a reprise of December 14 [1825, the date of the Decembrist insurrection]." (Vyazemsky)

On July 10, 1831, the court arrived in Tsarskoe Selo, taking refuge both from the epidemic and from popular agitation. It is said that as the imperial couple strolled through the streets, they were pleasantly struck by Natalie's loveliness and by how unusually docile Pushkin seemed at his very young wife's side. Miss Zagryazhskaya's intrigues and the good offices of Zhukovsky, the doting "teacher surpassed by his pupil," did the rest: at the end of 1831 the poet reentered the civil service with an annual stipend of 5,000 rubles and the rank of titular counselor. Though formally posted to the Ministry of Foreign Affairs, he would actually be working on a history of Peter the Great. He moved to Petersburg, where prices were high. He tried to help his parents by assuming the onerous management of Mikhailovskoe and became entangled in exasperating family squabbles. Inspiration abandoned him for long stretches. He was fascinated by his new historical work, but the laborious research took time and would certainly never make him richer. His *History of the Pugachev Revolt*, published in 1834, sold only about a thousand copies. Censors – the Tsar personally as well as dull-witted guardians of literary decorum – strewed countless obstacles in his path, delaying and sometimes preventing publication of what he wrote. He tried his luck at cards and lost, as players besieged by need always do. Peace and happiness kept slipping through his fingers like wriggling snakes. The breaking point came with that jester's uniform, an intolerable insult to his age, his fame – and his unbounded pride. Vyazemsky was quite right when he said, "Despite our friendship, I will not deny that he was shallow and sensitive to social status. A kamerger's key would have been an honor he would have appreciated."

> *It's time, my friend, it's time. The heart demands peace.*
> *Day flies after day, and every hour steals*
> *a crumb of life: meanwhile we delude ourselves*
> *that we are living, and look: we are already dying.*
> *No happiness is here, but peace exists.*
> *and freedom. A weary slave, I've long pursued*
> *a dream of flight to a far-off*
> *refuge of work and pure delight.*

Every year on July 1 the Empress's birthday celebration was held at Peterhof, a party of incomparable pomp and magnificence, a festival in the grand northern style, somber, mournful, thousands of Russians trudging through the streets in sepulchral silence, without a trace of laughter, one behind the other like disciplined shades emerging from some crypt. Amid a sea of lights and lavish decorations the imperial family and the court would form a long cortege in sumptuous *lineiki*, offering themselves to their subjects' gaze. One of these parades once passed Pushkin as he strode briskly along the edge of the road, hurrying to who knows where. "*Bonjour*, Pouchkine!" the Tsar called in greeting. "*Bonjour*, Sire," replied the poet, respectfully but casually, without a hint of awe. Then one summer, probably in 1835, he, too, had to take his seat in one of the lineiki. "He draped his famous almaviva, noticeably frayed, over his braid-trimmed kamerjunker's uniform. His face seemed pained, rigid, and pale beneath the tricorne. Tens of thousands of people saw him, not in his glory as the nation's leading poet, but in the ranks of the apprentice courtiers."

March 11, 1831. Decree issued by His Imperial Majesty regarding uniforms for ranks in the Imperial Court:

... For ministers (if not of military rank), grand chamberlains, grand marshals, grand stewards, chief cupbearers ... the prescribed dress uniform is of dark green cloth with red collar and matching cuffs. The design currently in use to be embroidered in gold on collar, cuffs, and pocket flaps: wide for the aforementioned and on the edges, narrow on the seams and tails; on the chest embroidered frogs; gold buttons stamped with the government coat of arms.

... For chiefs of protocol, kamergers, and kamerjunkers an identical uniform is prescribed, but without embroidery on the seams, this being reserved exclusively for the first ranks of the Imperial Court.

For all the aforementioned ranks the prescribed everyday uniform, with sword, is similar to the dress uniform except that in place of the embroidery on the chest shall be sewn as many chevrons as buttons, plus another three on the sleeves and four on each tail.

For all members of the Imperial Court the prescribed regulation tailcoat is of dark green cloth with the underside of the collar black velvet. Matte gold buttons bearing His Imperial Majesty's monogram in three gothic letters beneath a crown.

Among those who "saw him as a lackey" was a band of new young writers who took literature *au grand sérieux,* even *au grand tragique.* They dreamed of marrying art to freedom, poetry to political rights, novels to social reform. These representatives of the fourth estate – still timid in word and deed, still respectful of the ancient gods – were climbing toward the throne of Russian letters, without covert palace scheming or bloody rebellion. In Moscow, Belinsky, the future Mad Vissarion, shed tears for the wane of Pushkin's talent, lamenting the mournful and ineluctable twilight of Apollo, now so rarely warmed by the rays of his ancient gift. Sons were on a war footing, and fathers wearied by past battles would have loved to be enraptured once more by the Pushkin of old, with his libertarian pathos, regicidal gestures, and Byronic pride, his exotic landscapes and Bakhchisaray fountains, his Gypsies and Circassians and demons, his *couplets sceptiques* and atheistic verses. Meanwhile, many minor-league critics, sharp-eyed hacks eager to please a broader philistine audience, taunted him cruelly: "Yes indeed, marvelous was the unforgettable time in our literature when Pushkin's lyre sounded and his name spread through Russia, along with his sweet songs! . . . But why has the poet's Muse fallen silent? Can it be that the poet's gift so swiftly ages? . . . That every beautiful thing on this earth is so short-lived?" Russian literature was mired in confusion. The writings of Marlinsky and Baron Brambeus were preferred to Pushkin's "slack and lazy prose," and his poems were eclipsed by the pomposities of Benediktov and the leaden lines of Kukolnik, rising stars fated to end as second-rate meteors leaving no more than fading streaks in Russia's literary firmament. And some suspected Pushkin of base envy when he ventured comments on the public's new darlings ("Why not? There are some good lines in Kukolnik, and supposedly some thoughts as well, they say").

We can picture many a poet pen in hand like an old lady knitting a sock: she dozes, but her fingers keep moving, and somehow the sock gets made. The result, however, is that many a pair of poetic legs wears socks with runs. (Vyazemsky)

Evening shadows fall on Olympus, in this case an apartment on the top floor of a building adjoining the Winter Palace.* It's a Saturday in the mid-1830s, and the "poets of the Pushkin era" have gathered: the master of the house, the elegiac Zhukovsky, whose every pore oozes kindness and goodness; the caustic Prince Vyazemsky; the Hussar Davydov, visiting Petersburg for several days; the mild-mannered Pletnev; the

---

* Zhukovsky was then living in a top-floor flat in "Shepelev's house." On December 29, 1835, Vyazemsky wrote to Turgenev: "On Saturday Zhukovsky invites the literary brotherhood to his Olympian attic . . . Krylov, Pushkin, Odoevsky, Pletnev, Baron Rosen, etc."

blind Kozlov. The others? "Some are no more, others are distant."*

Zhukovsky, Vyazemsky, and Pushkin are the survivors of the "aristocratic," "high society" wing of Russian literature, the notorious "art for art's sake" crowd, "knights of gentle Pegasus in the ancient uniform of old Parnassus," urbane, refined gentlemen sitting rather stiffly on Empire sofas and chairs. Worshippers of grace and elegance, they savor poetry like a vintage Lafitte; they revere Harmony, and they wince in horror at any awkward line or any rhyme that strains laboriously to scale the peaks of assonance. With them are Odoevsky, *le prince-chimiste*, a devotee of Schelling and storyteller enamored of Hoffmannesque witchcraft, and Count Vielgorsky, a fine musicologist and gourmet. There are a few young talents, too, obsequious and discreet, their faces frozen in expressions of reserve and modesty. Gogol alone shows signs of unease: turning his odd profile to the portraitist, he seems agitated, uncomfortable, impatient, as if eager to flee the salon, the city, Russia, and literature itself. Pushkin picks lazily at a cluster of grapes, taking no part in the general conversation.

A servant unobtrusively begins preparations for evening tea. The young withdraw with an understanding glance, leaving the masters to themselves. The host escorts them to the foyer, where Gogol, not bothering to wait for the servants, is already looking anxiously for his overcoat. Only a few are left in Zhukovsky's salon; Pushkin is chatting with someone, obviously telling him something very funny, since suddenly his gleaming white teeth are revealed in a resounding, boisterous laugh. Let us take advantage of this brief pause, this rapid and somewhat disorienting change of scene, to ask ourselves

---

* Delwig and Ryleev are no more, the latter executed after the Decembrist revolt. Küchelbecker is distant, exiled to Siberia (the December events again), as is Batyushkov, who is seriously mentally ill. Yazykov is in Moscow, as is Boratynsky, now separated from Pushkin by more than mere miles.

some quick questions about this little group of writers lingering on Mount Olympus on this evening in the mid-1830s.
Are they die-hard outcasts bypassed by history? Nostalgic
conservatives or even – not to mince words – reactionaries?
Remarkable geniuses that they are, can't they take notice of
things more serious than fine arts and fine women, or be more
useful to their vast country with its vast problems? What do
they think of good and evil, of freedom, of absolutism, of the
bondage of the serfs?

Yes, to the public they are die-hards (Pushkin, let's not
forget, was born in 1799), "miserable anachronisms striving
to resurrect the eighteenth century."

No, they are themselves living history. They awakened to
conscious life and literature at a time when Russia loomed
over Europe as a paradigm of grandeur and diversity: the
marvel of the steppes, sumptuous Byzantium, an invincible
power, barbaric and fierce, big and bold. They remember their
country's heroic, mythic infancy, and today they chat and
joke, think and create, steadfastly refusing to yield to its gray
old age. For something strange and terrifying has taken root
in the Russian organism, almost as if the frantic pace of its
initial growth spurt had disrupted its natural physiological
cycle and plunged it into premature senescence, marking that
powerful young body with the warts and wrinkles of blind
bureaucratic stupidity, of police inquisition, of rigid, stilted
formalism.

Nostalgic, yes. And conservative – of precious chunks of
the past.

Reactionary, yes: they react to bad taste, bad poetry, bad
government.

They can, and they do. But they shun the grim garb of
judge, muckraker, executioner.

God save us from asking them these questions, for they
would reply with an astonished stare, confused silence, deadly
cracks, scornful frowns, Pushkin with one of those boisterous
peals of laughter in which "he seemed to pour out his guts."

The talk has now curved in on itself, tracing a rapid circle back to that thunderous echo of a laugh. At its center lies the mystery of the "Pushkin era," once a radiant dawn and now already a darkening sunset. The mystery of a poet fated never to grow old (d'Anthès's bullet itself seems like part of some remote celestial plan) but who, in the shining maturity of his art, is widely rejected as an aged, useless ruin, a Prometheus chained to the rock of eternal childhood, a Methuselah scorned. Almost as if someone had forced him painfully to embody the tragic hiatus between two ages in his country's history, compensating him with a lifetime's harmonious growth in his art.

Countess Tolstaya used to say that she didn't want to die a sudden death, since it would be embarrassing to appear before the Lord out of breath. She said her first concern in the next world would be to find out the secret of the Iron Mask and of the breakup of the marriage of Count V. and Countess S., which had amazed everyone and had been the subject of much conjecture and talk in Petersburg society. The flood of 1824 made such a strong impression on her and got her so annoyed at Peter I that long before the Slavophiles she took pleasure in driving her carriage past the monument to Peter and sticking out her tongue! (Vyazemsky)

Vyazemsky was a good poet, a refined critic, a remarkable conversationalist and letter writer, a renowned, conceited conqueror of female hearts, an intelligent man, always bitter, sometimes cruel. Never one to get too excited about anything, he viewed the world with lucid disenchantment. He compared himself to a thermometer that registered temperature changes instantly and with maximum fidelity, a useless instrument, he observed, "in a place where things boil or freeze at random, where warnings earn no credence and no gauges are required." His notebooks – private diaries and titillating chronicles of soap operas past and present – record the wild and sudden swings of Russia's moral temperature in meticulous detail. For instance: "'I never did understand the difference between a cannon and a culverin,' Catherine II said to a general. 'There is a big difference,' he replied, 'which I will now explain to Your Majesty. The cannon, you see, is one thing, while the culverin is quite another.' 'Ah,' said the Empress, 'now I get it.'"

Pushkin loved stories about Peter, Elizabeth, Catherine, and Paul. He collected anecdotes about the daily habits, vices, weaknesses, comic sides, temper tantrums, and wisecracks of personalities already nimbed with the halo of legend. He enjoyed the inimitable "historic grace" of the conversations of Natalya Kirillovna Zagryazhskaya, a distant relative of Natalie's in her late eighties, and devoted a chapter of his unfinished *Table Talk* to them: "Orloff was a regicide at heart, it was like a bad habit. I met him once in Dresden, in a park outside the city. He sat down next to me on a bench. We started talking about Paul I. 'What a monster, how can they stand him?' 'Well, my dear friend, what would you do? Strangle him?' 'Why not, dearest?' 'Really? And would you let your daughter Anna Alexeevna get involved in a thing like that?' 'Not only would I let her, I'd be delighted.' That's the kind of man he was!" Thus was living history created by the living voices of old men and women who lingered into the new century like bizarre relics. Thus was the link between generations preserved by the still reliable memories of venerable eyewitnesses. Thus was *"le néant du passé"* kept at bay — ever a danger in a country with Russia's innate bent for wiping slates clean and rebuilding on a conflagration's ashes.

Many things in our past history can be explained by the fact that a Russian, Peter the Great, sought to make us Germans, while a German, Catherine the Great, wanted to make us Russians. (Vyazemsky)

"Pushkin's carriage!" the butler at the gate of a patrician Petersburg mansion called to the coachmen waiting to drive their masters home. "What Pushkin?" came a voice from the throng of men in livery. "Pushkin the writer," the butler replied. Lacking a noble title, he vanished from the salons of people who held literature in low esteem and who recalled of "the writer" nothing more than a few venomous epigrams; he entered the consciousness of young admirers of utility and progress as an apostate of liberty, a slave to Mammon and to power.

> *From Pindemonte*
>
> *I don't care much about high-sounding rights*
> *that just seem to make people's heads spin.*
> *I don't weep if the gods deny me*
> *the good fortune to fight over budgets*
> *or keep kings from waging war.*
> *It doesn't grieve me at all that the press*
> *whips blockheads, that the shrewd censor*
> *persecutes those who love jokes.*
> *All that is only "words, words, words."**
> *Other rights are dear to me. I love*
> *a higher and a better liberty:*
> *servant of the people or servant of power,*
> *is it not all the same thing? To be accountable*
> *to no one, to serve and satisfy*
> *oneself alone, not to bow*
> *one's head to crowns, to liveries,*
> *to wander as fancy dictates,*
> *to tremble, seduced, before beauty,*
> *to be moved by nature,*
> *the creations of the mind. That*
> *is happiness, there are rights!*

Although Pushkin's family origins went back quite far, names of his ancestors appearing in medieval chronicles, many would have laughed had the gentleman taken it into his head to call

---

* *Hamlet.* (Note by Pushkin)

himself an aristocrat. With his post as titular counselor, his rank of kamerjunker, and his status as poet, he rubbed elbows with a swaggering, arrogant, but newly coined aristocracy, most of them *anoblis* who could barely name their own grandparents and whose most ancient roots were at best traceable back to Peter and Elizabeth. "Orderlies, choristers, scullery boys in noble kitchens."

Table Talk again: "The late N. N. Raevsky was Prince Potemkin's favorite nephew. Potemkin wrote out a few rules for living for him, but N.N. lost them, remembering only the opening lines: 'To start with, try to test yourself to see whether you're a coward; if you aren't, bolster your innate courage by spending much time with your enemies.'"

Posterity was to revere Pushkin as an innocent victim martyred by the aristocracy and its salons. But sometimes the truth is very simple: Pushkin would never have set foot in those notorious salons if he'd hated them. Nobody forced him. He came late and left early, in accordance with the shifting whims of his own mind and the etiquette of the snob. But he loved the salons. They were the place to hobnob with the powerful, to discuss weighty issues as if chatting about the weather or the latest ball:

Wednesday I was at the Khitrovos'. Long conversation with the Grand Duke. . . . We started talking about the nobility. . . . I pointed out to him that in a state it isn't necessary, or at least it should be limited and accessible only by the sovereign's will. . . . As for the Third Estate, what else is our ancient gentry, with its holdings destroyed by so many divisions, its culture, its hatred for the aristocracy, and all its claims to power and wealth? No similar natural element of revolt exists in Europe. Who came out into the streets on December 14? Only the gentry. . . . Regarding the old gentry, I told him: *"Nous, qui sommes aussi bons gentilshommes que l'Empereur et Vous . . . etc."**

* "We, who are just as much gentlemen as the Emperor and you . . ."

Anyone in the salons with eyes in his head and a willingness to stand apart – in a corner near a window, say – was
treated to a fascinating cross section of Russian life, a kind
of mini-encyclopedia. No peasants or servants, of course,
but they were hardly at the head of Pushkin's list of concerns. The salons were ruled by manners, order's first line
of defense against Russia's greatest enemy, formless chaos.
Here you encountered rich people (and wealth breathes a
harmony all its own), and beautiful women (beauty bears
earthly witness to the order of other worlds). Here you moved
among glittering shards of reality reflected endlessly in
mirrors that gave a soothing illusion of amiable infinity;
you glided rapidly over gleaming waxed parquet, pausing to
linger at your whim, until time itself became a polished surface that could be vanquished solely by desire. With all the
nonchalance and elegance of a salon habitué, elegant, relaxed,
Pushkin's intelligence was refractory to systems, splintered
into lightning-like, sometimes contradictory thoughts. His legacy from the Enlightenment was an insatiable curiosity, and
he was already teaching the new century the heartrending art
of the fragment – always with a smile on his lips and a glow
of pride in his pale eyes. What Pushkin hated about the salons
– or about some of them – was the presence of stupid people,
bores, bluestockings who asked questions like "Haven't
you written some new little something?" And above all,
people who failed to pay proper homage to his genius and
uniqueness.

Suvorov always observed the fast days. Potemkin once laughingly
told him, "Apparently, Count, you wish to enter paradise astride
a sturgeon." The joke was clearly greeted with enthusiasm by His
Most Serene Highness's courtiers. Some days later one of
Potemkin's most servile worshippers, whom he had nicknamed
Senka the bandore strummer, had the bright idea of repeating the
line to Suvorov himself: "Is it true, Your Lordship, that you wish
to enter paradise on a sturgeon?" Whereupon Suvorov turned to

the jokester and said coolly, "Be advised that while Suvorov sometimes asks questions, he never answers them."

The words flow naturally and easily, never stumbling, never
exposing the well-plotted efforts, even torments, the hard-won
victories, the countless discarded variants. The art is the epitome of intimate familiarity with the world, of relaxed and
loving ease with the dire matters being discussed, respectful
but never submissive, on an equal footing established by an
ancient lineage of the spirit. Pushkin's poems afford us the
illusion that the sublime lies but a few steps away – kindly,
cordial, modest, sometimes even a bit comical.

> *And they tell me with a wicked smile:*
> *"You are a hypocrite, famous poet:*
> *you have no use for glory, you say,*
> *it's a small thing and vain. Why do you write,*
> *then?" "I? For myself." "Why then*
> *do you publish your verses?" "For money."*
> *"And you are not ashamed?" "I? Why?"*

In one story he called poetic inspiration *dryan*: rubbish, trash,
filth; he toyed with what was most sacred, the stern twins
Prophet and Poet. And in doing so he taught us that poetry
is also a place of indecency where the remnants of the soul's
solitary gluttonies end up.

> *. . . Vrai démon pour l'espièglerie.*
> *vrai singe par sa mine.*
> *beaucoup et trop d'étourderie –*
> *ma foi – voilà Pouchkine . . .**

Everything about him was strange, unusual. There was an
odd, mysterious fascination in the "negro monstrosity" of his

---

* "In mischief like a demon he, / his face just like an ape, / as careless
as a man can be – / good God, it must be Pushkin."

face: the dark brown hair, curly in a non-European style, the slightly swelling lips, "wide and very red," the snub-nose profile, the pearl-white teeth, the dusky skin so vividly highlighting his clear gray eyes with their flecks of blue. Thick sideburns joined by a strip of down on the chin. Very long fingernails, like claws. Short and thin, he moved quickly, with jumpy, nervous gestures. When, as a youth, he pirouetted in a waltz or mazurka, provincial ladies took him for a foreigner, a demon, or a Freemason. The climate of his soul displayed sudden shifts, from clouds of gloomy melancholy to luminous clear skies of childlike, rowdy joy. One minute impulsively merry, the next as dark as the sea before a storm, shy one minute and insolent the next, kind and refined and then scowling and unpleasant. His changes of mood were instantaneous and unpredictable. When gripped by depression – as he was ever more often in his last years – he would pace the room, hands deep in the pockets of his baggy trousers, lamenting, almost wailing, "How sad I am, what anguish!" There were times when the blood rushed so violently to his head that he had to hurry to douse it in cold water. Though quick to anger, he was imperturbable in the face of risk and death. In duels he was like ice. Within him were strangely joined a lucid, luminous intelligence and a lively impulsiveness that could suddenly deliver him defenseless to the mercies of life's trifling miseries. In large groups he was almost always serious and taciturn, often glum. At grand balls and crowded receptions he would stand in a corner or at a window, pretending to take no part in the general merriment; but sometimes, on the contrary, he was too outgoing and sparkled too much. Either way he never lasted long and was always among the first to leave. In smaller circles he would open up, telling jokes and playing with words, weaving lacy webs of banter, shifting unexpectedly from banal and even silly subjects to more profound matters. He would offer confessions, speaking with heartbreaking candor of his pain and torment. With enemies he was merciless, dispatching offenders with frigid silence or a few lethal words; with friends he was generous, lavishing treasures of tenderness. He had what Russians call "memory of the heart," and he had it in spades. His language, too, was twinned: pure Russian, warm and affectionately familiar; eighteenth-century French, cold and stern. But his peers chided him for a very different duality. One of them, V. I. Safonovich, recalled: "He was an enigmatic man, with two faces. He liked to be with aristocrats and wanted to be of the people, he went to salons and behaved coarsely, he sought to ingratiate himself with influential people and high society and was wholly graceless in his manners; his attitude was tinged with arrogance. He was both conservative and revolutionary. He welcomed the title of kamerjunker, while yet frequenting circles with little sympathy for the court. He lounged in salons and worked hard at literature."

Exegi Monumentum

"No hands have wrought my monument: no weeds
will hide the nation's footpath to its site.
Tsar Alexander's column it exceeds
*   in splendid insubmissive height.*

"Not all of me is dust. Within my song,
safe from the worm, my spirit will survive,
and my sublunar fame will dwell as long
*   as there is one last bard alive.*

"Throughout great Rus' my echoes will extend,
and all will name me, all tongues in her use:
the Slavs' proud heir, the Finn, the Kalmuk, friend
*   of steppes, the yet unnamed Tunguz.*

"And to the people long shall I be dear
because kind feelings did my lyre extoll,
invoking freedom in an age of fear,
*   and mercy for the broken soul."*

Obey thy God, and never mind, O Muse,
the laurels or the stings: make it thy rule
to be unstirred by praise as by abuse,
and do not contradict the fool.

He possessed – by blood, century, and stamp of the divine –
the gift of detachment. In art this enabled him to transport
what still sears the flesh and blood to a distance measurable
in eras, ages: a distance that makes things seem timeless. The
crystal ball of poetry allowed him to gain a distance from
events of the heart and the world that mere mortals are granted
only by suffering and forgetting. This amazing acceleration,
this miraculous alchemy that clots the blood of open wounds
at its first contact with the rarefied air of poetry, was his
secret. In life it gave him the air of blasé scorn that so many
found annoying. He was well aware of his own worth, and
the joking, humble, minor key in which he liked to speak of
himself – "I have written a little something," referring to the
Boldino prose and poems – was in part an antidote that taste
and intelligence administered to his overblown sense of self: "I
met Nadezhdin at Pogodin's. He struck me as common, vulgar,
boring, conceited, and utterly lacking in decorum. For instance,
he picked up the handkerchief I dropped on the floor."

"The chill of calm pride" was the earthly variant of the
archetypal sacred perfection that rules Pushkin's poetry from
a distant, ever hidden place. It is a negative divinity, the other
side of all the restless fidgeting, all the struggles, efforts,
yearnings, and passions of human beings. We are granted
only fleeting reflections of it – in art, in nature's majesty, in
the harmony of social forms, in the orderliness of rituals. Its
voice never reaches us, does not teach or command or punish.
It doesn't meddle in human affairs and is complete in itself
and content with itself. It seeks neither victims nor priests. It
is cold and unsharing, remote and unmoving. It cannot be
sought or followed or loved; only its contemplation is permitted.

Count Kochubey was buried in the Nevsky Monastery. The countess asked the sovereign for permission to put a railing around the plot of earth beneath which her husband lies. Old Mrs. Novosiltseva said: "We'll see if he makes it on the day of the Second Coming. He'll be stuck crawling around down there, trying to get through that railing, while the others are long since in heaven."

His shifting poetic masks were disconcerting and disorienting. His masterpiece was the narrator of *Eugene Onegin*, a novel in verse and in transit, in perpetual motion. He begins in the coach of a mail train taking Onegin to his dying uncle in the provinces, but then abruptly changes direction, returning to Petersburg to pursue the young hero as he arrives by sleigh at the most fashionable spot for a daily stroll, hastens to the Talon restaurant, flies to the theater, rushes home for a change of clothes, dashes in a rented carriage to a society ball, and finally goes home in his carriage to rest, at last, after the frenetic day. Truly a novel on two runners and four wheels. Even when the exhausted hero pauses, his creator's restless vagabond imagination keeps running, chasing fleeting associations and flashes of memory, digressing into confessions, reflections, lyrical effusions. "In this connection . . ." – and any connection is good for a chat: female feet, the magic of the theater, women's hearts, rustic customs, the scrapbooks kept by country girls, the laws of fate, the barren soul of modern man, Russia's wretched roads. Our young traveler is never silent.

He stuns us with his maxims of simple wisdom. "Foes upon earth has everyone, / but God preserve us from our friends!" "The less we love a woman / the easier 'tis to be liked by her." "He who has lived and thought can't help / despising people in his soul." "The amiable sex is light as fluff." At times he sounds like a decrepit, sullen misanthrope, letting fly against vapid, wicked society, the world's cold cruelty, the tyranny of fashion. Are these really the children of the age, the Romantics, the Russian Byrons? At times he sounds like a nostalgic old man singing dithyrambs to the good old days. Yet his voice is full of youthful grace, luminous joy. He is never silent, this strange traveler of ours, and even invites us to have our say:

> *Hm, hm, gent reader,*
> *is your entire kin well?*
> *Allow me; you might want, perhaps,*
> *to learn now from me*
> *what "kinfolks" means exactly?*
> *Well, here's what kinfolks are:*
> *we are required to pet them,*
> *love them, esteem them cordially,*
> *and, following popular custom,*
> *come Christmas, visit them,*
> *or else congratulate them postally,*
> *so that for the rest of the year*
> *they will not think about us.*

Our kinfolk are all fine, thank God. Do we feel like finding out a little more about Eugene? Of course we do. Well, he and Eugene, we should know, are the same age and old friends – old in spirit, withered beyond repair. Invalids, their feelings maimed, they drag themselves along without purpose or pleasure. Sometimes they turn dreamily to the past, to the beginning of their young lives, like listless prisoners serving life sentences in some dark cell suddenly transported to a sun-soaked verdant forest. Truly a wonderful image. And what a cruel fate for two noble souls. We are already wiping away a tear when all at once our garrulous traveler gives himself away as this little phrase slips out:

> *Can it be true that really and indeed,*
> *without elegiac devices,*
> *the springtime of my days is fled*
> *(as I in jest kept saying hitherto) . . .*

In other words, he was joking, mimicking fashionable foreign writers, talking just to kill time, as so many travelers do. But also to trick us, for what do we know of him, of who he really is? An idle country squire, an inspector general incognito, a subversive on the run, a poet? Or perhaps a caricature of one, "this angel, this arrogant fiend"? Reaching our destination, we thank him politely for his company and his fine words, for we can't deny the words were lovely, warming our hearts even while singing of the cold.

When, like death, the silence falls, we begin to understand something of our enigmatic traveler. He who talks like this, gliding over subjects as over the polished parquet of a Petersburg palace, is a man who knows the empty depths of existence and can imitate perfectly its glittering appearances. He who rambles like this, driven along by motion, is a man who has had terrifying glimpses of the goal and, in dread fascination, has averted his eyes: the cold is daunting yet alluring. Thus do poets, or some of them, enjoy making up stories.

Delwig did not like mystical poetry. "The closer one gets to heaven," he said, "the colder it is."

On the world's stage, Pushkin had been attended — as if by tireless, devoted stagehands — by reversals of fortune, by condemnation and calamity. For the six years preceding the great pardon he had lived in exile, first in the South, then at Mikhailovskoe. Distance befits myth: he had been dubbed the great hope of national literature and then the greatest in the land — in absentia. His eccentricity — homage to Byron, aristocratic charm, a dandy's ways, instinctive dislike of monarchy's ossified forms — was perfectly embodied in his absence, in his being always elsewhere, in some real or imaginary backwater that, far from hiding him from Russia's eyes, cast an even brighter spotlight on him as he stood stage center in the blazing aura of a martyr, lonely titan, eternal nomad. The punishments that so unfailingly followed his excesses —

whether political, poetic, or even amorous – afforded him ideal settings: lonely rockface, roaring waves, inviolable peaks, rustic hideaways, his very own St. Helenas and Missolonghis. In banished exile he became the focus of the public's interest, attention, and avid curiosity. "Pushkin is all sugar with a rump of apples," people would tell their children.

Restored to freedom, he remained the invisible poet, the wandering spirit, restless and ever on the move, traveling between Petersburg, Moscow, and the country houses where he deliberately placed himself under house arrest in an effort to prod languid inspiration. "Where's Pushkin? What's he up to?" friends and admirers were constantly forced to wonder, and in all probability they could imagine the answer: in a Petersburg salon, yawning or downing an ice cream; at Tanya the Gypsy's house of ill repute in Moscow, or the famous Sofya Astafevna's in the capital; in some secluded dueling ground; at the faro tables in a dusty inn on one of Russia's great highways, frittering away the money his latest poem had earned; on the Turkish front with soldiers who took one look at his frock coat and top hat and mistook him for a chaplain; in chaste tête-à-tête with the Muse in some hotel room; or in bed in another hotel room, burning with fever, his head shaved, racked by Venus' revenge.

Weary, he tries to pause, but Fate soon sees that this is but another attempt to elude her by donning the disguise of a fat and happy middle-class man trying to slip away into normalcy and anonymity. It is not to be. He is sent to Petersburg, summoned to court, invited imperiously to the Anichkov. Being in the center of things does poets no good: it mars the legend, corrodes the soul, bares the nerves. Let's leave aside Natalie's passion for balls and her hatred of rural life; leave aside the Tsar's proscriptions and the obligation to ask his permission for the slightest little movement, the most innocuous trip; leave aside the 135,000 rubles in debts – or rather, let's think of them as the agents and clerks of Fate. They have condemned Pushkin to being there, condemned him to all the searing glances and the flashes of a thousand lorgnettes — which are no longer sparkling with benevolent curiosity about the mysterious stranger making a sudden, sensational return. His fragile domestic intimacy, his "at home,"* the place he'd chosen as the ultimate, fortified refuge of the mind, was suddenly revealed for all to see, shielded only by glass, scored in places but transparent still. And lying in wait is obsession, enemy of detachment.

At a German spa a young Frenchman was courting a beautiful Russian lady not wholly indifferent to his attentions. Her rustic husband had no inkling of the affair that was about to begin under his very eyes. A more perceptive friend advised him to take his wife back to the country forthwith, reminding him that the hunting season had begun and adding, "Just in time, too, since the horns are already sounding." (Vyazemsky)

During the Ochakov campaign Prince Potemkin fell in love with Countess * * *. He managed to get an appointment and was having a tête-à-tête with the woman in his headquarters, when he suddenly and inadvertently pulled the cord of the bell, whereupon all the cannon around the camp thundered. Upon learning the reason for the cannon fire, Countess * * *'s sarcastic and immoral husband commented with a shrug, "What a lot of noise about nothing!"

Old K * * *, a tender and loving husband but forgetful father, would sometimes ask his wife, "Dear one, who did you say was the father of our second son? I just can't seem to remember." Or, "Our younger son's father's name? It's on the tip of my tongue."

---

* "Youth has no need of *at home* [English in the original]; middle age fears its own solitude. Blessed is he who finds a companion — go, then, far away, back home. Oh, to be able to move my Penates to the countryside — fields, gardens, peasants, books; working on poems — family, love, etc. — religion, death." These were Pushkin's notes on the themes and thoughts he meant to develop as he continued working on "It's Time, My Friend, It's Time," which he never finished.

On October 19, 1836, he was seen to weep at the annual festivities marking the solemn anniversary of the lyceum's glorious first class, always attended by all surviving students. He arrived with a brand new poem, warned friends that he hadn't had time to finish it, and began to recite:

> *Our tumultuous celebration has come to an end*
> *with the years it has grown calm, like all of us,*
> *and sober, and now is silent, thoughtful,*
> *the clink of the tankards is muted and sad . . .*

at which point he was choked by sobs and had to stop, withdrawing to a corner so as not to make a spectacle of his own emotion. It must be said that Pushkin was very tired that day, having already put the finishing touches on *The Captain's Daughter* and sketched the rough draft of a lengthy reply to Chaadaev's "Philosophical Letter":

. . . As for our historical insignificance, I definitely cannot agree with you. . . . What about Peter the Great, himself a universal history? And Catherine II, who brought Russia to Europe's threshold? And Alexander, who led you to Paris? And tell me (cross your heart), do you see nothing grand in Russia's present situation, nothing that will strike future historians? Do you believe they won't see us as part of Europe? Although personally warmly attached to the Tsar, I am far from admiring all I see around me; as a man of letters I am grieved, as a man of principle offended – but I swear on my honor that not for anything in the world would I wish to change my homeland or to have a history different from that of our ancestors, such as God has given us.

How low have we fallen since Catherine's day! . . . Then there was something chivalrous about all the adulation and toadying. The fact that the Tsar was a woman had a lot to do with it. But later it all took on an air of lackey humility. . . . Consider, for instance, the difference between Panin and Nesselrode, that lackey dwarf, which term I intend not in the ethical sense – since in that sense he's not even a dwarf but a depraved runt, *vermisseau né du cul de feu son père*, or rather, recalling his father's habits more accurately, *un vent lâché du cul de feu son père* – but the physical: he is a dwarf. . . . Say what you will, Russia needs physical presence in its high officials. And what by God has this Lilliputian got? The words of Paul, epitome of despotism, are now established law: "Be advised that in my Court he alone to whom I speak is great, and only while I'm speaking." (Vyazemsky)

He was walking along the Nevsky Prospect with Count Nesselrode, vice-chancellor of the Russian Empire, and Count Vorontsov-Dashkov, chief of protocol and member of the Council of State. "Posterity will tax me with no sin," writes N. M. Kolmakov, "if I mention that Pushkin's *bekesh* was missing a button in the back, at waist height. The button's absence troubled me whenever I encountered Alexander Sergeevich and noticed it. Clearly they were not looking after him . . ." The tiny flaw in Pushkin's outfit troubles us as well, but while it piques our curiosity, we will not lose historical perspective as Kolmakov did. Not looking after him? There were many servants in Pushkin's house, and contrary to what the memoirist suggests – hinting at an impossibly anachronistic middle-class household complete with a disenchanted, lazy, slovenly wife – seeing to his wardrobe would not have been Natalya Nikolaevna's job. Surely it is too much to believe that the button's absence was deliberate or intentional, but it is hard not to see it as a ray of light in Pushkin's gloomy kamerjunker career, a mocking symbolic comment, a grinning, coded message from the Russian Empire's very last dandy.

"L'exactitude est la politesse des cuisiniers."

Let us imagine the waist at the back of Pushkin's *bekesh* as a line of verse. Doesn't the missing button perhaps resemble the stress accent that suddenly breaks loose from the iamb and vanishes into the void, thus mocking the etiquette of prosody, freeing the line from servile metrical obedience, making it ever new and mobile, changeable, unpredictable, whimsical, boundlessly elegant and free?

Mÿ vsyé ŭchílis' pōnemnógu

("All of us had a bit of schooling" – learning, for example, that an iambic tetrameter has the form — / — / — / — /.)

chemú-nĭbŭd' i kák-nĭbŭd'

("in something and somehow": three accents have disappeared in just two lines, engulfed by the void that sickens Onegin, Petersburg, and the age.)

Vorontsov-Dashkov's martingale: — / — / — / — /
(the strong syllable, /, standing for the button, the weak, – , for the pleat)

Pushkin's martingale: — / — — — / — —

Voilà.

The Anonymous Letters

Liza was here in the city
with her daughter Dolly,
and was called in society
"naked Eliza."
Now Liza is all dressed up
at the Austrian Mission,
naked old truth
with her shoulders on display.
— attributed to Pushkin

In 1826 Elizaveta Mikhailovna Khitrova, daughter of General Kutuzov, the man who defeated Napoleon, returned to her beloved motherland after a long absence. Three years later her daughter Dolly came to Petersburg as the wife of the new Austrian ambassador, and in 1831 Khitrova joined her daughter and son-in-law in the lavish Quarenghi mansion, where the Austrian mission was housed. Until recently the majestic building on the Neva had belonged to the Saltykovs, who were known for punishing servants by ordering their heads shaved, but Count and Countess Ficquelmont brought a luminous renaissance to the residence that banished medieval gloom and made it into a cultured and elegant window on Europe. The mother's morning receptions and the daughter's soirées became obligatory stops on the social and intellectual rounds of the capital. Petersburgers, Vyazemsky recalled, "had no need to read newspapers, just like the Athenians, who lived, studied, philosophized, and savored the pleasures of the intellect under the stoas and in the agora. Similarly, the two Ficquelmont salons supplied all the day's news, from the latest political pamphlet or parliamentary speech by a French or English orator to the novel or dramaturgical creation of some darling of the literary times." Pushkin was a regular guest at the Austrian Embassy; Nashchokin claims he had a brief but intense fling with the lovely Dolly, a one-night stand whose passion was untimely enough to last until dawn, and only quick action by an enterprising, seasoned French maid prevented the cuckolded husband from finding out. If the episode really occurred (the much-courted Countess Ficquelmont's conjugal fidelity was legendary), it would be a none too shabby entry in the already impressive catalogue of Russia's most famous Don Juan. Quite well documented, however, is the deep affection felt for Pushkin by Dolly's mother, a massive, opulently endowed woman who believed herself statuesque and was proud even of her facial resemblance to her illustrious father, as valiant as he was graceless.

Morning callers would sometimes find Mrs. Khitrova still in bed. As the embarrassed visitors looked around for somewhere to sit, they would hear, "No, not there, that's Pushkin's chair; not that sofa, that's Zhukovsky's place; not that chair, it's Gogol's; sit on my bed, that's everyone's place."

"Eliza the bare," also known as Dodo (from *dos-dos,* or "back-back"), was wont to expose her flourishing but aging shoulders – target of countless jokes and even verses ("Is it not high time to cast a veil over the past?" ". . . and with every fresh winter / she awes us with the vast nakedness / of those senescent shoulders") – in a plunging backline that cut so deep it sometimes grazed the tailbone. The rare occasions when she failed to bare her celebrated back were immortalized in parodies of the society pages: "She covered it like an alabaster vase lest flies sully it." Also proverbial was a wistful comment Dodo liked to repeat at a fairly advanced age: "How singular my fate – still so young and already twice widowed." Pushkin paraphrased it in late 1830, when Grand Duke Konstantin Pavlovich was forced to withdraw from insurgent Poland: "Now he, too, can say: Still so young and already twice widowed – of an empire and a kingdom."

While admiring the virtues of the pious, patriotic Eliza – her heroic friendship, her generosity with favors – many scoffed at her two consuming passions, one "Christian" (for Archbishop Filaret), the other "pagan" (for Pushkin). Though she yearned to minister to the poet's soul, to lead him from the pastures of impiety and recklessness to the fold of faith and temperance, his slightest physical indisposition plunged her into despair, and his everyday problems kept her in a terrible state of anxiety. Ever vigilant and solicitous, she showered him with attention and advice, interceded on his behalf with the powers that were, kept him up-to-date on news of the capital and Europe, and got him books delivered by speedy and secret diplomatic pouch from Paris, Vienna, and London. Grateful for these countless favors and respectful of this ample, half-naked vestige of the motherland's history, Pushkin did his best to dampen the "old fanatic's" ardor without wounding her pride. He once eluded her martial embraces by emulating the biblical Joseph, who fled Potiphar's wife while leaving his coat in her hands; Pushkin, he said, left his shirt in Khitrova's corpulent arms. Among friends he claimed to be a Tancred hectored by an overweening love, jokingly imploring them to strive to replace him in Ermina's enraptured heart. Fearing posterity's judgment, he was carefully concise in his replies to the raging torrent of letters with which Eliza, heedless of her beloved's coolness, bombarded him in Petersburg, Moscow, the countryside, and even on the road. But one day he lost patience: "That's what you're like, all of you, which is why the thing I fear most in the world is a respectable woman of lofty sentiment. Give me a seamstress anytime!" Undaunted, Khitrova persisted in playing her amorous trumps, until the poet informed her of his impending marriage. Only then, pain in her heart, did she resign herself to manifesting her "burning tenderness" in new ways: "From now on my heart, my inner thoughts will be an impenetrable mystery to you. . . . Between us will lie an ocean, but *sooner* or *later* you will always find in me – for yourself and for your wife and children – a friend like a rock against which all will be dashed. Count on it for life and death, come to me for anything without hesitation. . . . I am invaluable to my friends: it costs me nothing, I can speak to people in high places, I seek them out again and again, and nothing daunts me, neither time, the age. . . . My diligence in *serving* others is on the one hand a gift of Heaven and on the other a result of my father's social position."

In early November 1836 Khitrova's soul was racked by three anxieties: the painful abscess in the side from which Nicholas I was suffering (whenever Eliza had occasion to utter the word "tsar," she added a religious pause meant to mark her limitless devotion to the House of Romanov) consequent to dismounting too carelessly from his horse; Chaadaev's frenzied libel; and the controversy surrounding "The Great Leader," the lyric in which Pushkin had had the bright idea of extolling Barclay de Tolly no less, Russia's unfortunate, forgotten defender against Napoleon's armies. She knew, of course, that the poet had no intention whatever of insulting the memory of her father, sole true Hero of the Great Patriotic War, and was quick to make the point to everyone, but her darling's every line stirred outrage and indignation all the same, and she suffered unspeakable pain with every assault. "Dear Friend," she wrote on the morning of November 4, 1836, "I have just been informed that the censor has approved an article confuting your verses. . . . They torment me endlessly on account of your elegy – I am like a martyr, dear Pushkin, and therefore love you even more and believe in your admiration for our Hero and your sympathy for me! Poor Chaadaev. What a great unhappiness it must be to bear such hatred for

one's country and one's countrymen in one's heart." She
had just added her impressive signature – Élise Hitroff, née
Princesse Koutouseff-Smolensky – when she was handed an
envelope that had arrived in the municipal post. She was
curious, for the *petite poste* was still a novelty in the capital.
She therefore opened it immediately. Inside was a single sheet
of paper – folded, sealed, and addressed to Pushkin. Astonish-
ment soon gave way to painful anxiety. Her sixth sense, finely
honed by long experience of the world and its baseness, told
her that the mysterious missive must surely have come from
one of the poet's enemies. Eliza spent a few silent moments
absorbed in thought, a vague, melancholy smile on her lips
as she savored the impending pleasures of maternal solicitude:
once again she would protect Pushkin, standing rock-solid
and shielding him with her imposing body. Upon suddenly
returning to reality, she ordered that both letters – the one
she'd just written and the one she'd received, its seal unbroken
– be forwarded to the poet at Princess Volkonskaya's mansion,
No. 12 on the Moyka.

On that same morning of November 4, 1836, Pyotr
Andreevich Vyazemsky was hard at work on his correspondence when his wife entered his study to give him the strange
item that had just arrived in the morning post: a single sheet,
completely blank, within which was enclosed another sheet
addressed to Pushkin. The worried Princess Vyazemsky, suspecting something nasty, was not sure what to do. Vyazemsky,
trusting in his long friendship with the poet, decided to open
the second sheet. He read it aloud and cast it into the fire
with a grimace of disgust. He and his wife agreed not to tell
anyone about it. What he didn't know was that the insult
was doing its slimy work elsewhere as well, seeping through
Petersburg like an oil slick.

On that same morning of November 4, 1836, Alexandra
Ivanovna Vasilchikova sent for her nephew, at the time a

guest in her home on Bolshaya Morskaya. "Isn't this odd? I've received a letter addressed to me, and inside is another letter, sealed, with this written on it: 'To Alexander Sergeevich Pushkin.' What should I do with it?" The twenty-three-year-old Vladimir Sollogub, an aspiring writer and an official at the Ministry of Internal Affairs, suspected that this very strange business was an aftershock of an unpleasant incident that had occurred nearly a year earlier.

He blushed as he recalled his first encounter – and first faux pas – with "the titan of national poetry." A student at the University of Dorpat, he was spending his Christmas holiday in Petersburg when one night his father pointed out the great Pushkin, sitting right in front of them at the theater. Count Alexander Ivanovich Sollogub introduced his son to the poet during the intermission: "My little boy – already a scribbler, you know?" As the second act ended, the lad – eager to make a good impression on his idol by showing that he was already acquainted with "*les gens du métier*" and spent time in their company – respectfully asked Pushkin whether he would have the pleasure of seeing him again at the Wednesday literary gathering of a certain writer. "I stopped going to such houses once I got married," the poet frostily replied, and the clumsy student felt like vanishing into the City of Peter's swampy innards. Since graduating from the university he had seen Pushkin several times at the home of the Karamzins, where, one evening in October 1835, Natalya Nikolaevna Pushkina had spoken jokingly of one of Sollogub's grand, ill-starred passions. "Have you been married long?" the resentful young man replied, suggesting that she had no business making light of a serious problem of the heart since she was herself hardly a child; he then immediately began talking about Lensky, a Pole highly skilled in the mazurka, a favorite escort of the Empress, and much sought-after by Petersburg's most fashionable ladies. Sollogub's words, blown out of proportion by the imaginative ladies present (was he trying to remind Natalya Nikolaevna of her wifely duties

or insinuating something about her relations with Lensky?),
seemed intolerably defamatory to the oversensitive Pushkin.
Having been dispatched to the provinces on a lengthy work-
related assignment, Sollogub found out only two months later
that the poet had sent him a written challenge to a duel and
had interpreted his silence as a dishonorable refusal. Sollogub
wrote to him, and in early February 1836 Pushkin replied,
postponing the encounter of honor to late March, when he
would be passing through Tver. The young man bought the
pistols and named a second, but the poet never showed up.
Instead, Pyotr Valuev arrived in Tver to report that Georges
d'Anthès was flagrantly courting Natalya Nikolaevna in
Petersburg. The two friends had a good laugh: Pushkin would
be dueling with one man while his wife flirted with another.

Time passed. In May Sollogub had to leave Tver for a few
days. On his return he learned to his dismay that Pushkin,
stopping briefly in the city on his way to Moscow, had been
looking for him. Afraid of really looking like a coward this
time, poor Sollogub hitched a ride on the postal troika to
Moscow that very night. The poet, a guest of Pavel Nashchokin, was still asleep when Sollogub arrived. He came into the
drawing room in his dressing gown, his hair tousled, eyes red
with sleep. Polishing his clawlike nails, he apologized for
having been forced to postpone the encounter so long and
asked his opponent who his second would be. The ice having
been broken, the conversation turned to literary matters,
specifically *The Contemporary*. "The first issue was too good,"
the fledgling publisher commented. "I'll try to make the
second a little more boring: mustn't spoil the public." At that
point in came Nashchokin, even sleepier than Pushkin after
a night at the green-felt tables of the English Club. Despite
a splitting headache and considerable irritation at the
unreasonably early morning visit, the master of the house
forthwith sought to make peace: the misunderstanding at the
root of this dispute was not worth a duel, he insisted. "Do
you think I enjoy fighting a duel?" Pushkin himself said to

Sollogub. "But what am I to do? It is my misfortune to be a public man, which as you know is worse than being a public woman." After long negotiations an honorable way out was finally found: the public man settled for a letter of apology addressed to his wife. As if suddenly relieved of a burden, Pushkin marked the cessation of hostilities by shaking Sollogub's hand and then dissolved into a cheerful, talkative mood. Later, when the young man returned to Petersburg, they saw each other often, walking together to the little outdoor market where they bought warm oven-fresh loaves of white bread to nibble on the way back, thus outraging the fops who strolled the Nevsky Prospect with their languid peacock strut. Pushkin discussed literature with Sollogub, praising his first efforts, encouraging him. In short, they were friends now, and the alarmed Sollogub wondered what this mysterious missive might mean. Surely nothing good; he felt that in his bones. Without sharing his misgivings with his aunt, he asked her to give him the still-sealed sheet and headed straight for the poet's house.

"On that same morning of November 4, 1836 . . ." at more or less the same hour, the same scene was repeated like a monotonous sordid ritual (the postman, the double letter, surprise, vague unease, indignation if the second letter was opened), in the homes of at least three other Petersburg families: the Karamzins, Count and Countess Vielgorsky, and the Rosset brothers.

Sollogub crossed the Nevsky Prospect briskly and walked along the canal. There were occasional ripples in the softly flowing waters of the Moyka, not yet completely frozen, a bleak gray with a greenish tint through the middle, along the line farthest from the banks, white with ice and stone. Arriving at No. 12, he climbed the short flight of steps. A servant let him in, announced him, and led him to the door of the study. Pushkin was sitting at his desk, a large rectangular table of pale wood. He unsealed the sheet and quickly skimmed the first few lines. "I've seen it already," he said. "I received an identical letter from Elizaveta Mikhailovna Khitrova today. It's a slander against my wife. Give me your word of honor you won't mention it to anyone. Anyway, it's like touching shit: not exactly pleasant, but wash your hands and it's all over. If they spit on my clothes from behind, it's the servant's job to get them clean. My wife is an angel, completely above suspicion. Listen to what I'm writing to Mrs. Khitrova about this . . ." He spoke calmly and with no apparent emotion, seemingly aloof, as if attaching no special importance to the disagreeable, vulgar incident.

Indeed, he had received his own copy of the very same letter that morning. He'd read it several times and by now knew the text by heart. Short, written in French in crude, widely spaced block letters, it said:

THE SUPREME COMMANDERS AND KNIGHTS OF THE MOST SERENE ORDER OF CUCKOLDS, GATHERED IN THE GRAND CHAPEL UNDER THE PRESIDENCY OF THE VENERABLE GRAND MASTER OF THE ORDER, HIS EXCELLENCY D. L. NARYSHKIN, HAVE UNANIMOUSLY NAMED MR. ALEXANDER PUSHKIN COADJUTOR TO THE GRAND MASTER OF THE ORDER OF CUCKOLDS AND HISTORIOGRAPHER OF THE ORDER.

PERMANENT SECRETARY, COUNT I. BORKH

A cuckold like Dmitry Lvovich Naryshkin, grand master of the hunt at the Romanov court and husband of Princess Marya Antonovna Svyatopolk-Chetvertinskaya, once a beauty of beauties and for fourteen years official favorite of Tsar Alexander I.

A cuckold like Count Iosif Mikhailovich Borkh, titular counselor and translator for the Ministry of Foreign Affairs. Of Lyubov Vikentevna Golynskaya, his wife since 1830, we know only what Pushkin himself said to Danzas one day as they passed the Borkhs' carriage: "The wife is sleeping with the coachman."

Anonymous letters and cryptic coded messages were all the rage in Petersburg at the time. In late October Andrei Nikolaevich Muravyev, a poet and high official of the Holy Synod, received a copy of Chateaubriand's new translation of *Paradise Lost* in the mail, and was said to have wept with rage when he grasped the allusion to his own murky role in the shocking dismissal of Nechaev, the Synod's chief procurator. And in December the ambassador from Baden-Württemberg was to write this from Petersburg: "Troubling the serenity of families by sending anonymous letters has already been a regrettable custom for some time here, but the disgraceful authors of such missives are now doing worse, going so far as to harass the city authorities with their writings . . ."

Let us try to imagine the writer. How did the odious act occur to him? Did an evil smile cross his lips as he savored the insult, the impotent rage, in advance? How long did it take him laboriously to copy out the defamatory message so many times, apparently trying to vary his handwriting? Did he do it in the isolation of a *cabinet privé*, in the solitude that befits this base act, or at a table strewn with the remains of a lavish banquet and copious libations, in an atmosphere of drunken, irresponsible merriment?

Perhaps the anonymous perpetrator was trying to twist the knife of affront by slanderously equating Naryshkin's wife and Pushkin's – the former Tsar Alexander's lover, the latter supposedly Tsar Nicholas's – thereby suggesting a similarly slanderous equation of the husbands, the former a man who had gladly accepted titles, privileges, and fabulous riches along with his horns, the latter a poet the charms of whose beautiful wife had supposedly earned him the Tsar's favors, not least the title of kamerjunker. There is no evidence – not a single diary entry, memoir, allusion, or bit of gossip – to support the suspicion that Natalie Nikolaevna had an affair with the Tsar (while Pushkin was alive). But it was no secret that Nicholas I singled her out among the ladies of the Anichkov Palace. Pushkin himself once told Nashchokin that the Emperor was courting Natalie like some small-time official, passing back and forth under her windows in the hope of stealing a glance or a smile. But we know no more than that, and the Tsar's extramarital affairs always came to light eventually, especially when they lasted and had a story behind them.

Pushkin must have suspected the possible allusions as he read between the lines of his cuckold certificate, just as we have. And he was blinded by indignation. Two days later, on November 6, he wrote to Count Kankrin, the Minister of Finance:

I owe the Treasury 45,000 rubles, of which I must repay 25,000 within five years. Today, wishing to retire my debt immediately and in full, I encounter an obstacle that can easily be removed, but only by you. I possess 220 souls in the province of Nizhny Novgorod, 200 of them mortgaged for 40,000 rubles. According to the terms set by my father, who bestowed this property upon me, I have no right to sell them in his lifetime, though I can mortgage them either to the Treasury or to private individuals. But the Treasury has the right to demand its due regardless of any private arrangement, so long as such arrangements have not been sanctioned by the Emperor. . . . May I be so bold as to burden Your Excellency with another entreaty important to me? Since it is a matter of scant account that falls within the scope of routine procedure, I most earnestly beseech Your Excellency not to bring it to the attention of His Majesty the Emperor, who, in his magnanimity, would probably reject such a repayment (even though it is in no way burdensome to me) and perhaps might even order the forgiving of my debt, which would put me in a situation both awkward and embarrassing, since I would then be duty bound to reject the Tsar's favor, an act that could appear unseemly, vainglorious, and even ungrateful.

With the deepest respect . . .

He was asking a government minister to compel him to repay a loan before it was due, to disregard a legal document signed by Sergei Lvovich Pushkin, and to keep the Tsar, who had ordered the granting of the loan in the first place, in the dark about the anomalous request. Pushkin was to write many other letters that November, some of unprecedented violence, but the one to Kankrin is disconcerting in its absurdity, a blind leap of pride and distress, a desperate effort to unravel the Gordian knot binding him to the Tsar, the court, and Petersburg "immediately and in full." Even the style is bombastically turgid, a rarity for Pushkin and a reflection of the anxiety he was mired in.

Dispatches out of Petersburg after his death carried Pushkin's name to distant lands he'd never had the chance to visit while he lived, reaching the ears of kings and statesmen who had never even known of his existence. All foreign ambassadors in the Russian capital sent their governments long reports of the duel, its tragic consequences, and the punishment inflicted on d'Anthès. With one exception: Baron Aimable-Guillaume de Barante, the French ambassador, who waited until April 6 to make this laconic comment on d'Anthès's fate: "placed in an open sleigh and conveyed to the border like a vagrant." But the "vagrant" was a French subject, and the man who served as his second in the duel was an official of the French Embassy. Moreover, Barante, a brilliant man of letters, knew Pushkin personally and had a high regard for his work. The French ambassador's silence therefore piques our curiosity. The dispatches received from St. Petersburg at the Tuileries during the nineteenth century are stored in the archives of the Ministry of Foreign Affairs in Paris, all in good order, bound by year. No. 7 of 1837, dated February 4, consists of several utterly blank pages. No one at the Quai d'Orsay is able to explain this void, which suggests revelations so sensational that someone was inclined to censor them. And consider the source. Let's not forget that exactly three years later the ambassador's son Erneste set out from the Barante house to fight a duel with Mikhail Lermontov. It is as if the French Embassy in Petersburg played some mysterious, ruinous role in nineteenth-century Russian letters, as if the elegant mansion on Bolshaya Millionnaya Street were the custodian of all the secrets that still shroud the duels of Russian poets. I yearned to get my hands on the draft of that silenced dispatch, stored, it turns out, in an archive in Nantes. At the top it bears the suggestive label SECRET – as I suspected, as I had hoped.

"Monsieur le Comte," Barante wrote to the French Foreign Minister on February 4, 1837, "at the Emperor's instructions Count Nesselrode has given me the attached translation of a letter . . ." The letter in question was again anonymous, this time written in Polish and intercepted in Poland. "We here," it said, "are still hunting the beast that appeared in 1830; this is the third time we have fired on it; the Miller's shot missed, nor was my own attempt successful: still unwell, I am unable to go out, rifle and dog remain inactive." The allusion to Meunier ("Miller," in French), whose attempt on the life of Louis Philippe d'Orléans failed in 1836, is even clearer in the translation. In other words, as if his countless enemies at home were not enough (legitimists, republicans, Fourth Estate hotheads) *le roi citoyen* also had to worry about Polish patriots who never forgave him for leaving their insurgent country prey to bloody Russian repression in December 1830. Setting their disappointment aside, we are struck by an intriguing detail: the unknown conspirator was writing to a "Mr. Mitkiewicz" of Poniewiedz – surely a member of the large family of Adam Mickiewicz, father of modern Polish literature. Mickiewicz had been a friend of Pushkin's, but they had a painful parting of the ways precisely because of the events of 1830–31, for Pushkin rejoiced when Russian banners fluttered once more over the Polish capital and imperiously denounced the West for trying to interfere in a "conflict between Slavs, an ancient family conflict already settled by fate." A section of the public became disenchanted with Pushkin for these verses – "*delenda est Varsovia*" – accusing him of having abandoned liberalism to become a courtesan poet and servant of the powerful.

All this came to mind during my melancholy return trip, as I pondered with amazement and admiration the marvelous arabesques that history weaves from the threads of so many enigmas, mysterious events that are parallel yet unrelated. A dream: all is white; barking dogs sniff out fresh tracks on snowy ground, eventually flushing their prey; Barante slowly levels his weapon at Pushkin, but misses, blinded by the slowly falling snow; Georges d'Anthès slowly stretches out his arm, but the slow, slow snow clogs his pistol's barrel, and the Miller's rifle misfires . . . A dream suddenly interrupted by Vyazemsky's bitter words: "They shoot at our poetry more accurately than at Louis Philippe."

A variegated and lively company used to gather almost every evening, sometimes late into the night, at the home of the widow of Nikolai Mikhailovich Karamzin: famous men of letters, old friends of the late historian, new young talents whose mere presence in his house earned them a kind of moral recognition bestowed by his illustrious shade, fashionable ladies on their way home from the theater or a ball, diplomats and statesmen, foreign travelers, young officers and civil servants who happened to be friends of Andrei and Alexander. The soul of this salon with no pretensions to luxury – one comfortable ottoman and a supply of armchairs upholstered in faded red wool, lit by a large lamp hanging over a table always set for tea – was Sophie, Karamzin's daughter from his first marriage. Past thirty now, she played her old maid's role with resigned irony, her acid tongue rarely missing an opportunity for a wicked gibe or pungent comment.

She was a skilled conversationalist capable of igniting flashes of wit in even the dullest minds. "You can't imagine how much this man is unaware of," she replied, like Mme Récamier, to those who expressed amazement at her ability to hold up her end of a chat with a fool. An expert strategist, every evening she cleverly arranged the armchairs so as to put all guests at ease, able to talk about whatever they wanted with just the right neighbor, thereby fostering new friendships, new acquaintances, and new loves. Queen of the samovar, she was always ready with cups of tea served with cream more delicious than any other in Petersburg, and delicate canapés of black bread and fresh country butter. She was a busy little bee who was never still, and when the number of guests grew too large (some evenings as many as sixty people packed the red drawing room), she would have chairs brought in from other rooms to accommodate the crowd, while simultaneously making sure that the conversation kept moving along, that no one was bored. And no one ever was: card-playing was proscribed; instead, people talked of Russian and foreign literature, political events, music, the theater. The atmosphere, never dogmatic or doctrinaire, was lightened by wit and by the joking and chatter of the young.

The Karamzins' home on Mikhailovskaya Square was probably Pushkin's favorite Petersburg address. He was drawn to it by its cordial and relaxed ways, by the maternal attentions of the still beautiful mistress of the house (for whom, as a youth, he'd had feelings rather more ardent than filial devotion), by the absence of formality, and by the certainty of almost always finding intelligent, cultured, knowledgeable, witty people to talk to, along with many lovely women. Natalie and her sisters were also treated like family by the Karamzins and rarely missed an evening appointment, despite the fact that the average age of the bachelors present was too young to offer suitable catches for Catherine and Alexandrine.

Sollogub wrote that the "anonymous letters" had been sent to members of "the Karamzins' inner circle." One might well wonder why. Some have speculated that it was an attempt to force Pushkin to act, since he could hardly fail to respond to an offense that the people dearest to him had been lured into witnessing. Or perhaps the intent was to induce him to take steps that could prove useful to whoever it was hurling insults from the cover of darkness (temporarily withdraw from social life, leave Petersburg). But neither Zhukovsky, Pletnev, nor any of his former lyceum classmates – friends to whom Pushkin was bound by the closest links of affection and intimacy – received copies of the letters. And Khitrova and Vasilchikova did not belong to "the Karamzins' inner circle." Moreover, after making inquiries of his own, Pushkin said that "seven or eight" people other than himself had received the cuckold certificate. We know of only five of them.

In the spring of 1837 Prince Hohenlohe-Kirchberg, Baden-Württemberg's ambassador to Russia, sent to Stuttgart a long, detailed "Notice sur Pouschkin," the text of which was published in Russia in 1916. In it we read: "Long before this lamentable duel, several anonymous letters, written in French and signed by N. as president and Count B. as permanent secretary of the society of C., were distributed and delivered to all Pushkin's acquaintances, either by servants or by the municipal post." The subsequent publisher of this document believed that the names were abbreviated to initials in an outburst of posthumous discretion by the archivist who made the copy of the "Notice" to send back to Russia. That seems convincing. It is hard to imagine the ambassador believing that he could enlighten his minister by identifying the people involved in this piquant Russian affair solely by their initials. But let us continue with this interesting document: "Many letters even came from the country's interior (among them that of W. de P.)." The fact that some of the certificates were sent from the countryside raises the possibility of a mini-conspiracy carefully prepared to the smallest detail, ensuring that the Russia-wide postal system and the Petersburg city mail would deliver the infamous double letter at the same time. Plus which, the mysterious initials "W. de P.," designating a man (or woman) who supposedly received it from the provinces, seem to correspond to no one who ever crossed paths with Pushkin in this life, a fact worthy of note for anyone who has no choice but to grasp at the smallest straws, the slightest clues. The enigma seemed worth a visit to the State Archives in Stuttgart, where another hammerblow of disappointment awaited me: the names are initials even in the original, and "W. de P." turns out to be a mere phantom, a homunculus born of a slip of the pen, an error of transcription of the manuscript's clearly legible "M. de P.," which no doubt simply stands for "Monsieur de Pouschkin."

The "Notice" was recopied not only by the inattentive German scribe but by Johan Gevers, the Dutch diplomat who replaced Baron Heeckeren in April 1837. He sent it to The Hague in a restricted report purporting to be an "impartial summary of the various opinions" he had gathered in Petersburg. The lackadaisical Gevers, however, introduced several slight variations in the text, and the passage that interests us most reads: "Many letters even came from the country's interior (that sent to Madame de Ficquelmont)." But Dolly Ficquelmont knew very little about the fatal certificates. "Some wicked hand," she writes in her diary, "sent the husband offensive and cruel anonymous letters in which all the nasty rumors were repeated and the names of the wife and d'Anthès were joined with the cruelest and most bitter irony." Did she, too, send Pushkin the second sheet without opening it? Or did Gevers have "the Ambassadress" mixed up with her mother? Did any of the certificates really come from the countryside?

We may as well give up. We shall never know for sure how many people received the anonymous letters on the morning of November 4, 1836; we shall never learn all the names. It therefore seems risky and scarcely profitable to speculate about the intent and hence the identity of the anonymous author on the basis of his choice of recipients. All we can really conclude is that he knew the Karamzins and some of the red salon's habitués, as well as their addresses.

In early December 1836 Sollogub saw George d'Anthès's adoptive father in possession of "a number of printed forms of various parody certificates of various ridiculous titles" similar to the one Pushkin received: basically blank forms where all you had to do was fill in your chosen victim's name along with those of his comrades in ignominy. On the same occasion Sollogub learned that a number of fun-loving lads had distributed similar "forgeries" in Vienna the winter before. It seems, then, that in recopying the certificate of coadjutor of the Order of Cuckolds, our anonymous prankster simply inserted Pushkin's name along with Naryshkin's and Borkh's. But barring stunning coincidence, there is a piece of evidence that he was in fact responsible for one, let us say, creative addition: the mention "Historiographer of the Order." Whoever put those words in knew about Pushkin's *History of the Pugachev Revolt* and was aware of his research on Peter the Great. In other words, he was a man of at least some culture, and he was up-to-date.

Only two copies of the certificate have survived – two sheets of heavy letter paper made in England, 11.5 by 18 centimeters, bearing no watermark – and a single copy of the sheet in which it was enclosed: the one addressed to Count Vielgorsky.

Let's start with the handwriting. The limited mastery of the Latin alphabet (Cyrillic letters resembling those needed for the French text crop up occasionally), lack of familiarity with grave and acute accents ("sécrétaire" or "sécretaire" instead of "secrétaire"; "pérpétuel" instead of "perpétuel"), and unconventional transcription of the second vowel in "Nar-*y*shkin" (a phoneme intractable to foreigners, who in fact always wrote "Nar*i*shkin") leave little doubt that the certificate was almost certainly written by a Russian, probably the same person who printed Vielgorsky's address, using the colloquial "Mikhail*a*," instead of the more correct "Mikhail" yet displaying unexpected accuracy in the spelling of the surname, often distorted to "Velgorsky" or "Velgursky" even by the count's own friends. The words "To Alexander Sergeevich Pushkin," on the other hand, seem to be the work of a different hand, though also Russian. Reading it, Sollogub was struck by the "lackey's slanting handwriting."

Both certificates clearly bear the imprint of an unusual seal: two drops dripping down from the top, with a prominent A in the middle (perhaps for Alexander, possibly meaning Pushkin, possibly Tsar Alexander I – also possibly a monogram, a J or an I entwined with an A) embedded in a figure reminiscent of a portal or a Greek or Cyrillic letter *P*, most of the length of whose crossbar is topped by a series of small vertical lines in turn closed by a horizontal line (forming what looks like a comb or a fence); to the right of the figure resembling a Π we can make out the profile of what may be an animal with a notable belly, which some have interpreted as a penguin with its beak thrust into a tuft of grass but is more likely a less exotic bird, while the blades of grass bear a greater resemblance to two ears as enormous as they are improbable; from the lower edge of the mysterious creature's body, reaching out to close off the bottom of the ersatz Π, is what seems to be a feathery tail (but might also be a palm frond). The sole unequivocal insignia is the one at the left edge of the emblem: a half-open compass, definitely a Masonic symbol.

Let us therefore take a fresh look at the other figures in the light of this one comprehensible mark: not a Π but a highly stylized Temple, or an altar on which a Bible has been laid; not raindrops but the tears for the death of Hiram that appear in many Masonic emblems. The trouble is that the bird (if that's what it is) on the right bears no resemblance to a dove, pelican, or eagle – the birds most common in Freemason iconography. And it's all so crude, murky, and muddled – almost a parody of a Masonic seal. Perhaps the certificates were sold in Vienna together with the printed forms: a complete kit for pranksters.

Fairy tales about the anonymous letters began to circulate while Pushkin was still alive: "They say, among other things, that he received in the post a certificate with gilded horns, signed by prominent society people admittedly part of the confraternity, who write that they are proud to have such an illustrious man in their ranks and hasten to send him the said certificate as they would to a member of their society, to which they joyfully welcome him." Marya Mörder claimed to know of an anonymous letter in which "a head with horns was drawn atop a complete list of names of husbands whom all Petersburg knew had been betrayed, followed by a note saying that a husband who permits himself to beat his wife cannot hope to escape the usual fate." When Pushkin died, scarcely anyone who told absent friends of the dreadful tragedy or confided their dismay to diaries and memoirs, failed to recall the events of November 4: "One lady, in love with d'Anthès, began writing Pushkin anonymous letters warning him, mocking him, informing him that he'd been accepted as an active member of the Society of Cuckolds." ". . . began to receive anonymous letters in which he was warned about his wife and cruelly mocked." "He was informed of the plot in an anonymous letter as vulgar as it was treacherous." "He began to receive anonymous letters in which he was congratulated for his horns." In these fanciful tales – slight variations on an already robust legend that might be called "The Death of the Poet" – the anonymous letter writer assumes the status of Pushkin's "true murderer," his "moral assassin." For everyone believed, as Danzas put it, that "without those letters there would have been no duel between Pushkin and d'Anthès." I too am convinced of that.

There is a gap of a few crucial hours after Sollogub left the house on the Moyka. What did Pushkin do on the afternoon of November 4, 1836, the day that launched him on the path to death? Did he seek help or advice? If so, from whom? Sobolevsky was out of town on a trip. The Smirnovs were away, too, in Baden-Baden. And many people who felt a warm affection for him were absent in spirit. Khitrova wrote to him immediately about the letter she'd received: "To me it is truly a disgrace, I assure you I am all in tears – I thought I'd done enough good in this world not to be treated to such horrible slanders! I beg you on my knees not to speak to anyone at all about this lamentable affair. I am dismayed at the thought of having such a cruel enemy – as to your wife, dear Pushkin, she is an angel, and they are attacking her only so as to lay hands on my voice and to strike at my heart." "To me," "my voice," *her* enemies – a raving, hysterical narcissist who surely couldn't have been much comfort to the poet. Pushkin was right: "Give me a seamstress anytime." It seems most likely that he spent that terrible afternoon alone in his study, alone with his suspicions, his rage, his thirst for revenge. Then – we may imagine – he decided to speak to his "Angel," a long, agonizing discussion during which he discovered much he'd never known. At that point he decided to challenge Georges d'Anthès. It had been dark in Petersburg for several hours by then.

The annals of dueling in Russia list no case in which satisfaction was demanded for anonymous letters, but this was hardly Pushkin's first violation of ritual and custom. The surprising element lies elsewhere: a duel with d'Anthès would seriously compromise Pushkin's wife, for the social set, unaware of the certificates, would buzz with whispered pearls of stereotypical tongue-wagging – "no smoke without fire," "he who strikes with his horns." Offenses far more serious than an overly diligent courtship would be ascribed to Natalya Nikolaevna's admirer. But Pushkin, a seasoned connoisseur of "the whispered snickering of fools," a man well versed in the laws of "the shallow social scene," somehow overlooked this. What prevailed instead was wrath and pain, a yearning to escape a now intolerable situation, a keen sense of his own honor, outrage. These prevailed, and in the process dispelled any dictate of prudence or good sense. As we know, the poet was rich in neither of these.

> *Liza was here in the city*
> *with her daughter Dolly,*
> *and was called in society*
> *"naked Eliza."*
> *Now Liza is all dressed up*
> *at the Austrian Mission,*
> *naked old truth*
> *with her shoulders on display.*

· 8 ·

Suspects

THE LUNGE

In the concluding lines of the "Notice sur Pouschkin" we read: "There are two widely held opinions about these anonymous letters. The one enjoying greater credibility among the public points to O——" This time there is no doubt: "O" stood for "Ouvarov," meaning Uvarov, a most important surname in nineteenth-century Russia that had already appeared in the "Notice" in its traditional French transliteration.

The mansion of Count and Countess Sheremetev began rising from the waters like a miracle back in Petersburg's dawning days, soon after a branch of that "nameless little river," the Neva, was christened Fontanka. In the 1830s the magnificent residence belonged to Dmitry Nikolaevich Sheremetev, the still young and single proprietor of 600,000 desyatins (about 1,627,000 acres) and a couple of hundred thousand serfs. One sad day in the autumn of 1835, the female population of the capital was stunned by the news that Sheremetev, Russia's most eligible bachelor, had been felled by a grave illness at his estate of Voronezh. A horde of servants lit votive candles and held holy Masses, praying that God would restore their master to them. But finally a mournful message arrived from the South: Count Dmitry's time was up, death was expected at any moment, all that could be done now was to pray for his soul. The Minister of Public Education, Sergei Semyonovich Uvarov, gripped by a febrile anxiety, schemed and pulled strings to see to it that the palace of the Russian Croesus was placed under lock and key; related by marriage to the dying man, he coveted the fabulous riches contained in the mansion on the Fontanka and was determined to thwart other, less opportunistic heirs. When the Council of Ministers discussed Sheremetev's imminent demise, one member ascribed it to a particularly nasty case of "scarlet fever." At which point Count Litta turned to Uvarov and thundered, "And you, Sergei Semyonovich, have a bad case of expectation fever!" It all happened, they say, in the autumn of 1835, by which time a silent swordplay between Pushkin and Uvarov – feints and touches, probes and grazes – had been going on for years.

Theoretician of the notorious triad "Orthodoxy, Autocracy, National Spirit,"* apostle of a new culture that was to be a bulwark "against so-called European ideas," champion of ultrapatriotic reforms designed to turn the universities into hothouses growing docile slaves, Uvarov was the scion of a good family that had fallen on hard times in the late eighteenth century. His father, Semyon Fyodorovich, managed to recover some of the line's lost luster as valiant man at arms and valorous lover of Catherine II during an interregnum between her two favorites, Alexander Lanskoy and Alexander Dmitriev-Mamonov. For a time he also won Prince Potemkin's favor, and spent many an evening entertaining His Most Serene Highness with his bandore, an ancient stringed instrument which he played masterfully, enlivening his concerts with frenzied exhibitions of prisiadka dancing: squatting low, arms crossed, feet flashing. Discharged from the Empress's bedroom with generous thanks (though not with the lavish riches the Great Catherine bestowed upon other boudoir veterans), Uvarov became a regimental commander of the Grenadier Guards and married a Golovina. Rumor in Petersburg had it that his wife's dowry included both substantial capital

---

* A formula that appeared for the first time in a report on the state of the universities which Uvarov sent to the Tsar in December 1832.

and an unborn child conceived with Prince Stepan Apraskin. The child was Sergei, who was orphaned soon after his coming into this world when his legal father fell ill during a campaign against the Swedes and subsequently died. After receiving an excellent education from private tutors, young Sergei embarked on a diplomatic career. In 1807 he was posted to the Russian Embassy in Vienna, where he continued his studies, corresponded with Goethe, Schelling, and the Humboldt brothers, and became a friend and confidant (a faithless one, as it later turned out) to Madame de Staël. After three years in the Austrian capital he left the diplomatic service and returned to Russia to take charge of a patrimony more or less completely squandered by his mother's ineptitude and dissipation. Soon he tied the knot with Countess Ekaterina Razumovskaya, a woman older than he but with a sizable dowry and a well-placed father: the new Minister of Public Education, who even before the wedding had his future son-in-law named education superintendent of the Petersburg district. Having successfully staved off the nightmare of poverty, Sergei Semyonovich Uvarov was able to devote himself quietly to research. He was, in fact, an erudite and esteemed scholar of classical antiquity, though some suspected him of being rather too cavalier in drawing on works published abroad. But he was concerned with more than gods and myths: he was also among the founders of Arzamas, the informal literary grouping whose devotion to Karamzin and rejection of traditionalism united Zhukovsky, Batyushkov, Turgenev, Vyazemsky, and the very young Pushkin. He had a reputation as an innovator in politics as well. In 1818 he was elected president of the Academy of Sciences, and on the day of his investiture, at the tender age of thirty-two, he delivered a speech so ringingly libertarian that a few years hence, people said, he would have sent himself to prison in Siberia for such an inflammatory declamation.

Uvarov's brilliant rise came to a screeching halt when the ideological wind shifted toward the end of Tsar Alexander's reign. Ousted from his superintendent's post, the Academy president could have retired comfortably on his income and his studies, but he was a stubborn man who loved power, quite prepared to roll up his sleeves when circumstances required. In 1822 he went to work at the Ministry of Finance, long a refuge for subjects with a whiff of disgrace about them. But his post, while prestigious, fell short of his desires and grandiose plans. Uvarov was a man who thought big, dreaming of triumphs that would cleanse his resumé of the embarrassing shadow of his father, Senka the bandore strummer. So yes, he thought big, and colleagues, subordinates, and friends were stunned by his fawning. Not a day passed that he didn't find some reason to drop by the home of his minister, Count Kankrin, bringing files, running errands, dandling the children (at first the little Kankrins, mistaking him for a doctor, stuck out their tongues when Uvarov set foot in the nursery). A soft spot for the children of powerful men, however, was not the sole weakness of the director of the Department of Manufacturing and Internal Trade. He also liked wood, particularly the Treasury's holdings of birch, larch, and poplar, and took advantage of his high office to acquire as much of it as he could for illegal trade. In the meantime, he pressed on with his studies and writings, pondering the future of Russian culture, clawing his way upward. Having distinguished himself for his patriotic zeal and his sweeping plans for education reform, he was named Vice-Minister of Public Education in 1832 and Minister in 1834. As Minister of Public Education he was also head of the central censorship directorate. Satisfied at last, he felt that he had the culture of the motherland at his feet.

Russia's most skillful chameleon and social climber approached Pushkin with a shrewd tactic of cooptation, letting it be known that he wanted him as an honorary member of *his* Academy, ingratiating himself by translating some of his poems into French, introducing him to university students in terms so flattering as to border on adulation, while in his heart resolving to subdue the "haughty and insufficiently servile" poet. Sometimes he didn't quite manage to conceal his hostility. In 1830, for instance, he let this comment slip at the home of Alexei Nikolaevich Olenin: "Why in the world is Pushkin so proud of being descended from that Negro Hannibal whom Peter the Great bought for a bottle of rum at Kronstadt?" Faddey Bulgarin couldn't resist repeating this leaden crack in his *Bee of the North*, and the poet flew into a rage. Consumed by a potent mixture of envy and megalomania, Uvarov couldn't endure the idea that the Tsar honored Pushkin with his own personal censorship, and he battled the Tsar and Count Benckendorff for the honor of watching over the works and days of his all too famous colleague in the arts of the mind. Pushkin, for his part, viewed the minister with hatred and scorn, though relations between them were formally correct. In February 1835, when he had to suffer the bitter humiliation of ordinary censorship for works not personally approved by the Tsar, Pushkin exclaimed: "Uvarov is a scoundrel . . . a cad and a charlatan. Renowned for his corruption. . . . They say he started out as a whore and then became a wet nurse." And two months later: "This is a bleak year for our academies: barely had Sokolov passed away at the Russian when Dondukov-Korsakov was named vice president at Sciences. Uvarov is a juggler and Dondukov-Korsakov his clown – one cavorts on the tightrope, the other on the floor below him." But all this was confined to diary entries and letters to trusted friends; himself a seasoned swordsman, Pushkin studied his opponent, parrying his more insidious lunges, biding his time. Until at last his patience was rewarded.

> *Vice-president of the Academy is*
> *Prince Donduk. They say such an honor*
> *is not fitting for Donduk.*
> *Why is he sitting there? He's the best censor,*
> *and above all he has something to sit on,*
> *and with his seat he knows whom to please.*
> — certainly by Pushkin

The mansion on the Fontanka was all sealed up and solemn funeral rites for Count Sheremetev were being prepared when wonderful news arrived from the South: the patient had suddenly, miraculously rallied; he was going to make it. Uvarov scurried furiously to cover the tracks of his cupidity, but it was too late to stop Petersburg from talking. Pushkin took advantage of Uvarov's spectacular blunder to deliver his own merciless lunge: he wrote "On the Convalescence of Lucullus," tripping up the censor by passing this "ode" off as "adapted from the Latin":

> *You were dying, wealthy young man!*
> *. . . and meanwhile the heir of your possessions,*
> *a greedy crow, glutton for carrion,*
> *grew pale, shaken by shivers,*
> *gripped by a fever for hoarding*
> *. . . He thought: "I won't have to sing lullabies*
> *to the children of high officials*
> *. . . or deceive my wife in the accounts,*
> *or continue to steal*
> *wood from the state!" . . .*

"My compliments to the translator," Alexander Ivanovich Turgenev wrote to Vyazemsky from Paris, "unfortunately from the Latin and not the Greek," thereby metaphorically adding homosexuality to the savage portrait of Lucullus' disappointed heir. (Everyone knew of the bond between Uvarov and Dondukov-Korsakov, the ignorant second-rater whom the minister had promoted to be chairman of the Censorship Committee and vice president of the Academy of Sciences.) Uvarov complained in high places, and Pushkin was summoned to the Third Section.

When Count Benckendorff demanded to know to whom the incriminating lines referred, the poet replied, "You." Benckendorff chuckled skeptically. "You don't believe it? Why, does someone else think I had him in mind?" The next day he wrote: "All I ask is that it be shown that I have named him – which feature of my ode can be ascribed to him?" This time Pushkin had it covered from all sides: any measure taken against him or the Moscow review that had published the so-called adaptation would mean that the Tsar himself recognized the eager vulture as one of his own "high officials," one of his own ministers. Uvarov swore to himself that Pushkin would pay. In the Ministry corridors someone heard him shout: "Let not one, but two, three, and four censors be assigned to the works of this scoundrel!"

The thinly veiled identification of Uvarov in the "Notice sur Pouschkin" was a reference to a popular rumor, an accusation not supported by evidence, the understandable reaction of a city in which the laughter provoked by "Lucullus" still echoed, for the laughter had been universal, even among the many who publicly condemned this latest unforgivable provocation on the poet's part. The reasoning was simple: Pushkin called Uvarov a thief and a lackey; Uvarov countered by calling Pushkin a cuckold. The logic seems ironclad, but it's far too simple. If there'd been the slightest evidence against the "crow," wouldn't Pushkin have used it to deliver the final thrust?

THE "BOMBE À LA NESSELRODE"

On February 17, 1837, Alexander Ivanovich Turgenev wrote in his diary: "Evening at Bravura's . . . then Valueva's. Vielgorsky was there. Zhukovsky talked about spies, Countess Yulya Stroganova, and the 3–5 packets she took from Pushkin's study . . . *Suspects. Countess Nesselrode.* Discussion with Zhukovsky about Bludov and other things." A passage in the memoirs of the elderly prince Alexander Mikhailovich Golitsyn, written early in the twentieth century, reads: "Tsar Alexander Nikolaevich, dining at the Winter Palace in a small group, said aloud, '*Eh bien, on connait maintenant l'auteur* *des lettres anonymes qui ont causé la mort de Pouchkine: c'est Nesselrode.'** I heard it from someone seated next to the sovereign." Some have concluded from this testimony that Countess Marya Dmitrievna Nesselrode was the author of the murderous certificates.

From his early youth Karl Vasilievich Nesselrode had been a virtuoso of blini, master of flambé, consummate artist of frosting. One of his puddings became a staple of Russian cuisine, and his dessert surprise – an ice-cream ball with a hot chocolate center – was immortalized internationally as *"la bombe à la Nesselrode."* The sarcastic government official and memoirist F. F. Vigel reports that Nesselrode's delicacies touched the heart of the capital's preeminent gastronome, Gurev, the Minister of Finance, whose daughter, a girl "ripe and even somewhat faded . . . dangling proudly and sadly from the family tree like a succulent fruit, willingly let herself be picked by Nesselrode. A shower of gold poured down along with her."

Armed with the "weakness of character" and dullness of intellect that can seem like virtues to an absolute ruler, Nesselrode rose rapidly in government ranks after a brief, unhappy stint in the Navy. He served as diplomatic adviser to the Russian ambassador in Paris, then adviser to the Tsar himself, and finally Foreign Minister and Vice Chancellor of the Russian Empire. (In 1846, nine years after Pushkin's death, he became Chancellor.) His wife, a rigid, haughty woman known for her imperious penchant for command, soon enough became the former adviser's most influential adviser, striking fear in the hearts of diplomats halfway across Europe. Fanatically devoted to the *ordre établi* and the Holy Alliance, she patterned her ideas and even her style after Metternich's living example. With her iron character and tireless energy, Marya Dmitrievna Nesselrode – "an extortionist, a gossip, a real witch" – staked

---

* "Well, now we know who wrote the anonymous letters that caused Pushkin's death: it's Nesselrode."

out an impregnable position at Russia's social summit, flattered
and feared by the throng of courtiers waiting at the foot of
the mountain in the hope of beginning their own daunting yet
potentially profitable ascent. She loved making and breaking
careers, fortunes, and reputations; her enmity was as terrifying
and dangerous as her amity was fervent and active. She seemed
deliberately to suppress all traces of femininity (of which she
had few in either body or face in any case). She scorned salon
small talk in favor of politics, high finance, royal weddings,
and sometimes literature (provided it was "serious"), and
despite her wholehearted devotion to the throne, she was
unsparing in her criticism and censure of the way the government functioned: *ce bon Monsieur de Robespierre*, Grand Duke
Mikhail Pavlovich jokingly called her. She would receive
guests half-reclining on a sofa's arm, silent and distant,
absorbed in her own inscrutable thoughts, raising her eyes to
show some sign of life only when her exclusive salon, which
many found fatally boring, was graced by the entrance of the
chosen few, the leading representatives of *la société dans la
société*, the members of the oligarchic Areopagus of the sort
who gathered at Sophie Swétchine's salon in Paris or Melanie
von Metternich's in Vienna.

Marya Dmitrievna Nesselrode hated Pushkin for an epigram about her father, Dmitry Alexandrovich Gurev, from
whom some felt the countess had inherited her unbridled
passion for other people's money: "While Golitsyn was indoctrinating Russians, Gurev was robbing them blind." In fact,
the epigram may not have been Pushkin's, but the public
attributed it to him, mindful of the many nasty things he had
indeed said and written about Mrs. Nesselrode, whom he
heartily detested. Natalya Nikolaevna once went dancing with
the Nesselrodes at the Anchikov without her husband's knowledge; Pushkin lost his temper and impolitely told the haughty
countess, "I don't want my wife going to places I don't go
to."

Those who argue that Marya Dmitrievna Nesselrode was

the perpetrator marshal other, circumstantial evidence. Sollogub recalls that on the morning of November 4 Pushkin
"suspected a woman whose name he even mentioned." In the
days when Petersburg was seething with scorn for the
foreigner who had shed Pushkin's blood, the Nesselrodes
stood firmly with Georges d'Anthès and the Dutch ambassador. Three years later, Countess Nesselrode expressed soli-
darity and concerned solicitude for Erneste de Barante, the
young Frenchman who fought a duel with the man she called
"the officer Lermontov": Mikhail Lermontov. Is this enough
for an indictment? Granted, Mrs. Nesselrode was hardly a
fervent admirer of either poet and in any case could not have
been familiar with their work, since she spoke and wrote
Russian only haltingly, just like her husband, in whose veins
German blood coursed and who held the court of Vienna in
such high esteem that some called him "the Austrian Minister
of Russian Foreign Affairs." Marya Dmitrievna Nesselrode's
lack of facility in Russian should exonerate her, since the
certificates were almost certainly written by a Russian, unless
we assume the complicity of a scribe, servant, or friend, which
surely would have been too risky for a person of her rank.
Nor are her accusers very well versed in French: autocrats
may not be subject to the same standards of etiquette as
ordinary mortals, but it seems doubtful that Tsar Alexander
would have said, *"C'est Nesselrode"* – without *"Madame de"*
or *"la Comtesse de"* – if he were naming a lady, especially
when sharing such a weighty revelation with his guests.
Common sense and grammar therefore suggest that if the
comment was made at all, the Tsar was referring to the Nesselrode who would have required no further specification, namely
the minister.

For the nearly fifteen years that he served as an official staff
member of the Ministry of Foreign Affairs, Pushkin was under
Nesselrode's supervision, at least formally. Although they
could sometimes be seen walking together on the Nevsky

Prospect in the mid-1830s and met frequently at Petersburg receptions, at court, and in the Ministry, the vice chancellor and the poet could not be called friends. But they weren't enemies either. True, on December 14, 1833, Pushkin noted in his diary: "Kochubey and Nesselrode have received two hundred thousand rubles each to feed their starving peasants, and the whole four hundred thousand will remain in their pockets." But even the ample reserves of his fiery, passionate character would have failed to suffice if he'd felt hatred for everyone in Russia who got rich in underhanded ways. As for Nesselrode, he seems not to have harbored any particular ill will for the poet, at least judging by the surviving documentary evidence. In 1820 he had this to say about Pushkin in a letter to General Inzov: "There is no excess in which this hapless young man has not indulged, and no perfection beyond the reach of the sublime superiority of his talent." His attitude to Pushkin seems not to have changed with time, despite the fact that even in his maturity the "hapless youth" continued to find ways of landing himself in scrapes that meant fresh trouble for Nesselrode, not to mention extra work and new stacks of files on his desk. No doubt this annoyed him. The vice chancellor was endlessly, breathtakingly lazy – and his laziness would seem to testify to his innocence in the matter of the certificates, since their preparation would have required time, commitment, and attention. Nesselrode had had more than his fill of paperwork; the moment he managed to shake off the burden of history from his feeble shoulders, he devoted himself exclusively to gastronomy, flower growing, and, on special occasions, what many considered his third hobby: extortion.

How much more pleasurable and relaxing it must have been to invent new recipes and test new orchid grafts than to fritter time away copying some stupid cuckold certificate, over and over, in block letters! But then what are we to make of Alexander's alleged "It's Nesselrode"? Was it posthumous gossip, a product of belated inquiries, a conjecture, a joke? Had the Tsar had a little too much to drink that day? It bears remembering that Prince Golitsyn was reporting a comment "heard by someone sitting next to the sovereign" at an event that must have taken place at least twenty years earlier, since Alexander died in 1881. He might have mixed something up, or perhaps whoever told him the story mixed up or misunderstood something. But it strains credulity to the breaking point to believe that the guests at an imperial dinner could have maintained such complete and inviolate secrecy about the solution to an enigma that had vexed and was to vex and agitate Russia for more than a century and a half, that nothing more would have ever been leaked about either Nesselrode, Count or Countess.

LE DIABLE BOITEUX

Pushkin's younger daughter recalled: "My mother always believed that the author of the anonymous letters was Prince Pyotr Vladimirovich Dolgorukov. . . . The other person my mother pointed to . . . was Prince Ivan Sergeevich Gagarin."

Dolgorukov, Gagarin. More sensitive observers avert their gaze. An acrid smell of sulfur wafts over the stage, purple flashes rend the darkness, a trapdoor swings open with a sinister creak, and lo and behold! Satan, making his appearance in the roles that the Russian popular imagination has assigned him since time immemorial: apostate like the Jesuit Ivan Gagarin, lame like the hobbling Dolgorukov (whose physical disability earned him the nickname *le bancal*, the wobbly). Dolgorukov displayed additional marks of Luciferian origin: a squat, ill-shaped body, irregular features, an evasive gaze shielded by thick eyeglasses, a poisonous tongue, a flair for the underhanded, an enthusiasm for gossip, intrigue, swindles. He was abrasive, repellent, stingy, and conniving, full of himself and full of contempt for his fellows, a treacherous man always at war with the world – in short, a regular Antichrist.

*

Klementy Rosset was also a recipient of the double missive on November 4, 1836, which was delivered to the house he shared with his brother Arkady and Nikolai Scalon, a former colleague in the Corps of Pages. The Rosset boys owed their friendship with the greatest writers of the era to their sister, the beautiful, intelligent, cultured Alexandra Osipova, who had married Nikolai Mikhailovich Smirnov in 1832. Pushkin was fond of both Rossets and a few days earlier had even asked Klementy how *The Great Leader* had been received by his fellow soldiers. Their reaction, Pushkin said, was far more important to him than the opinion of aristocrats and power holders. Klementy Rosset unhesitatingly opened the letter addressed to Pushkin and immediately showed it to his brother and his friend, sharing his impressions with them. He felt that the writer must have been familiar with their little apartment on Mikhailovskaya Square, for the address had been spelled out on the envelope with unusual care: "Zanfteleben building, on the left, third floor." He thought he recognized the stationery and handwriting, too – where had he seen them before? Then he remembered, and the next day he went looking for Prince Gagarin.

Gagarin – twenty-two years old and recently returned from a long stay in Munich, where he worked for the Russian mission – loved good writing and the company of writers: Vyazemsky, Chaadaev, Pushkin himself. It was he who introduced Pushkin's circle to the lyric poems of the absent Tyutchev. In the autumn of 1836 Gagarin lived on Bolshaya Millionnaya Street with another young man of good family and culture with whom Rosset was also well acquainted: Prince Pyotr Dolgorukov. Rosset lunched with Dolgorukov and Gagarin but made no mention of the purpose of his visit while the servants were present. Only later did he and his two friends withdraw to the study, where he showed them the certificate, discreetly trying to feel them out by observing their reactions as he wondered aloud who might have written it and what its consequences might be.

That conversation, perhaps along with other considerations unknown to us, must have aroused Klementy Rosset's suspicions, since just after the duel the names of the two princes began to circulate as the authors of the fateful certificates that provoked it. On January 31, 1837, Alexander Ivanovich Turgenev noted in his diary: "Lunch with Mrs. Karamzin. Discussion about Heeckeren and Pushkin. Prince I. Gagarin under suspicion again." Turgenev kept an eye on Gagarin at the poet's funeral the next day: if he failed to approach Pushkin's body for the final farewell, it would be indirect confirmation of his guilt. But the young man, who seemed "devastated by some secret grief," went to the bier and brushed the corpse's ashen forehead with his lips. No one but Turgenev was reassured by this pious gesture: in 1843, when Gagarin entered a French Jesuit college as a novice, many believed that, driven by remorse, he was withdrawing from Russia and the world to expiate the misdeed that weighed on his conscience.

But these were whispered rumors, and no one seems to have named Gagarin or Dolgorukov openly until 1863, when a little-known poet named Ammosov published a slim volume reconstructing the events leading to Pushkin's tragic death "on the basis of the account of his former lyceum classmate and second, Konstantin Karlovich Danzas." Now all at once Russians could read in black and white: "After Pushkin's death many suspected Prince Gagarin; today suspicion falls on Dolgorukov. . . . Once he was out of the country, Gagarin admitted that the anonymous letters had in fact been written on his stationery – not by him, but by Prince Pyotr Vladimirovich Dolgorukov."

Pyotr Dolgorukov had not yet turned twenty in November 1836. He'd completed his studies in the Corps of Pages, but in 1831 was divested of the title of Page of the Bedchamber (which he'd earned earlier that year), "for bad behavior and laziness." The low rank and attestation of ineptitude that accompanied his dismissal from the corps precluded the brilliant career in the Guards to which his title and property would otherwise have entitled him. Instead, he was forced to settle for an ill-paid post in the Ministry of Public Education, where he could count on Uvarov's benevolence and protection. As sole heir to a substantial fortune, the young man had no financial worries and plenty of free time, devoted mainly to his social life and his hobby, genealogy. His *Notice sur les principales familles de Russie* was published in France in 1843 under the pseudonym Count d'Almargo, arousing the ire of the Tsar, the attentions of the secret police, and the resentment of many compatriots. Their rancor was further aggravated by the passage of time and the continuation of Dolgorukov's prolific publishing program, for the prince liked to supplement the facts he dug out of archives with pungent salon anecdotes, thereby exposing and taunting sycophants who garnered titles and positions of power through flattery, intrigues, marriages of convenience, and erotic exploits. Gazing down from the lofty heights of his own millennial lineage (his family's origins reached back to the Varangian warrior Rurik, ninth-century prince of Novgorod), Dolgorukov saw the Romanovs themselves as little more than parvenus. An ominous summons from Nicholas I brought him back to the motherland knowing that the Tsar's punishment awaited him, and so it did: he had to spend a year confined to remote Vyatka, where he struck the pose of a "Wallenstein in disgrace." Upon his release he devoted himself exclusively to his studies and to genealogical charts that remain invaluable to this day. In 1859 he fled the country secretly, taking refuge in France, where he was granted official status as a political exile. There he continued to publish his merciless "truths about Russia"* in newspapers, pamphlets, and memoirs, issuing fiercely sarcastic broadsheets exposing the vices of his homeland's aristocracy and autocracy.

---

* *The Truth about Russia* was the title of a book of Dolgorukov's published in Paris in 1860.

He died in exile in 1868, by which time many in Russia were convinced – and some who had passed on had stated with certainty – that he was the man ultimately responsible for Pushkin's death. That accusation, based on indirect evidence and analogy, continues to enjoy widespread credibility today.

In 1848 Chaadaev, then living in Moscow, received a letter from a Louis Colardeau, a fictitious Parisian neuropathologist, offering to cure the Russian thinker of his serious case of *mania grandiosa*. Around the same time, many of Chaadaev's friends and acquaintances also got letters calling upon them to urge the state-certified madman to place himself in the care of this foreign physician who, by curing him, might "hope for a post as physician to Count Mamonov and thereby assure himself of a permanent position." Chaadaev had no trouble figuring out who was responsible for this prank and wrote Dolgorukov a scathing reply, which he eventually decided not to send.

In June 1856 Prince Mikhail Semyonovich Vorontsov, taking the waters at Wildbad, received a deeply disturbing letter from Russia. In it Dolgorukov, preparing Volume IV of his *Russian Genealogy* for the printer, asked Vorontsov for new documents confirming the antiquity of his lineage, since an examination of the old acts and chronicles had turned up no evidence for the authenticity of the charts Vorontsov had earlier provided. The letter was accompanied by a disconcerting note, unsigned and apparently the work of a different hand: "His Highness has a *guaranteed* method of having his genealogy published . . . just as he wants it: by granting Prince Pyotr Dolgorukov a gift of fifty thousand rubles; in that event *all* will be done according to his desires. But there is no time to lose." Vorontsov died soon afterward, and three years later his son, Semyon Mikhailovich, sued Dolgorukov for publishing libelous information in *Le Courier de Dimanche*. The trial ended on January 3, 1861, the judges finding the prince guilty of slander and ruling that he had disguised his handwriting to pen the anonymous note blackmailing the late Vorontsov.

In the first issue of the magazine *Future*, published in Paris in September 1860, Dolgorukov wrote of Pushkin's friend Odoevsky: "In his youth he lived in Moscow, eagerly studied German philosophy, scribbled ugly little so-called poems. He tried his hand at chemistry experiments without success and assailed his acquaintances' ears with incessant musical exercises. . . . Today Odoevsky is known in social circles as a literary man and in literary circles as a socialite. He has a backbone of rubber and an insatiable thirst for decorations and court invitations; by constant groveling left and right he finally obtained the rank of Master of the Court."

Odoevsky dashed off an indignant riposte: "Until now the ignorant gentleman has confined himself to gossip and the distribution of anonymous letters, in which field he has acted with great success, causing many quarrels and family catastrophes, including, among other things, an enormous loss that Russia still laments even now." But he could not publish his reply: writing about forbidden writings was forbidden in Russia.

On February 7, 1862, Sergei Alexandrovich Sobolevsky, a friend of Pushkin's whose relentless efforts to unmask the author of the certificates continued even after the poet's death, wrote to the younger Prince Vorontsov: "I have just learned that d'Anthès himself intends to file suit against Dolgorukov, maintaining that he has proof that it was Dolgorukov who wrote the infamous anonymous letters. . . . I know that the memoirs (whether real or forged) of Princess Dolgorukova are circulating in Petersburg. . . . If you come across them, it would be worth your while to see what they have to say about the Pushkin affair, which would be of special interest, since the princess has always maintained (and used to tell anyone willing to listen) that her husband told her he was the author of the entire intrigue."

On February 8, 1862, the printer E. I. Weimar wrote to

the same Prince Vorontsov to tell him of a nasty incident that occurred after he printed the third volume of Dolgorukov's *Genealogy*: "On March 2, 1856, I brought the bill to his house. . . . He threw himself upon me, saying that some of the copies were spoiled. . . . 'Sign the receipt,' he said. I signed. He took the bill, went to his study as though to fetch money, and returned some minutes later to say: 'What are you waiting for?' 'What do you mean, what am I waiting for, Excellency? My money!' 'You got your money, you signed the receipt!' . . . He began to insult me in the most offensive terms, called the butler, and ordered him to show me out." Weimar sued, but later withdrew his claim, wary of having to challenge "a powerful and illustrious person" like Dolgorukov in a public trial.

In 1863 Dolgorukov perpetrated yet another mockery of his motherland's rituals, this time in the fifth issue of *Feuilleton*: "From Petersburg we hear that our wise government means to mark Russia's entry into its second millennium of chaos by preparing the establishment of two new decorations, to wit: the Order of Jackass First-Class, honoring persons famous for their devotion to autocracy and its dim intellectual capacities; the Order of Crap Chatter, honoring loyal writers who rattle off gibberish in defense of autocracy."

In his *Memoirs*, "Dolgorukov merrily tells of another, earlier *anonymous* lampoon (also French) that 'pranksters' sent all over Petersburg in the name of the mother of V. V. Levashev (later Count Levashev) on the occasion of the wedding of her son, the product of a liaison lacking the sanctity of marriage: '*Miss* Akulina Semyonovich is honored to announce the marriage of her son' . . ."

In 1892 the editor of *Russian Archive* revealed that he'd been told by the late Count Adlerberg: "In the winter of 1836–37, at a grand Petersburg reception, standing behind Pushkin, the young Prince P. V. Dolgorukov (later a noted genealogist) nodded toward d'Anthès and held up a hand with his fingers extended like horns."

In 1895 *Russian Archive* published Baron Fyodor Andreevich Büler's notes on an unpublished letter of Pushkin's. In them we read: "At one of Prince V. F. Odoevsky's literary-musical Saturdays in the forties, I happened to linger until four of us remained in his study: he, I, Prince Mikhail Yurievich Vielgorsky, and Lev Sergeevich Pushkin, then known as Levushka. . . . Levushka listened to Count Vielgorsky's detailed and highly interesting account of the many baleful provocations that led his brother to fight that duel. Even now I find it impossible to reveal all I heard on that occasion. I will say only that the name of Prince P. V. Dolgorukov figured on the list of authors of the provocative anonymous letters."

In Dolgorukov's mind the claims of Pushkin's second, Danzas (who was still alive when Ammosov's little book came out and issued no denials), seemed yet another link in the chain of slander forged by his many enemies in Russia, the very same people who, he was convinced, had no compunction about corrupting judges, experts, and documents during the Vorontsov trial. In 1863 he sent an open letter, previously published in Alexander Herzen's magazine *Bell*, to *The Contemporary*. In it he indignantly rejected every imputation and cited in his own defense, among other things, the fact that Pushkin's friends and intimates continued to associate with him after the tragedy. But not all of them, and in the margin of a page of a book published in Berlin in 1869 in which the prince-genealogist's guilt in the matter of the anonymous letters leading to Pushkin's death is recalled, Vyazemsky wrote: "The thing is still not proved, though Dolgorukov was capable of committing such an infamy."

*

Gagarin raised his own aggrieved voice for the first time only two years later, in 1865. In a letter to *News of the Exchange*, a widely circulated Petersburg newspaper, he countered Danzas's assertions by citing his long-standing esteem for the prematurely deceased poet, the ties of friendship that had always bound them, and above all his own honor. As for the stationery used for the certificates, he claimed that it was hardly surprising that it resembled his, since thousands of others bought the very same paper at the English Store in Petersburg.

Sobolevsky wrote to Semyon Mikhailovich Vorontsov (in the letter we quoted from earlier): "I have too much respect for Gagarin to harbor the slightest suspicion in his regard; nevertheless, last year I questioned him closely about the matter; he replied without so much as a thought of defending himself, certain as he was of his own innocence, but while exonerating Dolgorukov, he told me much that seemed to me to demonstrate the latter's guilt."* In 1886, four years after Gagarin's death, Nikolai Leskov took up his defense in the pages of *The Historical Messenger*, calling for "extreme caution in speculating about him." Justice and mercy, he wrote, demanded as much. No one, however, spoke up for Pyotr Vladimirovich Dolgorukov, except another Russian exile, Alexander Herzen, who while he saw nothing likable about "Peto Vladimirovich," "Prince Hippopotamus," felt duty-bound to stand shoulder-to-shoulder with such a proud opponent of the autocratic regime. Many years later, the limping devil found another admirer in Lenin, who preferred him to mendacious liberal historians and hailed the publication of his political writings in a Russia freed from the tsarist yoke.

Sollogub had this to say about the certificates: "It would suffice for experts to analyze the handwriting, and the name

---

* Sobolevsky must also have shared his impressions with his friend Danzas, who reported them as established facts.

of Pushkin's true murderer would be known, despised for all eternity by all the Russian people. That name is on the tip of my tongue." It has been the prey of "experts" aplenty in the twentieth century as well, but it lies for all eternity on the tip of Sollogub's overly discreet tongue.

In 1927 Shchegolev submitted samples of the writing of Gagarin, Dolgorukov, and Heeckeren to a handwriting expert named Salkov, who decided that the handwriting of the two surviving copies of the certificate was indubitably Prince Pyotr Dolgorukov's.

In 1966 the Pushkin biographer Yashin, supported by an expert named Tomilin, detected the hand of Prince Ivan Gagarin in the flourish at the end of the certificate and of Vasily Zavyazkin, a servant of Gagarin's father (who had been living in Moscow at the time), in the indication "To Alexander Sergeevich Pushkin." Another expert, Lyubarsky, challenged Tomilin's findings, demonstrating that they were unfounded.

In 1974 the expert Tsipenyuk argued that Salkov's methods and conclusions were devoid of scientific foundation; Dolgorukov's guilt therefore could not be incontrovertibly proved.

CAUSES AND EFFECTS

Why does an entire nation argue endlessly about the identity of the presumed perpetrators of what was after all a crime no more serious than libel? Simply because the offense, however minor in strictly legal terms, triggered a deadly sequence of events. The nation in question, apparently trying to reestablish proper proportions in face of a dismaying, disorienting gap between cause and effect, relentlessly strives to identify the person morally responsible for Pushkin's death: Minister Uvarov, Countess Nesselrode, Prince Gagarin, Prince Dolgorukov. Many would be incredulous and some downright offended if an impossible miracle were to reveal that the beginning of the end for Pushkin could be traced to a mere plebeian – someone like Faddey Bulgarin (journalist, flagrant plagiarist, author of third-rate novels, active collaborator with the Third Section), who tormented Pushkin with the sharp stings of *The Bee of the North*, or some even more obscure malefactor. "*C'est Nesselrode*," Tsar Alexander II is supposed to have said. But no one ever considered the possibility that he was referring to Dmitry Karlovich Nesselrode, the count's son, a man of scant quality or significance who enjoyed a respectable career purely by dint of his powerful family connections.

Of the younger Nesselrode we know that in 1836 he was, like Pushkin, a staff member of the Foreign Ministry, that he once lent the poet a copy of Dumas père's *Angèle*, that he was "unintelligent, arrogant, and rude," and that the Tsar felt "he wore his hair a little too long." All of which of course proves nothing, but neither does the fact that his mother once accompanied Natalya Nikolaevna to the Anchikov. Far be it from us to sully Dmitry Nesselrode's already lackluster memory, but it is significant that no suspicion has ever fallen on him in the endless search for the anonymous perpetrator, now more than a century old. That search has always focused on powerful enemies whose standing was commensurate with the poet's, at least in rank, title, and social position. Enemies, we said, and their name is legion.

Was Nesselrode's or Uvarov's hostility, for instance, any less intense than Countess Kossakovskaya's? Once, in a sour literary mood, she rashly provoked the poet: "You know, sir, your *Godunov* may be of some interest in Russia." To which Pushkin frostily replied: "Just as you, Madame, can pass as a beautiful woman in your mother's house." From that day on she trembled with rage and disgust at the mere mention of his name. And what about the parvenu noblemen Pushkin mocked in "My Genealogy," his pungent poetic reply to Uvarov's crack and Bulgarin's article?

> *... My grandfather wasn't a pancake seller,*
> *didn't polish the Tsar's boots,*
> *or sing with the toadies of the court,*
> *he didn't jump up among princes in a single leap*
> *from Ukraine, nor was he a deserter*
> *from the powdered troops of the Austrian kingdom;*
> *so what sort of aristocrat would I be?*
> *I am a plain bourgeois, thank God ...*

The Menshikovs, Kutaysovs, Razumovskys, Bezborodkos, Kleinmikhels were quite recognizable in those lines, handwritten copies of which were still circulating in 1836, stirring resentment and thirst for revenge. There were many people who didn't like Pushkin, who had, or thought they had, good reason to do him harm. But the leading suspects, Gagarin and Dolgorukov, were not among them. If one (or both) of them really wrote and sent the certificates, it was clearly just a prank – mean-spirited and deadly, but nevertheless a prank. Those who refuse to believe this grasp at far-fetched hidden motives, claiming, for instance, that Dolgorukov was part of the circle of "shamelessly dissolute young men" around Heeckeren who shared the "Asiatic vice" (as an erotic preference by men for men was then called). There is a similar reluctance at least to take note of, if not necessarily credit, what Alexander Vasilievich Trubetskoy said in his muddled *Account*: "In those days a number of idle young men – including Urusov, Opochinin, Stroganov, *mon cousin* – started sending anonymous letters to cuckolded husbands." Well, why not? Because the idea that a mere joke caused a great man's death affords no satisfaction or consolation and therefore fails to convince. And evil as an end in itself – including the evil of a wretched prank – disorients and dismays.

Moreover, if it's enemies we're looking for, what about the enemies of Georges d'Anthès? Granted, they were few in number, for the *chevalier garde* was good at getting people to like him. But some ladies must have harbored grudges: the

"Wife" he jilted in the late autumn of 1835,* for example, or other wives whose hearts he'd broken. A woman would have had both motive – jealousy – and purpose: to get d'Anthès and his new flame in trouble. They're still there.

THE JESUIT HYDRA

Many twentieth-century Russians learned in school and later read in books and magazines that Pushkin, "friend" of Decembrists, was the victim of a covert plot of the regime, a nefarious alliance uniting the Tsar, the secret police, and a clique of aristocrats, a conspiracy in which d'Anthès was either a dupe or a willing tool. The Soviets, not generally known for their imagination, toyed at length with the notion of conspiracy.

In 1836 I. S. Gagarin returns to St. Petersburg. . . . He becomes an intimate at Countess M. D. Nesselrode's salon. Everyone in this carefully disguised underground Jesuit den – the woman, her husband, the regular visitors – was an implacable enemy of Russia and her national genius. . . . Pushkin's moral character struck fear among the Tsar and his circle, disgusted by his democratic spirit. . . .

---

* It has not been possible to establish this woman's identity. The only available clue was d'Anthès's brief remark in a September 1, 1835, letter to Heeckeren: "I have my poor Wife, who is in the greatest despair; the poor woman just lost one child a few days ago and is now threatened by the loss of the other." I could find no genealogical record of the death of a child in St. Petersburg in the second half of August 1836. We might therefore assume that the "Wife" was not a member of the aristocracy, except that genealogical records often fail to specify the date of a child or adolescent's death, instead simply noting: "died a minor." I also consulted the four-volume *Peterburgsky Nekropol* (St. Petersburg, 1912–13), but in vain. The Historical Archive of St. Petersburg, where all nineteenth-century city church registries are kept, would surely contain some record of the unfortunate child's burial, but it has been closed for several years for restoration. Which is too bad, since there may be something to the hypothesis that the author of the anonymous letters was a woman jealous of d'Anthès, perhaps even the woman Pushkin mentioned to Sollogub on the morning of November 4.

But what Nicholas I feared most was Pushkin's Decembrism. Yes, in the fiber of his being, in all his character and all his art, Pushkin reminded the Tsar of the hated Decembrists. . . . And so Pushkin was doomed. The Jesuits' diabolical international game, a game aimed at the political conquest of Russia on behalf of Catholicism, hastened the ruin of the great Russian citizen. . . . What the police headed by Nicholas I were unable or unwilling to do openly was carried out by the Third Section subsidiary: the police-Jesuit salon headed by Countess Nesselrode and her close aide Gagarin. . . . The whole Jesuit salon of Countess Nesselrode, temporarily transferred to Heeckeren's home, anxiously awaited the result of the duel between Pushkin and d'Anthès . . . the arrival of the foreigner who, in accordance with the prearranged plan, was to kill the national pride of Russia. . . . D'Anthès himself is very close to the "servants of God" . . . not a dashing drinking companion, dancer, and womanizer, but a Jesuit, and not just any Jesuit, but a leader whose experience and authority entitle him to give advice and instructions to others. . . . "Judge not, lest ye be judged." Meaning that the Jesuits and their agents deserve immunity from the judgment of history, the judgment of progress? No. . . . Gagarin's black Jesuit cloak is also stained with Pushkin's blood, with "the poet's righteous blood." [1973]

Quite apart from the fact that d'Anthès, with his French nonchalance and utter lack of culture, cuts a ludicrous figure in the dark robes of a Jesuit "capo," the Soviet conspiracy theory raises another troublesome question as well: if Pushkin was a sworn enemy of Tsarism and a blot on the landscape in the eyes of the Tsar from whom the diabolical Jesuits were striving to snatch political and spiritual power over heretical Russia, then why would the Jesuits have been so tenacious in seeking his death? If anything, they ought to have considered him an ally, an accomplice, a secret agent.

9

Twelve Sleepless Nights

On November 3, 1836, there was an inspection of the Horse Guards in preparation for a review the next day in the presence of General Knorring. Lieutenant Georges d'Anthès was given five punitive tours of guard duty because of "the ignorance of the men in his platoon and the carelessness of his dress." Beginning on the afternoon of November 4, then, he had to spend most of his time in the barracks, physically removed from the events that were to lend his fate such a sudden and unexpected twist.

On the evening of November 4, the Hussar Ivan Goncharov, Natalya Nikolaevna's younger brother, delivered Pushkin's letter of challenge to the Dutch Embassy. D'Anthès was on guard duty, so it was Heeckeren, alarmed at the mere mention of Pushkin's name, who opened the letter. He froze with fear when he read it, but after recovering his wits decided that the first thing he had to do was to observe the formalities stipulated by the code of honor. On the morning of November 5 he went to Pushkin's home to accept the challenge in the name of his son, absent owing to military duties. In view of that absence and those duties, he asked that the twenty-four-hour waiting period prescribed by ritual be doubled. This brief delay, he said, would also give the challenger time to reflect on his act with greater calm. The postponement was granted.

*

On the morning of November 6, Pushkin received a short letter from Jacob van Heeckeren requesting another deferment of the duel and informing him that he would be coming to see him later that day. In the meantime, Zhukovsky received an unexpected visit from Ivan Goncharov in Tsarskoe Selo, where he was tending to his duties as tutor to the Tsar's heir. Young Goncharov told Zhukovsky of the challenge and begged him in the name of his sisters and his aunt to hurry to Petersburg to try to dissuade Pushkin from his sanguinary plans. When Zhukovsky arrived at his friend's, he chided him kindheartedly, reminding him of his duties as father and husband: was he aware of the possible consequences of this ill-considered act? Even if he was lucky in the duel, the law's punishment would await him. There would be a new, long period of disgrace. What would his family live on? Were those contemptible anonymous letters really worth his life, his children's future, and his wife's honor? For it wasn't hard to imagine what nasty insinuations the wagging tongues of Petersburg would make about Natalya Nikolaevna. Who would placate the Tsar's legitimate indignation this time? And with what arguments?

Pushkin was silent, grim. Zhukovsky continued to plead his mournful cause until Baron Heeckeren was announced, at which point he thought it more useful and discreet to withdraw. Alone with the poet, the ambassador explained that he had not yet told his Georges of the challenge and would do so only at the last moment; he still hoped Pushkin would change his mind, because – and to this he swore – at no time had his son ever committed any affront to his honor. He spoke of his enormous affection for the youth, who was now all he had in his lonely life; he said a duel would mean the utter ruin of the entire edifice of his hopes, for even if the *chevalier garde* came out alive, his career would be dead. "Touched by the father's distress and tears," Pushkin agreed to a two-week delay, giving his word that he would take no further initiative until then and that if he encountered d'Anthès, he would act as though nothing had happened. Zhukovsky learned of the postponement when he returned to No. 12 on the Moyka. Clearly relieved, he went to see Count Vielgorsky and then Prince Vyazemsky. Having lived in Petersburg longer than he had, they would surely be able to help him get his bearings in this affair, much of which still seemed murky and incomprehensible.

On the afternoon of November 6, the Dutch ambassador had a brief chat with d'Anthès in the barracks on Shpalernaya Street. He told him of the challenge and of his two meetings with Pushkin, urging d'Anthès to wait patiently to see how the steps he'd already taken worked out. Heeckeren said he could not stand idly by and watch the collapse of everything he'd built at the cost of so many sacrifices; his own diplomatic career would be seriously damaged if his adoptive son fought a duel, whatever its outcome. Promising to keep d'Anthès informed of developments, he headed for the Winter Palace to see Ekaterina Ivanovna Zagryazhskaya, the Goncharov sisters' aunt.

When Zhukovsky got home on the evening of November 6, he found a letter from Zagryazhskaya asking him to stop by the next morning to discuss the unfortunate events. Zhukovsky had trouble sleeping that night. He kept thinking about the many times he'd had to intervene to bring the Pushkin boy to his senses (he was sixteen years older and still thought of Pushkin as a boy). His intense, impulsive character seemed to lure him irresistibly to the road to ruin. Two years earlier, when Pushkin had had the bright idea of retiring, it was Zhukovsky who gave him the scolding he deserved: "Stupidity! Lamentable, selfish, unspeakable stupidity!" "I don't understand what's come over you. It's as if you've turned into an idiot. You ought to do a stint in an insane asylum or get yourself flogged with sticks to get your blood moving again." Which was more or less how he felt about this new whim: disheartened and dismayed like an anxious loving father. So it was that the complex, uncontrollable events we are about to witness would see two fathers doing their utmost to save their beloved adoptive sons from disaster. These were loves of different natures but of equal intensity. Jacob van Heeckeren was clearly the more cunning of the two fathers, ready to do anything.

D'Anthès to Heeckeren [evening of November 6]: My dearest friend, I thank you for the two notes you sent me. They calmed me a little, which I needed, and I write these few words to tell you once again that I place myself completely in your hands whatever you decide, convinced in advance that you will act better than me in this whole business. My God, I don't wish this on the wife, and I'm glad to know she's all right, but this is serious heedlessness or madness that I don't understand, nor what its purpose is. Write me a note tomorrow to let me know if there's anything new overnight. You didn't say whether you saw the sister at the aunt's, or how you know she owned up to the letters. Good night, I kiss you from my heart. . . .

In all this Catherine is a fine person behaving admirably.

Georges d'Anthès's tortuous style (now further garbled by worry and haste) drags us deeper into a swamp of confusion. Who was guilty of "serious heedlessness or madness"? The "wife," Natalya Nikolaevna? If so, what kind of madness? Who "owned up to the letters"? The "sister" d'Anthès mentioned? Which one, Catherine or Alexandrine? What letters? The anonymous ones, by any chance?

Perhaps we ought to rein in imagination and stick to clearer testimony. From Vyazemsky we know that the arrival of the certificates "led to demands for explanations in the Pushkin household. . . . The wife, guilty of frivolity, thoughtlessness, and compliance in tolerating d'Anthès's persistence, made a clean breast of it, telling her husband everything about her own mistakes and the young man's behavior toward her." I believe that on that stormy occasion Natalie told her husband that she'd received letters from the *chevalier garde*. The husband demanded to read them, and Natalie showed them to him. That was the "serious heedlessness or madness." A few days later Pushkin confronted d'Anthès with "the idiocies he had gone to the trouble of writing" to his wife, idiocies which, at his trial some months later, d'Anthès would dismiss as "short notes accompanying books and theater tickets."

Right. Mournful as the impending events may be, it is hard to read those words with a straight face: *d'Anthès* sending *books* to *Pushkin's* wife! The study in the apartment at No. 12 on the Moyka was home to one of Russia's richest private libraries, with books on every subject from A (Agoub, J.; Alexeev, P.; Alfieri, V.; Alhoy, M.; Alipanov, E. I.; Ampère, J. J.; Anacreon; Ancelot; Ancillon; Andrei Ioannov; Androsov, V.; Annenkov, N. E.; Antoine, A.; Antommarchi, F.; Apollodorus; Ariosto; Aristophanes; Arnaud; etc.) to Z (Zschokke, J., *Histoire de la Suisse*). The ones d'Anthès sent Natalie were probably silly romance novels that Pushkin would never have had on his shelves.

On the morning of November 7, Zhukovsky headed for the Dutch Embassy after talking to Ekaterina Ivanovna Zagryazhskaya. Heeckeren greeted him as heaven-sent, telling Zhukovsky of his anxiety and his desire to prevent the duel at any cost. There was, he maintained, no justification whatever for it, apart from the poet's extreme touchiness, well known to all. The baron admitted that his son had always paid homage to Natalya Nikolaevna's beauty, but who in Petersburg hadn't? True, his son's head had been turned by Pushkin's enchanting wife, but in all good conscience was this a crime? Luckily, time soon heals the wounds in young men's hearts, and the lad's initial infatuation had given way to a deeper and more mature feeling for Mrs. Pushkin's sister. "Alexandrine?" the utterly bewildered Zhukovsky asked, and the ambassador straightened him out. No, his son was in love with Catherine Goncharova and had already told her of his intention to marry her, even though he, Heeckeren, opposed the idea quite firmly. Of course he had the highest opinion of Mademoiselle Catherine, a wholesome girl from an excellent family and maid of honor to the Empress, but he had hoped for a more suitable match for his Georges. His modest ambassador's stipend could not guarantee the boy the comfortable future every father wishes for his son, and it was no secret that the Goncharovs' fortunes were not exactly prospering; granted, the aunt's munificence allowed the nieces to glow elegantly in Petersburg's salons, but not even Mademoiselle Zagryazhskaya, highly esteemed as she was, could assure Catherine a suitable dowry. That was why he had long opposed the marriage, but now that his son's very life was at stake, he would no longer stand in his way. Pushkin, he added, was to be told nothing of what this father racked by pain now felt it was his right – nay, his duty – to reveal. Zhukovsky promised to keep everything in the strictest confidence, whereupon the ambassador decided to treat him to an even more sensitive revelation which in other circumstances he would never have shared with anyone: it was Heeckeren blood that ran in Georges's veins – but no, out of respect for the late Baroness d'Anthès he could say no more. Barely able to believe his ears, Zhukovsky swore he would never say a word to anyone about the baron's secret.

Zhukovsky felt that what he'd just been told about Catherine Goncharova and Georges d'Anthès changed the situation unexpectedly, offering a glimmer of hope for peace. He went straight to Pushkin – just as Heeckeren had secretly wished he would – to report the stunning news he had sworn to keep to himself. But far from softening Pushkin's resolve, Zhukovsky's report drove him to a fury. Blinded by rage, he erupted in a stream of insults: the ambassador was a brazen liar, a vile pimp, a sordid wretch who would stoop to anything, no matter how base; as for d'Anthès, the mere threat of bullets was enough to make him hastily abandon his great, sublime passion and scurry to hide behind his papa's tailcoat. Zhu-

kovsky missed much of what Pushkin was saying – or shouting
– but long experience had taught him that when the hot
African blood rose to Pushkin's head, your best bet was to
leave him alone until he got it out of his system. Zhukovsky
left. Meanwhile, Pushkin realized that he was now hemmed
in by the good intentions of family and friends who, having
fallen for Heeckeren's fine words and slick maneuvers, would
stop him from fighting the duel. He had to find a way to flush
d'Anthès out and challenge him again – not in writing this
time. Whom could he trust? He decided to turn to Klementy
Rosset, who knew d'Anthès well and would be able to track
him down, in the barracks or wherever else the coward was
hiding.

D'Anthès was at the Dutch Embassy, still dazed, at a loss
to find his way in this whirlwind of events that had occurred
in his absence and unbeknownst to him. Klementy Rosset
went to see him on the afternoon of November 7. D'Anthès
announced that he would be at the poet's disposal as soon as
the two-week postponement was over. He spoke at length
with his adoptive father, explaining that although he had complete faith in his wisdom and experience and would take his
advice as always, things had now gone too far: honor
demanded that he visit Pushkin to accept the challenge in
person and find out the reasons for it, as was his inalienable
right. In fact, he would do so that very evening. Heeckeren
had a hard time stopping him. He forbade him to let himself
be carried away by the recklessness that had already caused
such serious trouble, but he also tried to appease him by
admitting that he understood how d'Anthès felt and by assuring him that he would convey his request for a meeting with
Pushkin, either through Mademoiselle Zagryazhskaya, with
whom he was to meet the next day, or through Zhukovsky.

In recounting this story, I am far from being an omniscient
narrator, and closer to being a patient conservator poring over
a mosaic with too many missing tiles, sifting through the few

remaining fragments – a handful of letters, brief passages in memoirs, the laconic and often enigmatic notes jotted down by Zhukovsky shortly after the event – in an effort to reconstruct the shape and shading of a picture long faded by time. One is guided by logic and an intimate familiarity with the protagonists hard-earned by long research. Yet doubt often assails one, as it must anyone laboring in good faith. Is it really true that d'Anthès learned of the challenge only on the afternoon of November 6? I believe Zhukovsky but cannot rule out the possibility that he was naïvely taken in by Heeckeren. Did Pushkin really send d'Anthès a second challenge? Conflicting testimony can be reconciled only by assuming that he did. According to the Vyazemskys, Ivan Goncharov was the bearer of the challenge; according to Danzas, it was Klementy Rosset. The Vyazemskys could be mistaken, of course, and Danzas may have conflated events that occurred later, but other circumstances lead one to suppose that there was indeed a second note. On November 9, 1836, Zhukovsky referred to a "first challenge" from Pushkin (implying that there was a second), which never "got into the hands" of d'Anthès (implying that it was written); Sollogub, for his part, recalls having seen d'Anthès's second holding Pushkin's letter of challenge, but at the trial d'Anthès stated that he'd received a *"cartel verbale"* (oral challenge), and Pushkin himself wrote to Benckendorff: *"Je le fis dire à Monsieur d'Anthès"* ("I had Mr. d'Anthès told"). Countless other details are obscure, fail to coincide, or are flatly contradictory. A diabolical, brain-vexing puzzle.

On the morning of November 8, Baron Heeckeren repeated to Miss Zagryazhskaya what he'd already told Zhukovsky: he would no longer stand in the way of his son's love for Catherine Goncharova or oppose their marriage, but the matter of the challenge had to be honorably settled first. To this end a frank, sincere meeting between the contending parties seemed opportune, even indispensable. But the challenger, he repeated (once again hoping for exactly the opposite), must know nothing of his son's matrimonial intentions. Meanwhile, Zhukovsky was talking to Pushkin. Finding him somewhat calmer, he took the opportunity to try to soothe him, to make him see reason. He reminded him of his own flirtations, of Natalya Nikolaevna's jealousy and the tears she had shed on account of the women he'd courted quite crudely (assuming it went no further than courting), of the ugly rumors about his relationship with his sister-in-law Alexandrine. Since Pushkin had not exactly been a shining example to his young, socially inexperienced wife, he ought to forgive her if she'd been unable to halt Georges d'Anthès's advances in the proper way. He was in no position to judge anyone. The anonymous letters, Zhukovsky said, were the filthy, vulgar face of Nemesis. Pushkin wept.

That evening Pushkin took the three certificates in his possession to Mikhail Yakovlev, a former lyceum classmate who now headed the Typographical Office of the Imperial Chancery's Second Section. Yakovlev examined them with his expert's eye. They were written on excellent paper, undoubtedly foreign, since none of that quality was made in Russia. Customs exacted a high duty on such stationery, which meant, he said, thinking out loud, that it was probably from an embassy. That night Pushkin was racked by insomnia, as he, too, grappled with the diabolical puzzle whose pieces finally seemed to be falling into place, revealing a monstrous design.

On November 9 the indefatigable Zhukovsky resumed his patient peacemaker's work, meeting again with Baron Heeckeren, who now treated him to new "revelations": it seemed that the amorous link between his son and Catherine Goncharova had unfortunately overstepped the bounds of propriety. Dismayed to hear it, Zhukovsky felt that they could no longer limit themselves to informal talks. Just then d'Anthès arrived from an early-afternoon release from military duty. He and his adoptive father had a heated discussion, a real set-to, in

Zhukovsky's presence. After yet another sleepless night spent weighing the facts and pondering his future, d'Anthès had now grasped the ridicule he was risking: sooner or later news of the challenge would leak out, Petersburg would sneer at him, the regiment would accuse him of cowardice, perhaps even discharge him. At this point he was dying to fight, he hated Pushkin, and he was sure he would kill him. He didn't care if he was imprisoned, demoted, or transferred to the Caucasus. He could no longer bear to stand by while others toyed with his fate and good name, however honorable their intentions. Heeckeren, in turn raising his voice, asked d'Anthès whether it had perhaps slipped his mind that he owed that very fate and good name to him and him alone. He categorically forbade him to take any initiative; he was to leave everything to Heeckeren. Pressing on with his conciliation proposals (not only between Pushkin and d'Anthès, but now also between d'Anthès and his adoptive father), Zhukovsky asked the baron for a letter formally granting him the authority to negotiate.

Heeckeren to Zhukovsky, Petersburg, November 9, 1836: "As you know, sir, until now everything has been handled through third parties. My son received a challenge, his first duty was to accept it, but he is at least owed an explanation, in person, of the reason for the challenge. An interview between the two parties therefore seems to me opportune, obligatory, in the presence of a person like yourself, sir . . . who can assess the true basis of the sensibilities that have provoked this turn of events."

Did the ambassador really admit to the illicit affair between Georges d'Anthès and Catherine Goncharova? It is hard to imagine what other "revelations" he might have offered Zhukovsky that would have been serious enough to bring about mediation forthwith. And Ekaterina Ivanovna Zagryazhskaya's urgent and repeated meddling after November 4 definitely suggests that Catherine's honor had been compromised: elderly Russian aunts, even those of solidly eighteenth-century mettle, never interfered in male issues like duels, but they moved heaven and earth to keep tainted young girls' skeletons in the closet long enough to whisk them to the altar. We must suppose that Catherine, too, shared secrets – with her sisters, with her aunt – in the hectic days following the challenge. Moreover, Zhukovsky (naïve but neither stupid nor blind) was soon to receive "material evidence" from Heeckeren that the subject of marriage had been broached prior to November 4. Since we know for a fact that d'Anthès was not in love with Natalie's sister, the marriage in question must have been meant to make amends: dank but magical Island nights, a woman hopelessly in love, the man aroused by less accessible charms, an eclipse of reason, and *voilà* – the shame of seduction, promises from the seducer, the flat refusal of a stern father. It is not hard to imagine that the *chevalier garde* might have seriously considered such a marriage: he would do the honorable thing, and incidentally be able to frequent Pushkin's home and its beautiful mistress with utter freedom. We can also understand why Heeckeren, who had good reason to detest all the Goncharov females, might have found that marriage repugnant. Now, however, he grasped it like a lifeline.

Catherine Goncharova to her brother Dmitry, Petersburg, November 9, 1836: I am happy to know, dear friend, that you are still content with your lot, my wish is that it may always be so; knowing that you, at least, are happy is a true consolation to me in the tribulations with which Heaven has seen fit to beset me. As for myself, I have long since given up on happiness, and am convinced that she and I are never to meet in this hapless world. The sole favor I ask of Heaven is that a life as useless as mine might soon be ended. Happiness for all my family and death for me – that is what I need, for that I pray to the Almighty without respite.

Vyazemsky tells us that while the post-challenge negotiations were under way, "father and son had the audacity and dishonor to have someone secretly ask Mrs. Pushkin for a letter to d'Anthès entreating him not to duel with her husband. Obviously she indignantly rejected this vile proposal." Why would d'Anthès have asked for such a letter to himself? What could he have done with it? It seems more likely that Heeckeren, unbeknownst to his "son," might have tried to get such a document from Natalya Nikolaevna. We know that he was ready to do anything to prevent the duel, and as he knew very well by now, Natalie alone was capable of touching his Georges's heart and mind. Around that time he also forced d'Anthès to write to Pushkin's wife "stating that he renounced any and all claims upon her" – an implicit attestation of faithfulness with which, Heeckeren said, she could prove to her husband that she had never violated her conjugal vows.

On the afternoon of November 9, Zhukovsky went to Pushkin's again to show him the ambassador's letter, along with a reply he had drafted. The poet stated flatly that he would meet d'Anthès only on the field of honor. He had nothing else to say. Zhukovsky left the house dejected and discouraged. He tried to gain time by lying to Heeckeren, writing him that his friend wasn't home and therefore he could not reply to him yet. Then he wrote to Pushkin again, with desperate tenacity: "It is still possible to call a halt to all this. You decide what I should say in my reply. Your response will decide the matter once and for all. But for the love of God, come to your senses. Grant me the joy of saving you from an insane crime and your wife from complete dishonor. . . . I am now at Vielgorsky's and will be staying for lunch."

Pushkin hurried to Vielgorsky's to vent his rage on the obstinate mediator. From now on, he said, Zhukovsky was not to interfere in his private life. Didn't he realize that Heeckeren and that bastard of his – or nephew, or whatever he was – were leading him around by the nose? What would he come up with next? Would he tip off the police, the Tsar? How dare he mention Natalya Nikolaevna's honor! Whose side was he on? Zhukovsky had neither the heart nor the time to reply, for he'd been invited to the imperial table for dinner. Late that night, when he got home, he wrote once more to his stubborn, feckless friend:

I don't want you to get the wrong idea about d'Anthès's part in this business. Here is the story. You already know what happened to your first challenge, how it never reached the son's hands but went instead to the father, the son learning of it only after the twenty-four hours were up – in other words, after your second meeting with the father. . . . Once he found out how things stood, the son wanted to meet you at all costs. But the father, dreading the very idea of such an encounter, turned to me. Not wishing to witness or be part of a tragedy, I offered to mediate; that is, I tried to do so by writing a reply to the father, the draft of which I showed you but did not and will not send. That is all. This morning I will tell the elder Heeckeren that I cannot perform any mediation. . . . I am writing all this to you because I considered it my sacred duty to bear witness to you that d'Anthès had no say at all in what his father did, that he is as prepared to duel with you as you are with him, and that he, too, fears that the secret might somehow come out. And to give the father his due as well, he is desolate, but here is what he told me: *"Je suis condamné à la guillotine, je fais un recours à la grace, si je ne réussis pas, il faudra monter: et je monterai, car j'aime l'honneur de mon fils autant que sa vie."** With this testimony the role I have played so badly and with such lack of success now comes to an end.

On the morning of November 10, Zhukovsky saw d'Anthès and informed him that the meeting he wanted with the poet would not take place. He then wrote to the ambassador to say that a final talk with Pushkin had convinced him that

* "I am sentenced to the guillotine, I ask for mercy; if I am denied, I will have to mount it, and I will, for I cherish my son's honor as much as I do his life."

there was no further possibility of conciliation. With great regret he was therefore bound to decline the task ascribed to him. Heeckeren begged him to intervene again despite everything: he alone could avert the tragedy. He now gave him permission to reveal what he had so far asked him to keep secret, if he thought it would be helpful in negotiating. Zhukovsky, no longer an official mediator, went to see Pushkin again and encountered yet another wall of rage and dismal obstinacy. To him it seemed truly insane.

Natalie's aunt did not give up when she learned from Zhukovsky that negotiations were stalled. Instead, she summoned him urgently on the morning of November 11. Zagryazhskaya reported that Pushkin had asked her niece Alexandrine to tell him the truth about the relationship between Catherine and d'Anthès, and it was not hard to imagine what kind of mood he was in now: doubly furious, doubly determined to go ahead with the duel. But Pushkin had also said something interesting to Alexandrine: everyone knew that d'Anthès suffered from lung problems; he should therefore have no trouble at all getting permission to take the waters abroad, slipping out of Russia never to return. That fool Catherine would spend the rest of her life waiting for him, a disgraced old maid. Well, Zagryazhskaya thought, if that's what Pushkin was afraid of, he could be reassured by a solemn proposal of marriage from d'Anthès and an equally solemn pledge that the wedding would take place as soon as possible.

Informed of this suggestion by Zhukovsky, Heeckeren declared his willingness to offer all possible guarantees, but demanded, in his son's name, that the challenge be formally withdrawn. If Pushkin still refused to meet with him or Georges, he said, it would suffice for him to put in writing the reasons both for the challenge and for his decision to desist. The ambassador's request was quickly conveyed to Pushkin.

*

Sometime around November 12, Sollogub asked Pushkin whether he had ever managed to identify the author of the certificates. Pushkin said he wasn't sure yet, but he did have a suspect. "If you need a second or a third," Sollogub said, "I am at your disposal." Pushkin replied seriously to the play on words: "There will be no duel, but I may ask you to witness an explanation at which I would like a man of the world to be present, for the appropriate disclosure whenever it should be necessary." He and Sollogub then went to the arms dealer Kurakin, where he was shown two pistols and he inquired about the price. Sollogub thought it strange behavior for someone who'd just said, "There will be no duel."

On the evening of November 12, the ambassador was summoned by Zagryazhskaya, who informed him that Zhukovsky's yeoman powers of persuasion and the entreaties of family members had finally worked a miracle: Pushkin was prepared to discuss peace terms with Natalie's aunt. That night they all enjoyed a long and tranquil sleep, unaware of the thoughts and plans now churning in the poet's mind, unaware that his sudden malleability was not the product of pity for Catherine alone.

Charles X, the King of France who had abdicated in August 1830, died in exile on November 12. Tsar Nicholas I declared the court in mourning and, as the Bavarian ambassador wrote some days later, insisted that it be observed "more scrupulously and strictly than is usual here. I was told that when the Empress noticed a maid of honor with white feathers in her hair, she plucked them out with her own hands."

On November 13 Pushkin listened in silence to Ekaterina Ivanovna Zagryazhskaya. She and Baron Heeckeren had now agreed that Georges d'Anthès would marry Catherine; Dmitry Goncharov would arrive in a few days to ratify the family's agreement by his presence. Did Pushkin want a family member's blood on his hands? By this marriage, d'Anthès would make amends for all his wrongs – *all*, Zagryazhskaya repeated gravely, including any that may have offended a husband's justifiable and comprehensible sensitivities. Pushkin had only to give her or Zhukovsky a letter officially renouncing the duel and above all promising that he would tell no one of how this wedding had come about, since any indiscretion might bring it to grief. Pushkin promised. Last, she asked him to come back the next day to meet with Baron Heeckeren in her presence. Pushkin agreed.

That afternoon Pushkin gave Zhukovsky a draft of his withdrawal of the challenge to be submitted for review by the interested parties. A copy of it remains among Zhukovsky's papers: "Baron Heeckeren did me the honor of accepting a challenge to a duel on behalf of his son, Baron G. d'Anthès. Having learned by chance from public rumors that Mr. G. d'Anthès had decided to request the hand of my sister-in-law Miss C. Goncharova in marriage, I ask Baron Heeckeren please to consider my challenge as never having been issued. For behaving toward my wife in a manner intolerable to me (if Mr. d'Anthès requires the reason for the challenge)."

Zhukovsky was so relieved to receive this scribbled draft of the letter he so yearned for that he took no notice of the latest volley of insult hurled at d'Anthès and Heeckeren. He took the piece of paper to the Dutch Embassy and then, exhausted, went on to the Karamzins' for some nice hot tea and a little relaxation in the company of personal friends. But what he heard from the mistress of the house and her stepdaughter plunged him into dismay anew, giving him yet another short night of fitful sleep.

Zhukovsky to Pushkin [night of November 13–14]: You are treating me in an extremely reckless, ungenerous, and downright unfair manner. Why did you tell Catherine Andreevna and Sofya Nikolaevna everything? What do you want? To make what was to end in the best way for you impossible? After long pondering over what you told me yesterday, I find your hypothesis utterly improbable. And I have reason to be sure that d'Anthès had nothing at all to do with what was done to avert the conflict. . . . I had further evidence of this *yesterday*. When I received from the father material evidence that the matter now in question had been considered long before your challenge, I advised him to act as he has, basing myself on the fact that if *the secret is kept,* no dishonor will befall the son. . . . You owe it to yourself to keep the secret as well, for there is much in this matter of which you ought to say: I am at fault.

On November 14 Pushkin and the Dutch ambassador met at Miss Zagryazhskaya's home to seal the peace. Pushkin promised to keep quiet, Heeckeren to ask for Catherine's hand on his son's behalf as soon as d'Anthès officially received the poet's withdrawal of the challenge. That letter, he added, would have to be slightly different from the draft Zhukovsky had shown him; d'Anthès had been so kind as to jot down some notes in this regard. Heeckeren then read from a piece of paper: "I cannot and must not agree to the sentence about Miss G. appearing in the letter; here are my reasons, and I think Mr. Pushkin will understand them. From the way the issue is posed, it could be interpreted: 'marry or fight.' Since honor prevents me from accepting any such condition, the phrase would leave me with the sad duty of accepting the latter proposal. . . . It therefore must be clearly stated that I ask for Miss Catherine's hand neither to make amends nor as an accommodation, but because she pleases me, because I desire it, and the matter has been decided by my will alone!"

Instead, d'Anthès wanted Pushkin to state the reasons for the withdrawal this way: ". . . having become convinced by chance, from public rumors, that the motives inspiring Mr. G. d'A.'s behavior were not of such a nature as to be prejudicial to my honor, the sole reason for which I felt duty-bound to challenge him . . ."

The Anichkov season opened on November 15 with a sumptuous ball at which a number of illustrious visitors to Petersburg were present: Lord and Lady Londonderry, Count Pallfy of Presburg, Count Mitrowsky, aide-de-camp of Archduke Ferdinand of Austria. As always, Natalya Nikolaevna was invited, but this time without her husband. In other circumstances Pushkin would have been all too happy not to have to appear in public in his kamerjunker tails; this time, however, he imagined that everyone knew of his shame and was plotting against him. He was upset, angry, exasperated. Natalie wrote to Zhukovsky for advice. His brief reply said that she must *absolutely* go to the ball. This was no time to open herself to any more gossip; as for Pushkin, some months ago he had himself told the Empress that he was shunning social gatherings while in mourning for his mother. Natalie went to the Anichkov alone. She was, as ever, a marvel. Alexandra Fyodorovna compared her to "an enchanting fairy."

Zhukovsky to Pushkin [night of November 15–16]: Last night I went to Vyazemsky's after the ball. Here is, *à peu près*, what you said to the princess the other day: *"Je connais l'homme des lettres anonymes et dans huit jours vous entendrez parler d'une vengeance unique en son genre: elle sera pleine, complète: elle jettera l'homme dans la boue."* * . . . It's a good thing you were the one who said it and that my good fairy let me know in time. It goes without saying that I told the princess nothing of what has happened. And now I say nothing to you either: do what you want. But I withdraw from this game of yours, which I don't like one bit. What if it occurs to Heeckeren to ask my advice? Will I not have to tell him to watch his step?

Here's a fable for you: Once upon a time there was a shepherd who was also a crack shot. The shepherd had some very fine sheep. One day a gray wolf began hanging around his flock. I think I'll gobble up that shepherd's favorite ewe, the gray wolf said to himself,

---

* "I know who wrote the anonymous letters, and in eight days you will hear tell of vengeance unique of its kind; it will be full, complete; it will cast that man into the mud."

but as he thought it over, he also licked his chops at the look of those other sheep. Then the glutton found out that the crack shot was keeping an eye on him, planning to shoot him. The gray wolf wasn't too happy about that, so he made various proposals to the shepherd, which the shepherd accepted, while wondering deep down, How can I stamp out that long-tailed ladies' man and make some nice little furs and boots for my kids out of his hide? So the shepherd went to his old friend Vasily. Vasily, pal of mine, he said, do me a favor and turn yourself into a pig for a minute and let your snorts drive that gray wolf out of the forest and into open ground. I'll get the neighbors together and we'll snare him. Listen here, brother, said Vasily, you want to catch the wolf, go right ahead, but why should I be a pig? I was godfather in your home. Good people will say that your son was baptized by a pig. That's not very nice. Besides, it won't look good for me. Maybe I'll be on my way to Mass, or sitting down to eat with people, or writing poems about pretty girls, and good people will say, A pig went to Mass, a pig is sitting at our table, a pig's writing poetry. Not good. Hearing this reply, the shepherd thought it over, but what he decided I don't know.

The unaffected, straightforward Zhukovsky probably never came closer to the truth than he did in this little fable. The deceptive shepherd had set a first-class trap indeed: by telling a few close friends — who he knew very well would not keep the secret for long — that d'Anthès was getting engaged in order to avoid a duel, he was tearing him to pieces morally. And while thinking about the nice little furs he would make for his kids from the greedy gray wolf's pelt, he was already savoring the even more beautiful, elegant fur he would make for himself from that papa wolf's hide. He'd had that second target in his unerring sights for several days now.

Godfather Vasily was a tenderhearted man who couldn't bear a grudge. On the morning of November 16, he overcame his irritation and went to see Pushkin again, begging him to delete that damned phrase about Georges d'Anthès's marriage from his withdrawal letter. His friend was implacable; he wouldn't change a single word. At last they arrived at a compromise: Pushkin authorized Zhukovsky to state orally that he no longer wanted the duel with the Frenchman, that he considered the matter closed for good and would not breathe a word about it to a living soul. Heeckeren reluctantly accepted these inglorious peace terms. But d'Anthès didn't. Obeying the dictates of his honor and disobeying his adoptive father for the first time since all this began, he suddenly acted on his own.

D'Anthès to Pushkin [November 16, 1836, about 1 p.m.]: Baron Heeckeren tells me that Mr. Zhukovsky has authorized him to inform me that the reasons why you challenged me to a duel no longer apply and that I can therefore consider your act as not having occurred. When you challenged me without telling me why, I accepted without hesitation as honor obliged me; now that you assure me that you no longer have any reason to want an encounter, before being able to release you from your word, I wish to know why you changed your mind, myself not having charged anyone to offer you the explanations that I alone can give you personally. You will be the first to agree that, before any withdrawal, explanations must be given by both parties so that we might henceforth hold each other in proper esteem.

"Letter from d'Anthès to Pushkin," Zhukovsky wrote. "Pushkin in a rage." Rage was the poet's sole reaction, and d'Anthès waited in vain for a reply.

Late in the afternoon of November 16, Pushkin received a visit from Olivier d'Archiac, attaché at the French Embassy.*

---

* Viscount d'Archiac's real name was Olivier and not Auguste, as all Russian sources indicate; he himself signed his name "Olivier" in several documents I found in the archives of the French Ministry of Foreign Affairs. It is not impossible, however, that Auguste was his middle name and that he used it as a forename.

Since the two-week delay granted by the poet was about to expire, d'Anthès had asked d'Archiac to inform Pushkin that he "was at his disposal." Pushkin told d'Archiac that he would let him know as soon as possible who his second would be. The emissary took a timid stab at conciliation: Pushkin had only to delete the phrase about d'Anthès's wedding plans and he was sure the whole thing would be settled without useless bloodshed. Pushkin dismissed him with brusque politeness.

On the evening of November 16, the Karamzins celebrated Mrs. Karamzin's birthday. Pushkin sat next to Sollogub at the dinner table. Amid all the merry chatter, the toasts and good wishes, he turned to his neighbor and surreptitiously whispered, "Come to my place tomorrow. I want you to go see d'Archiac to make arrangements for the duel. The bloodier the better. No negotiations." Then he went on chatting with the other guests. Sollogub "was dumbfounded but didn't dare object. There was a firmness in Pushkin's tone that brooked no objections." Later the entire company moved on to the Austrian Embassy for a gala reception that the Tsar and Tsarina were to attend. Pushkin arrived later than the others. On the grand marble staircase he ran into d'Archiac, who tried to resume the discussion interrupted several hours ago. All Pushkin would say was this: "You Frenchmen are very fine. You all know Latin, but when you duel you shoot from thirty paces. We Russians do it differently: the fewer the civilities, the fiercer the duel."*

When he entered the ballroom, Pushkin noticed that all the ladies were dressed in black for the death of Charles X except Catherine, who was wearing white. This meant that the Empress must have been aware of Catherine's impending marriage; otherwise she would have immediately ordered her

---

* There are one or two indecipherable words in Sollogub's account, from which this remark has been taken. "Civilities" seems the most likely solution in the context.

maid of honor to change her gown or leave the reception, since only girls soon to be married were allowed to wear white when the court was in mourning. As if that were not enough, d'Anthès himself was there beside her, clinging to her virginal dress, flaunting gestures of devotion wholly befitting a fiancé. In other words, everyone in the social world had already taken note of everything, including Natalya Nikola-evna's diplomatic absence. A menacing tide of whispers was already on the rise. Pushkin, deathly pale, approached the couple, ordered his sister-in-law not to speak to d'Anthès, and treated the officer to "some very rude words." A few minutes later, he left the Embassy, taking both sisters-in-law home with him. Sollogub exchanged a meaningful glance with d'Archiac. Then he, too, approached d'Anthès and asked him what kind of man he was. "I am a man of honor," d'Anthès replied, "as I hope soon to demonstrate. I don't understand what Pushkin wants. I will duel with him if I must, but I seek neither quarrel nor scandal."

Vladimir Sollogub awoke to what seemed a bad omen on the morning of November 17: an overcast, pallid white sky, thick falling snow swirling in dense midair eddies. It was a real blizzard: bright flakes flying into eyes and under turned-up fur collars, making it hard to breathe or walk. Even seasoned coachmen had to strain to coax their sleighs along streets raked by the wind. But Sollogub absolutely had to go out that day, and God alone knew when he might return. He'd decided to see Georges d'Anthès first. He knew him better than he did d'Archiac and could therefore be more open with him; who knows, perhaps he'd be able to dissuade him from a duel the reasons for which Sollogub still didn't even know. But d'Anthès refused to explain them and curtly referred him to his second for the necessary arrangements. Only after much insistence did he tell Sollogub: "Look, don't you understand that I'm going to marry Catherine? Pushkin has withdrawn his challenge, but I don't want it to look as if I'm getting married to avoid a duel. Nor do I want the name of any woman to come up in this whole business. My father has been refusing to let me get married for a year now." Only at this point, convinced that d'Anthès was not entirely in the wrong, did Sollogub go to see Pushkin, stopping off at his father's house on the Moyka to say a brief hello.

Pushkin soon realized that his young friend had violated his instructions by talking to his opponent. "D'Anthès is a wretch," he said. "Yesterday I told him what a scoundrel he is. . . . People say he's courting my wife. Some say she likes him, others not. It's all the same to me, but I don't want their names linked. I challenged him when I got those anonymous letters. . . . Now go see d'Archiac." Sollogub told Pushkin that d'Anthés didn't want the name of any woman to come up. Pushkin flew into a rage. "So what? What's it all about, then? If you don't want to be my second, I'll find someone else." The saddened Sollogub, now losing heart, finally had himself driven to the French Embassy. D'Archiac admitted that he hadn't slept all night either and would be delighted to see this duel called off, not only because he was a friend of d'Anthès and wished him well, but also because, even though he was French, he was well aware of what Pushkin meant to Russia. "Convince him to withdraw the challenge unconditionally," he told Sollogub, "and I'll personally guarantee that d'Anthès will go through with the marriage. Perhaps then we can avert catastrophe." Sollogub replied that Pushkin had to be considered a sick man: certain trifles were better overlooked. The two men decided to suspend their negotiations and to meet again later in d'Anthès's presence.

Annoyed at how Sollogub was acting, Pushkin headed for Mikhailovskaya Square — "the Zanfteleben building, third floor on the left" — to ask Klementy Rosset to be his second. Rosset refused. As second, it would be his duty to seek a peaceful solution, but he hated d'Anthès as much as Pushkin did and would be delighted to see his friend rid Petersburg of the swaggering little officer. He also said that his written

French was not up to the requirements of the preliminary negotiations, which now seemed fairly complicated, but he would be happy to assist the poet in the field and willingly accepted an invitation to lunch. The invitation was not without ulterior motive: Pushkin wanted to line up an alternate second in case Sollogub disregarded his orders again.

Negotiations between the seconds resumed at the Dutch Embassy at about three that afternoon. D'Anthès was present but took no part in the talks. Once place, date, and conditions were set, Sollogub wrote to Pushkin to inform him of the arrangements – but also to make one last attempt at conciliation. D'Anthès wanted to read this letter, but d'Archiac put his foot down. Instead, he read it himself. "I agree," he announced. "Send it." They waited almost two hours for a reply. D'Anthès sat in gloomy, brooding silence.

The dashing guardsman was now suddenly a statue, powerless and passive. His adoptive father had taken the situation firmly in hand, authoritatively interposing himself between Pushkin and the son. The seconds, still desperately seeking peace, were prepared for concession and compromise; d'Anthès himself, having swallowed his initial burst of pride, now wondered whether a duel might not destroy Natalie's reputation and Catherine's future. He felt trapped, under pressure to accept a humiliating surrender. For the first time we feel a twinge of pity for d'Anthès, for we do not consider him a coward – which was how Pushkin saw him and how Russia would see him forever – nor do we believe that he would have married Catherine Goncharova to save his own life. Pushkin's friends didn't believe it either, and they certainly had no soft spot for d'Anthès. "The young man," Vyazemsky wrote, "was probably himself entangled in his father's murky machinations." The marriage "was a sacrifice he made to him."

Sollogub to Pushkin [November 17, 1836, about 4 p.m.]: As you wished, I have gone to see Mr. d'Archiac to arrange time and place.

Since it is impossible for me to be free on Friday, we have agreed on Saturday, in the vicinity of Pargolovo, early in the morning, at ten paces. Mr. d'Archiac has added confidentially that Baron d'Anthès had firmly decided to announce his marriage plans but, lest he give the impression of wanting to avoid a duel, will be able to do so in good conscience only when everything is settled between you, and you have acknowledged verbally, in my or Mr. d'Archiac's presence, that you do not ascribe his marriage to calculations unworthy of a man of noble feeling. Not being authorized to promise on your behalf this step of which I wholeheartedly approve, I beg you in the name of your family to accept this accommodation, which will satisfy both parties. It goes without saying that Mr. d'Archiac and I vouch for d'Anthès.

Sollogub

Please inform me of your reply without delay.

Sollogub ordered his coachman to take the letter immediately "to the Moyka, where he'd been that morning." The poor driver, not sure which of the two Moyka houses he'd stopped at a few hours ago was meant, took a second look at the address: *"À Monsieur Pouchkin, en mains propres."* This was a man who could barely make out the letters of the Russian alphabet, let alone the French. He opted for the house of Sollogub's father, where he'd taken the young count so often before. Privy Counselor Alexander Ivanovich Sollogub hesitated to open a letter addressed to Pushkin, but since he'd been told that the matter was urgent and recognized his son's handwriting, he finally decided to read it. He nearly had a fit.

A snowstorm, a vital letter delivered to the wrong address – it's almost as if Fate were aping a Pushkin story. In *The Captain's Daughter* young Grinyev is rescued by a vagabond to whom he gives his fur coat during a snowstorm. The stranger turns out to be the bloody populist rebel Pugachev, who saves Grinyev's life in memory of that generous gesture. A nighttime snowstorm also figures in one of the *Tales of*

Belkin: under cover of darkness in a godforsaken little country church, a stranger marries a girl waiting at the altar for her lover, who has lost his way; meeting by chance many years later, the stranger and the victim of his childish prank are joined in a happy, legal marriage. Would that the Pushkin snowstorm, whimsical, fickle ally of benevolent chance, could be our accomplice in writing our very own surprise happy ending to this story: *"Deeply shaken by what he read, appalled at the idea of Russia's greatest poet fighting a duel (a crime doubly serious in that his own son would be called to account by the law), Privy Counselor Alexander Ivanovich Sollogub took extreme measures, hurrying to see Count Benckendorff and report what he knew and what he guessed. Without even consulting the Tsar, the police chief quickly dispatched his men to the place where arrangements for the criminal design were being settled. So it was that at the last minute, in a bizarre, freakish turn of events, Pushkin's life was saved by the very man who had poisoned it in so many ways for the past fifteen years."*

But that's not how it happened. Recovering from this most unwelcome surprise, Alexander Ivanovich Sollogub handed the letter back to the messenger, who spurred his horses to No. 12 on the Moyka. There is no need for excessive regrets: the encounter of honor set for November 21, 1836, "in the vicinity of Pargolovo, early in the morning, at ten paces" would not take place. But no reason for inordinate rejoicing, either: another duel was already germinating, so far in words alone. It was now that the die was cast, and the consequences would be fatal.

Pushkin to Sollogub, November 17, 1836 [around 5:30 p.m.]: I shall not hesitate to put in writing what I am willing to state orally. I challenged Mr. Georges d'Anthès to a duel, and he accepted the challenge without regard to explanations. It is I who ask the worthy witnesses in this matter to please consider the challenge as not having been issued, *since I have learned from public rumors that Mr. Georges d'Anthès had decided to declare his proposal of marriage to*

Miss Catherine Goncharova after the duel.* I have no reason to attribute his decision to considerations unworthy of a man of noble spirit. I ask you, Count, to make whatever use of this letter you deem most suitable. . . .

The now exhausted coachman – Vasya? Vanya? Grishka? It would be nice to know the name of this bit player so unfairly forgotten by history – delivered Pushkin's reply to the Dutch Embassy. D'Archiac skimmed it and said, "This may be enough." Once again he refused to show d'Anthès the letter, instead congratulating him on his impending marriage. The *chevalier garde* then turned to Sollogub and said, "Go to Mr. Pushkin and thank him for agreeing to put an end to our quarrel. I hope that we will now meet as brothers." The two seconds went straight to No. 12 on the Moyka, where the poet was dining with family members and Rosset. He withdrew with Sollogub and d'Archiac to the study. Tense and pale, he listened in silence to the Frenchman's ritual words of gratitude and spoke only when Sollogub said, "For my part, I took the liberty of promising that you would treat your brother-in-law as a friendly acquaintance."

"You shouldn't have done that!" the irritated Pushkin exclaimed. "That will never happen. The houses of Pushkin and d'Anthès can never have anything in common." A brief pause, then he added, "But in any event I acknowledge, and am prepared to repeat, that Mr. d'Anthès has acted as a man of honor."

"I need nothing more," d'Archiac interjected, and quickly left with Sollogub.

Pushkin returned to the dining room and told Catherine, "My congratulations. D'Anthès has asked for your hand in marriage." His sister-in-law – whose nerves were shattered, her dark eyes stained by the tears of many a sleepless night

---

* The italics are mine, added to highlight a sentence that cuts like a knife. If it is believed, then Pushkin wins without a duel.

during the terrifying roller coaster of hope and anguish of the past few days – abruptly threw her napkin onto the table and as abruptly rose and ran to her room. Natalie followed. "What a man, this d'Anthès!" Pushkin said to Rosset with a little grin.

The engagement of Catherine Goncharova and Georges d'Anthès was announced that very evening at the Saltykovs' regular Tuesday-night ball, an ordeal for Petersburgers forced to endure the stifling sultriness of the improbably jammed little rooms. Pushkin attended but snubbed his future brother-in-law. He spoke only to Sollogub, who thought him bitterly merry and animated. After chiding his friend for having agreed to negotiations he had expressly forbidden, Pushkin added more calmly that he was ready to bet that the marriage would never take place. And in fact they did bet: Pushkin's complete works against Sollogub's walking stick.

Georges d'Anthès to Catherine Goncharova [Petersburg, November 21]: My dear, good Catherine, you see that the days pass, and one does not resemble the next. Yesterday lazy, today active, though I am returning from a horrible tour of guard duty at the Winter Palace, which I complained of this morning to your brother Dmitry, asking him to tell you so that you could give me some little sign of life. . . . This morning I saw the lady in question and as always submitted to your supreme orders, my love. I formally stated that I would be most grateful if she would call a halt to these absolutely useless negotiations; that if her husband was not intelligent enough to understand that he alone was playing the fool in this business, it was a waste of her time to try to explain it to him.

10

Remembrance

When for mortal men the noisy day is silent,
and in the streets and muted squares
semi-transparent shades of night thicken,
and sleep descends, the reward of daily toil,
then in the quiet the torturous time
of waking drags slowly on:
in the night's stillness the snakebites of conscience
burn more cruelly,
fantasy seethes,
in a mind oppressed by anguish
heavy thoughts throng,
before me memory silently unrolls
its infinite parchment,
and I read my life with disgust, I shiver
with dismay, and curse, and cry,
but the bitter tears of regret
do not delete the melancholy lines.

The Deleted Lines

Sollogub went to see Pushkin late in the afternoon of November 21, a Saturday. The poet raised the subject of the aborted duel. "You were d'Anthès's second more than mine," he complained yet again, "but still I don't want to do anything without your knowledge. Let's go to my study." There Pushkin closed the door and said, "I'm going to read you a letter I've written to Heeckeren. With the son it's all over. Now I want the old man." He let his guest get comfortable, then sat down at his desk, picked up two sheets of light-blue, gold-trimmed paper, and began to read. His trembling lips and bloodshot eyes were frightening to look upon. Sollogub later wrote that it was only then that he realized "that he was truly of African origin."

Two drafts of Pushkin's letter to Heeckeren have survived, one of which is undoubtedly the document the poet read to Sollogub that afternoon. Though torn up by Pushkin (perhaps on the eve of the fatal duel), the shreds were discovered after his death by someone who preserved them like precious relics until 1880, when they were reassembled and published by *Russian Antiquity* – though not in their entirety, since some pieces had in the meantime been lost. By matching up the edges of the remaining fragments, filling in the gaps in one copy with what remains of the other, nearly all the first draft can be reconstructed. In it Pushkin refers to a duel, which suggests that it may have been written during a breakdown of the fragile truce, when circumstances led him to believe that he would indeed be facing off against d'Anthès. In other words, the afternoon of November 16 or the morning of the seventeenth. But the phrase itself – "A duel is no longer enough for me . . . and whatever the outcome . . ." – suggests a different hypothesis: once the conflict had been peacefully resolved by the efforts of the two seconds and the sudden surrender of Georges d'Anthès, Pushkin was trying to force Heeckeren to fight. He would thereby settle accounts with "the old man" in blood and simultaneously shame the youth who had lacked the courage to face his bullet. It is hardly surprising to find ambiguity here: in this play of thick shadows and rare glimmers, words can bear more than one meaning at a time. Everything becomes doubtful and double-edged when philology's tools must be supplemented with those of psychology, itself a double-edged sword, as the great Porfiry Petrovich maintained.

Pushkin to Heeckeren [sometime between November 16 and 21, 1836]:

Dear Baron,

Allow me first of all to summarize what has just happened. Your son's conduct, perfectly well known to me, could not be a matter of indifference; but since it remained within the bounds of propriety and, furthermore, I knew how much my wife deserved my trust and respect, I was content merely to observe, intervening only when I considered it appropriate. I knew very well that a handsome mien, an ill-starred passion, two *years'** persistence always *wind up* making some *impression* on a young person's heart, and that the husband, unless he is a fool, quite naturally becomes his wife's confidant and guides her behavior. I will admit I was not without

---

* The italics indicate restorations suggested by context; but I have not marked those made by completing surviving word fragments or interpolating words or groups of words from the second draft, which in many places is identical to the first. Ellipsis indicates words or passages whose reconstruction is doubtful or outright impossible.

misgivings. An incident that would have been most disagreeable at any other time fortuitously extracted me from embarrassment: I received some anonymous letters. I saw that the moment had come, and I seized it. You know the rest: I made your son look so grotesque and pitiful that my wife, stunned by such baseness, could not help but laugh, and any emotion she may have felt for his great sublime passion faded into far calmer and much deserved disgust.

But you, Baron, what was your role in this whole affair? You, the representative of a crowned head, acted as pimp for your so-called bastard; the young man's entire behavior was guided by you. It was you who dictated to him the platitudes *that were being* spouted and the idiocies that were undertaken *to be written*. Like an obscene old woman you lay in wait for my wife so as to talk to her about your son at every opportunity, and when he was bedridden by his treatments for syphilis, you, vile as you are, told her he was dying of love for her; give me back my son, you implored her.

You see that I know everything: but wait, there is more; as I was saying, the affair got more complicated. Let us return to the anonymous letters. You may well imagine that they may be of interest to you.

On November 2 you had delightful news from your son. He told you ... that my wife was afraid ... that she was losing her head ... to strike a decisive blow.... *I received three* copies of the anonymous letter (*of the ten that* were distributed). *This letter* was so carelessly fabricated that I picked up the author's tracks at the very first glance.... I was sure I would find my villain and worried about it no further. Indeed, after less than three days of investigation I knew what to do. If diplomacy is no more than the art of knowing what goes on in others' houses and beating them at their own game, you must give me my due by acknowledging that you were vanquished in all respects.

I now come to the purpose of my letter. You may wish to know what has so far forestalled me from bringing dishonor upon you in the eyes of our court and yours. I will tell you.

I am a good, plain man ... but I have a sensitive heart.... A duel is no longer enough for me ... no, and whatever the outcome,

I will feel adequately vindicated neither by the ... your son nor by the letter I have the honor to write you now, a copy of which I am keeping for my personal use. I would like you to take the trouble to *find* reasons that might persuade me not to spit in your face and liquidate even the slightest trace of this wretched affair, which could easily serve as an excellent chapter in my history of cuckoldry.

    I have the honor to be, Baron,

        your most humble and obedient servant

                                        A. Pushkin

Pushkin claims that he guessed from the very first glance that his "villain" was Heeckeren, yet we know from Sollogub that on the morning of November 4 he suspected a woman. (And if the ambassador was truly a suspect, would Pushkin have received him and allowed himself to be moved by his tears?) He claims that his wife now felt nothing but serene disgust for d'Anthès, that she was laughing at him, yet Dolly Ficquelmont tells us that Natalie, "loath to believe that d'Anthès preferred her sister, in her innocence, or rather, in her amazing idiocy, talked to her husband about whether such a change of heart was possible in someone whose love she may have cared for out of vanity alone."

    Reading over the first draft of his letter to Heeckeren, Pushkin deleted three lines: "On November 2 you had [delight]ful [news]* from your son. He told you ... † that my wife was afraid ... that she was losing her head ... to strike a decisive blow ... copies of the anonymous let ... were distributed)." Despite the gaps, the sense of what Pushkin meant is clear: on November 2, after receiving some good news from his adoptive son, the ambassador decided that the time had come to strike the "decisive blow" – the anonymous

---

* "*nouvelle qui vous fit beauc ...*" has been reconstructed from the remnant tops of an *n*, an *f*, a *t*, and a *b*.

† Here there remains only the tail end of a word: "... *ité*," which lends itself to more than one reconstruction.

letters. It is also clear that Pushkin was eager to eliminate even the briefest mention of the substance of the alleged conversation between d'Anthès and Heeckeren on November 2. Why?

He'd been thinking about this letter – pondering it, savoring its every word – since November 13, when he told Princess Vyazemskaya: "I know who wrote the anonymous letters, and in eight days you will hear tell of vengeance unique of its kind; it will be full, complete; it will cast that man into the mud." Eight days: the meticulous, chilling tenacity of his hatred is evident in the precision of the timetable. Eight days meant November 21, when the two-week delay he'd granted Baron Heeckeren on the morning of November 6 would expire.

"How was I to react to such destructive distress?" Sollogub wondered at the time. "I forced myself to hold my tongue." Nor do we dare comment on such delusions of grandeur, omnipotence, omniscience: a single dazzling sleight of hand, and the victim of a trivial prank, pitiable husband with a whiff of the cuckold about him becomes the supreme master of circumstance and event. He knows all – even what his persecutors are plotting in deepest secret – and can do all – even seize upon an idiotic, wicked insult to eradicate from his wife's heart whatever feeling she "may" have had for her persistent admirer. We watch in amazement as the romantic intermezzo draws to a close. The blushing, quivering ingenue and her frenzied lover exeunt, ceding the starring roles to two characters of greater age, intelligence, experience. Having deftly rid himself of a vulgar *coureur d'alcôves*, the ever vigilant and wise Russian husband now unleashes all his venom on a target whose words and deeds ooze vile abasement and malicious design, whose unfathomable wretchedness is matched by his own boundless nobility. In the livid glare of Pushkin's hatred, Heeckeren assumes the stature and countenance of a demonic creature, dark power of evil.

*

Faithful to the principles of his art even in epistolary prose, Pushkin never wonders or explains why an "old man," a father, a nobleman, scion of a royal line, would stoop to pimping for his "so-called bastard" or concoct a sordid hoax. Instead, he merely insults the Heeckeren bloodline, provoking him on his own slippery ground, challenging him to see if he can avoid a scandal, threatening him with ruin without revealing how and when he will activate his plans, hinting that he might show others the letter, a copy of which he is keeping for his own "personal use." And incidentally treating us to an eighteenth-century intrigue straight out of Laclos, a whole new chapter of *Les Liaisons dangereuses* in which we imagine Tourvel striving to thwart the schemes of the Marquise de Merteuil, outdoing her in cunning and iniquity.

Pushkin also crossed out other lines as he edited the first draft of his letter to the Dutch ambassador: "You may wish to know what has so far forestalled me from bringing dishonor upon you in the eyes of our court and yours. I will tell you." This passage was now moot, since on November 21 he acted on his threat, writing to Benckendorff:

Dear Count,

It is my right, and I consider it my duty, to inform Your Excellency of what has recently happened in my family. On the morning of November 4 I received three copies of an anonymous letter affronting my and my wife's honor. From the look of the paper, the style of the letter, the manner in which it was worded, I realized immediately that it was the work of a foreigner, a man of high society, a diplomat. I began investigations. I learned that seven or eight people had received copies of the same letter that day, sealed and addressed to me in a double envelope. Most of those who received it, suspecting an outrage, did not pass it on to me.

The general reaction was indignation at such a wicked and gratuitous insult; but while reiterating that my wife's conduct was above reproach, people said that the pretext for this villainy was Mr. d'Anthès's persistent courtship of her.

I was not at all pleased to see my wife's name linked to anyone else's in this manner. I said so to Mr. d'Anthès. Baron Heeckeren came to see me and accepted a duel in the name of Mr. d'Anthès, asking me for a delay of fifteen days.

As it happened, Mr. d'Anthès fell in love with my sister-in-law, Miss Goncharova, during the period of this delay, and asked for her hand. Having heard public rumors to this effect, I sent word to Mr. d'Archiac (Mr. d'Anthès's second) that my challenge was to be regarded as null and void. I meanwhile ascertained that the anonymous letter came from Mr. Heeckeren, something I consider it my duty to bring to the attention of the government and society.

Being sole judge and guardian of my and my wife's honor, and consequently requesting neither justice nor vengeance, I cannot and will not reveal to anyone the evidence for what I maintain.

In any case, Count, I hope that this letter may stand as proof of the respect and trust I bear for you.

It is with these sentiments that I have the honor to be . . .

Pushkin was sure that his letter to Heeckeren would result in a duel (indeed, he read it to Sollogub so as to make sure of his services as second), although by now not even a duel was enough to slake his hatred. But he also knew that his letter to Benckendorff would make a duel impossible: the police, the Tsar himself, would intervene, and his already copious roster of enemies, unaware of what had happened over the past two weeks, would deride the poet who turned people into the Third Section rather than washing his dirty laundry at home or – better still – in some secluded corner in the outskirts of Petersburg. This – along with circumstances and events yet to be related – must have been what stopped him, convincing him not to send either letter. But he did not destroy them. Instead, he put them in a safe place. They might yet prove useful.

*

Vyazemsky wrote to Alexandra Osipovna Smirnova on February 2, 1837: "Yes, it was certainly society that killed him. Those disgraceful letters, that disgraceful gossip coming back to him from all over, his passionate, gloomy character were the cause of the catastrophe. He didn't consult us, and I don't know why he was always so fatally impelled to go off in the wrong direction." But within a few days the tone of Vyazemsky's letters to friends and acquaintances changed significantly, counteracting picturesque interpretations of the tragedy and bequeathing a more detailed, albeit already largely hagiographic, version to contemporaries and posterity.

On February 9 he wrote that "perverse and still obscure machinations" had been mounted against Pushkin and his wife. "Perhaps time will bring them to light," he added. And on February 10: "The more you think about this loss, and the more you learn of the so far unknown circumstances that time is little by little beginning to reveal, the more your heart bleeds, weeps. Diabolical plots, diabolical maneuvers, were organized against Pushkin and his wife. No one can say whether time will reveal all, but what we already know is enough. The Pushkins' marital happiness and harmony were targeted by the most depraved and insidious schemes of two people prepared to do anything to dishonor Mrs. Pushkin."

And on February 16: "Pushkin and his wife were victims of a disgraceful trap." There has been speculation that in the second week of February 1837 close friends of the murdered poet learned something that turned pity for "the unfortunate victim of unfortunate circumstances and of his own passions" into violent, uncontainable execration of d'Anthès and Heeckeren — something very serious that they tried to keep secret forever.

In the words of Alexandra Arapova and in her unmistakable style, with the additions, emendations, and slips of her fervent imagination:

The sending of the infamous certificates was the first poisoned dart forcing Pushkin to take notice of his wife's overly enterprising admirer. . . . He began to chide her for flightiness and flirting, demanded that she refuse to receive d'Anthès, scrupulously avoid any conversation with him in public, and put an end to his offensive hopes with icy resistance. Docile as ever, Natalya Nikolaevna bowed to her husband's wishes, but d'Anthès was not the sort of person to be easily discouraged. And at this point a person whose ambiguous role is truly inexplicable enters the unfolding drama. I speak of the Dutch ambassador himself. The social world has an ugly interpretation of his abject infatuation with his adoptive son, but that never stopped him from doing all he could to bring the young officer and Mrs. Pushkin closer, thus luring the latter onto a dangerous path. The moment she avoids meeting d'Anthès or speaking to him, Heeckeren, pursuing her everywhere, appears before her like a shadow, cleverly finding ways to whisper of the mad love for her of his son, capable of killing himself in an outburst of despair, painting pictures of his suffering, expressing indignation at her coldness and cruelty. Once, at a ball of the Assembly of Nobles, apparently deciding that the ground had now been properly prepared, he insisted on laying out a plan, arranged down to the smallest particulars, to flee abroad under his diplomatic aegis, holding out the most alluring future for her; and to sap the resistance of her guilty conscience, he reminded her of her husband's repeated and widely known cheating, which entitled her to the freedom of avenging herself. Natalya Nikolaevna let him finish and then, raising her radiant gaze to him, replied: "Even if we admit that my husband has done me the wrongs you impute to him, if we admit that in the bewilderment of a passion that, at least on my side, does not exist, these wrongs were of such a nature as to cause me to forget my duties to him, you are still losing sight of a crucial point: I am a mother. If I went so far as to abandon my four children at their tender age, sacrificing them to a love that is culpable, I would be the vilest of creatures in my own eyes. We have nothing else to say to each other, and I demand that you leave me alone." . . . There is reason to believe that her explanations did not satisfy the baron, and that he continued to direct events on their fatal course.

The source of Pushkin's information – and of his ire and accusations – must have been Natalya Nikolaevna; we know from Vyazemsky that after the certificates arrived, the wife made a clean breast of things to her husband, not only about her own missteps and the young man's behavior toward her, but also about the conduct "of old man Heeckeren, who had sought to divert her from her duties and to draw her into the abyss." To this day, the source of our information and our doubts has been the scant handful of facts transmitted by a few witnesses. Danzas recalled that after the summer stay at the Islands and the fresh, unstoppable wave of gossip, Pushkin "ceased receiving d'Anthès." According to Dolly Ficquelmont, however, "he made the great mistake of allowing his wife to go out into society without him" – and Natalie continued to see d'Anthès at receptions, the theater, and friends' homes and "was unable to repel or halt the displays of that crazed love. . . . She seemed to pale and tremble at his gaze, but had clearly lost any capacity to keep the man in check, and he was determined to carry her to the end. . . ." Princess Vyazemskaya was the only person who tried to warn Natalie, opening her heart to her as to one of her own daughters: she was not a child anymore, she told her, and ought to realize the possible consequences of her behavior. At last Natalie spoke: "I have fun with him. I like him, that's all. It will go on as it has for the past two years."

Marya Baryatinskaya wrote nearly identical words about Georges d'Anthès: *"Il m'amuse, mais voilà tout."* To her we also owe an account of an interesting conversation in a Petersburg salon around the middle of October 1836. Mrs. Petrovo-Solovovo, happening upon a cousin of Princess Baryatinskaya, asked, "So, has your cousin's engagement been settled?" "To whom?" asked the dumbfounded relative. "To d'Anthès," replied the lady, as though the Frenchman's matrimonial intentions were common knowledge, and she went on to plead the cause of the *chevalier garde*, who, she claimed, would have been in despair had he not been granted Miss Baryatinskaya's hand. The girl herself was stunned by the conversation, and commented on it angrily in her diary: "*Maman* found out from Trubetskoy that d'Anthès was rejected by Mrs. Pushkin. Maybe that's why he wants to get married – *out of spite!* . . . I will know how to thank him if he dares ask for my hand."

There is one last thing we know about the months, perhaps even the days, before November 4 – but here we must bring in a new character: Idalya Poletika, illegitimate daughter of Count Grigory Alexandrovich Stroganov, the Russian *grand seigneur*, echoes of whose erotic exploits may be found as far afield as in Byron's *Don Juan*. Ambassador to Spain in the early nineteenth century, Stroganov stole the stunningly beautiful Juliana da Ega from her lawful husband and brought her back to Russia along with Idalie, their little bastard child. A cousin of the Goncharov sisters through the Stroganovs, the enchanting Idalie was like family for the Pushkins; the poet mentions her affectionately in letters to his wife and once scolded Natalya Nikolaevna for not "staying at Idalie's" instead of receiving distant male relatives at home in his absence. Apparently he trusted Idalya Poletika. That was a mistake. Married to Alexander Mikhailovich Poletika, regimental colonel of the Horse Guards and therefore d'Anthès's direct superior, Idalya was very friendly with the French officer and on at least one occasion did him a most delicate favor, one that may have been critical in the events we are trying to reconstruct: "At d'Anthès's insistence, Mrs. [Poletika] invited Mrs. Pushkin to her house and then went out. Mrs. Pushkin told Princess Vyazemskaya and the princess's husband that when she and d'Anthès were alone, he drew a pistol and threatened to shoot himself unless she gave in to him. Mrs. Pushkin was at a loss how to extract herself from his insistence; wringing her hands, she began to speak as loudly as possible. Luckily the unknowing daughter of the mistress of the house came into the room, and the guest threw herself upon her."*

The Vyazemskys' testimony had not yet been published and therefore could not possibly have influenced Baron Gustav Vogel von Friesenhof, Alexandrine Goncharova's husband, when in 1887 he gave Arapova his description of the days leading up to Georges d'Anthès's engagement: "He saw your mother only in social settings, and there were no meetings or exchanges of letters between them. But there was one exception to each of these circumstances. Old man Heeckeren wrote your mother a letter trying to convince her to leave her husband and marry his adoptive son.† Alexandrine recalls that

* Until a few years ago it was taken for granted in all reconstructions of Pushkin's last days that the meeting between d'Anthès and Natalya Nikolaevna at Idalie Poletika's house took place in late January 1837 and that Pushkin, informed of the fact by yet another anonymous letter, reacted by writing to Heeckeren, thereby provoking the fatal duel. This was the version offered by Arapova, who also says that the broker of the secret rendezvous was none other than her own father, Pyotr Petrovich Lanskoy, who was Idalie Poletika's lover in the 1830s and became Natalya Nikolaevna Pushkina's second husband in 1844. But if it really happened the way Arapova says, then the meeting had to have occurred long before January, since Lanskoy left Petersburg on October 19, 1836, and returned in February 1837.
  Abramovich – relying on the chronological order in which Baron von Friesenhof told Arapova of the facts related to him by his wife – maintained for the first time (in *Pushkin v 1836 godu*) that the meeting at Poletika's house occurred before November 4. Abramovich's arguments seem plausible (and I would add one that appears decisive: in their later testimony neither the Vyazemskys nor Friesenhof drew any direct link between the trap d'Anthès set for Natalya Nikolaevna and the events of January 26–27, 1837), but I am not so sure about the claim that the meeting actually took place on November 2, the date Pushkin cited in the first draft of his letter to Heeckeren.
† I doubt the ambassador would leave such compromising material evidence and believe instead that it was d'Anthès who wrote that desperate proposal of marriage (or rather of flight, since divorce was rare and very difficult in Russia, and the abandoned husband would not have stood idly by), albeit with his adoptive father's help, at least with grammar and syntax. As we have seen, Pushkin himself accused Heeckeren of "dictating" the letters d'Anthès was writing to Natalie.

your mother replied with a decisive rejection, but cannot remember whether it was orally or in writing. As for the meeting, your mother once received an invitation to visit Mrs. Poletika, and upon her arrival found d'Anthès instead of the lady of the house; falling to his knees before her, he begged her for what his adoptive father had written. Your mother told my wife that this meeting lasted only a few minutes, since she left forthwith after immediately rejecting him."

Even in her husband's account of events, Natalya Nikola-evna heeds the "obscene old woman" who tracks her down wherever he can to badger her about d'Anthès's amorous yearnings. Even in her daughter's patently euphemistic and fictionalized version, she agrees to intimate discussions with the cruel Shadow lying in wait for her. Why didn't she send him straight back to the hell from which he came? Why didn't she call a decisive halt to those awkward, painful talks? Why didn't she tell her husband about them right away? And why – when, where, how – did Heeckeren seek to "lure" Pushkin's wife "onto a dangerous path"? The ambassador wrote to Nesselrode on February 13, 1837: "I am said to have encour-aged my son's courting of Mrs. Pushkin. In this regard I appeal to the lady herself. Let her be questioned under oath, and the accusation will be seen to collapse. She can tell you everything I said to her so often to make her aware of the abyss toward which she was heading. If she is unrestrained by considerations of pride, she will tell you that in my talks with her I was frank to the point of employing words that must have hurt her but at the same time opened her eyes: or at least so I hoped. If I could not have Mrs. Pushkin's con-fession, I would ask the testimony of two ladies of distinction to whom I always confided my unease, informing them daily of all my efforts to break that deadly bond."

Two counterposed scenarios loom before our disoriented eyes: a perverse corrupter prodding a young wife toward the abyss of adultery; a wise counselor restraining a young woman striding rashly to the brink of that same abyss, ready and willing even to offend her with his crudeness if only to keep her from the ruinous leap.

Paris, early summer of 1989, 152 winters and 153 springs after Pushkin's death. Among the papers of Georges d'Anthès's descendants are three letters labeled "strictly personal." We are already familiar with two of them: the one d'Anthès wrote to Heeckeren on April 30, 1836, and the one we have dated November 6. Our heart skips a beat when we read the third:

D'Anthès to Heeckeren: My dear friend, I wanted to talk to you this morning but had so little time it was impossible. Yesterday I happened to spend the evening in tête-à-tête with the Lady in question, and when I say tête-à-tête I mean I was the only man, for at least an entire hour, at Princess Vyazemskaya's, you can imagine the state I was in, at last I summoned my courage and played my part fairly well and was even fairly happy. In short, I held out until eleven, but at that point my strength forsook me and I was gripped by such great weakness that I barely had time to leave the room, and once out on the street began to weep like a real idiot, which in any event was a great relief, however, because I was about to burst, and back in my room I found I had a raging fever and couldn't sleep all night and suffered in mind till I thought I'd go mad.

So it is that I have decided to turn to you and to beg you to do what you promised tonight. It is absolutely necessary that you speak to her and that I know once and for all how to behave.

She is going to the Lerchenfelds' this evening, and if you give up your card game you'll find the right moment to speak to her.

Here's how I see it: I think you ought to approach her frankly and ask her, making sure her sister doesn't hear you, if by any chance she was at the Vyazemskys' yesterday, and when she says yes, tell her that you thought so and that she can do you a great favor; then tell her what happened to me yesterday as if you'd witnessed everything that happened when I got home: that my servant took fright and went to wake you at two in the morning, that you asked me many questions but managed to learn nothing from me* and were convinced I'd quarreled with the husband and it was to avert my unhappiness that you were turning to her (the husband being absent). This will prove only that I told you nothing about the evening, which is absolutely necessary, since she has to believe that I am acting without your knowledge and that it is only as a father concerned for his son that you are questioning her. It wouldn't hurt to give her the impression that you believe that the relations between us are far more intimate than they are, because when she protests her innocence, you will find a way to make her see that they ought to be, given the way she behaves with me. Anyway, beginning is the hard part and I think this is the right way, because as I said, she absolutely must not suspect that the thing has been planned and she must see this step of yours as a completely natural feeling that you must be worried about my health and my future and you must ask her most urgently to keep it secret from everyone and most of all from me. But it would be prudent not to ask her to receive me right away. You can do that next time, and be careful not to use phrases that might be in the letter.† I beg you once again, my dear, to help me. I place myself wholly in your hands, because if this continues without my knowing where it is to take me, I will go mad.

You might even frighten her and make her realize that *[three or four illegible words]‡*

I ask you to forgive me for the disorder of this note, but I assure

---

* The following lines were added obliquely in the margin: "that besides I didn't have to tell you, you knew very well that I'd lost my head for her, that the change in my behavior and character proved it to you and consequently even her husband was aware of it."

† The one, I imagine, in which he asked her to flee abroad with him.

‡ D'Anthès deleted the entire sentence (the words *"Tu pourrais aussi lui faire peur et lui faire entendre que"* are barely legible). In fact, he probably never even finished it, instead drawing a pen stroke through it and smudging the ink to obliterate the last words so thoroughly that not even the finest instruments for deciphering old manuscripts can tell us how he wished to frighten Natalie. Was it dramatic posturing ("I will kill myself") or a more prosaic threat ("I'll tell her husband . . .")? Not even the latter hypothesis would surprise us.

you that my head has never felt like this, it burns like fire and I am sick as a dog. Anyway, if this information is not enough, please be so kind as to come by the barracks before going on to the Lerchenfelds'. You'll find me at Béthencourt's.

I embrace you.

Georges d'Anthès could not have written this letter before the summer of 1836, when Natalie first saw him again after at least three months of housebound isolation (while mourning for her mother-in-law and awaiting the birth of her daughter). It was written from Petersburg: in other words, after everyone had left the Islands. It could not have been written before the very end of September (since it was only around the twentieth of the month that Vera Fyodorovna Vyazemskaya reopened her salon after a long stay in Norderney), and it obviously predates Pushkin's challenge. It must go back to a day when d'Anthès was on guard duty, since it was written from Shpalernaya Street, and only a compulsory evening and night in the barracks could have stopped the *chevalier garde* from rushing to the home of Maximilian von Lerchenfeld, the Bavarian ambassador, where he knew he would find Natalie. And of those days of guard duty, it was probably the one closest to October 19, when the regimental physician put d'Anthès on medical leave: we know how delicate his health was, and the sudden weakness, burning brow, and "raging fever" sound like symptoms of another lung infection as well as consuming lovesickness.

One may therefore surmise that the letter was written on the afternoon of October 17: the night before, having left the Vyazemskys' drenched in sweat and having paused in the street to vent his excitement, d'Anthès was caught unawares by the sudden frigid northwest wind that swelled the Neva's waters.

One can begin to understand. There must have been some confrontation between d'Anthès and Pushkin* — a demand

---

* Only in this case could Heeckeren have pretended to believe that there had been a quarrel between them when talking to Natalie.

for explanations, perhaps a violent argument – as early as October 1836, probably when the poet told d'Anthès to stay away from his house. Something dramatic and decisive must also have happened between d'Anthès and Natalie, probably the rejection Alexander Trubetskoy mentioned to Marya Baryatinskaya's mother. The mere sight of Natalie now drove d'Anthès to tears, requiring herculean efforts to maintain his lighthearted, playful image. His merry cockiness was no more than a public charade, as least from the time he fell for Pushkin's wife. And here we'd smiled at his claim that it was torture to act cheerful and carefree while there was "death in his heart," here we'd suspected that his ostensible professions of love concealed devious ulterior motives, even doubting it was love at all! It must be said, though, that d'Anthès had good reason to feel distressed, anxious, and uncontrollably nervous at the time, for he had also gotten himself into a fine mess with the oldest of the Goncharov sisters.

There is proof, then: it was d'Anthès who "guided the behavior" of the ambassador, designed his pimp's trap, and implored him to speak to "the Lady in question," probing her feelings and intentions, stirring her pity, trying to sap her strenuous resistance. "What a man, this d'Anthès!" – we can say with Pushkin – who doesn't balk at asking the man who loves him to intercede on his behalf with the woman he cannot bring himself to lose. And that latter man rushes to help, acting as the messenger of the maniacal passion that alarms, pains, and offends him. Hardly a disinterested observer, he realizes that only by possessing the intractable beauty will the young man recover "life and peace," along with time, attention, and affection for him. But he is not acting out of calculation alone, for he cannot bear seeing his "son" languish in body and mind in a state very near madness. He is therefore ready for anything, up to and including taking Pushkin's wife by the hand and leading her to the patient's bed. Tears in his eyes, he seeks Natalya Nikolaevna out and tells her that d'Anthès is wasting away, dying of his love for her, murmuring her name even in his delirium, begging to see her one last time before death takes him. "Give me back my son!" Heeckeren entreats her, and his words are ingratiating, double-edged: reproach and prayer, pain and incitement.

One breathes a sigh of relief: at least as of October 1836, Pushkin was not a cuckold. As Heeckeren wrote to Nesselrode, Natalya Nikolaevna "had never *completely** forgotten her duties," and as Vyazemsky wrote to Grand Duke Mikhail Pavlovich, she could boast of "a fundamental innocence." But her paradoxical guilt, the cause of the disaster, lies precisely in that "fundamental," that "never completely." She rejected d'Anthès (for the second time that we know of, now partly no doubt out of jealousy – of her sister Catherine, of Princess Baryatinskaya), but she could not and would not call a halt to the delicious game of pallors and tremors, languid gazes and wheedling sweet nothings, furtive little love notes. "It wouldn't hurt to give her the impression that you believe that the relations between us are far more intimate than they are ... to make her see that they ought to be, *given the way she behaves with me.*" In other words, out of love for Georges d'Anthès, fear of her husband, a bizarre conception of virtue, and her deadly pettiness of spirit, Natalie was acting like an *allumeuse*, a provocative flirt. She offered the young Frenchman herring and caviar but refused to slake the burning thirst that she herself incited.

One would like, now, to ring the curtain down on an event in which Love – in all its variants, acceptations, deviations – sowed only ugliness. But we cannot, for Fate has already bolted from its starting post. We wish we might close the courtroom door once and for all on the odd trio that has stood in the dock ever since that painful day when Pushkin lost his life: the ardent little officer, the heedless beauty, the equivocal ambassador. But at least one of the charges still

* My italics. What a snake the ambassador was!

pending against Baron Heeckeren requires further investigation.

Vyazemsky to Grand Duke Mikhail Pavlovich, Petersburg, February 14, 1837: Pushkin suspected that Heeckeren was the author of the anonymous letters from the moment he received them, and he died convinced of it. We have never managed to clarify the basis of that conjecture, which until his death we considered inadmissible. Since then a fortuitous accident has afforded it a degree of plausibility. But since neither legal nor concrete evidence exists, it must be left to the judgment of God and not of men.

What would Heeckeren's motive have been? We are hardly the first to have wondered about that. This was Anna Akhmatova's answer: "Eager to separate d'Anthès from Natalya Nikolaevna, he was convinced that upon receiving such a letter, *'le mari d'une jalousie révoltante'* would get his wife out of Petersburg forthwith, dispatching her either to her mother's house in the country (as he did in 1834) or to some other place, thus bringing it all to a peaceful end. That's why the certificates were sent to Pushkin's *friends* and not his enemies, who obviously would have been in no position to encourage the poet with their good advice."

I am not convinced. Surely the astute ambassador could have concocted a less intricate stratagem for separating d'Anthès from Natalya Nikolaevna. One would think that "a man of calculation more than of depravity" could have predicted that when Pushkin received those cuckold certificates from multiple sources, he would unleash his ire at the *chevalier garde* even if d'Anthès's name never appeared in them. Jealousy? Heeckeren does not strike one as the sort of man to act in the heat of even the most blinding passion or to be driven by a fleeting lust for vengeance. But above all, would he have risked his honor, his career, his life itself (not to mention his adoptive son's) by using paper, a style, a "way with words" that could be traced back to him "from the very first glance"? And would he have relied on the sworn silence of at least one other person? Remember, even those who believe him guilty admit that he could not have acted alone, that his odious plan required a Russian accomplice.

In his own and d'Anthès's defense,* Heeckeren, too, wondered, *"Cui prodest?"* To Nesselrode he wrote: "My name has been linked to the disgrace of the anonymous letters! To whose advantage could this weapon worthy of the vilest assassin, of a poison-spewing individual, have been used? My son's, Mr. Pushkin's, his wife's? I blush merely in venturing to ask the question. And at whom were these absurd but nonetheless disgraceful insinuations aimed? A young man now facing the threat of the death penalty and of whom I am forbidden to speak, since his fate depends on the sovereign's clemency. Could my son, then, have been the author of these letters? Once again, toward what purpose? To have his way with Mrs. Pushkin by leaving her no choice but to throw herself into his arms, ruined in the eyes of the world and repudiated by her husband?"

Yes, many have claimed, precisely for that purpose – except that the two sordid malefactors simply blundered. But those who make this claim forget that Heeckeren was a seasoned diplomat. Fifteen years in the field had taught him not to let personal feelings transpire in what he wrote to kings, ministers, or men of state.

In the twentieth century a note decisively exonerating the Dutch ambassador was found in the secret archives of the Third Section. Heeckeren wrote to d'Anthès:

---

* After the poet's death many suspected d'Anthès as well. For his part, Pushkin was somewhat unsure of the role played by the Frenchman. In the second draft of his letter to Heeckeren he hesitated between "villain" and "villains"; in the draft of his letter to Benckendorff he wrote: "I knew for certain that the anonymous letter came from Messrs. Heeckeren," and only later decided on "Mr. Heeckeren."

If you mean the anonymous letter, I can tell you that it was sealed with red wax, carelessly, without much wax; a rather unusual seal, if memory serves, an *a* in the center, in this shape: *A*, with many symbols around it; I couldn't make the symbols out clearly, because as I said it was carelessly sealed, but it seems to me there were flags, cannon, etc., but I'm not sure. I think I remember they were on several sides, but I'm not sure of that either. In God's name be careful and don't hesitate to use my name about these details, since it was Count Nesselrode who showed me the letter, written on the same size paper as this note. Mrs. N. and Countess Sophie B. have been telling me to say many nice things to you, they're both taking a warm interest in us. May the full truth be brought to light – such is my heart's fondest wish; yours with heart and soul. . . . Why are you asking me for all these details? Good night, sleep tight.

In other words, all Heeckeren knew of the fatal certificates was the copy Count Nesselrode showed him. Yet some still wonder whether the ambassador might not have written this note after Pushkin's death (a most difficult time for him), just in case he ever needed proof of his own innocence. Once again we are dubious: is it plausible that the old fox could come up with no more substantial evidence in his own defense than a hasty and somewhat disjointed note that openly cites Nesselrode, his sole and last defender on Russian soil? It seems hard to believe, but there are other questions to which we have no answers. When was the note written? While d'Anthès was under arrest and preparing his defense, as the phrase "don't hesitate to use my name about these details" suggests? But it is unlikely that d'Anthès would have needed any information about the seal on the certificates in February 1837, since he'd at least looked at the "copy of the insulting letter" that Sollogub saw in Olivier d'Archiac's hands on November 17. Heeckeren's brief note would therefore seem to date back to the first half of November 1836, when notes and messages were flying back and forth between the barracks of Shpalernaya Street and the Nevsky Prospect. But how in

the world did Nesselrode get his hands on one of the certificates back then? Did he, too, receive a copy on the morning
of November 4? Or had a friend or acquaintance of Pushkin's
been quick to supply him with one? If so, who and why? We'll
never know. But nothing prevents us from speculating that some
Third Section functionary may have come across the ambassador's note in the archives many years later, and that the phrase
"it was Count Nesselrode who showed me the letter" (hastily
interpreted in ignorance of all we know today) was the genesis
of Tsar Alexander II's alleged *"C'est Nesselrode."*

There is an isolated fragment – "... *à cacheter* ..." – in the
draft of Pushkin's letter to Beckendorff, apparently an allusion
to the seal on the certificates, one of the clues, along with
those deduced from the paper, style, and wording, that supposedly led the poet to Heeckeren. Danzas recalled that Pushkin
suspected Heeckeren "because of the similarity of the handwriting." Since none of Pushkin's arguments against the
ambassador hold up when tested against the two copies we
have today, it has been suggested that one or more of the
certificates may have been written on different paper, in a
different hand. "The paper and the seal," Anna Akhmatova
argued, "would have come up during Natalya Nikolaevna's
confessions if, for example, some of d'Anthès's notes bore the
same seal. It is no accident that Heeckeren describes the seal
to d'Anthès in his 'fraudulent note.' Why would the size of
the paper on which a prank certificate is written or what is
depicted on the seal matter to an innocent man?"

It would matter a great deal if the man had been challenged
to a duel on the basis of the prank. Confined to his barracks
and unable to act, Georges d'Anthès racked his brains over
the cause of his troubles and asked Heeckeren for every detail
about those damned letters. Nothing in his conduct suggests
that he bore any hatred for Natalya Nikolaevna or thirsted
for revenge for her repeated rejections, and those are the only
feelings that might have inclined him to dishonor her and her

husband.* But even if we suppose that his curiosity was born of guilt — a far-fetched, unlikely hypothesis — then that would make Heeckeren an innocent dupe of a "fraudulent note" in which d'Anthès tries to divert his adoptive father's suspicions by asking for information about the seal. As for the existence of other certificates that supposedly would reveal Heeckeren's perfidious hand, let us recall that Pushkin spoke of the "same letter" and that Danzas described the anonymous letters as having "the identical content, word for word." If the "style" and "wording" were identical, we have to believe the same of the paper, the handwriting, and the seal. But above all there is this: whatever our opinion of Natalya Nikolaevna's intelligence, it is truly curious that she blamed the certificates on Dolgorukov and Gagarin. She was, after all, the best informed person. Much better informed than her husband — of that we may be sure.

Of Jacob van Heeckeren's countless Russian accusers, we, too, have made our choice in a Gotha of the imagination: Anna Akhmatova, poet of genius.

In dealing with the ambassador, Pushkin was eager to flaunt his own diplomatic abilities, demonstrating that he knew "what was going on in other people's houses": *"Le 2 de novembre Vous eûtes de Mr. votre fils une nouvelle qui vous fit beaucoup de plaisir, Il vous dit . . . ité, que ma femme craignait . . . qu'elle en perdait la tête."* The evidence against Heeckeren lay not in the content or look of the certificates but in the facts alluded

---

* His only less than loving words about her are reported by Sollogub: *"C'est une mijaurée"* ("She's a flirt") he said of her at the Austrian Embassy on the evening of November 16. But that was a time when he had to prepare society for the news of his engagement to "the ugly Goncharova" and was feeling generally spiteful because he hadn't had the chance to duel with Pushkin. We may imagine that when Natalie learned that the *chevalier garde*'s attentions to her sister were not entirely platonic, she would have been unable to conceal her disappointment, indignation, and offense, and would have been the first to claim that the marriage was a sop. Whatever may have moved him to call her a flirt, d'Anthès was not entirely wrong. But he said it *after* November 4.

to in those three deleted lines – crossed out, but not so thoroughly as to fail to pique our imagination. The second part of the sentence can be reconstructed to a fair degree of verisimilitude: *"que ma femme craignait un scandale* au point qu'elle en perdait la tête"* ("that my wife so feared a scandal that she was losing her head"). The first part is far more problematic: *"Il vous dit* [from twenty to no more than twenty-five missing letters] . . . *ité."*

What could d'Anthès have told Heeckeren that would have filled him with such joy as to convince him to unleash the offensive of the certificates? How many French words end in *ité*? Plenty: abstract feminine nouns like *fatalité, possibilité, sincérité*; participles like *convoité, débité, profité*; concrete nouns like *comité, cité*; and a few others. We can eliminate those incompatible with Pushkin's vocabulary or the context – from *anfractuosité* to *villosité*. A mischievous urge inclines us to consider those appropriate to a risqué situation, from *infidelité* to Catherine Goncharova's *virginité*, or for that matter pre-marital *maternité*, which many suspected when her unexpected engagement was announced. But none of these can be coherently inserted into the existing text, and Pushkin, we may be sure, would never have committed them to paper in any case. We must also forget about fresh insults directed against d'Anthès or Heeckeren – *avidité, bestialité, immoralité, nullité, pusillanimité, stupidité, vulgarité* – for again we cannot devise a sentence that makes sense or discern any connection between yet another expression of Pushkin's contempt and the ambassador's satisfaction or Natalie's fears.

Let's put our imagination to work. Natalie and d'Anthès meet, she warns him that her husband has received an anonymous letter,† he's furious, beside himself, God knows what

---

* Or: *un éclat, une histoire.*

† Why not? If the letter Pushkin thought Heeckeren had written was the "decisive blow," there could have been similar ones before it. Many spoke of other anonymous letters, a regular "hailstorm" of them falling upon the poet on several occasions.

he has in mind, she is dying of fright. *"Il vous dit que j'étais très agité"* (or *excité, irrité*). Too short. And too vague: specific facts, serious facts, it seems to us, are required to support such peremptory charges – a new and more violent altercation between Pushkin and d'Anthès, for example, but all that imagination and a dictionary can suggest is a very un-Pushkin-like *"Il vous dit que je l'avais maltraité* ("He told you I had mistreated him"), which is as improbable as it is vacuously generic.

We had better look elsewhere. "Furious at Natalya Nikola-evna's coldness . . . d'Anthès was so bold as to pay her a visit, but as luck would have it, in the hallway he encountered Pushkin, who was on his way in." Thus Arapova. Should we believe her for a change? Let's see if it fits: *"Il vous dit qu'il avait abusé de mon hospitalité . . ."* A little too long, and in any event d'Anthès could not have "abused" a "hospitality" that had already been denied him in what we imagine were no uncertain terms. Let us return to the facts we are sure of: the meeting at Poletika's house. *"Il vous dit qu'il avait commis une énormité . . ."* But would d'Anthès have described the trap he himself had set for Natalya Nikolaevna as an "enormity" – an act reckless beyond all reason? If anything, that was Pushkin's assessment of what he'd done, and Pushkin, on the contrary, sounded as if he'd witnessed the conversation between d'Anthès and Heeckeren on November 2, as if he'd been eavesdropping, lurking behind a door somewhere in the Dutch Embassy. So we will have to continue the hunt for the right noun that rhymes with our own stubborn *tenacité*.

Informing his mother of d'Anthès's marriage (which he had heard about from the Bavarian ambassador and from Heeckeren himself, Otto von Bray-Steinburg wrote from Paris: "They say that the young man was courting Mrs. Push-kin and that the husband happened upon a suspicious letter which, to avoid embarrassment, they claimed was addressed to the marriageable sister-in-law. The marriage seems to have arisen out of this whole entanglement." In *Mémoires d'un royaliste* Count Frédéric Falloux, who visited Russia in the summer of 1836, offered a more fanciful version of events, which he said he had heard from an "unimpeachable source": "One morning d'Anthès saw Pushkin in his room. . . . 'How is it, Baron, that I've found letters written by you in my house?' He held in his hand letters that indeed contained expressions of ardent passion. 'There is no cause for offense,' d'Anthès replied. 'Mrs. Pushkin agreed to receive them only so as to pass them on to her sister, whom I wish to marry.' 'In that case, get married.' 'My family will not consent.' 'Then make them do so.'"

Is this no more than a tall story invented by d'Anthès as a way of saving face, or the product of unbridled salon fantasies? Pushkin comes upon a passionate missive signed "Georges de Heeckeren" and asks his wife what's up. The panicky Natalya Nikolaevna declares that the love letter was actually meant for her older sister. D'Anthès, having been warned by Natalie, confirms the wife's story when the husband suddenly turns up, imperiously demanding explanations. His chivalrous lie now fluttering from his lance, the *chevalier garde* immediately becomes Catherine Goncharova's fiancé: *"Il vous dit qu'on avait fiancé d'autorité, que ma femme . . ."* Pushkin imagines that once informed of the event, the ambassador decides to provoke a scandal that will make this most unwelcome wedding impossible. But in that case the news brought by d'Anthès would *not* have pleased the ambassador. Ruler in hand, we find that the empty space will easily accommodate a negative: *"une nouvelle qui ne vous fit beaucoup de plaisir."*

Weary now, loath to go on, we would be only too willing to sign off on this last reconstruction – albeit fragile as a child's house of cards, an arbitrary foray into the unknown – were it not for what Alexander Karamzin wrote to his brother Andrei on March 13, 1837: "D'Anthès was suffering from consumption at the time, steadily losing weight. Old Heeckeren told Mrs. Pushkin that his son was dying for her and begged her to save him, threatening her with revenge if

she didn't; two days later the anonymous letters cropped up."
Two days later – the baleful November 2 again, but this time
with a completely altered script: Now the ambassador sees
Natalie and threatens vengeance if she does not yield to his
son, Natalie tells d'Anthès she's frightened to death, d'Anthès
goes home and tells his adoptive father that . . . But here we
are halted, because the little white space ending in *ité* seems
quite refractory to any mention of threats, and it seems
unlikely that d'Anthès would have informed the ambassador
of what the ambassador himself had said or done.

But even if we assume that the three now irrevocably silent
lines did refer to Heeckeren's dark threats, why did Pushkin
cross them out? Far from compromising Natalya Nikolaevna,
they reiterated her persecutor's infamy. Yet logic rears and
snorts: if there were any way of linking the sense of Heeckeren's menacing words to the sending of the certificates ("I
will dishonor you in the world's eyes," for instance), then
Heeckeren would have been turning himself in, signing his
own name to the defamatory and no longer anonymous letters.
Nor could the ambassador rely so blindly on Natalie's silence,
for she did in fact speak: she alone could have been the source
of the information reported so confidently by Karamzin. So
Pushkin must have been writing about something else. Once
again: *absurdité, calamité, fatalité, gravité, hostilité, identité,
malignité, opportunité, susceptibilité, témerité* . . . This is not
complete madness. What we would like above all to read
in the deleted lines are the feelings that dictated the poet's
accusations. For either it was only a suspicion, to which rage
and rancor gave the consistency of certainty, in which case
Pushkin reconstructed what happened at the Dutch Embassy
on November 2, using his imagination and contempt to recast
what his wife had confessed to him; or he really knew something that could not be revealed even to his dearest friends,
something that drove him to tortured circumlocutions,
deletions, corrections. Once again we have two counterposed
visions: a man in the wrong hurling accusations without proof,

blinded by his yearning to "cast into the mud" the man who was trying to lead his wife astray; a man in the right constrained to silence by another monstrous offense that cannot be confessed but that contains the evidence for what he maintains, evidence that he cannot and will not "reveal to anyone at all."

Yet all this cannot be mere accident.

A few missing words in one of Pushkin's letters and we find ourselves confounded, our hands tied, compelled to admit our impotence, silenced. We know the place, date, and time of his last duel; we know how high the sun stood above the horizon; we know the temperature and the way the wind was blowing; we know the size of the hole the bullet made in his black frock coat. But at every step we must also acknowledge what we do not know.

We sit in our box seat, in the dark, straining to follow truth's endless tricks and costume changes. Truth – that most famous and coveted actor *en travesti* of the human comedy. At the end of the show we applaud, which only confirms the abyss that still divides us from it.

With his death Pushkin lures us to a place where everything we know and feel sure of suddenly seems decayed beyond recognition, like goods long stored in a crumbling warehouse. A place where knowledge seems to shade into blackness. A place where the margin dividing cause from effect, once believed to be narrow and richly explored, becomes a boundless desert of inscrutable hieroglyphs, deceptive shadows, indistinct presences, mirages and traps.

Poetry's lesson. Mystery's lesson. Lesson of the sacred.

Perhaps *verité* itself is the word hidden behind that suffix so dear to our hearts. In that case, we would have to accept the most widespread reconstruction of the passage: "He told you that I suspected the truth, that my wife so feared a scandal that she was losing her head." The truth – nothing more or less. But what truth?

Having led our patient readers into a labyrinth whose exit still eludes us, we haven't the heart simply to leave them there. They are at least owed a guess, a conjecture. So here it is, based on the feeblest of clues and on what a faint, wheedling voice has long been murmuring from the proscenium pit: Pushkin had no evidence; it wasn't Jacob van Heeckeren who wrote or commissioned the certificates. Let us order one last line-up of the suspects, silent and dusty with the ashes of time: the conceited, arrogant Minister of Public Education; the sullen female Metternich; the Jesuit with the angelic look; the lame jester. If the choice must fall upon one of these four, we point the accusing finger at Pyotr Dolgorukov.

One evening early in November 1836, at a table strewn with the remains of a rich banquet and copious libations, someone passed around copies of the insulting forms that had long entertained Vienna: certificates of thief, miser, cuckold, lackey. The cuckold certificate immediately piqued the interest of the assembled company, a handful of young denizens of Petersburg society, and in an atmosphere of drunken, irresponsible merriment, the happy group began to draw up a list of fellow citizens at whose expense they might have a little fun. But it was quite a long list ("Morality in Petersburg is plummeting," Pushkin used to say, "and the debacle will soon be complete") and night was almost gone. Implementation of the delightful project had to be postponed. The next morning, as yet another idle, empty day began, last night's revelry came to Prince Pyotr Dolgorukov's mind. How was it no one had thought of Pushkin? Now there was a story! His wife was cheating on him with d'Anthès and he was cheating on his wife with his sister-in-law Alexandrine; d'Anthès was cheating on Heeckeren with Natalya Nikolaevna and on Natalya Nikolaevna with her sister Catherine. The haughty, puffed-up poet should have written a History of Cuckoldry rather than of Peter the Great. Pleased with his own cleverness, Dolgorukov decided to follow it up. Reconstructing the brief text from memory, he added the title of Historiographer to that of coadjutor of the Order of Cuckolds. He had no doubt whom to name Grand Master of the Order; Permanent Secretary required a moment's thought, but at last he settled on Iosif Borkh, whose situation offered the full gamut of wifely infidelity, from coachman to the Tsar. Now he needed a seal that would do justice to his work. He took a sheet of paper and drew a circle with a motley collection of Masonic emblems in the center. Let Pushkin rack his brains trying to remember all the teeming Freemason groups in Petersburg. To tickle the poet's curiosity further, he devised a bizarre monogram: the *J* of Jacob van Heeckeren entwined with the *A* of d'Anthès, representing the amorous entanglement that the beautiful, faithless Natalie now threatened to unravel. He completed his design with a cuckoo, the poor little bird whose name had become the symbol of the cuckold, and endowed the creature with an unambiguous pair of horns, lest there be any doubt about its meaning. Inspired now, he added a thick tail in the shape of a goose-quill pen just like the gift from Goethe that Pushkin proudly displayed on his desk. Let him write his treatise on cuckoldry with that! He handed his design to a servant to be taken straight to the engraver who had already served him with discretion and solicitude on several occasions in the past, then recopied the brief, defamatory text in fake, distorted handwriting. After all, why send it only to Pushkin? This certificate was a minor masterpiece; to keep it from Petersburg society would be a shame. Besides which, it would be nice to get maximum use out of a seal that cost money (the manufacturing cost, plus a generous tip to guarantee the craftsman's silence). He was out of paper. He took some sheets from Ivan Gagarin's study and went back to work. Eight copies, maybe nine. That would have to do, for he was tired now. Next he chose the recipients: friends and acquaintances of Pushkin – the first who came to mind, those whose addresses he remembered or had close at hand. Everything was ready by the time the servant returned with the newly

minted seal. Dolgorukov had him write "To Alexander Sergeevich Pushkin" on the back of each certificate, and a few
minutes later he sent him with the packets to one of the city's
many postal drops – not in the neighborhood, he specified.
And all this happened, as the hidden, evil designs of Chance
would have it, on November 3, 1836: the unexpected boot in
the rear from the god of quirks and coincidences was the
most Pushkinian thing that could have happened to Pushkin,
encouraging him to see a link between this coordinated
libelous attack and certain other events that had occurred in
recent days. In the winter of 1836–37 the Petersburg postal
system delivered other cuckold certificates to other victims of
this same band of merry men, which had finally set to work.
Those sheets wound up in the fireplace after arousing rage,
indignation, a few family squabbles – but no duels.

Admittedly, we have no proof. And we have nothing personal against Dolgorukov. Despite a long and often suspicious
tradition, we would have preferred to point the finger elsewhere, perhaps at one of those mentioned by Trubetskoy:
"Urusov, Opochinin, Stroganov." But we don't know whether
any of them, like Dolgorukov, was close to Heeckeren and
morbidly fascinated by his amorous travails, as well as friendly
with Pyotr Valuev (from whom Dolgorukov could have heard
about the storms raging in the Pushkin household), Lev Sollogub (from whom he could have known that Lev's younger
brother Vladimir was a guest of Aunt Vasilchikova in early
November 1836), and the Rosset brothers, whose address the
lame prince, a comrade of Karl Rosset's in the Corps of Pages,
knew very well. Nor do we know if any of them was a regular
visitor at the Karamzin home, as Dolgorukov was. But most
of all, the *bancal* was a perfectionist prankster. And Fate always
knows where to recruit its day laborers.

Anna Akhmatova also thought Dolgorukov guilty – but
in league with Heeckeren and d'Anthès. And she accused
him of something else as well. Wondering, as we have,
about the lines Pushkin deleted, she drew these conclusions:

Obviously, Natalya Nikolaevna could not have known that a document tarnishing her honor was being manufactured at the Embassy. To this I would add that Pushkin was very proud of his information and unshakably convinced of its veracity. This has to be understood as follows: someone witnessed the conversation between Heeckeren and d'Anthès; the *coup décisive* of the anonymous letters was decided in the presence of this person, who then went to Pushkin and told him everything, thus making it possible for Pushkin to sling mud at the ambassador, but clearly, for very understandable reasons, the person wished to remain anonymous.... We can speculate that Dolgorukov was playing a double game. Assume that he was the one who informed Pushkin, thus supplying him with the material for his letter.

Let us try to amend this interesting conjecture: to amuse himself further by fishing in the murky waters he himself has troubled, Dolgorukov tells Pushkin that on November 2 he witnessed a talk between Heeckeren and d'Anthès – a very important talk, he says, during which they decided to pillory the poet and his wife. We would then understand why Pushkin flaunted the certainty – I was about to say the presumption – of eyewitness testimony when writing to the Dutch ambassador. But how could Dolgorukov account for his presence at such a delicate conversation without arousing the poet's suspicions? Clearly Heeckeren and d'Anthès would have spoken of the "decisive blow" only in front of an accomplice, not a casual guest. Once again we cannot agree with Anna Akhmatova.

Alexander Karamzin to his brother Andrei, Petersburg, March 13, 1837: D'Anthès was a nobody when he got here, comical for his combination of lack of breeding and natural wit, otherwise completely insignificant both morally and intellectually. If he'd never gone any further, he would have been no more than a nice lad, but then he was adopted by Heeckeren, who, for reasons still completely unknown to the public (which gets its revenge with innuendo), being a very intelligent man and the most refined pig the world has ever seen, had little difficulty taking control of the mind and soul of d'Anthès, who was far less endowed than Heeckeren with the former and perhaps totally devoid of the latter. For some diabolical reason that eludes me, these two men persecuted Mrs. Pushkin so unrelentingly and persistently that, taking advantage of her simplicity of mind and her sister Catherine's appalling idiocy, within a year they had nearly driven her mad and destroyed her reputation. D'Anthès was suffering from consumption at the time, steadily losing weight. Old Heeckeren told Mrs. Pushkin that his son was dying for her, begged her to save him, then threatened vengeance. Two days later the anonymous letters cropped up. (If Heeckeren was the author of these letters, it would be an appalling and incomprehensible absurdity on his part, though people who should know something about it now say that it is virtually proven that it was him!)

From whom did Pushkin's close friends learn of the "perverse machinations," the "diabolical plots," the "disgraceful trap," when the poet was already dead and buried in the Svatye Gory cemetery? Mostly from Pushkin himself – via the copy of the letter to Heeckeren that he carried in the pocket of the frock coat he wore to his duel on January 27, 1837: his statement to posterity, the consecration of the future infamy of the ambassador and *chevalier garde.* But also from the letter to Benckendorff that he hadn't quite convinced himself to send two months earlier. Discovered among his papers on February 11, it was transmitted to the Third Section, and the diligent Miller quickly distributed copies to the murdered poet's friends.* The grieving widow must have told them

---

* It's possible that the rediscovery of this letter was the "lucky accident" that later afforded Pushkin's suspicions some "plausibility." We may imagine that Vyazemsky would have had a hard time believing that the poet would have sent the police commander such a violent indictment without evidence, which would have been demanded of him during the inevitable investigation. But Vyazemsky overlooked the fact that the letter was never sent – or perhaps he didn't know it then.

some things, too, and they would have reconstructed others from the memory of incidents they themselves had witnessed. It is worth recalling that these were people still stunned by the tragedy, tormented by terrible feelings of guilt for having laughed at Pushkin, for having failed to help him when they were still unaware of many things, not knowing that d'Anthès had resorted to deception to arrange his private talk with Natalya Nikolaevna, that he was trying to get her to leave her husband, that Baron Heeckeren, acting as pimp, was in cahoots with his adopted son. I am convinced that these were the "unknown circumstances" gradually revealed to Pushkin's close friends. More than this they didn't know, and by the time they found out, the era itself, despite its broad-minded morality, had turned its back in horror and disgust on the two men who had inexplicably acted in concert against a woman's virtue. That alliance seemed all the more loathsome and monstrous to those who guessed its secret motivation. The admittedly unsavory, ignoble, and inelegant acts of Georges d'Anthès and Jacob van Heeckeren – in their own way two "poor devils" madly in love – could therefore seem like a satanic plot.

When he left Pushkin on that Saturday afternoon of November 21, Sollogub went to Prince Odoevsky's weekly literary-musical gathering. There, as he hoped, he found Zhukovsky and brought him up-to-date on what he'd seen and heard. Zhukovsky hurried to his friend. He convinced him not to send the letter to Heeckeren. The next day he asked the Tsar to bring his fatherly advice to bear to stop Pushkin from fighting a duel over a matter of honor.

So it was that for the second time in as many weeks Pushkin had to change his course, call his own impulsive self to order, take a step back. The twofold retreat is upsetting. What stopped him on November 21? Zhukovsky's judicious arguments surely played a role: the scandal that would engulf his family, his children's future, his sister-in-law's painful position, the Tsar's disapproval and grief, and so on. Perhaps he also had some doubt about the truth of his own accusations. But there was something more as well, something whose roots went deep into a dark region of being far below the precincts of reason. Not fear of death, which Pushkin had always faced with icy resolution, but regret for life, which forced him at every pause to look back in horror and disgust on the road he'd just traveled. He had committed no crime, never killed or betrayed anyone, never broken his word of honor. What he regretted was something else: having lived and written poetry. Existence itself is the original sin that gnaws at the conscience of poets versed in the lightness and purity of nothingness. And now he felt a new regret, as he realized that "with almost supernatural and, so to speak, tangible force, he had become infatuated with death." He was aware of that almost palpable force, was drawn to it, but the deadweight of his mind kept him anchored to the earth. Weighed down by this immense burden, he was forced to linger in this world – so it is that wayward cherubim get trapped, wings snagged in bramble, when they pay their secret visits to human valleys. And during all that time demanded by life, most merciless of creditors, he felt a mysterious scent wafting around him, a scent he detected in much that he did, said, and wrote: the bitter odor of reprisal, repellent yet as intoxicating as a drug.

At a few minutes after three on November 23, 1836, after his customary afternoon stroll, Tsar Nicholas I received Pushkin in his private study at the Anichkov Palace. It was the second extraordinary audience the sovereign had granted the poet. Ten years earlier, on September 8, 1826, a courier had come to Mikhailovskoe to escort Pushkin to the new Tsar's Moscow study. "What would you have done if you'd been in Petersburg on December 14?" the Tsar asked. Pushkin, undaunted, replied with words that became famous: "I would have stood with the rebels." The meeting lasted more than an hour. "Today I had a long talk with the most intelligent man in

Russia," the Tsar remarked that same evening at Marshal Marmont's ball.

No one knows what Pushkin and Nicholas said to each other on that November afternoon. Two laconic witnesses tell us only that the poet promised "not to fight a duel for any reason" and gave the Tsar his word of honor that "if the issue flared again, he would take no step to resolve it without first letting him know."

At the Karamzins' Zhukovsky told Sollogub he could relax, he'd managed to stop Pushkin from sending the letter to Baron Heeckeren. And when Sollogub set out for Moscow at the beginning of December, his mind was indeed at rest. He was convinced that Pushkin no longer needed a second.

12

The Bold Pedicurist

Sophie Karamzina to her half brother Andrei, Petersburg [November 21, 1836]: I have another remarkable bit of news for you, about the marriage Mama mentioned: have you guessed? You know the couple very well, we've even talked about it, but never seriously: the young man's behavior, compromising though it was, nevertheless compromised only one other person, for who can look upon an ordinary painting next to a Raphael Madonna? Well, the painting in question has found itself an admirer, perhaps because it didn't cost as much: have you guessed? Well yes, it's d'Anthès, young, handsome, insolent (and now rich) d'Anthès, who is to marry Catherine Goncharova, and I swear he seems quite content, even gripped by a kind of fever of madness and merriment. . . . Natalie is nervous, tense, and her voice is strained when she speaks of her sister's marriage; Catherine is walking on air and says she still can't believe she's not dreaming. People are amazed, but since very little about that business of the [anonymous] letters has come out, the marriage has a very simple explanation. It's only Pushkin who'll wind up arousing suspicion and conjecture − what with that restlessness of his, those sibylline remarks he makes to anyone who'll listen, his curt treatment of d'Anthès and the way he avoids him in society. Vyazemsky says he seems more irritated than his wife that d'Anthès isn't courting her anymore. . . . Knowing that I'm writing to you, d'Anthès asks me to tell you that he's delighted and that you ought to congratulate him for his happiness.

Only to a few close friends did the Dutch ambassador speak of the "sense of moral rectitude that led his son to rescue the reputation of the woman he loved by tying himself down for life." In public he concealed the weariness and tension of the stormy days of negotiation, squelching his bitterness and contempt, striving to seem satisfied with his adopted son's impending marriage, devoting every spare minute not taken up by work or social commitments to feverish preparations for the big day. It was he who furnished (with exquisite taste) the bride and groom's love nest in the new house he was about to move into; he selected draperies, furniture, paintings, carpets, silver, porcelain, knickknacks, tending to every detail to make sure that everything was beautiful, costly, elegant, so that it would all arouse admiration and even a dash of envy, thus muting the clamor triggered by the announcement of this unexpected wedding.

Meanwhile, d'Anthès tried to act like a loving fiancé. There was more at stake than merely convincing the suspicious, gossipy social set that his feelings were genuine, for Catherine, still unable to believe what was happening to her, was racked by jealousy and doubt. Since Pushkin refused to receive him, d'Anthès was able to visit his intended only for a few hours before lunch, at Miss Zagryazhskaya's, and even then they couldn't be alone: the elderly aunt was a strict, old-fashioned chaperone. Given the impossibility of proving his love for Catherine with his most persuasive arguments – passionate kisses and embraces – d'Anthès resorted to written notes: "I love you . . . and want to tell you so out loud, with the sincerity that is at the root of my character and that you will always find in me. Adieu, sleep well, rest quietly, the future smiles upon you. . . . No clouds in our future, banish every fear, and above all never lose faith in me; it matters little who is around us; I see no one but you and never will; be calm: I am yours, Catherine, you can count on it, and since you doubt my word, my conduct will prove it."

In short, d'Anthès did the best he could, and for a while even took the ambassador's advice to avoid social situations where he might run into Natalya Nikolaevna and her husband. He had few free evenings anyway, since on November 19 he was given five more tours of guard duty for lateness. But neither his nor his adoptive father's efforts were able to silence public whispers.

Sophie Bobrinskaya to her husband Alexei, Petersburg [November 25, 1836]: Never since the world began has there been an uproar like the one now in the air in all the salons of Petersburg. D'Anthès getting married!! Now there's something to keep rumor's hundred mouths wagging and weary! Yes, getting married, and Madame de Sévigné would have treated him to the full torrent of epithets she once bestowed on the late lamented Lemuzot! Yes, a marriage set today that will not easily take place tomorrow. He is marrying the oldest Goncharova, ugly, dark, poor sister of Pushkin's wife, who is beautiful, fair, and rich in poetry. If you ask me any questions, I will reply that I myself have done nothing but ask questions for a week, and the more I hear about this unbelievable affair, the less I understand. It's a mystery of love, of heroic devotion, it's Jules Janin, it's Balzac, it's Victor Hugo. It's the literature of our time. It's sublime, it's ridiculous. A sneering husband publicly gnashing his teeth. A pale and lovely wife destroying herself with dancing that lasts entire evenings. A pale and thin young man laughing convulsively. A noble father playing his part, his twisted expression betraying the diplomat for the very first time. In the shadow of a mansard of the Winter Palace a tearful aunt making preparations for the wedding. A single white dress amid the strict mourning for Charles X, and the fiancée's virginal gown has the look of the lie about it. In any case, her veil hides tears enough to fill the Baltic. What we are seeing is a drama so sad as to silence even gossip. Anonymous letters of the most disgraceful nature have rained down on Pushkin, and the rest is vengeance worthy of the scene where the mason walls up the wall.* . . . It

* In *Maçon*, by Auber, libretto by Scribe and Delavigne.

remains to be seen whether heaven will allow a single avenger so many victims.

On November 25 Pushkin went to Shishkin's to pawn one of his wife's cashmere shawls – black, with a wide fringe, scarcely worn – for 1,200 rubles.

The magnificent sable coat the Tsar gave Amalya Krüdener, natural sister of Maximilian von Lerchenfeld and cousin to the Tsarina, the diamonds and emeralds of Lady Londonderry, who with her husband had been a guest in the city for some time, the virtuosity of the Belgian violinist Artôt, the new canvases from London that enriched the Hermitage collection (Raphael, the Carracci, Leonardo, Domenichino) – none of this managed to distract the denizens of Petersburg's salons from the French *chevalier garde*'s "unbelievable," "incomprehensible" engagement. Only when the restored and redecorated Grand Theater reopened for the long-awaited premiere of *A Life for the Tsar* (music by Glinka, libretto by Baron Rosen) did people find something else to talk about for a few days. Everyone who was anyone in Petersburg was there for the November 27 premiere, naturally including Pushkin, accompanied by his wife, Zhukovsky, and Alexander Turgenev. The latter, a friend of the poet's from the Arzamas days, had arrived from Moscow only two days earlier and had been in Paris a few months before that. He was therefore unaware of much that had happened and went to greet the Dutch ambassador in his box. Pushkin forgave him the unwitting gaffe, but must have confided in him later that same evening at the Karamzins'. The next day Turgenev wrote of the poet's being "concerned about a family matter"; subsequently he reportedly discussed that very matter with mutual friends, marveling at the hostility to Pushkin and defending him against charges of insufferable behavior toward his wife and blind, insensate hatred of d'Anthès.

"What in the world does he want?" many people close to him asked of Pushkin. "It's crazy! He's acting like a braggart!" Their reasoning was simple: by forcing his wife's overly ardent suitor to marry "the ugly Goncharova," Pushkin had humiliated him, made him look ridiculous; this represented full satisfaction. Some outsiders saw it that way, too: "Either the marriage is in good faith, in which case it eliminates any reason for vengeance, or it is a safe-conduct, and as such adequate punishment." One might be inclined to agree, were it not for knowledge of the poet's "disastrously passionate character." The rumors raging in the salons stung him like slaps in the face – that some serious, mysterious outrage had supposedly upset the Pushkins' conjugal life, that d'Anthès had to improvise an engagement to salvage Natalya Nikolaevna's honor. "Ruining his future for the love of a woman! What altruism, what self-sacrifice!" sighed a touched and admiring Petersburg. "Devotion or sacrifice?" the Tsarina wondered. Even Andrei Karamzin, sipping fine coffee in Baden-Baden, racked his brains over the reasons for the marriage: "What the hell is this all about? . . . Could it really be self-sacrifice?" Dazed public opinion, inclined to romantic fantasy as it was, began to see d'Anthès as the heroic champion of a woman's honor, a martyr to Love. And Pushkin couldn't bear it.

One evening as he left the theater with Natalie and his two sisters-in-law, the "Pasha with three pigtails" ran into Konstantin Karlovich Danzas, his former lyceum classmate, now lieutenant-colonel in the Corps of Engineers. The two friends greeted each other cordially, and Danzas naturally congratulated Catherine on her impending wedding. "My sister-in-law isn't sure whether she'll be Russian, French, or Dutch," Pushkin jokingly remarked. He was in a good mood that evening. Usually the mere mention of the marriage plunged him into gloom, and he would mutter menacingly, "You're the fellow who wanted her, Georges Dandin!" (Everyone got the nasty pun on "d'Anthès": Dandin was

Molière's fatuous, ill-starred social climber doomed to misery by a marriage of convenience.)

On December 1 Pushkin postponed until March repayment of 8,000 rubles he'd borrowed from Prince Nikolai Nikolaevich Obolensky at the beginning of the summer. He also owed his quarterly rent of 1,075 rubles, but didn't have it.

Winter came late that year. Unseasonably mild temperatures broke the ice on the Neva in late November – an exceptional event that had last occurred back in 1800. But the inhabitants of Petersburg had little time to enjoy the Indian summer, for a cloak of yellowish fog soon descended on the city, bringing many days of that bleak mixture of rain and snow that spreads bronchitis and influenza far and wide. "I feel so feverish and cold all over, I just can't seem to warm up," Pushkin complained one evening in early December, as he was putting on his coat and boots to leave the house of Nikolai Ivanovich Grech (where he'd stayed no more than a half-hour, but long enough for the other guests to notice that he was uneasy, glum, and upset). "This bearish climate of ours is so unhealthy. To the South, the South!" To the South – for a little warmth, a little respite from his ghosts.

On December 12 the flu epidemic struck even the Tsar. Georges d'Anthès fell ill that same day.

D'Anthès to Catherine Goncharova [Petersburg, December 22, 1836]: The baron wants me to ask you to save the first polonaise for him and also to tell you to keep a bit of distance from the court so that he can find you. I did not need your note to know that Mrs. Khitrova is Pushkin's confidante. It seems she still has the habit of sticking her nose into matters that are none of her business; do me a favor: if they mention this to you again, say that Mrs. Khitrova would do better to tend to her own behavior rather than that of others, especially when it comes to propriety, something

I believe she has lost all memory of long ago. . . . It's annoying that you cannot get the carriage for tomorrow morning, but since I think you know better than I what means you have for going out, I have no advice to give you on the subject. But in any case I don't want you to ask formal permission from your dear aunt.

Sophie Karamzina to her half brother Andrei, Petersburg, December 30, 1836: Coming back to the gossip, let me start with this d'Anthès business: if I told you all the rumors it would be endless, but since I'd have to add "who knows?" to every item, I'll confine myself to informing you that the wedding will be celebrated in all earnest on January 10. . . . Of Catherine and with Catherine, d'Anthès speaks only with feeling and apparent satisfaction, and what is more important, Papa Heeckeren adores her and dotes on her. Pushkin, on the other hand, continues to behave in the most idiotic and absurd possible way; he walks around like a tiger and gnashes his teeth whenever he speaks of the subject, which he does willingly enough, always glad to find a new audience. . . . For her part, Natalie is acting in a somewhat unorthodox fashion: when her husband is present she is careful not to greet or look at d'Anthès, and when Pushkin is not around, she starts up again with her flirty tactic of lowered eyes, nervous and awkward conversation, and he goes back to standing right in front of her and treating her to lingering glances, apparently ignoring his fiancée, whose expression changes as she suffers pangs of jealousy. In short, it's never-ending playacting whose secret no one really knows, and Zhukovsky had a good laugh about your claim to have figured it all out while sipping coffee in Baden. In the meantime, poor d'Anthès is very sick with an inflammation in the side that has frightfully transformed him. The other day he turned up again at the Meshcherskys' – very thin, pale, attractive, and subdued with all of us, as one is when one is very upset or perhaps very unhappy. He came again the next day, and this time his fiancée was there, too, and, more to the point, so was Pushkin: the poetic scowls of hatred and rage began again; black as night and with furrowed brow menacing like an angry Jove, he broke his grim, awkward silence only with a few quick, ironic comments and an occasional burst of demonic laughter: it's really very funny, I assure you! ... To change the subject, let me mention that the fourth issue of *The Contemporary* just came out and contains a Pushkin story called *The Captain's Daughter*. They say it's delightful.

A few weeks earlier Countess Bobrinskaya couldn't decide between the sublime and the ridiculous, tragedy and comic opera, but Sophie Karamzina now opts firmly for comedy. She was, of course, a grown-up girl who liked to spice her stories with a pinch of arsenic, often repeating the caustic remarks of her Uncle Vyazemsky, yet one cannot dissent completely from her assessment. What was now being played out before an attentive audience eager for salon drama looked more and more like farce. Pushkin knew well that the distance from sublime to ridiculous could be very short, at times imperceptible, and he had always been quite cautious in what he did, but he was now driven by an uncontrollable force, prey to a restless beast. "Full of hatred for his enemy and long steeped in revulsion, he could not control himself and did not even try. He shared his rage and hatred with the city and its salons." "He was disturbed, upset, painful to observe." Worse: he was risible.

As this sinister, hybrid tragicomedy rushed toward its denouement, it was not events but a man, "Russia's most intelligent," who was hurtling toward what he most feared and found most repellent. A long, ghastly fall, a long, ghastly, obsessive spectacle. We, too, would like to cover our eyes or avert our gaze – as some soon did out of offended morality – so as not to see this Pushkin, tedious as a cartoon figure, unremittingly comic as a masked man in a fairground play, persisting in his grimaces of poetic fury, snarling and gnashing his teeth, eager to regale anyone who will listen (and they are fewer and fewer in number) with every detail of the abject behavior of Georges d'Anthès and Jacob van Heeckeren, meeting more and more often with embarrassed silence and even compassionate little smiles. We yearn for the other Pushkin, the ironic, disdainful lover of refinement, master of the remote. Only in one respect do the two incarnations merge, the two Pushkins come together: in awareness of his own greatness. To anyone who tried to placate him by telling him that his friends and the social world were as convinced of his wife's innocence as he, that the young Frenchman's behavior was itself proof of that innocence, he replied that the opinion of this or that countess or princess was not enough for him, for he belonged not to this or that circle but to Russia itself, and his name had to be immaculate wherever it might be uttered, in whatever language – "in that of the Slavs, the Finns, the still savage Tungus, the Kalmucks, friends of the steppes."

He spent the last night of the year at the Vyazemskys'. The prince and princess had earlier refused to receive d'Anthès, but now that the young man had regularized his position in the eyes of the public, they had no choice but to invite him, as the fiancé of Pushkin's sister-in-law and close friend of their daughter and son-in-law. D'Anthès never took his eyes off Natalie during the entire night that turned 1836 into 1837, asking her to dance, entertaining her with witticisms of all kinds, drawing more than a few smiles. Meanwhile, the wrathful Jove was so terrifying to behold that Countess Natalya Stroganova told Princess Vyazemskaya, "My God, I'd be afraid to go home with him if I were his wife."

January 6, 1837: *raout* at the Austrian Mission. Long line of carriages at the entrance, fur coats made of the pelts of rare animals of the North hanging in the grand vestibule, thousands of flickering candles, discreet men in livery, buzzing throngs, sumptuous glamour, fabulous jewels, high-ranking uniforms, the steady, harmonious ebb and flow of men and women in motion like stars in a planetarium, parting and coming together in ever new and ephemeral constellations as required by the mysterious laws of salon migration. Elizaveta Mikhailovna Khitrova, spouting words of inspiration as she spills out of her clinging gown, lectures the fine-looking young Olivier d'Archiac on the superiority of spiritual over carnal love. Turgenev listens to the lofty argument for a few minutes, then joins a nearby cluster of gentlemen in tail-coats locked in animated discussion: Pushkin, Prince Vyazemsky, Baron von Liebermann, Baron de Barante. Were we to stop and lend an ear, we'd be treated to juicy news of Talleyrand and his yet unpublished memoirs, fascinating anecdotes about Goethe, Catherine II, Montesquieu.

How many things they talked of that evening in the palace on the English Embankment! Brabant, for instance, mentioned that (with the author's help) he would love to translate *The Captain's Daughter*, a truly splendid creation of the poet and historian, a Russian challenge to the well-deserved fame of Sir Walter Scott. The pervasive elegance, the brilliant, cultured conversation, and the welcome absence of the court (which otherwise would have monopolized minds and glances as always) gave Turgenev the momentary feeling of being back in Paris. Pushkin, on the other hand, had no need to glance outside at the fortress spire, the House of Peter, or the pale blue glow of the river firmly shrouded in its prison of ice to know that this was indeed Russia, his country, land that could be . . . No, wait. The rhetoric is getting out of hand: Pushkin had never been abroad, had never been given permission. "At least take a quick look at Lübeck, my friend. That's all I have to say to you," the cosmopolitan Turgenev had once replied to one of Pushkin's Russophilic rants. But it's also true that Pushkin was well acquainted with the history, life, and scent of places forbidden to him. Books and his own mind enabled him to travel, observing, comparing, deducing.

On January 7 Tsar Nicholas I put in an appearance, alone and for no more than half an hour, at Princess Marya Grigorievna

Razumovskaya's ball. He immediately noticed Natalya Nikolaevna among the crowd filling the white marble ballroom with
its vaulted sky-blue ceiling studded with gold stars. So it was,
that night and always: men would pick her out among a
thousand other women. He approached her, paid customary
homage to her dress and beauty, but then warned her of the
risks to which that beauty exposed her. She had to be more
cautious, he said, pay closer attention to her reputation – for
her own sake, of course, but also for the happiness and well-
being of her husband, whose frenzied jealousy was known to
all. Actually we cannot be sure of the exact date of this
conversation, which certainly came after Pushkin's November
23 audience with the Tsar. It could have occurred on any of
the many social occasions of the especially rich Petersburg
winter calendar, none of which the poet missed, for as Dolly
Ficquelmont somewhat reproachfully recalled, far from abandoning society, Pushkin "was bringing his wife everywhere
– to balls, the theater, the court." It was his way of demonstrating that he took no notice of the vulgar chatter of vulgar
salon gossips. But now the Tsar himself was discussing his
private life with Natalie, treating her to sermons on virtue.
When Pushkin found out, he felt he'd tasted the very dregs
of shame and humiliation.

The marriage which all Petersburg had doubts about (including the bride, who suffered horrible nightmares) took place
on January 10, 1837 – twice, in fact: first in a Catholic, then
in an Orthodox ceremony. "Count and Countess Stroganov,
the young woman's uncle and aunt, served her as godfather
and godmother . . . Prince and Princess di Butera were the
witnesses." The Orthodox priest Nikolai Raykovsky listed
Catherine Goncharova's age as twenty-six in the registry of
the Church of St. Isaac; in fact she was twenty-nine, nearly
four years older than the groom. Obeying the orders of her
husband, who showed up at neither service, Natalya Nikolaevna returned home directly after the ceremonies and did not

attend the reception. Pushkin lost many copies of his works that day, for Sollogub was far from the only taker of his bet that the wedding would never take place.

The Dutch ambassador yearned to establish at least formal peace between d'Anthès and Pushkin, partly to keep up appearances, partly so that the background to this much-talked-about marriage might finally sink into oblivion, and perhaps also because he'd been told by confidential sources that the Tsar had been most displeased to hear of the barely averted duel. Immediately after the wedding d'Anthès wrote to Pushkin at his adoptive father's urging. Now that everything had been settled, he said, it was time to forget the past. Pushkin did not reply. On January 14 Count Grigory Alexandrovich Stroganov fêted the newlyweds with a gala dinner. After the last course, the excellent wines having put him in a somewhat expansive mood, Baron Heeckeren approached Pushkin. With all the affability he could muster, smiling as broadly as he could, he told him that he was sure Pushkin's attitude toward his son would now change; henceforth, he hoped, he would treat him as a relative, a brother-in-law. Pushkin curtly replied that he would have nothing at all to do with d'Anthès.

Despite everything, d'Anthès brought his wife to see Pushkin. He was not received. He then wrote to his brother-in-law a second time. Pushkin took the letter to Ekaterina Zagryazhs-kaya without so much as opening it, intending to ask her to return it to its sender. But when he happened to run into the ambassador in Natalie's aunt's apartment, he requested that he take the letter back to his son, explaining that he would not read what d'Anthès had written and never wished to hear his name again. Striving valiantly to control himself, Heeckeren objected that he could not accept a letter neither written by nor addressed to him, whereupon Pushkin hurled it in his face, shouting, "You'll take it, scoundrel!" The ambassador met this insult in silence. But he now began to complain publicly about this man who was acting like a savage worthy of his African origins, a raging Othello, a man out of his senses.

On February 26, 1837, Georges d'Anthès was to write a long letter to Colonel Brevern, president of the military court that was trying him. Striving to minimize his own guilt in legal terms by demonstrating that he'd had no choice but to fight the duel, the *chevalier garde* listed Pushkin's many provocations:

. . . in Mrs. Valueva's presence he said to my wife: "Be careful, you know I'm evil, and I always cause pain in the end when I want." . . . After my marriage, every time he saw my wife with Mrs. Pushkin, he would come and stand beside her, and one day, when she remarked upon this, he replied: "It's to see how you are together and what kind of faces you make when you talk." This happened at the French ambassador's ball. At dinner that same evening he took the opportunity of a brief absence of mine to come over to my wife and propose that she drink to *his* health! When she refused, he repeated the invitation, receiving the same reply. He then walked away furious, saying to her, "Be careful, I'll bring you grief." Aware of my opinion of this man, my wife did not dare report that statement to me, lest we quarrel. Moreover, Pushkin had now reached the point of striking fear in all the ladies, because on January 16, the day after a ball at Princess Vyazemskaya's at which he treated the two women in his usual way, Mrs. Pushkin, replying to Mr. Valuev, who'd asked her how she could let herself be treated so badly by such a person, said, "I know it's not right, that I ought to rebuff him, because every word he speaks to me makes me tremble"; I don't know what he said in reply, because Mrs. Valueva reported only the first part of the conversation to me.

D'Anthès did not tell Colonel Brevern how he himself behaved with "the two ladies." Zhukovsky knew something about that:

"After the marriage, two faces.* Morose in her presence, merry behind her back. *Les révélations d'Alexandrine.* In the aunt's presence, affectionate with his wife; in the presence of Alexandrine and others who might talk about it, *des brusqueries.* At home, however, merriment and great harmony." In other words, d'Anthès treated Catherine affectionately in front of her aunt and in the privacy of their own home, but with bitterness and outright rudeness in front of anyone who might report his words and deeds back to Natalie. At social gatherings he was his usual cheerful, high-spirited self, but bleak melancholy clouded his blue eyes at the mere sight of Natalie. It was his way of showing her that relentless *amour fou* had gripped him yet again now that, as a relative, he could see her and be close to her with impunity. But the combination of languishing looks and discourteous remarks, of melancholy and flamboyant gaiety, was also a way of showing the world that he was not the coward Pushkin was calling him left and right, that he was not afraid of the jealous husband and was even deliberately provoking him, gladly accepting the consequences of his unquenchable passion. At the same time, according to Vyazemsky, Natalie "in her relations with d'Anthès found herself almost at the same point as before the marriage. Nothing to be guilty about, but a good deal of ambiguity and too much self-assurance." Baron Heeckeren felt fresh nibbles of jealousy and feared new scandals and disasters; whenever he saw Natalya Nikolaevna, he would shower her with warnings and advice, "paternal exhortations" to "break the deadly bond." Catherine suffered, too. She acted deliriously happy in public, but her sister Alexandrine guessed her secret pain: "She has gained in composure, I believe; at home she seems better than in early days: more calm, but

---

* Zhukovsky's notes don't say whose were meant. Most commentators claim the reference is to d'Anthès, but some have supposed he meant Pushkin. I myself hesitated for some time before ascribing the cryptic reference to d'Anthès, and for good reason: at the time one could have said it of either.

sometimes, I think, more sad than calm. But she is too intelligent to let him see it, and too proud as well."

An old serving woman who had once worked for the Goncharova sisters told the adult Arapova of an incident engraved in her memory: one day, realizing she'd lost the little cross she wore around her neck, Alexandrine Goncharova looked high and low for the precious object – in vain. The missing cross eventually turned up in Pushkin's bed, found by the servant preparing it for the night (Natalya Nikolaevna had recently given birth, and the couple were sleeping separately). For once Arapova's story seems confirmed – by Zhukovsky's notes (to which she could not have had access when she was writing); indeed, it seems to explain and comment on the enigmatic *"histoire du lit"* that the forthright Zhukovsky mentions laconically immediately after the passage about the two faces of d'Anthès. We have no way of knowing whether the "business about the bed" had the ticklish implications the servants ascribed to it, but we can well imagine that Heeckeren and d'Anthès might have dusted it off to show just what kind of a man Pushkin was and how debauched was the pulpit from which he presumed to preach and defame. In any event, open warfare was now raging between the Heeckeren and Pushkin households, a war of gossip, insults, and accusations.

And let's not forget the role played by the chorus, the denizens of the salons. Eager to glean maximum enjoyment from the many elements of the show – the Moor's wrath and the Frenchman's bravado, Natalie's tremors and Catherine's jealous glances – high society was in a frenzy, with everyone telling everyone what everyone was saying about everyone else, deliberately organizing balls and receptions to create as many opportunities as possible for the two couples to meet. It became a favorite pastime of a city now divided into two antagonistic factions, each loudly and fervently backing its own champion as if this were a clash of gladiators, a horse race, or a cockfight.

One day late in January, Pushkin met with Vladimir Dal, a young doctor and writer from whom he wanted a story for *The Contemporary*. Dal was enamored of the living language of the people, and Pushkin was quite fond of him; he loved his rich repertoire of proverbs and sayings, the notebook in which he jotted down picturesque expressions, his ability to mimic turns of phrase and to capture the spirit of Russia's most remote and unknown reaches. It was at this meeting with Dal that Pushkin first heard the word *vypolzina* (from *vypolzat*, "to creep or crawl out"), designating the skin sloughed off by snakes every year. "We call ourselves writers," he exclaimed, "yet we are ignorant of half the words of the Russian language!" When he saw Dal again the next day, he was wearing a black frock coat fresh from the tailor. "Do you like my new skin?" he asked with a laugh. "This one's going to last me quite a while. I won't shed it soon." In fact, he was to wear it for just a few days, and when he was compelled to shed it – arduously and in pain – it was stained with blood leaking from a hole near the waist.

On another day in late January, Pushkin went for a walk with Pyotr Alexandrovich Pletnev, the poet and professor of Russian literature at the University of Petersburg. They had a long, intense talk about Providence and its secret designs. "Glory to God in the highest and peace to men of goodwill," Pushkin commented, quoting Luke. He told his friend that he saw in him what he prized most in men: goodwill toward others, a virtue, he confessed, that he himself lacked and envied.

I managed to see Pushkin just once, a few days before his death, at a morning concert at Engelhardt's. He was standing at the door, leaning against the frame, arms crossed on his broad chest as he looked around with a discontented air. . . . He seemed to be in a bad mood.

I went to Pushkin's house shortly before his death. One of the things he touched on as we chatted alone about this and that was married life, and he was most eloquent in describing the bliss of a successful marriage.

Shortly before his death Pushkin pensively told a friend that the most important events in his life always happened on Ascension Day and said he firmly intended to have a church dedicated to Our Lord's Ascension built at Mikhailovskoe someday.

Contemporary memories, honed by pain and dismay, retain details that would otherwise be lost: the final pages of biographies are packed with random words and deeds amplified, magnified, raised to the level of omens of the impending end. This is only natural, for the death of a great man is a funnel of echoes, a magical magnifying glass. But of all the many witnesses to Pushkin's last months and days, we are most grateful to those who offer us the other side of the coin of his sensuous attraction to non-being, those who portray him as lucid and active, brimming with energy and plans. We are particularly grateful to Alexander Turgenev, whose letters from Paris, published under the title "A Russian's Diary," had given *The Contemporary* a glittering European touch. Turgenev had unearthed some documents on eighteenth-century Russia in the Paris archives and was now preparing them for publication in Pushkin's magazine. At the Demout Hotel, just a stone's throw from Princess Volkonskaya's mansion, he told Pushkin about his research and about his meetings with European writers. He talked about history and literature, recalling the past, commenting sharply on the present, never rubbing salt in the wound by so much as mentioning the subject everyone else was talking about. With Turgenev Pushkin was able to relax: alert, impassioned, amused, he managed to forget his everyday miseries.

Furthermore, Pushkin didn't just go "to balls, the theater, and court" in December 1836 and January 1837; he also spent time at artists' studios and bookstores, visited the Academy of Sciences and the university, went to Pletnev's Wednesdays and Zhukovsky's and Odoevsky's Saturdays. He continued work on his history of Peter I, which he called a murderous undertaking: the Great One's gigantic shadow darkened his path, forcing him to grope forward blindly; he would still need much more time. He began collecting texts and ideas for a critical edition of *The Song of the Band of Igor*. He looked for new contributors to *The Contemporary* and began some essays of his own for the journal. Commenting on Chateaubriand's having translated Milton "for a crust of bread" in order to avoid having to come to terms with the new rulers of France, he reflected once again on the dignity and independence of free minds. In a strange little work called *Joan of Arc's Last Relative* he invented a descendant of the Maid who in 1767 challenges the aging Voltaire to a duel because of a work demeaning to his ancestor's reputation. Once again the tenacious, unavoidable themes of honor and duels, but brightened by reason and humor.

Among the four hundred guests invited to the Austrian ambassador's gala ball on January 21, 1837, were Pushkin and wife, d'Anthès and wife. This was no place for literary conversation, and it was talk of quite another kind that was overheard by Marya Mörder, lady-in-waiting, spy, and our most diligent, invaluable informant:

D'Anthès spent part of the evening not far from me. I saw him speaking with great agitation to an elderly lady who, as I could tell by the words that reached my ears, was scolding him for his hot-headed behavior. And really: to marry a woman so as to have the right to love another, your own wife's sister – Good Lord, you need plenty of cheek for that! I couldn't hear what the lady was whispering. But d'Anthès replied out loud, with a hint of wounded pride: "I see what you mean to say, madame, but the fact is, I'm not at all sure that I've done anything foolish." "Prove to the world that you can be a good husband and that all these rumors are baseless." "Thank you, but the world has only to see for itself." A minute later I saw A. S. Pushkin pass by. What a monster! They say – but how dare I believe everything I hear?! – that Pushkin once came home to find d'Anthès alone with his wife. The husband, warned by his friends, had been looking for a way to confirm his suspicions for some time; he managed to control himself and joined the conversation. Suddenly he had the idea of turning off the lamp. D'Anthès asked him to light it again, to which Pushkin replied: "Never mind, anyway I have to go take care of a few things . . ." The jealous husband hid behind the door and a minute later heard something that sounded like a kiss.

D'Anthès's viewpoint and supporters were carrying the day: Pushkin was being turned into a character in a tale out of Boccaccio, a roving anecdote, like one of those stories that plied the roads in days of old, supplying copious material for ribald European yarns. The anecdote kept circulating for years, even decades. Frédéric Lacroix used it in *Les Mystères de la Russie*: "P. suspected that his wife was unfaithful. . . . Determined to ascertain the truth, he devised this stratagem. He invited the friend to dine. Afterward they retired to the drawing room. Two candles were burning on a little table. As he walked by, P. put one out and, pretending to try to relight it, extinguished the other as well. In the darkness he rubbed lampblack on his lips and, taking his wife in his arms, planted a kiss on her lips. A moment later he returned with a lamp, took one look at his friend, and saw black traces on his lips. All doubt was removed: concrete evidence of her infidelity. The next day the unfortunate husband fell in a duel, mortally wounded by his rival."

Alexander Vasilievich Trubetskoy told the story this way: "Returning from the city and finding his wife in the drawing room with d'Anthès, Pushkin did not greet them but went straight to his study; there he smeared soot on his thick lips, then entered the drawing room a second time, kissed his wife, greeted d'Anthès, and left the room saying it was time to dine. Immediately thereafter d'Anthès, too, said goodbye to Natalie, they kissed, and of course the soot on Natalie's lips came off on d'Anthès's."

Pushkin's body was not even in the ground when a student at the University of Petersburg noted in his diary: "At one ball Mrs. Pushkin had more suitors than usual. Pushkin noticed and sulked. His wife came up to him and said, 'Why so pensive, poet mine?' And he replied:

> *'Alas my dear one, for your poet,*
> *the great fast has now begun;*
> *I love you, shining comet,*
> *but your tail has too many by one.'*

I heard this from Kramer, who was there himself."

It would be hard to imagine a sadder, more sinister sound track than the unrelenting clamor that accompanied Pushkin's death and did more than a little to provoke it: "They say," "Apparently," "They told me," "I heard with my own ears." A loathsome, faithless requiem for a man still drawing breath. It would be hard to imagine a more merciless punishment for the author of a novel in verse whose music owes so much to salon *bavardage*, to fierce and fatuous social chatter. Too much in this story seems grotesquely plagiarized from *Eugene Onegin*, except that the poem's light touch of grace becomes real life's witless, leaden thump, and poetry's broad skies become real life's cage, prison, and torture chamber. Alexander Blok, himself suffocating in the old capital of a new empire, put it this way: "It wasn't d'Anthès's bullet that killed Pushkin. It was lack of air." Pushkin's oxygen was cut off by the airless stench in Peter's proud city, pervading the salons, the sites of power, the homes of friends. Always the same people. A narrow-minded province of gossips, vultures, voyeurs, whose unyielding, deadly rituals Pushkin not only declined to shun but actively, zealously took part in. It would be hard to imagine a more appalling way of killing oneself than by sinking into it.

At Count and Countess Vorontsov-Dashkov's grand winter ball, Pushkin thanked the Tsar for the good advice he'd given Natalya Nikolaevna. "Could you have expected anything else from me?" asked the Tsar, naïvely falling into the trap. "Not only could I," Pushkin replied, "but I must admit I suspected you of courting my wife yourself." Nicholas I tells us nothing about Pushkin's expression as he made this remark, but we imagine him grinning and self-assured, a victorious glint in his pale eyes. Once again we cannot be sure that this conversation took place at the Vorontsov-Dashkovs', but we do know that d'Anthès and his wife were present that evening, as well as Pushkin and Natalya Nikolaevna, and that the *chevalier garde* was more than ever in the mood for drollery. Helping himself at the fruit table he remarked, *"C'est pour ma légitime,"* emphasizing the last word as if to summon the very beautiful shadow of his second, illegitimate companion. He danced many dances with Natalie and positioned himself opposite her in the quadrilles several times, managing to chat with her briefly, asking whether she was happy with the pedicurist Catherine had recommended. "He claims," d'Anthès added, "that your *cor* is more beautiful than my wife's." It was considered inelegant to speak of a lady's feet, but the real outrage was that the French words for "corn" and "body" (*cor* and *corps*) are pronounced alike. Presumably d'Anthès had brought smiles to the lips of many a cunning lady in Paris, Berlin, and Petersburg with this leaden play on words.

Perhaps it even drew a laugh from Natalie. But not from Pushkin, who heard the lamentable pun from his wife. It seems Natalya Nikolaevna hadn't changed. She still told him everything – or almost.

Chaadaev to Alexander Turgenev, Moscow [January 20–25, 1837]: Insane as I may be, I hope Pushkin will accept my congratulations on his enchanting baby [*The Captain's Daughter*]. . . . Please tell him that what enchants me most is its utter simplicity and good taste, both so rare nowadays, so difficult to attain in this fatuous yet reckless century strewn with tinsel and mired in filth, truly a whore in an evening dress, her feet in the mud.

On January 24 Pushkin pawned his sister-in-law Alexandrine's silverware. But this time the 2,200 rubles he got from Shishkin didn't go to cover debts. Instead, it was earmarked for an important purchase: a pair of pistols.

Pushkin and his wife spent that evening at the Meshcherskys'. Arriving a little late, Arkady Rosset went to greet Meshchersky in his study and found him playing chess with the poet. "I suppose you've already been to the drawing room," Pushkin said to his young friend. "So is that fellow sitting next to my wife yet?" "Yes, I saw d'Anthès," Rosset stammered. Pushkin laughed at his obvious embarrassment.

Sophie Karamzina to her half brother Andrei, Petersburg, January 27, 1837: Sunday there was a big *réunion causante* at Catherine's: the Pushkins, the Heeckerens (still acting out their sentimental comedy for the public's delectation. Pushkin gnashes his teeth and makes his tiger face. Natalie lowers her eyes and blushes under her brother-in-law's lingering, burning glances – the whole thing's getting more immoral than usual; Catherine jealously eyes both husband and sister, and just to make sure that everyone has a role in the play, Alexandrine flirts steadily with Pushkin, who is seriously in love with her, jealous of his wife as a matter of principle but of his sister-in-law out of genuine feeling. In short, it's all very strange, and Uncle Vyazemsky says he covers his face and averts his eyes from the Pushkin household).

On January 25, 1837, Pushkin got together with Zizi Vrevskaya, who'd been in Petersburg for several days. He'd first met her more than ten years earlier in Trigorskoe, in the rustic little world, the frivolous yet soothing female universe that had enlivened his confinement in Mikhailovskoe. Steadily hectored by requests for money from his brother-in-law, in December Pushkin had asked Zizi's mother, Praskovya Alexandrovna Osipova, whether she would be interested in buying Mikhailovskoe: he said he would be happy to see the estate remain in friendly hands and that he would like to hold on to the old manor house, along with a dozen or so serfs. Mrs. Osipova was either unable or unwilling to take on the acquisition, but her son-in-law, Zizi's husband, seemed interested in becoming the property's new master. Pushkin and his friend now talked about Mikhailovskoe and its distant, joyous memories – until Vrevskaya brought up the rumors about Natalya Nikolaevna and Georges d'Anthès, echoes of which had apparently made it all the way to Trigorskoe. Pushkin needed no prodding. He quickly filled Vrevskaya in and felt the usual slight relief after the outburst. But he also realized that d'Anthès, as Vyazemsky put it, "continued to stand as a third party between him and his wife" – everywhere now, even in the provinces.

After visiting the Hermitage gallery with Baroness Vrevskaya, Pushkin went to see Krylov. He chatted with the elderly poet and his daughter, played with his granddaughter for a while, sang the little girl a few nursery rhymes. He left suddenly, as if waking from a dream.

January 25 was a Monday; some think it was the day Zhukovsky was referring to when he wrote in his notes, after Pushkin's death: "Monday. Heeckeren arrives. Quarrel on the steps."* Others have a different interpretation: on January 25 the Dutch ambassador showed up at No. 12 on the Moyka, Pushkin wouldn't even let him in, and the ensuing altercation was the immediate cause of the new challenge. It's not impossible that this is how it happened, but I am convinced no straw was needed to break this camel's back: Pushkin's hatred would have exploded even without the deadly spark of this most unpleasant visit, if indeed it occurred.

He shut himself up in his study. He took out the sheets of light-blue stationery he had put in a safe place and carefully reread them. Then he laid them out on the desk in front of him, took a clean sheet, and began to write:

Baron,

Allow me to summarize what has just happened. Your son's behavior has been known to me for some time and could not leave me indifferent. I resigned myself merely to observe, prepared to act when I considered it appropriate. An incident that would have been most unpleasant at any other time fortunately occurred to extract me from the impasse: I received the anonymous letters. I saw that the moment had come, and I seized it. You know the rest: I made your son look so ridiculous that my wife, astonished by such cowardice and baseness, could not help but laugh, and whatever emotion she may perhaps have felt for this great, sublime passion died in the most serene disdain and well-deserved revulsion.

I cannot resist pointing out, Baron, that the role you played was less than seemly. You, the representative of a crowned head, acted as fatherly pimp to your son. His entire behavior (rather clumsy, incidentally) seems to have been guided by you. It was probably you who dictated the vulgarities he has been uttering and the stupidities he has gone to the trouble of writing. Like an obscene

* February 1, the day of Pushkin's funeral, was also a Monday. Perhaps the ambassador made an untimely appearance at the dead man's home to present his condolences and one of Pushkin's friends treated him rudely when denying him entry. Or perhaps Heeckeren went to see Zhukovsky, whose normal gentle calmness failed him. By now it is impossible to say.

old woman, you lay in wait for my wife wherever you could, talking to her of the love of your bastard, or so he is called; and when he was home in bed with syphilis, you told her he was dying of love for her; give me back my son, you murmured.

You realize, Baron, that after all this I cannot allow my family to have anything whatever to do with yours. Only on this condition did I consent not to pursue this sordid story and not to dishonor you before our court and yours, as I had the power and intention of doing. I do not want my wife to be treated to any more of your fatherly exhortations. After his despicable behavior, I cannot allow your son to dare to so much as speak to my wife, let alone regale her with barracks remarks, feigning devotion and ill-starred passion, whereas he is nothing but a coward and scoundrel. I am therefore obliged to address myself to you to ask that you put an end to all these intrigues if you wish to avert a new scandal, in face of which I will certainly not retreat.

It is my honor to declare myself, Baron, your most humble and devoted servant. . . .

The letter he'd decided not to send in November thus proved useful after all. He made some changes, adding the allusion to the vulgar puns of d'Anthès (whom he had now openly called a coward on two separate occasions), toning down several assertions with qualifiers like "it seems" and "probably," and eliminating many passages. For example, he no longer accused the ambassador of having written the anonymous letters. This could be the confirmation we've been waiting for: Pushkin was no longer sure that things had gone as he'd been ready to insist with such assurance two months earlier. But one tiny detail prevents us from drawing definitive conclusions: in November he'd written, "I received *some* anonymous letters," whereas this time he wrote, "I received *the* anonymous letters." Was this because the matter of the certificates was now public knowledge, along with his charges against Heeckeren, and therefore no longer worth talking about?

That same evening of January 25, he went to the Vyazem-skys' with Natalie and Alexandrine. D'Anthès and his wife were there again. At one point, staring straight at his brother-in-law, Pushkin said to Vera Fyodorovna Vyazemskaya, "What amuses me is to see this man enjoying himself with no idea of what's waiting for him at home." "And what might that be?" Princess Vyazemskaya asked in dismay. "Have you written to him?" The poet nodded in assent and added, "To his father." She asked if he'd already sent the letter. Another nod of assent. "Today?" Pushkin rubbed his hands and nodded again. "We were hoping it was all over . . ." "What do you take me for, a coward? I told you before that it was all over with the young man, but the father's a different story. I warned you my revenge would set the world's tongues wagging." As the guests took their leave, the mistress of the house took Count Vielgorsky aside and told him what she'd just heard, sharing her anxiety, entreating him to wait for her husband and discuss the bad news with him. But Prince Vyazemsky came home very late that night, too late, his wife said, to do anything.

Jacob van Heeckeren received Pushkin's letter on the morning of January 26. He reasoned coolly, coming to a quick decision: "Could I let it go unanswered or lower myself to the level of such a letter? A duel was inevitable." "Challenge the author of the missive myself? . . . If victorious, I would dishonor my son, since evil gossips would go around saying that once again I'd been obliged to settle a matter in which my son exhibited scant courage; were I to fall a victim, my son would surely avenge me, and his wife would be left without support. In any event, I did not wish to rely on my own view alone, and so immediately consulted my friend Count Stroganov; finding that his opinion coincided with mine, I informed my son of the letter, and a written challenge was issued to Mr. Pushkin."

Heeckeren to Pushkin [January 26, 1837]:
Sir,

Not being familiar with your handwriting or signature,* I have consulted Viscount d'Archiac, the bearer of the present note, to confirm that the letter to which I hereby reply came from you. Its content is so far beyond any limit that I refuse to respond to all the details of the missive. You seem to have forgotten, sir, that it was you who withdrew the challenge issued to Baron Georges de Heeckeren and accepted by him. Proof of what I here assert exists, written in your own hand, and is still in the custody of the seconds. It remains only for me to advise you that Viscount d'Archiac comes to you to agree upon the place where you will meet Baron Georges de Heeckeren and to inform you that the said encounter can on no account be delayed. In the future, sir, I will be able to see to it that you acknowledge proper respect for my position, which no act on your part could infringe upon. I am, sir, your most humble servant, Baron Heeckeren. Read and approved by me, Baron Georges de Heeckeren.

Alexander Turgenev saw Pushkin at Demout's on the morning of January 26, "merry, full of life . . . We talked for a long time about many things, and he joked and laughed." When the poet took his leave, he promised his friend he would come to see him again. Viscount Olivier d'Archiac brought him the letter of challenge early that afternoon. He accepted it without even reading it. They agreed that the encounter of honor would take place the next day.

Late that afternoon Pushkin went out to call on Baroness

---

* In fact, he would have known both quite well if he intercepted Pushkin's letter to d'Anthès on November 4. But at this point we will not step back and change our story to claim that Pushkin sent only a *"cartel verbale."* Nor will we follow all Russian commentators in accusing Heeckeren of simply being his usual lying self. Aware that what he wrote to Pushkin would be widely publicized, we believe, the ambassador was striving to conceal from contemporaries and posterity his own decisive role in the November events, the background to the aborted duel, which was not very flattering to d'Anthès. In this he did not succeed.

Vrevskaya. He told her he was going to fight a duel. She tried to dissuade him: What would become of his children, would they now be orphans? "It doesn't matter," Pushkin flatly replied, almost annoyed. "The Tsar knows all about it, and he'll take care of that." On the way home he stopped in at Lisenkov's bookshop, where he and Boris Mikhailovich Fyodorov had "a long and interesting chat about the whole literary world." Back home he found a note from d'Archiac: "The undersigned informs Mr. Pushkin that he will wait at his own home until eleven this evening, and after that hour at Countess Razumovskaya's ball, for the person assigned to deal with the matter to be concluded tomorrow." Since it was already after eleven, Pushkin immediately headed for the mansion on Bolshaya Morskaya Street. There he would find all of Petersburg high society (except the Heeckerens, who had prudently decided to stay home) and perhaps, he hoped, a second. On entering the ballroom, he had a private chat with Arthur Charles Magenis, a counselor at the British Embassy reputed to be a loyal and honest man. He asked Magenis to serve as his second in a duel that was to take place the next day – actually later that same day, since it was now past midnight.

Did he turn to a virtual stranger because he no longer trusted friends and acquaintances? Did he pick a foreigner so as not to expose a Russian to legal sanction, a diplomat so as to ensure that his act would have repercussions in the milieu from which the insult had come? Or was it simply that Magenis was the first person he happened to run into? In any event, the "sick parrot" – as the Englishman was called because of his pallor and his long nose – said he would have to talk to d'Anthès's second before giving his answer. Taking his leave of Magenis, Pushkin exchanged a few words with d'Archiac. Someone noticed and told Vyazemsky, who immediately came toward them. Pushkin hurriedly said goodbye to the Frenchman and spent several minutes talking to his friend, asking him to write to Prince Kozlovsky to remind him about the

essay he was supposed to be writing for *The Contemporary*.
Soon afterward he left the ball. At two in the morning he
received an urgent note from Magenis: having learned that
there was no possibility of conciliating the parties, he was
compelled to decline the admittedly flattering mission Pushkin
had proposed to him.

January 27, 1837. "He awoke cheerful at eight," Zhukovsky
later wrote – in Russian *Vstal véselo v vósem chasóv*, a sentence
whose rhythmic stress and euphony of alliteration give it the
solemn ring of inadvertent verse, as if Zhukovsky's notes,
hieroglyphs of a man in a desperate search for truth, were
themselves now imbued with new peace and harmony – the
very peace and harmony that took root in Pushkin's soul once
he was sure he would duel with d'Anthès.

So Pushkin woke up in a fine mood on the morning of
January 27. After tea he wrote to Danzas asking him to come
over for a matter of the greatest importance. A little after
nine he received a note from Viscount d'Archiac: "It is indispensable that I meet the second you have chosen as soon as
possible. I will wait in my apartment until noon; before that
hour I hope to receive the person you will be so kind as to
send to me." Pushkin still didn't know if or when he would
have a second, but he found a way to use even that embarrassing fact to heap scorn on d'Anthès:

Pushkin to d'Archiac, January 27, 1837 [between 9:30 and
10:00 a.m.]: Viscount, I haven't the slightest intention of sharing
my family concerns with the idlers of Petersburg; I therefore reject
any negotiations between seconds. Mine will appear with me only
at the site of the encounter. Since Mr. d'Anthès is the challenger
and the offended party, he is free to select one for me if he wishes;
I accept him here and now even should it be his footman. Regarding
time and place, I fully accept his decisions. By the customs of us
Russians, this is sufficient. I ask you, Viscount, to believe that this

is my last word on the matter, that I have no more to say, and
that I shall move only to repair to the site.

At eleven he had breakfast with Natalie, Alexandrine, and the
children. He rose from the table before the others and began to
pace up and down, "unusually cheerful," humming, repeatedly
glancing out the windows at the Moyka. Outside, snow
sparkled in the sun. At last he saw a sleigh draw up at the
gate: Danzas, his left arm in a sling, an irritating reminder of
a battlefield wound. Pushkin went to the door, greeted his
friend with joy and relief, then withdrew with him to the
study. He explained that he *had* to duel with d'Anthès that
very day, in just a few hours, there was simply no choice –
and he still had no second. Would Danzas do it? Danzas
hesitated, holding up his injured arm, begging him to approach
other friends. The favor Pushkin was asking was too sorrowful. But he was at his disposal for any practical help. The poet
asked him to pick up the pistols he had chosen at Kurakin's gun
shop and gave him the money he'd need. They agreed to
meet again in an hour. When his friend left, Pushkin summoned Nikita Kozlov, a former serf from the Boldino estate
who'd taken care of him in his childhood and youth and
returned to his service several years ago. He had Kozlov
prepare a bath, requested clean underwear, washed and
dressed. Viscount d'Archiac's reply arrived a little before one:
Pushkin had to respect the rules, any further delay would be
tantamount to rejection of the satisfaction requested. The poet
asked Kozlov for his *bekesh*, the old one with the missing
button, and went out, telling the aged servant that he would
not be back before late afternoon.

Zhukovsky: "He ordered him to bring him the *bekesh*, went
out to the steps. He turned back. He ordered him to bring
his long fur coat and walked to a carriage for hire." In other

words, Pushkin retraced his steps – literally this time – a stunning surprise, since there is a Russian superstition that anyone stepping back across the threshold of his home immediately after going out faces inevitable disaster, and God knows, Pushkin was superstitious. Sometimes, when he was about to go out on important business, he would order the horses unhitched from the waiting carriage simply because a servant or family member ran back in to get something for him – a handkerchief, a watch, a manuscript forgotten in haste. And it is no myth that on the death of Tsar Alexander, when Pushkin heard of the chaotic hiatus during which the Decembrist revolt ripened, he decided to return to Petersburg from Mikhailovskoe in secret and would have done so – "I would have arrived at Ryleev's house just in time for the December 13 meeting . . . I would have wound up with the others in Senate Square" – except that bad omens convinced him to abort the journey he had barely embarked upon. Had Pushkin been completely honest with Tsar Nicholas I, his famous "I would have stood with the rebels" would have been amended by: "except a hare crossed my path and I ran across a priest."

And now, on the day of this duel, Pushkin goes back into the house to exchange his *bekesh* for a fur coat. Creating or accelerating disaster by his own hand? Not at all. He was going out to kill – to kill d'Anthès and with him the sullied, wounded part of himself, so he could finally begin to live again, putting an end to all truck with death. But all at once he recalled Frau Kirchhof's words. He was still a boy when he'd gone to consult her, more or less for fun, and the German soothsayer had predicted that he would soon receive unexpected money and a job offer. In the more distant future, she said, great fame, two exiles, and a long life awaited him, providing he did not die in his thirty-seventh year because of a white horse, white head, or white man. Everything she read in the cards came true, and even before turning thirty-seven

Pushkin was always on his guard when dealing with a *"weisser Ross, weisser Kopf, weisser Mensch."* Leaving his house at one in the afternoon on January 27, 1837, he suddenly realized that he was on his way to a duel with a man with blond hair (in Russian *belokury*, or "white-haired") who loved strutting around in the white dress uniform of the *chevaliers gardes*. So it might be a good idea to be especially careful. The sun he'd seen from the windows was deceptive: in fact, it was bitter cold, with a strong west wind. Better play it safe and wear his warmest coat. Otherwise an inadvertent shiver might make him miss his target.

He hired a carriage on the Nevsky Prospect and had himself driven to the Rosset brothers'. He remembered Klementy's promise: "If it comes to blows, I'm at your disposal." But the Rossets weren't home. He went on to Danzas's, a few hundred yards away, and asked him to follow him to the French Embassy. There he would explain everything, and his friend could decide. In Olivier d'Archiac's presence he read the copy of his letter to Heeckeren that he'd brought with him and explained with cold concision the facts that had impelled him to write it. "There are two kinds of cuckolds," he added. "The real ones know what they must do; the others, who acquire their status by dint of public comment, find themselves in a more awkward position. Such is the case with me." He concluded with these words: "Now I have only to tell you that if the matter is not settled this very day, the first time I encounter a Heeckeren, father or son, I will spit in his face." Only at this point did he nod at Danzas, saying, "This is my second." Then he turned to him and asked, "Do you agree?" Danzas said he did; he then discussed the duel's modalities with d'Archiac.

Pushkin went home to a silent, empty house: Natalie had joined the children at Catherine Meshcherskaya's; Alexandrine was in her room; Nikita Kozlov, assuming the master would not return before dinnertime, had withdrawn to the servants' quarters. Pushkin shut himself up in the study. He wrote to Alexandra Osipovna Ishimova: "Dear Madam, I am truly sorry to be unable to accept your invitation for today. Meanwhile, it is my honor to send you the Barry Cornwall. . . . Today I happened to open your *History in Stories* and became engrossed without meaning to. This is what writing should be! With the deepest respect . . ." He took a book, *The Poetical Works of Milman, Bowles, Wilson and Cornwall* (on the last page, where the titles were listed, he'd made crosses on Cornwall's five "Dramatic Scenes," which Ishimova was to translate for *The Contemporary*), wrapped it and the letter in thick gray paper, handed the packet to a porter, and told him to take it to Furshtadskaya Street. Then he went out. At a little after three-thirty he entered Wolf and Bérenger's pastry shop on the third floor of a building at the corner of the Moyka and the Nevsky Prospect, where he had an appointment with Danzas. Before long his friend arrived with a sheet of paper. D'Archiac, he explained, had insisted that the terms of the duel be put in writing.

1. The two adversaries will stand twenty paces from each other, each five paces from two barriers set ten paces apart.

2. Each armed with a pistol, they will be able to use their weapons at an agreed-upon signal, each advancing toward the other but never crossing his own barrier.

3. It is further agreed that once a shot has been fired, neither of the two adversaries may change position until the one who fired first has been exposed to return fire at the same distance.

4. After the two parties have fired, if there is no result, the procedure will begin again, the adversaries standing at the same distance of twenty paces, maintaining the same barriers and observing the same conditions.

5. The witnesses will be the sole intermediaries of any clarification between the adversaries at the site of the duel.

All Pushkin wanted to know was the time and place: five

o'clock, Chernaya Rechka, near the fortress commander's dacha. As for the terms, he listened to what he needed to know without even deigning to glance at the document drafted by the seconds. He drank some water with lemon. He told Danzas that he was carrying a copy of his letter to Heeckeren in the pocket of his frock coat and authorized him to make whatever use of it he saw fit if things went badly. It was about ten minutes to four in the afternoon when Pushkin and Danzas got into the sleigh that was waiting for them in the street.

13

Table Talk

Pavel Isaakovich Hannibal was a good-natured man . . .
Pushkin, barely out of the lyceum at the time, was quite
fond of him, which did not stop him from challenging him
to a duel because during one of the dances at a cotillion
Pavel Isaakovich stole young Loshakova from him. Pushkin
was madly in love with her even though she was ugly and
had false teeth. The quarrel between uncle and nephew
ended ten minutes later in conciliation, followed by fresh
amusements and dancing, and during dinner, under the
influence of Bacchus, Pavel Isaakovich made this toast:
Though it was just at the height of a ball
that you challenged Uncle Hannibal to a duel,
as God is my witness, Pavel Hannibal
would not ruin a ball with a row! . . .

Pushkin loved his friend Küchelbecker, a classmate at the
lyceum, but often made fun of him. Like many young poets
of the day, Küchelbecker used to drop in on Zhukovsky,
pestering him to read his poems. Once Zhukovsky was
invited to an evening at someone's home but failed to show
up. When asked why, he replied, "To start with, I had an
upset stomach the day before; then Küchelbecker came
over, so I stayed home." Pushkin found it amusing and
began hectoring the tiresome poet with these verses:
The night before I ate enough to burst,

and the cook made plenty of wurst,
so I had an attack of diarrhea
and what's worse, friends, kukelbekorrhea.

Küchelbecker flew into a rage and demanded a duel. No
one could talk him out of it. It was winter, Küchelbecker
fired first and missed. Pushkin threw his pistol down and
went to embrace his friend, but the furious Küchelbecker
shouted, "Fire! Fire!" Pushkin had a lot of trouble
convincing him that he couldn't, because his barrel was
jammed by snow. The duel was postponed, and the rivals
later made peace.

Pushkin and Korff were living in the same building;
Pushkin's servant, under the influence of Bacchus, burst
into Korff's antechamber to pick a fight with Korff's
servant. . . . Modest Andreevich came out of his room to
see what was going on and, impetuous as he was,
prescribed the *argumentum baculinum* for the man guilty of
fomenting the disturbance. The beaten servant complained
to Pushkin. Alexander Sergeevich was in turn incensed and,
acting in his servant's defense, forthwith challenged Korff
to a duel. Modest Andreevich replied in writing to the
written challenge: "I do not accept your challenge for such
a trifle, not because you are Pushkin, but because I am not
Küchelbecker."

One morning at exactly 7:45 I went into the next room,
where my major lived. I had just stepped in when three
strangers entered from the antechamber. One was very
young, slender, not tall, with curly hair and a Negro
profile, wearing a tailcoat. Two officers came in behind
him. "What do you want?" Denisovich asked the fellow in
civilian clothes, rather curtly. "You ought to know," he
replied. "You told me to be here at eight" – at this point
he took out his watch – "a quarter of an hour from now.

Which gives us time to choose our weapons and name the place." ... My Denisovich, turning red as a beet and stumbling over his words, replied, "That's not why I asked you to come. ... I can't fight with you, you're too young, I don't know you, and I'm an officer of the General Staff." The young man in civvies insisted, "As my companions will confirm, I am a Russian gentleman, Pushkin, so there is no dishonor in dealing with me." The evening before, Pushkin had been to the theater, where, as fate would have it, he had sat next to Denisovich. The play was lousy, and Pushkin spent the whole time yawning, whistling, exclaiming loudly, "This is unbearable!" His neighbor was apparently enjoying the show. Afterward Denisovich buttonholed Pushkin in the aisle. "Young man," he said, "you prevented me from hearing the play. That was rude and impolite." To which Pushkin replied, "True, I am not old, Mr. Officer of the General Staff, but it is even more impolite to tell me so here, and so pompously. Where do you live?" Denisovich gave him his address and told him to be there at eight. In the end Denisovich apologized and held out his hand, but Pushkin didn't take it. "You're excused," he muttered, and left with his companions.

In late October 1820, Colonel Fyodor Fyodorovich of the Uhlans, General M. F. Orlov's brother ... came to Kishinev for a few days. We decided to go to Golda's billiard room. ... Orlov and Alexeev were playing billiards for money and after the third game ordered a pitcher of punch, which was soon brought. ... A second pitcher had quite an effect, especially on Pushkin. ... He got very boisterous, strolled up to the table, and started disturbing the game. Orlov called him a schoolboy and Alexeev added that schoolboys had to be taught a lesson. All of a sudden Pushkin stepped away from me, scattered the balls, and told them where to get off. He wound up challenging both of them to a duel and asked me to be his second. They were to meet at my place at ten in the morning. It was almost midnight. I asked Pushkin to spend the night at my house. . . . "It's a dirty, rotten business," he said when we were almost there, "but what can I do?" "Simple," I said. "You're the one who challenged them. If they propose peace, your honor won't be tainted." He was silent for a long moment and finally said, in French, "Nonsense, they'll never agree; maybe Alexeev, he's a family man, but Fyodor never; he's always wanted a violent death, and dying by Pushkin's hand or killing him is better than staking his life against anyone else." I went to Orlov's before eight. When he wasn't there, I went on to Alexeev's. The moment they saw me standing there at the door they announced in unison that they were about to come and see me to get advice about how to resolve last night's stupid incident. "Come to my place at ten as agreed," I told them. "Pushkin will be there, and you can tell him straight out to forget yesterday's punch just as you have." Pushkin seemed to calm down. The only thing he was clearly sorry about was that the quarrel took place at a billiard table and in a fog of punch. "Otherwise how I would have fought! My God, what a duel it would have been!"

Pushkin and Lyudmila were taking a walk in a garden near Kishinev. The boy who used to stand guard during these trysts signaled them that Inglezi was on the way. He'd long been suspicious of Pushkin and Lyudmila and was trying to catch them together. Frightened not for himself but for her, Pushkin galloped off with her in the opposite direction, trying to throw the bloodhounds off the track by bringing her to my house. But it didn't work; the next day Inglezi locked Lyudmila up and challenged Pushkin, who accepted. . . . The duel was set for the next morning . . . but someone alerted Governor-General Inzov. . . . Inzov put Pushkin under arrest in the guardroom for ten days and sent Inglezi a note giving him permission to go abroad with his wife for a year. Inglezi got the message, and he and Lyudmila left Kishinev the next day.

Once he was talking to a Greek who cited a literary work. Pushkin asked him to loan it to him. "What, you're a poet and you don't know this book?" the astonished Greek said. Pushkin found the remark offensive and wanted to challenge the Greek to a duel. The matter was resolved this way: When the book was delivered to him, he returned it with a note saying he'd already read it, etc.

Usually we played *stoss*, *écarté*, and especially *banque*. Once, Pushkin happened to be playing with one of the Zubov brothers, an officer at headquarters. Pushkin noticed that Zubov was cheating; he lost; when the game was over, he mentioned to the other players, laughing and completely casually, that gambling debts in this kind of game were never paid. Zubov heard about it, demanded an explanation, and challenged Pushkin. . . . According to many witnesses . . . Pushkin showed up at the duel with some cherries in his hand and nibbled at them as his opponent took aim. . . . Zubov fired first and missed. "Are you satisfied?" Pushkin asked him when his turn came. Instead of demanding that he fire, Zubov rushed to embrace his opponent. "Let's not get carried away," Pushkin said, and left.

One evening at the casino in Kishinev . . . a young officer of the Egersky Regiment ordered the orchestra to play a Russian quadrille, but Pushkin, who with A. P. Poltoratsky had already agreed to have a mazurka played, clapped his hands and called out to the musicians to play it. The novice officer repeated his order, but the orchestra obeyed Pushkin. Colonel Starov watched the whole incident and summoned the officer, advising him at least to demand an apology from Pushkin. The intimidated youth was reluctant, saying that he didn't know Pushkin from Adam. "In that case I'll speak to him on your behalf," the colonel replied. . . . The duel was to take place at nine in the morning, a couple of versts from Kishinev. N. S. Alexeev was Pushkin's second. But a snowstorm and a strong wind made it impossible to aim. They decided to postpone it. . . . Luckily they didn't have to try again. Poltoratsky and Alexeev managed to get the rivals to meet at Nicoletti's restaurant. "I have always held you in great esteem, Colonel," Pushkin said, "which is why I accepted your challenge." "And well you did, Alexander Sergeevich," Starov said in turn. "I too must say, if the truth be told, that you are as good facing bullets as you are when you write."

There was a rumor he'd been flogged at the Secret Chancery, but it's humbug. He fought a duel over this in Petersburg. And this winter he wants to go to Moscow to duel a Count Tolstoy, "the American," the man mainly responsible for these rumors. Since he has no friends in Moscow, I offered to be his second.

Once, in Moldovia, he had a duel with a German coward they had a hard time convincing to fight. Goaded by fear, the German of course fired first; Pushkin advanced to his own barrier and, if you'll excuse the expression, took a shit. With this the duel ended.

I don't recall the details of the other duel – in Odessa if I'm not mistaken; all I know is that Pushkin's opponent didn't resist, that Pushkin let him go in peace, but this, too, in his own way, tucking the still-loaded pistol under his arm, stepping slightly aside, turning, and . . .

Pushkin used to carry a heavy iron walking stick. "Why

do you carry such a heavy stick?" my uncle once asked him. "To strengthen my arm," Pushkin replied, "so it won't tremble in case it has to fire."

An old friend of the poet . . . went to Vasily Lvovich's, where he found Pushkin dining. And Pushkin, still in his traveling clothes, told him to deliver a challenge to Count Tolstoy, the famous "American," the very next morning. Fortunately things worked out: Count Tolstoy wasn't in Moscow, and the rivals later made peace.

> *Now they have stepped five paces more,*
> *and Lenski, closing his left eye,*
> *started to level also — but right then*
> *Onegin fired. . . . Struck have*
> *the appointed hours: the poet*
> *in silence drops his pistol . . .*

> *Gently he lays his hand upon his breast*
> *and falls. His misty gaze*
> *expresses death, not anguish.*
> *Thus, slowly, down the slope of hills,*
> *in the sun with sparks shining,*
> *a lump of snow descends.*

14

The Man for Whom
We Were Silent

The sleigh set out toward the Neva. At Palace Quay it crossed paths with the Pushkins' carriage: Natalya Nikolaevna on her way home with the children. Danzas recognized her and for an instant hoped for a miracle – "but Pushkin's wife was nearsighted, and Pushkin was looking the other way." "You're not taking me to the fortress, are you?" Pushkin asked his friend as they drove onto the frozen river. He was joking, but in the bottom of his heart he still feared that something or someone might stop him. Petersburg high society had taken advantage of the unusually clear day to take their chic little sleds out to snowy hills on the Islands, and every time they passed a returning carriage Danzas hoped it would be friends of the poet who would get suspicious when they saw him leaving the city as the sun was setting and would alert someone, even the police. Many recognized Pushkin. "You're late!" Baron Lützerode's daughter called out to him, and he replied, "No, Mademoiselle Augustine, I'm not." From another carriage two young acquaintances, Prince Vladimir Golitsyn and Alexander Golovin, called, "Where are you going at this hour? Everyone's on their way home!" Only Countess Vorontsov-Dashkova, who'd also seen d'Anthès and d'Archiac heading for the Islands, guessed what was happening – but she didn't know "whom to turn to, where to send someone to stop the duel." Iosif Mikhailovich and Lyubov Vikentevna Borkh, the "Permanent Secretary of the Order of Cuckolds" and his wife, were also on their way back from the Islands. "*Voilà deux ménages exemplaires*," Pushkin commented when he saw them. When Danzas looked puzzled – why two? – he explained, "The wife is sleeping with the coachman, the husband with the postillion." They reached the commander's dacha in about forty minutes, arriving almost simultaneously with d'Anthès and d'Archiac.

The two carriages stopped. The occupants got out and followed a narrow path into the gentle fields ringing the dacha. Danzas and d'Archiac looked for a suitable place. They found it a little more than three hundred yards from the road, just past three lone silver birches, in a small thicket of pines sheltered from the wind and from the view of coachmen or occasional passersby. Pushkin's second asked him if he was satisfied with the choice. "It makes no difference to me," he replied. "Let's just try to hurry it up." The snow was knee-deep. With Georges d'Anthès's help, the seconds trampled enough of it to form a lane less than a yard wide and the necessary twenty paces long. The poet sat on a mound of snow, taking no part in the preparations, simply watching with an expression of utter indifference, breaking his silence only to ask impatiently, "So, are you finished?" They were. After pacing off the distance, d'Archiac and Danzas removed their coats and laid them in the snow to mark the barriers. They loaded the pistols and handed them to the rivals, each of whom stood five paces behind his own barrier. Danzas waved his hat. The opponents moved forward. Pushkin had stopped at his barrier, turned slightly sideways, and was taking aim; d'Anthès was still a step away from his second's coat when a crystalline shot rang out in the hollow, frigid air. Pushkin fell. "I think my thigh is broken," he said a moment later. The seconds rushed toward him, d'Anthès himself made a move in his direction, but Pushkin, lying in the snow, stopped them. "Wait!" he said. "I have enough strength to take my shot." D'Anthès stood motionless behind his barrier, turned slightly sideways, right hand on his chest, waiting for

Danzas to give Pushkin a second pistol; the barrel of the first, having fallen, was full of snow. Bracing himself with his left arm, Pushkin aimed, fired, saw d'Anthès reel and fall. "Bravo!" he cried to himself, tossing the pistol into the air. "Is he dead?" he asked d'Archiac. "No, wounded in the arm and chest." "Strange, I thought it would please me to kill him, but that's not how I feel." D'Archiac tried to utter words of peace, but Pushkin gave him no chance. "It doesn't matter anyway; if we both recover, we'll have to do it again." The snow beneath his bearskin coat was turning red. Twice he lost consciousness briefly. The seconds agreed the duel could not continue. When they lifted Pushkin, they saw it was impossible to bring him back to the road: he was unable to stand, and he was gushing blood. They ran to call the coachmen, and with their help took down a small fence to let the sleighs in. They gently placed the wounded poet on the seat. The sleigh's runners sank into the snow all the way to the rough ground beneath. Pushkin grimaced in pain with every bump. The carriage that had been dispatched to Chernaya Rechka by the farsighted Baron Heeckeren was waiting on the road. The two Frenchmen offered it to Pushkin. Danzas accepted without telling his friend whom it belonged to. He helped him in and sat down beside him. Casting one last glance at his opponent now receding in the distance, Pushkin said, "It's still not over between us."

Under his bearskin coat Pushkin was wearing the new frock coat, a dark vest, a shirt, and black trousers. How d'Anthès was dressed that day is not the pointless detail one might imagine. "It was only a heavy contusion that knocked d'Anthès down," Zhukovsky wrote. "The bullet pierced the fleshy part of his right arm, which he was holding over his chest; its force thus diminished, it then struck the button attaching his trousers to his suspenders." And Sophie Karamzina: "The bullet passed through his arm, wounding only the flesh, and stopped at belly height — he was saved by a button on his clothes, suffering only a slight bruise on his chest." The life-saving button is also mentioned by Vyazemsky, Danzas, and the ambassadors of Prussia and Saxony. It seems as clear as day: Fate blocked Pushkin's bullet with the makeshift shield of a little metal disk.* Apparently the wayward goddess, ever a friend to d'Anthès, was also miffed at the Russian poet for having violated one of her minor commandments by returning home to change his coat. We would also be willing to wager that d'Anthès was wearing a flannel undershirt beneath the coat and vest of his *chevalier garde* uniform on that frigid January afternoon – minus 5°C, according to the thermometer. But his attire gave rise to fresh suspicions and ingenious new deductions in the twentieth century.

In an article published in *Siberian Lights* more than fifty years ago, the engineer M. Komar expressed doubt that it was possible for a bullet a centimeter and a half in diameter with a muzzle velocity of about 300 meters per second to "ricochet like a Ping-Pong ball" against a button. The button, he felt, should have shattered, its deadly shards ripping the Frenchman's chest. The "despicable executioner hired by Nicholas's aristocratic lackeys and Nicholas himself," Komar concluded, "went to the duel wearing a breastplate . . . of steel scales or plates under his uniform" – one of those nineteenth-century coats of mail, a device available in Berlin at the time. The clever Heeckeren, it seems, had ordered the precious item back on November 5, 1836, after the first challenge, and had requested the two-week delay precisely so as to allow time to take delivery.

In 1950 Ivan Rakhillo recalled the sensational tale he'd heard in the early 1930s from a Siberian man of letters: he

---

* The oblique, rising trajectory, the piercing of several layers of cloth and especially of the fleshy part of the forearm protecting his rival's chest, robbed Pushkin's bullet of its impact, halting its no longer lethal journey when it collided with a button on d'Anthès's overcoat, vest, or suspenders.

had chanced to discover in an old registry that a messenger from the Dutch ambassador had arrived in Arkhangelsk in November 1836 and that the mysterious traveler spent a few days on Armorers' Street – apparently to order the treacherous cuirass, which he then brought back to Petersburg.

"Duel or homicide?" one V. Safronov wondered in the pages of *Neva* in 1963. Homicide, he replied – since apart from the fact that the pistols used by the opponents "might have been . . . of different calibers,"* d'Anthès was wearing a single-breasted jacket; the row of buttons was therefore nowhere near the point where his body was hit, whereas the buttons on his suspenders – flimsy objects of horn, wood, or fabric – could not have resisted the impact of lead, and even if the bullet had ricocheted off a suspender button, small traces of it would have remained on d'Anthès's clothes, and "none of the contemporaries mentions that."† Conclusion: The chest of the "Russian Army's hireling" was shielded by a "protective device," a coat of thin metallic plates.

Tass spread the word to every corner of the Soviet Union: "Experts Accuse d'Anthès." In *The Criminal Will Out*, a small book nearly a million copies of which were printed in 1963, A. Vaksberg triumphantly declared: "Last winter the mystery of Pushkin's death was definitively resolved. . . . After experiments and analysis of numerous original documents (more than fifteen hundred) as well as court records in the archives, criminologists were able to review all the particulars of d'Anthès's bloody crime in detail." In fact, more reliable Russian scholars promptly rejected the hypothesis of Safronov and the imaginary committee of experts. Three genuine

* He forgot that ensuring that the weapons were of equal power was one of the prime tasks of the seconds in any duel, and Danzas himself recalled that Pushkin's and d'Anthès's pistols were "absolutely the same."
† And of course we can imagine the "contemporaries" in question – Sophie Karamzina, Zhukovsky, Prince Vyazemsky, Danzas, the Barons von Liebermann and von Lützerode – suddenly ballistics experts all, poring over d'Anthès's clothing, carefully scrutinizing the material in search of revealing clues. Presumably in a drawing room at the Dutch Embassy.

experts declared that while d'Anthès was of course capable of any and every infamy, "one thing he couldn't do was wear armor to a duel: the slightest wound to his neck or shoulder would have resulted in his disgraceful unmasking." To argue otherwise "requires utter lack of knowledge and above all lack of understanding of the way of life and traditions of that milieu."

The dust seemed to have settled when, in 1969, concluding a long essay on Pushkin's death, M. Yashin established the truth of the disputed question once and for all: the Horse Guards wore two types of regulation jackets, both of green cloth with silver buttons. The first type, double-breasted, had two rows of six buttons each, the second, longer and single-breasted, one row of nine buttons. If d'Anthès was wearing the double-breasted jacket on January 27, 1837, it is quite clear how the bullet struck his forearm and was halted by the fateful button, leaving only a slight contusion. "For the moment," Yashin nevertheless concluded, "there is no solid basis for wholly ruling out the hypothesis that the idea of wearing something like a cuirass on the day of the duel might have occurred to d'Anthès." He added that there would have been no need to go to Berlin or even Arkhangelsk to acquire such an object: old archival documents revealed that it was precisely in 1835 and 1836 that the Horse Guards experimented with body armor invented by Dr. Popandopoulo-Vreto.

Dr. Popandopoulo-Vreto: delightful! Amateur surgeon, engineer, inventor, arms dealer, charlatan. Of Greek and Patagonian extraction, native of Gogol's baroque and merry lands. We dissolve in laughter, unable to read on. And once again we marvel at the bias that has tainted and so often vitiated the thousands of pages written about Pushkin's death in Russia in recent decades – and not only by weekend sleuths. But let us end by asking ourselves whether it is not perhaps unfair to laugh at the Yashins and their ilk, for behind the depressing ideological clichés and the massive ignorance – of the times, of the era's customs and rituals, of its second (and sometimes primary) language: French – behind all the arcane conjectures of murky plots and surreptitious shields, you sense a genuine, throbbing hatred. Should we not instead admire a land that never stops mourning its poets?

Prince and Princess Vyazemsky recall: "Pushkin did not conceal the impending duel from his wife. He asked her whom she would weep for. 'For the one who is killed,' Natalya Nikolaevna replied."

Pushkin bore his pain with courage. On the way home he tried to chat and even joke with Danzas. But the pangs in his abdomen were rising in frequency and intensity, and he began to realize that the wound was serious. "I'm afraid it's like Shcherbachev's," he said. Mikhail Shcherbachev had fought a duel with Rufin Dorokhov in 1819; a bullet punctured his abdomen, and the young man died after two days of appalling agony. But Pushkin's main concern was for his wife. He asked Danzas not to frighten her if she was home when they arrived, to keep silent about his true condition. The ambassador's carriage reached No. 12 on the Moyka at about six in the evening. Danzas rushed into the main-floor apartment and asked for the mistress of the house. He was told she was not home. Breathless, he quickly explained what had happened and sent some servants out to the street; he then walked unannounced into Natalya Nikolaevna's boudoir – or more exactly into her screened-off corner of the conjugal bedroom. He found her with Alexandrine, told her that her husband had fought a duel with d'Anthès but that there was no cause for alarm: he'd been slightly wounded in the side, no more.
    Meanwhile, Nikita Kozlov helped Pushkin out of the carriage, mounted the short flight of steps with his master in his arms, and entered the house. "You must be sorry to have to carry me like this, aren't you?" Pushkin asked. Natalie screamed and fainted when she saw her bleeding husband in the hallway. Pushkin insisted on being brought to the study

and ordered the sofa prepared for the night. He took off his
own bloodstained clothes, put on clean linen, and lay down.
Only then did he send for Natalie. Having come to, she had
tried to enter, but Pushkin had stopped her with a robust
"N'entrez pas!" She had waited in the drawing room, wringing
her hands, accompanied by her sister and Pletnev, who had
come to his friend's house driven by a gnawing foreboding even
while expecting him for the usual Wednesday get-together.

"Calm down, none of this is your fault" were Pushkin's
first words to his wife. Meanwhile, Danzas was out looking
for a doctor. Neither Arendt nor Salomon nor Person was
home. Person's wife advised him to try the nearby orphanage.
Dr. Wilhelm von Scholtz was on his way out when Danzas
arrived. Scholtz was an obstetrician but promised to find someone more skilled in treating wounds, and a few minutes later
arrived at the house on the Moyka with Zadler, who was on
his way back from the Dutch Embassy, where he'd just seen
to d'Anthès's arm. After examining Pushkin, Zadler left to
get proper instruments: he thought an operation might prove
necessary.

Pushkin was now alone with Scholtz. "What do you think
of this wound?" he asked. "Just after the shot I felt a heavy
blow in the side and a burning pang in the gut; I lost a lot
of blood on the road. Tell me the truth, what do you think?"
"I can't tell you it's not serious." "Fatal?" "I feel it's my
duty to tell you: I can't rule that out. But let's hear what
Arendt and Salomon have to say; they're on their way." *"Je
vous remercie, vous avez agi en honnête homme envers moi; il
faut que j'arrange ma maison."** A few minutes later: "I'm
losing a lot of blood, don't you think?" Scholtz examined the
wound – the bleeding seemed to have stopped – and applied
a new cold compress. He asked Pushkin if he wanted to see
any of his closest friends. "Farewell, friends," Pushkin said
softly, glancing around, perhaps taking leave of his books.

---

* "Thank you for being honest with me; I must put my affairs in order."

"Do you think I have less than an hour?" he asked. "Oh no," the flustered obstetrician stammered, "I just thought you might like to see some of them. Mr. Pletnev is here." "All right, but I'd like Zhukovsky. Give me some water, I feel sick to my stomach." After checking Pushkin's pulse – "feeble and rapid, as during internal bleeding" – Scholtz left the study to ask for water and to convey the patient's wish.

As Dr. Scholtz left, History and Legend slipped unseen into the rectangular room crowded with books, books covering the walls all the way to the ceiling and piled on a shelf shielding the sofa from view. Impatiently awaiting the poet's corpse, they began even now to take possession of his words and deeds. Even a chronicler as sober as Alexander Turgenev, some of whose letters were written at a table in the drawing room while Pushkin lay dying next door, had Russia and posterity partly in mind as his audience. On at least one point these letters and those written soon afterward by Zhukovsky and Prince and Princess Vyazemsky differ from the testimony of Spassky, the doctor who arrived shortly after seven that evening, and from the recollections of Danzas. And the point is an important one. According to Turgenev (and Zhukovsky and the Vyazemskys), Pushkin accepted the sacraments *after* Tsar Nicholas I sent Dr. Arendt to urge him to die a Christian. Spassky and Danzas, however, say that Pushkin confessed and took communion *before* receiving the sovereign's message. We are inclined to the latter version, since we would like for once to afford Pushkin the freedom to decide for himself, especially in a matter so delicate. But also because we take irresistible pleasure in imagining the Tsar's historic message being received after the fact by a soul already saved. And since no one had the heart to tell him the truth, the Tsar could say in good faith, "We managed to convince him to die a Christian," thus inventing an edifying fable for all good subjects, one that spread far and wide, crowding out the truth.

*

Zadler returned to No. 12 on the Moyka almost simultaneously with the arrival of Dr. Salomon and Nikolai Fyodorovich Arendt, Russia's most famous doctor, physician to the court. Arendt confirmed his predecessors' prognosis: there was no hope of recovery; Pushkin might not survive the night. He felt that surgery would be futile and might even aggravate the internal bleeding; he prescribed ice packs, sedatives, purgatives. Next to arrive was Spassky, the Pushkins' family doctor. "Yes, it's bad," the poet said when he saw him come in, waving him away when Spassky uttered a few words of hope. There was no need to lie to him, he knew the truth. Arendt left the house. "At the request of relatives and friends" Spassky asked Pushkin if he wanted to receive the sacraments. He did. "Whom do you want us to call?" "The nearest priest, whoever it is." He remembered that early that morning he'd received the announcement of the death of young Nikolai Grech. "If you see the father," he told Spassky, "say hello to him for me and tell him I deeply share his grief." The elderly Father Pyotr arrived from the little church at Royal Stables Square, close by the Moyka. Arendt came back. "The patient confessed and took communion." When Spassky returned to the study, Pushkin asked him how his wife was holding up. The doctor put his mind at rest: Natalya Nikolaevna was calmer. "Poor thing," Pushkin said, "she's suffering even though she's not to blame and may suffer even more in the public's judgment." He was wrestling with two conflicting feelings: he wanted his doctors and friends to conceal the gravity of his condition from Natalya Nikolaevna, yet he feared that his wife might harbor hope that could be mistaken for indifference: if she was seen to be calm at a time like this, he said, society would tear her apart. "Poor girl, poor girl," he kept saying. He asked to see Arendt. "Ask the Tsar to pardon me," he implored him, "and ask him to pardon Danzas. He's been a brother to me. He's not to blame, I ran into him on the street and made him come with me." Once again taking his leave, Arendt promised to come back later. In the meantime, he turned Pushkin over to Spassky's care. "The patient's exceptional presence of mind never deserted him. Now and then he quietly complained of the pain in his stomach and lost consciousness for a few seconds at a time." Shortly after eleven Arendt returned, bringing Pushkin a short, hurriedly written penciled note from the Tsar: "If God wills that we do not meet again upon this earth, accept my pardon and my advice to take communion and die a Christian; do not worry for your wife and children. They will be like children to me, and I shall take them under my protection." Spassky, back at Pushkin's bedside, asked if there were any arrangements he wanted made. "Everything goes to my wife and children." He requested that Spassky bring him a piece of paper with Russian writing on it — the doctor recognized the poet's hand — and burn it. Then he said, "Call Danzas." He asked to be alone with his friend. He dictated a list of personal debts for which there were no letters of liability or other documentation, then signed it with an unsteady hand. Danzas murmured that he would like to avenge him by challenging d'Anthès to a duel. Pushkin flatly forbade him. He let his wife come in only a few times, and for a very few minutes. Natalie veered between outbursts of hysterical despair and moments of frenzied hope when she kept repeating, "He's not going to die, I know he won't die." Alexandrine and their elderly aunt, along with Princess Vyazemskaya, made sure she was never alone, staying up all night with her on the sofas in the drawing room; Danzas and Vyazemsky made do in the hallway. Other friends rushed to the house when they heard the news and left very late: Zhukovsky, Vielgorsky, Prince Meshchersky, Valuev, Turgenev. But none of them was allowed to see the patient. Spassky stayed with Pushkin. In a quiet moment the poet told him that the number 6 had always been bad luck for him: "His misfortune began in 1836, when he turned 36 and his wife was 24 (2 + 4 = 6); in the sixth chapter of *Eugene Onegin* there was a kind of presage of his own death, and so on. In other words, as he lay dying Pushkin himself thought of the sad parallel between him and Lenski." The pain worsened toward four in the morning, his moans turning into hoarser, wilder cries. "Why such torture?" he asked Spassky. "Without this torment I would die in peace." They had to summon Arendt, who prescribed an enema; the highly painful procedure worsened the patient's suffering. Several times Pushkin's convulsions nearly threw him from the sofa, his forehead bathed in cold sweat, eyes seemingly about to pop from their sockets. During the night he decided to kill himself. He asked Nikita Kozlov to bring him the case with the pistols. The servant obeyed but alerted Danzas, and the pistols, already hidden under the sheet, were taken away. When the sky began to lighten, Pushkin asked for his wife. Natalie was sunk in a kind of lethargic slumber just when the most wrenching cries came from the study; she heard only the last scream, which they told her had come from the street. Pushkin now gave his young wife his last advice: "Go to the country, wear mourning for two years, then get married again, but not to a scoundrel." He wanted to say goodbye to his friends. Zhukovsky, the Vyazemskys, Vielgorsky, Turgenev, Danzas came into the study one by one. A few words of farewell, a feeble handshake. Then Pushkin wordlessly asked to be left alone. Zhukovsky asked him, "If I see the Tsar, what do you want me to tell him?" "Tell him I'm sorry I'm dying because it leaves me no way of expressing all my gratitude; I would have been completely his." He asked for Pletnev and the Karamzins. Ekaterina Andreevna Karamzina was sent for. He asked to see his children. They were led into the study still half asleep. Pushkin looked at them, blessed them, touched the back of his now cold hand to the mouths of Masha, Grisha, Sasha, Tasha. His wife stubbornly refused to believe what was happening. "*Quelque chose me dit qu'il vivra,*" she whispered as people came out of the study, eyes reddened, distress on their faces. Mrs. Karamzin arrived. This farewell, too, lasted little more than a minute. Moving away from the sofa, she made the sign of the cross in the dying man's direction, then started for the door. Pushkin called out to her, asking her to bless him again. Then he had his wife brought in. It was finally time to tell her the truth: Arendt had passed sentence, he had little time left, perhaps just a few hours. Natalie threw herself to her knees before the icons, wailing, sobbing. The foyer was filling up as friends, acquaintances, and strangers crowded in to find out how Pushkin was. The door from the main entrance kept opening, the noise disturbing the patient. It was decided to bar it with a chest of drawers and to open the servants' entrance. Someone wrote *Pushkin* on the tiny, shabby door with a piece of charcoal. A brief bulletin, drafted by Zhukovsky, was posted, too: "The first half of the night was restless, the second calmer. There are no new dangerous crises, but nor can there be any improvement either." At around noon came the return of Arendt, from whom Pushkin was impatiently awaiting news that the Tsar had pardoned Danzas, thus allowing him "to die in peace." But the only comfort the court physician could provide was a few drops of opium, which Pushkin eagerly consumed. Until then he had refused all treatment during that entire horrible, pain-racked morning. Meanwhile, back in his study in the Winter Palace, Tsar Nicholas I was telling Zhukovsky of his satisfaction that Pushkin had accepted a good Christian's final duty; as for Danzas, the Tsar said he could not change the laws but would do all he could. It was during this conversation that the Tsar instructed Zhukovsky to seal the poet's study upon his now inevitable death; he also ordered him to examine all remaining papers – subsequently and at his leisure – and to destroy any compromising material that turned up. When he returned to the Moyka, Zhukovsky was able to reassure his dying friend about Danzas's fate. Elizaveta Mikhailovna Khitrova arrived. She wept, tore her hair, blamed the whole world for the tragedy. She was not allowed into the study. Dal arrived at about two in the afternoon. "Things are bad, friend," Pushkin greeted him. He was exhausted now, sometimes assailed by a torpor not unlike unconsciousness. His wife and friends were taking turns at his bedside a few moments at a time. "All of us still have hope," Dal tried to comfort him, "you should, too." "No, I'm not going to live here. I'm going to die, clearly it must be so." He suffered horribly again when the effects of the opium wore off. He clenched his fists and bit his lip to keep from screaming. His condition seemed to worsen suddenly at about six that evening; his pulse raced to 120, his temperature rose, the signs of agitation and discomfort mounted. Following Arendt's instructions, Spassky and Dal tried leeches. It was Pushkin himself who placed them on his stomach, all around the wound. He did not want anyone else to touch it. The remedy's effect was rapid: his pulse returned to normal, his temperature fell, his distended belly deflated. That evening Dal seemed to brighten with a glimmer of hope – his heart talking rather than his mind. When he saw his friend display some relief, Pushkin, too, thought there might be some remote possibility of survival, but he soon abandoned the illusion. Another night of agony descended. He kept asking Dal what time it was and seemed enraged by the answer. "How long do I have to go on suffering? Faster, faster, please!" He was talking to his own death now, measuring its approach by constantly taking his own pulse, issuing his own reports of its snail's-pace advance. "It's here," he said several times. He spent that second night of torment holding Dal's hand. Every now and then he picked up a glass of water and helped himself to tiny sips from a spoon. He rubbed his own forehead with small pieces of ice, changed the compress on his stomach himself. Worse than the pain, he said, was the terrible anguish that choked him, crushing his heart. He would ask Dal to help him sit up or to turn him on his side or to turn the pillow over, but then would interrupt him: "That's fine, it's perfect, that's enough, it's all right now," or "Let it be, there's no need, just pull me up a little by the arm." Dal told him not to be ashamed of the pain: "Scream, it'll help a little." "I can't, my wife would hear, and it's silly to let this stupidity get the better of me, I don't want to." A new bulletin was posted on the morning of January 29: "The patient's condition is most grave." His breathing was rapid and ragged, his pulse fading by the hour. Pushkin called for his wife several times on that last morning of January 29, 1837; it was hard for him to talk now, and he only held her hand. Sometimes he didn't recognize her. Natalie was at his side when Pushkin asked Danzas if he thought he would soon be dead, adding, "I think I will, or at least I hope so. Today I'm calmer, happy they've left me alone, yesterday they tortured me." At around noon he asked for a mirror. He took a quick look at himself and waved a hand in annoyance. The doctors noted that his arms and legs were cold now. His face, too, was suffering an appalling metamorphosis; yet death did not come. *Tu vivras, tu vivras!* Natalie kept saying, though the doctors would not let her stay with her husband for long. He waited for death stretched out on the sofa, one knee raised, the back of his head propped on his forearm – the position in which he had created poems in other days. At about one-thirty Mrs. Khitrova was admitted to his bedside. Eliza dissolved in sobs, fell to her knees. When she left, Pushkin said to Dal again, "Tell me, will it be over soon? I'm so tired of it." And a few minutes later: "Lower the blinds, I want to sleep." He really seemed to be sleeping when all at once he opened his eyes and asked for cloudberries. There were none in the house; someone hurried out to buy some. Pushkin, impatient, almost irate, kept saying, *Moroshki, moroshki!* He wanted his wife to feed them to him. Kneeling beside the sofa, Natalya Nikolaevna brought the small spoon to his lips, helped him to eat two or three berries and drink a bit of juice, then leaned her face close to her husband's forehead. He stroked her head. "Don't worry," he said, "it's nothing, thank God everything's all right." He sent her away. "You'll see," she said to Spassky on her way out of the study, "he's going to live, he's not going to die." Dal checked his pulse again. He could no longer find it; Pushkin's whole body was cold. He walked over to Zhukovsky and Vielgorsky and said, "He's going."

"Lift me up," Pushkin said with his eyes closed, "come on, higher, higher! Come on, let's go!" He roused himself from the partial faint that had clouded his thoughts and explained to Dal, almost apologetically, "I was dreaming we were climbing these books you and I, high on these shelves, and I got dizzy." A few seconds later he took Dal's hand and started again: "Let's go, please, let's go together." He fell back into an unconscious haze. He came to again, asked to be turned onto his right side. Dal and Danzas lifted him gently, by the armpits; Spassky put a pillow behind his back. "That's good," he said, and then: "Life is done." Dal misunderstood the barely whispered words and answered, "Yes, of course we're done." But all at once he guessed and asked, "What's done?" "Life," the poet said, with utter clarity. And then: "I'm having trouble breathing, I feel a weight." His chest was nearly still when he let out a very faint sigh. A little later – at 2:45 in the afternoon – Dr. Andreevsky closed his eyes. They hadn't let Natalya Nikolaevna in; at his bedside were Dal, Spassky, Zhukovsky, Vielgorsky, Princess Vyazemskaya, Turgenev. At three o'clock Turgenev sat down at the table in the Pushkin drawing room and wrote: "His wife still doesn't believe he's dead: she still doesn't believe it. And meanwhile the silence is broken. We speak out loud – and the sound is dreadful to our ears, for it speaks of the death of the man for whom we were silent."

15

The Ambassador's Snuffbox

Dal: When the abdominal cavity was autopsied, all the intestines were found to be severely inflamed; the small intestine was infected with gangrene in one place the size of a half-kopeck coin. In all probability this was where the bullet struck him. . . . From the bullet's direction it must be concluded that the deceased was standing sideways, in three-quarter profile, and that the trajectory of the shot was from high to low. . . . Time and circumstance did not permit the investigation to be pursued in greater depth.

They lowered the blinds and covered the mirrors. Zhukovsky sent for a sculptor to make the death mask. The body was washed, dressed, laid out on the dining-room table ("How light he is!" marveled Arkady Rosset), then placed in a coffin lined with purple velvet. Old Count Stroganov, who'd spent the past two days shuttling between the house on the Moyka and the Dutch Embassy, paid death's initial onerous bills. He did so on his own initiative, and without skimping. Was he perhaps consumed by remorse for having offered his friend Heeckeren that fatal advice? Not at all. Everyone knew a duel was inevitable after Pushkin's letter. "Frightful, frightful!" Alexander Turgenev exclaimed when Jacob van Heeckeren happened to run into him and treated him to a brief account of its contents. In those first hours of grief and mourning, many of Pushkin's friends thanked heaven that the life of Georges d'Anthès had at least been spared.

Late in the afternoon of January 29, the people who'd witnessed the poet's death agony silently raised their glasses in his memory at the home of a mutual friend: a birthday dinner for Zhukovsky became a sorrowful ceremony of commemoration. Between silent toasts and melancholy memories they discussed the fate of Natalya Nikolaevna and the children. What would they live on and where? Zhukovsky decided to appeal to the Tsar's kindness. The deceased, he wrote, had often expressed his desire to be buried at Svatye Gory, near his mother's grave and the land of his ancestors, but the Mikhailovskoe estate was about to be sold; it might be acquired by some crude provincial landlord who cared little for Pushkin's tomb, and Russians would then have no place to go to mourn their poet. Pushkin's family had to be protected along with his memory, and that meant saving them from financial ruin: a mere three hundred rubles had been found in his home at the time of his death. Zhukovsky humbly dared to suggest that His Majesty might help the widow with the initial expenses and then finance a complete edition of the deceased's works; proceeds from the sales could create a modest capital for the innocent orphans.

The immediate measures taken by Tsar Nicholas I went well beyond Zhukovsky's requests and hopes: as early as January 30, Petersburg learned that the sovereign would be generous to the murdered poet's family. On January 31 the imperial will was confirmed by decree: the Treasury would redeem the Mikhailovskoe estate from the auction block, settle all Pushkin's debts, and finance an edition of his works; the widow would receive a one-time subsidy of 10,000 rubles and an annual pension of 1,500; that same annual sum would be allotted to each of the male children (who were to enroll in the Corps of Pages) until such time as they began their civil or military careers, and to each of the female children until they were married. Russia was moved, and the astonished courts of Europe marveled at Nicholas's kindness: the Beneficent Angel had snatched *le beau rôle* from the dead poet. But it seems unlikely that Pushkin would have had any complaint this time. Never in his rosiest daydreams had he imagined such a happy solution to his financial woes. Meanwhile, demand for his books was soaring: the bookseller-publisher Smirdin sold 40,000 rubles' worth between January 29 and February 1, 1837.

The crowd coming to pay its last respects to the poet was growing by the hour, spilling past the gate and clogging nearby lanes. In those sad January days you had only to climb into a sleigh and tell the driver, "Pushkin's," and he would take you straight to No. 12 on the Moyka. Every coachman in Petersburg now knew the address by heart. Police officers controlled the flow of visitors waiting their turn to pass through the low servants' entrance, file through the storeroom, pantry, and drawing room (a screen concealed the door to the dining room, shielding family and friends), and make their way to the foyer: faint, flickering candlelight, yellowish floor and walls, air thick with incense. A deacon chanted litanies at one end of the bier, while at the other a servant in a blue coat with gold buttons "kept sprinkling the deceased's head with cologne and telling visitors tales of his death."

Apart from friends, acquaintances, and every member of the Petersburg intellectual and literary world, at least ten thousand people filed past the bier between the afternoon of January 29 and the evening of January 31. Most were ordinary souls come to salute their Poet, who in Russia was prophet, master, hero, and saint. They came to honor the nation's glory, the Russian killed by a foreign hand. They were, in Catherine Meshcherskaya's words, "women, the elderly, children, students, men of the streets, some in *tulup*, others even in rags." Sophie Karamzina described them as "officials, officers, merchants. . . . 'You see,' one of these strangers told Rosset, 'Pushkin was wrong to think his popularity was gone; it's all right here, except that he didn't look for it where hearts would answer.'" Words well worth noting: piety itself silences all blame, as if by dying Pushkin had absolved himself of his guilty truck with the aristocracy and the regime. "Poor Pushkin," wrote the grieving censor Nikitenko. "Such is the price he paid for his freedom of entry to the aristocratic salons where he squandered his time and talent."

But among the immense crowd paying their last respects to the poet, there were also many crocodiles, seemingly summoned by some dismal spell from beneath the Neva's ice, shedding their tears. Many who had buried Pushkin years before, announcing the decline of his popularity and most recently yawning over the pages of *The History of the Pugachev Revolt* or *The Contemporary*, now came to mourn him. Also honoring him were the new plebeian intellectuals, whose offspring would soon enough bury him again in the dusty Pantheon of pure and useless Art for Art's Sake. The death of Pushkin – "a twofold aristocrat, by nature and social position" – rallied the Second Estate and was a tacit appeal to the Third. But Mrs. Meshcherskaya's emotion led her to exaggerate where the rag-clad populace was concerned. Nikitenko's view was more astute; he noted that the church where the funeral rites were held could boast elegant private carriages and a great throng, "but no *tulup* or *zipun*" – no sheepskin jackets or rough-spun robes of the Fourth Estate.

"What time is it?" the dying Pushkin kept asking. It was not pain alone that tormented him, for he knew his country and his audience. By dying in that year and on that day he managed to bring his detractors and future debunkers together in a single enormous embrace, vanquished by his elegance, his timing. And without resentment: he understood the necessity of what was happening and would happen. Not for nothing was he the Russian Empire's new historiographer.

"I'm not going to live here," he protested when Dal tried to comfort him. "Here" meaning "in this century." And as he left the stage he bathed Russia in a final blaze of blinding Alexandrine brilliance, exhibiting the very same disregard for life that other Russians had displayed on the battlefield at the dawn of the nineteenth century.

"I feel sick to my stomach, I'm thirsty, call the nearest priest, I'm tired of it, I want to sleep." So had Pushkin spoken in his death agony. Simple, piercing phrases consonant with the terrible thing that was happening to him. Even in his delirium, when he saw death as the impossible scaling of books piled far too high, he had scarcely wasted a word. At 2:45 in the afternoon of January 29, 1837, Russian literature lost its muse of concision. Gone were charm, grace, and lightness, and the eclipse would be a long one, for a different stylistic era now ensued: rococo of the absurd, saraband of ambiguities, puffed-up grotesqueries, cheerful Grand Guignol, shrill laughter amid pathetic tears. Given what we were soon to witness, let no one claim that Gogol was not a realist author. Fantasies of amnesiac epigones.

One of those who came to pay his respects to the poet's remains was a student of whom we know only the initials: P.P.S. He asked Vyazemsky's son whether the portrait by Kiprensky, showing Pushkin serene and full of life, was available for viewing; young Vyazemsky went to the drawing room to convey the request. Count Stroganov's wife rushed into the bedroom screaming that a gang of university hotheads had burst into the house to pillory the woman responsible for the tragedy. She then wrote to her husband, at the Third Section at the time, asking him to send police reinforcements to defend the poor widow from the outrages of the irresponsible mob. But there was no need for that: the ever-diligent Benckendorff had already seen to everything. Apart from the uniformed policemen assigned to maintain order at Mrs. Volkonskaya's house, others in plainclothes filed past the bier; perhaps it was one of them who hurried to inform the authorities that the deceased was dressed in a black tailcoat instead

of his kamerjunker's uniform. The Tsar disapproved of Pushkin's last outfit. "Turgenev or Prince Vyazemsky must have
suggested it," he said.

Agents were also lurking in the crowd waiting at the gate,
eavesdropping on what people were saying in the streets and
in their homes. Police reports noted that the populace was
enraged at the foreigner who had dared to raise his sacrilegious
hand against the poet; there was talk of stoning the killer's
windows. Apart from the hated Frenchman, people also
wanted revenge against the doctors – Poles, Germans, Jews!
– who'd been unable to save their poet's life. Demonstrations
of public outrage were in the works. Vigilance had to be
redoubled to prevent rebellions and riots in the streets.

Writing about forbidden things was forbidden in Russia.
Everyone knew how Pushkin had died, but the newspapers
were not allowed to mention the duel. "He departed this vale
of tears after brief physical suffering." Do tell. A bad cold,
venereal disease, indigestion after eating tainted ice cream?
Indeed, much of the press, struck by sudden aphasia, didn't
even report the death. Still, the censors had not a moment's
peace during those hectic days after January 29. Strict orders
had been given: all obituaries must be free of excessive praise
or any hint of regret. Only the "Literary Supplement" of *The
Russian Wounded Veteran* managed to sneak in under the wire,
publishing Odoevsky's brokenhearted epitaph, unsigned and
in a black-bordered box: "The sun of our poetry is extinguished! Pushkin is dead, dead in the full flower of his life, in
the midst of his great journey! ... Pushkin! Our poet! Our
joy, our nation's glory! ... Can it really be that Pushkin is
no longer among us? We cannot take in the idea!" Kraevsky,
editor of the incautious paper, was summoned by Prince Dondukov-Korsakov the next day: "What was the meaning of the
black border around the report of the death of a man who
held no post in state service? ... 'The sun of our poetry'!!
Too much honor, don't you think? ... As Sergei Semyonovich says, writing little verses hardly amounts to a great jour-

ney!" Kraevsky, who was also an official in the Education Ministry and as such a subordinate of the said Sergei Semyonovich – namely Uvarov – was formally censured. Grech, too, was hauled before the Third Section and formally rebuked: Benckendorff felt that the brief item published in *The Bee of the North* was too insistent, almost a panegyric: "Afflicted by the deepest pain, we shall not waste words in our announcement. Russia owes Pushkin a debt of gratitude for his twenty-year achievement in the field of Literature, a string of the most brilliant and effective successes in works of every kind."

The notices sent out by Natalya Nikolaevna announced that the funeral would be held at eleven in the morning on February 1 at St. Isaac's – not the majestic cathedral it is today, but a large, beautiful church in the Admiralty complex, of which Pushkin was a parishioner when he lived in the house on the Moyka. On the evening of January 31, a police officer ordered the funeral chamber closed and declared that in the interest of public order the body would be moved that very night – not to St. Isaac's but to the Saviour of the Divine Image, a small church at Royal Stables Square. A heavy detachment of policemen arrived around midnight, and the unusual cortege (about a dozen of the poet's family and friends and twice as many officers) made its way through the empty streets, without torches, like a group of nervous criminals. Contingents of security forces ready to put down riots or rebellions were posted at every corner.

Many upstanding Petersburgers faced an awkward dilemma on the morning of February 1: what should they wear to the funeral? Uniform or civilian clothes? The Tsar's attentions to the family showed how highly he esteemed Pushkin; it was not out of the question that he might make a last-minute decision to pay his respects to the prodigal son, and everyone knew what a stickler he was when it came to dress. That would suggest uniforms. On the other hand, there was Pushkin's ambiguous past. Plus the fact that he died committing a crime: dueling. So maybe just frock coats. Nevertheless, the poet did hold a court rank, albeit a modest one. Uniform, then. In the end nearly everyone opted for dress uniforms with ribbons, stars, and decorations. Those who had not been informed of the change in plans turned up at the Admiralty, and their carriages had to fight their way through a crowd of students and workers who, violating the explicit prohibition posted at the university and elsewhere, were now streaming back toward Royal Stables Square. Admission to the little church was by invitation only. "Look at them, will you," Elizaveta Mikhailovna Khitrova said to an acquaintance, nodding at a group of men in tailcoats with clusters of multicolored ribbons on their lapels. "Have they no heart at all? They might at least shed a tear." Touching one of them on the elbow, she asked, "Why aren't you crying, my dear? Don't you feel any grief for your master?" The man in the tailcoat answered humbly, "If you please, Your Ladyship. We are the undertakers, you see."

A. I. Turgenev to A. I. Nefedeva, Petersburg, February 1, 1837: *One in the afternoon.* I returned from the Royal Stables church and from the crypt in the Stables building, where the bier is to be kept until being sent off. I arrived at the announced time of eleven, but the service had begun at ten-thirty. Countless crowds on the streets leading to the church and in Stables Square, but people weren't allowed into the church. There was barely enough room for the luminaries. A crowd of generals' aides-de-camp, Count Orlov, Prince Trubetskoy, Count Stroganov, Perovsky, Sukhozanet, Adlerberg, Shipov, etc. Ambassadors – including the French one, looking so exceedingly moved and sincere that someone, having earlier heard it said that few aristocrats were mourning Pushkin, commented: "Barante and the various Herrs *sont les seuls Russes dans tout cela!*" Ambassadors from Austria, Naples, Saxony, Bavaria, with their wives and retinues. High-ranking members of the court, some ministers, including even *Uvarov*: death makes peace. Beautiful women and many fashionable ladies; Mrs. Khitrova and her daughters, Count Bobrinsky; actors: Karatygin and others. Journalists, writers – Krylov was the last to say farewell to the body. A great many young people. The archimandrite and six priests officiated. A crush for the last kiss. Friends carried the casket out of the church, but there were so many who wanted to help that Prince Meshchersky's frock coat was torn in half in the crush. There was also Engelhardt, his teacher at the Tsarskoe Selo lyceum. "He's the eighteenth of mine to die," he told me – meaning from the lyceum's first graduating class. All his classmates from the lyceum were there. We carried the bier into the crypt in the other courtyard; they nearly trampled us.

Vyazemsky and Zhukovsky each placed a glove beside the body before the coffin was nailed shut: the swatch of suede was a symbolic strip of their souls. Police officials, immediately informed of the act by their spies, saw the gloves as a challenge to established institutions, the regime, the Tsar.

On February 2 Viscount d'Archiac left for Paris as a diplomatic courier.

On the morning of January 31, Zhukovsky had received an anonymous letter via the municipal post. "After this event," the writer asked, "is it possible for not only Dantest but also the contemptible Heckern to be tolerated in our midst? Can the government indifferently tolerate the scornful foreigner's act and leave this arrogant nonentity of a boy unpunished? You, a friend of the deceased . . . should do all you can to see to it that . . . those who dared desecrate the nation's spirit in the person of the deceased . . . are driven out." On February 2 Count Orlov, a member of the Council of State, received a letter from an individual signed "K.M." The handwriting suggests that this was the same man who'd written to Zhukovsky, but his tone was more menacing this time: "Depriving Dantest of all titles and confining him to barracks forever as a private cannot give Russians satisfaction for the deliberate, premeditated murder of Pushkin; no, the quick expulsion of the contemptible Heckern and an unconditional ban on foreigners' entering Russia's service will perhaps alleviate and somewhat soothe Your compatriots' grief. . . . Be so kind as to point out to His Majesty the necessity of acting in conformity with the desire of all . . . otherwise, Count, we shall pay bitterly for the outrage committed against the people, and soon."

Orlov hurried to inform the Third Section, and Bencken-dorff quickly replied: "This most important letter demonstrates the [secret] society's existence and activity. Show it to the Emperor immediately and then return it to me that I might track its author down before the trail goes cold." For reasons unknown to this day, Tsar Nicholas I told Benckendorff that he suspected the archpriest Alexei Ivanovich Malov, who had tried to read a funeral oration in the Royal Stables Church ("a devastating condemnation of the cruel prejudice to which we owe our Poet's death"), for which permission had of course been denied. Thorough investigations by the Third Section failed to identify the author of the two letters, who thus went unpunished. Let us acknowledge this anonymous patriot as the first Russian to state the hypothesis of deliberate murder, of a plot against an entire nation and its glory.

Sophie Karamzina to her half brother Andrei, Petersburg, February 2, 1837: In general this second society has displayed an enthusiasm, regret, and sympathy that must gladden Pushkin's soul if even an echo of earthly events reaches so far; among the youth of this second society there is also seething turmoil, threats, and indignation against his murderer; in ours, however, d'Anthès finds many defenders, and what is far worse and inconceivable, there are trench-ant accusers of Pushkin. . . . On Saturday evening I saw poor Natalie. . . . She's a ghost. . . . All at once she asked me, "Did you see my husband's face in death? Such a sweet expression, a brow so calm, a smile so nice – wasn't that a sign of happiness, of contentment? He saw that everyone's happy up there." And she sobbed convulsively, trembling. Poor miserable creature – and so beautiful, even in that state!

A benefit performance by Vasily Karatygin had been planned for February 2. The famous tragic actor was to have recited Pushkin's *The Avaricious Knight*. Postponed as a token of mourning, the show never took place.

Petersburg talked of nothing but the duel. The high aristocracy was divided. Some, quivering with disgust, went so far as to censure the Tsar's magnanimity: for them the rabble thronging to hail Pushkin was striking proof of just who his admirers and disciples were, not to mention their ideological leanings. The Nesselrode clan openly backed Georges d'Anthès and heaped insults on the dead poet; Benckendorff said over and over again that in fighting a duel Pushkin had behaved *"wie ein grosser Kerl"* ("like a common lout"). The Frenchman's fellow guardsmen were also on his side, as were many romantic souls.

From the diary of Marya Mörder: I've heard two conflicting versions of Pushkin's duel. My aunt tells one story, my grandmother another. I like Grandmother's better, in which d'Anthès seems truly chivalrous, Pushkin rude, uncouth. . . . I think B——n is right to say that women like dandies; to me, at least, d'Anthès is more likable than Pushkin. . . . You should never be in too much of a hurry. If d'Anthès didn't already have a wife, he could marry Mrs. Pushkin now or carry her off. . . . They say d'Anthès's arm will have to be amputated. Poor man! . . . Everyone's talking about Pushkin. Mrs. K——va condemns him. . . . Here's what she says: "If he'd challenged d'Anthès three months ago, before he got married, fine, then you could understand; but now, when d'Anthès married the sister of the woman he loved, sacrificing himself to salvage her honor, he should have respected him for that kind of sacrifice, especially since Mrs. Pushkin was the only woman in the world d'Anthès saw as an inaccessible goddess. She was the soul of his life, the ideal of his heart."

Baron Heeckeren had written to Count Nesselrode on January 30, imploring him to appeal to Nicholas I: he was anxiously waiting for His Majesty to offer the "few lines exonerating his personal behavior" that would amount to authorization for him to remain in Petersburg. Those lines never came. On February 2 the ambassador himself asked Baron Verstolk van Soelen for permission to leave Russia: "If I might be permitted to insist on one respectful consideration in a circumstance that concerns me personally, I would say that in the absence of any other charge, my recall would represent a resounding disapproval of my conduct. . . . I therefore aspire to a change of residence which, while satisfying a fatal necessity, may at the same time demonstrate that I have not lost the trust with which the King has deigned to honor me for so many years. . . . A faithful and devoted servant, I shall await His Majesty's orders, certain that . . . he will take due note of thirty-one years of unimpeachable service, the extreme modesty of my personal possessions, and the expenses now imposed upon me by a family of which I am the sole support and, given the condition of my son's young wife, will soon enough increase."

One wonders how Heeckeren could be so self-assured (and tactless) as to mention his daughter-in-law's "condition" a mere twenty-three days after her wedding. Was Catherine Goncharova carrying the fruit of sin in her womb even as she went to the altar?*

On February 3 the trial "of Baron d'Anthès, Kamerger Pushkin, and Lieutenant Colonel Danzas of the Engineering Corps for the duel held between the first two" began in a court-martial headed by Colonel Brevern.

Writing to his sister Anna Pavlovna on that same day, Tsar Nicholas I asked her to inform her husband, William of

---

* We suspect so, although Mathilde Eugénie de Heeckeren's official date of birth was October 19, 1837 (new style).

Orange, that the Tsar would soon send them a detailed report of the "tragic event that ended the career" of Pushkin – by courier, since the subject "would not withstand the curiosity of the Post Office." (What an amazing country, Russia, where the Emperor himself feared the prying eyes of his own postal service!) Nicholas wrote to his brother Mikhail Pavlovich as well: "The event has stirred countless rumors, most of them quite idiotic; only the condemnation of Heeckeren's conduct is just and deserved: truly he behaved as a disgraceful scoundrel, pimping for d'Anthès in Pushkin's absence, trying to get his wife to give herself to d'Anthès, who he claimed was dying of love for her." (What an amazing country, Russia, where the Tsar, himself the august censor who spent years deleting from Pushkin's manuscripts every suspect or overly bold word, even changing "chamber pot" to "alarm clock" in *Count Nulin*, now repeated the poet's insults virtually word for word!)

The Tsar, then, believed Pushkin, trusting his arguments and "evidence"* – yet another demonstration of faith and loyalty. One might be prepared to applaud if one didn't know that his keen contempt for the Dutch ambassador was of longer standing, dating back to a dispatch Heeckeren had sent to The Hague on May 23, 1836. Nicholas I had had a hard time convincing his brother-in-law William that he was in no way accusing him of mistreating his wife, and an even harder time proving that Alexandra Fyodorovna's unfortunate remark about the Prince of Orange's stubborn "propensity" for keeping an army stationed on the Belgian border was not tantamount to Russian interference in Dutch affairs. It was also during that fateful summer of 1836 that the Tsar had learned that Baron van Heeckeren was confidentially telling some of

---

* Prince von Hohenlohe-Kirchberg reported to Stuttgart: "There are two widespread views about these anonymous letters. The one enjoying greater credibility with the public points to U[varov]. The one shared by the powerful – based on sameness of punctuation, handwriting, and comparison of paper – incriminates H[eeckeren]."

his diplomatic colleagues that William of Orange believed that his children's long stay in Russia had done them no good; they visited the country in 1834 and returned, he said, "too enthralled by military ideas and infatuated with the absolutist ideal, not a good thing in a constitutional state." The dispute between the absolutist Tsar and the constitutional Prince, both of whom had a pronounced weakness for wars and armies, was finally brought to a peaceful end, but Nicholas was determined to get rid of that scoundrel of a Dutch ambassador at the first available opportunity. That opportunity came with the death of the *"trop célèbre Poushkin, le poète."*

Faddey Bulgarin to Alexei Storozhenko, Petersburg, February 4, 1837: I feel sorry for the poet, very much so, but the man was disgusting. He posed as a Byron and died like a hare. His wife, in all good conscience, is not to blame. Have you ever seen Pushkin? Was it possible to love him, especially when he was drinking?

Danzas had asked the Tsar for permission to accompany his friend's mortal remains to their final resting place. For a few days Nicholas let the man who had acted as a second in a duel where blood was shed walk free, but in the end the law had to take its course. He therefore assigned the dismal task of transporting Pushkin's body to Alexander Turgenev, "an old friend of the deceased and a man without employment." More to the point, Turgenev was the brother of a man who had been sentenced to death in absentia for his role in the events of 1825; a second brother, also with a whiff of Decembrism about him, had died prematurely in painful voluntary exile. The Tsar had pretended not to recognize Turgenev when he ran into him at Princess Baryatinsky's ball on December 22, but he suddenly remembered him now, thereby reminding Russia that he hadn't forgotten Pushkin's tumultuous youth. The bier would be accompanied by ghosts out of the past.

Benckendorff put the final touch to the carefully crafted

scenario by adding one more ghost, this one of flesh and blood, whose identity we shall keep to ourselves for the moment. The convoy set out on the night of February 3, once again in full darkness, like a contingent of evildoers unworthy of daylight's favor. The carriage of a police captain took the lead, followed by the cart bearing the coffin (with the faithful Kozlov aboard), Turgenev and a Post Office official bringing up the rear in a *kibitka*. The journey was nearly over when Turgenev encountered Kamerger Yakhontov, a representative of the local aristocracy, at a postal station near Pskov. Nothing unusual about his returning to his own estate. Turgenev stopped to take tea with him. They chatted about the weather, the latest Petersburg news, and Turgenev's sad mission. He then set out again – by now it was the evening of February 4, and there was no time to lose – while Yakhontov insisted on lingering in the foul-smelling inn, black with soot but warm and comfortable after the long journey in the cold.

"Winter! The peasant celebrating . . ."

On arriving in Pskov Turgenev went straight to the home of Governor Peshchurov, an old acquaintance. Finding that he had barged into a party, he had no choice but to join it. A little later a messenger appeared at the governor's residence with an urgent letter from a high official of the Third Section – quite an honor for a modest gathering of friends already gladdened by an unexpected guest who'd been kicking up his heels in Paris only a few months earlier. To impress his provincial audience, the governor began to read the missive from St. Petersburg aloud, adding parenthetical comments of his own:

Most esteemed Alexei Nikitich,

   Acting Counselor of State Yakhontov, who will deliver this letter to Your Excellency, will also relate the news from St. Petersburg. Pushkin's body [May God receive that rabble-rouser in glory!] is being taken to the province of Pskov [Saints of heaven! more headaches, another nuisance!] to be buried on his father's estate. In this regard I have asked Mr. Yakhontov to convey to you the instructions of Count Alexander Khristoforovich [Benckendorff! What instructions? I don't understand what he's talking about!], but it is also my honor to inform Your Excellency of the Sovereign Emperor's wish that . . .

Only when he came to the word "Emperor's" did it occur to Peshchurov that he had no business reciting such an important document in public. With a pained expression commensurate with the gravity of the event, he paled, fell silent (to the great disappointment of his listeners), and handed the highly confidential sheet of paper to his illustrious guest, who was from the capital and would surely know more about it than he did. In other words, he handed it to Turgenev – the very person from whom it was to be strictly concealed and ahead of whom Benckendorff had deliberately dispatched his top-secret courier, the warmth-seeking Yakhontov. Turgenev read the rest of the letter to himself: ". . . the Sovereign Emperor's wish that you prohibit any special demonstration, any outpouring of tributes, in a word, any ceremony beyond that normally celebrated according to the rites of our church when a nobleman is buried. . . ."

Burying this particular nobleman turned out not to be easy: a hard layer of ice resisted the shovels of the peasants who came from Trigorskoe and Mikhailovskoe to dig the grave, as though the earth itself were trying to reject a body everyone found so inconvenient. The mahogany coffin got into the ground only as day began to dawn on February 6. Turgenev, Kozlov, and Marya and Ekaterina Osipova wept; the police captain did not, nor did the peasants, by now yearning only to warm themselves with something strong. At no time during the journey or at Pskov or at Svatye Gory did the triumphant tributes feared by the Third Section materialize.

Sergei Grigorievich Stroganov to his father, Grigory Alexandrovich, Moscow, February 5, 1837: Moscow society is quite concerned about Pushkin's sad death, and he is mourned by all, as he should be.... You can almost guess from the expressions of those who speak of the poet what they admire in his works and what they think of the loss of an author who hadn't dirtied his obscene and regicidal pen for the past ten years. It seems to me that the government is taking good advantage of a circumstance of this kind to draw its own conclusions.

Benckendorff to Zhukovsky, Petersburg, February 6, 1837: Those papers that could damage Pushkin's memory must be turned over to me so that I may read them. Such a measure is being taken not with any intent whatsoever to harm the deceased, but solely for the exceptionally just necessity of hiding nothing from the surveillance of the government, whose vigilance must extend to all possible materials. Once I have read the said papers, if any such are found, they will be burned forthwith in your presence. For the same reason all other letters written to the deceased by third parties will, as you have kindly proposed, be returned to those who wrote them, but in all cases only after I have read them.

Heeckeren prepared his departure while waiting for The Hague to assign him to a new legation, in Paris or Vienna, he hoped. Believing it superfluous to take with him everything he had acquired in thirteen years, and being keenly aware of the expenses entailed by moving to a new life, he organized a private auction of furniture, porcelain, and silverware, to be held in his own home. "Many saw it as a chance to insult him. At one point, for instance, he was sitting on a chair on which a price was displayed; an official walked over, paid for the chair, and took it out from under him."

Leonty Vasilievich Dubelt, chief of staff of the national police, removed the seals from Pushkin's study on February 6; a police officer packed the poet's papers in a box to be taken to Zhukovsky's apartment. (Zhukovsky had begged Benckendorff not to insist that he perform his thankless censor's task in the offices of the Third Section.) The macabre ritual of posthumous search began on February 7 and took many days to complete. With a secretary's help, Zhukovsky and Dubelt read, assessed, and organized the papers. There was no bonfire – at least not in Zhukovsky's presence – but his soul burned with contempt. Forced to violate Pushkin's private life, he discovered that many had gone before him over the years. And he came to understand many other things as well.

On February 8 Dr. Stefanovich stipulated that Georges d'Anthès's physical condition no longer justified house arrest; the defendant could therefore be transferred to the guardroom.

Christian von Hohenlohe-Kirchberg to Count von Beroldingen, St. Petersburg, February 9, 1837: Just after the duel between Mr. Pushkin and Baron d'Anthès, there were declarations in the latter's favor, but less than twenty-four hours was enough for the Russian side to turn feelings toward Pushkin, and it would be imprudent of anyone to exhibit the slightest fondness for his opponent. Time will soothe their minds but will never manage to generate any true fondness for foreigners in Russian hearts. As for the Barons Heeckeren, it is true that they did everything to stir widespread dislike, and many who were once happy to honor the minister Baron Heeckeren now must regret having done so.

Georges d'Anthès appeared before the court-martial on February 10. He was asked (in French, and no Russian could have made sense of the tortured, ungrammatical question as recorded): "Of what expressions did the letters written by you to Mr. Pushkin or Mrs. Pushkin consist such that in the letter written by him to the Dutch ambassador he describes as idiocies?" D'Anthès replied: "Since I sent Mrs. Pushkin books and theater tickets accompanied by brief notes rather often, I suppose that among these there may have been some whose words might have hurt his feelings as a husband, which gave him cause to refer to them in his letter to Baron Heeckeren of January 26 as idiocies written by me." The next day Danzas was called to complete the testimony he'd given on February 9. His words were recorded thus:

At Mr. d'Archiac's, Alexander Sergeevich Pushkin began his explanation as follows: Having received letters from an anonymous source of which he considered the Dutch ambassador guilty and knowing that rumors damaging to his wife's honor were circulating in society, in the month of November, public opinion having pointed to Lieutenant d'Anthès, he challenged him to a duel; but when Mr. d'Anthès proposed to marry Pushkin's sister-in-law, Pushkin, desisting from the duel, demanded as a necessary condition from Mr. d'Anthès that there be no relations between the two families. Despite this, even after the marriage Messrs. Heeckeren, behaving insolently toward Pushkin's wife, with whom they met in society alone, continued to foster the spread of opinions offensive to his honor as well as his wife's. It was to put an end to this that on January 26 Pushkin wrote the letter to the Dutch ambassador that was the cause of Mr. d'Anthès's challenge.

D'Anthès was questioned again on February 12. He was asked, among other things: "Who in the month of November and *after** wrote the letters to Pushkin in the name of an unknown [sic] and who was guilty of it?" He replied: "I don't know who wrote Mr. Pushkin the anonymous letters in the month of November and after." He also stated: "I do not agree that I avoided the duel by proposing to marry his sister-in-law." But protests and explanations were of little use. Even the military tribunal held that his had been a marriage born of fear.

On February 13 the military judges decided that the facts of the case were clear and that a verdict could be issued. One

---

* My italics. I wonder, indeed, how the court-martial judges knew of the other anonymous letters Pushkin received even after November 4. As we have said, many contemporaries recalled the fact, but there was never any mention of it during the questioning.

Maslov, a court registrar, appealed against that decision the next day, arguing that legal statutes required that the police request certain explanations of Pushkin's widow. But the judges held that it was pointless "to insult Mrs. Pushkin for no reason by asking her for the explanations requested in Magistrate Maslov's report." The inquiry was closed.

The judges of the court-martial were doing the gentlemanly thing by refusing to question the widow. They knew, among other things, that their procedure was more or less purely formal anyway: they would sentence d'Anthès and Danzas to death, and as always in such cases at that time, the sentence would be commuted to some milder punishment by imperial decree. It is therefore understandable that they would try to wrap everything up quickly, with minimal publicity. Nor would any reasonable person hope to find anything of significance in the official record of judicial proceedings relating to the Pushkin–d'Anthès duel, published in one volume in 1900: 160 tedious and occasionally irritating pages notable for turgid language, procedural wrangles that move at a snail's pace, a few incredible mistakes (only on March 16, after questioning the relevant officials, was it discovered that Pushkin was a kamerjunker and not a kamerger, as he had been called until then), a farcical black-comedy decision to sentence the defendant Pushkin to be hanged but to "suspend sentence on account of his death," and the defendants' repeated lies (minor in Danzas's case, slightly more serious in d'Anthès's).

But one thing strikes us as we plow through the leaden, repetitive pages one last time. Maslov wanted Pushkin's widow to be asked: "(1) Whether she knew exactly what anonymous letters had been received by her late husband. . . . (2) What letters or notes the defendant d'Anthès wrote, as he himself admits . . . where all these papers now were, and *similarly the letter from an unknown person received by Pushkin back in the month of November in which the ambassador from Holland, Baron Heeckeren, is said to be responsible for the discord between the defendant d'Anthès and Pushkin.*"

The added emphasis is mine, marking genuine, belated surprise: a "letter from an unknown person" in which Heeckeren is said to be "responsible for the discord" between d'Anthès and Pushkin. In other words: an anonymous letter warning Pushkin that Heeckeren was trying to stir up trouble between him and d'Anthès – obviously by sending the certificates. These few lines may well contain the answer to a question that has plagued us all along, for they tell us how Pushkin knew who wrote the certificates – not from the paper, the wording, the handwriting, or the seal, but from yet another anonymous prankster. No wonder he couldn't and wouldn't tell anyone what his evidence was: the revelation came from a nameless, faceless source.

Prince Dolgorukov no doubt! Such was his "double game": first he sent the certificates; then he added to the amusement by sending Pushkin an anonymous tip saying that Heeckeren had done it and claiming to have heard with his own ears d'Anthès saying such-and-such and the ambassador saying such-and-such on November 2. That letter, combined with Natalie's admissions and Yakovlev's observations, channeled Pushkin's anger toward Georges d'Anthès's adoptive father. We can even establish when he received it: November 12, 1836. That was the day when, to everyone's surprise, he seemed flexible, willing to talk peace with d'Anthès, whereas the very next day he was boasting to Princess Vyazemskaya: "I know who wrote the anonymous letters." And here we were racking our brains! Chastened by previous disappointments, however, one might best douse the euphoria of discovery in cold water. What about everyone who read these proceedings before? How in the world did they miss this?

But let's assume that they did and play devil's advocate. How and from whom would Maslov have learned that there was another anonymous letter? There was no mention of any such document during any of the questioning. But the transcript of Danzas's February 9 deposition was missing from the file in which the trial records were stored for decades:

two sheets disappeared. No one knows how, when, or why. Someone other than the god of trifling coincidences must be at work here, someone with an interest in sowing confusion and distraction (though toward what end one cannot know). Instead of giving up, let us reread the invaluable text yet again, this time pondering every last word. The laconic accounts of the February 9 hearing seem to suggest that at least on this occasion Danzas claimed that he was drawn into the duel at the very last minute, by which time he could do nothing to avert it. But not all the testimony was recorded.

How and from whom did Maslov learn of the other anonymous letter? And exactly who was Maslov? We don't even know his first name or patronymic, just that he was a registrar of the XIII class, a clerk with a modest career. We also know that his Russian was halting and garbled, as twisted as a snake with a toothache. A nasty suspicion flits across our mind: that Maslov simply screwed up, his hasty goose-quill pen turning "anonymous letters for which he held the ambassador responsible" into "the letter in which the ambassador . . . is said to be responsible for the discord"; and that the offspring of the incestuous mating of ignorance and bureaucracy, now afforded a reality of its own, then set out on a long judicial journey, being cited many more times by as many careless people. In other words, a phantom letter. Cross our hearts, we cannot say whether Maslov was an illiterate bungler and dreamer or an overly conscientious servant of justice. And though the former hypothesis is far more alluring – marvel of clerkdom, a scribe's mirage, delirium of an Akaky Akakievich* – let us nevertheless suspend judgment. Whichever you were, registrar Maslov, incompetent clerk or zealous functionary, to you we owe an idea that had never crossed our mind. One well worth exploring.

Even the mild-mannered Zhukovsky became exasperated with the brazen, intrusive stupidity of Benckendorff's policemen

* The leading character in Gogol's *Overcoat*. Translator's note.

and spies. He wrote to the director of the Third Section: "I heard from General Dubelt that Your Excellency has been informed of the theft of three packets by a top-flight person [*de haute volée*]. I immediately guessed what it was about. . . . Not three but five packets could have been seen in the drawing room, or more exactly in my hat . . . they were simply Pushkin's letters to his wife, in his own hand."

Zhukovsky then took the opportunity to tell Benckendorff what was really on his mind: "First I will talk about Pushkin himself. . . . In all his twelve years under the Sovereign's magnanimous tutelage his situation never changed. He remained under close and painful surveillance, like an unruly little boy you were afraid to turn loose. . . . The thirty-six-year-old Pushkin was still regarded like the Pushkin of twenty-two. . . . In your letters I find reprimands because Pushkin went to Moscow, because he went to Erzerum. But where is the crime in that? . . . And these reprimands, of such little account to you, colored his whole life: he could not come and go at will, was deprived of the pleasure of seeing Europe, could not read his works to his friends. . . . Allow me to speak freely. By his personal protection the Sovereign meant to put Pushkin's mind at ease and to let his Genius blossom fully; but you turned this protection into police control." Zhukovsky understood that it was not a talented, irresponsible boy who had died but a manumitted, weary adult. In death Pushkin inspired words and thoughts worthy of a *frondeur* in this most devoted Russian subject.

Vyazemsky, too, lost patience when he realized that certain salons and government offices detected a whiff of conspiracy and subversion in the piety of the dead man's friends. He wrote to Grand Duke Mikhail Pavlovich: "What can you have to fear from us? What purpose, what ulterior motive on our part could be imagined without tarring us with lunacy or iniquity? Every possible absurd purpose has been ascribed to us. . . . What ignorance of the facts, what narrowness of vision it is to judge Pushkin this way! What trace of the politician was there in him, a poet above all else, poet and nothing but a poet? ... And what does politician, liberal, oppositionist mean in Russia? These are words *devoid* of meaning, borrowed from foreign dictionaries by the police and in ill will, inapplicable among us here. Where is the stage on which this borrowed role might be performed? What organs are available for such professions of faith? Barring madness, the only thing a liberal, an oppositionist can do in Russia is to take the Trappist vows, fall silent, and bury himself alive."

Pushkin himself never went so far in his chats with the imperial family.

The court-martial pronounced sentence on February 19: hanging for d'Anthès and Danzas, formally the same punishment for Pushkin. The sentence, along with the record of the proceedings, was conveyed to the authorities of the Guards for the ritual review.

Alexander Turgenev to Praskovya Osipova, Petersburg, February 24, 1837: Natalya Nikolaevna left on February 16. ... I saw her the evening before, we said goodbye. Her health is not so bad, and she is recovering mentally as well. It seems her sister Catherine went to say goodbye, and their aunt made no secret of her feelings when she heard her say, "I forgive Pushkin."

Sometime around February 20 Benckendorff wrote himself a note, "as a reminder": "Wasn't it one Tibeau, a friend of Rosset's on active duty at the General Staff, who wrote the obscenities about Pushkin?" At about that same time he asked d'Anthès for the address of the teacher who had once given him Russian lessons, a trick for getting a sample of the *chevalier garde*'s Cyrillic handwriting to be compared with the writing on the addresses of the certificates. In an effort to track his former teacher down, d'Anthès turned to a former servant of Otto von Bray-Steinburg, and it was he who wrote the address of one "Viskovskov" on a piece of paper. But even if d'Anthès had written the teacher's address himself, we already know that the second sheet, the one enclosing the certificates, was drafted by someone who had known the Russian alphabet all his life. Inquiries about "one Tibeau" led nowhere. Benckendorff's agents reported that no one of that name worked at the General Staff, though two Tibeaus, both titular counselors, were employed by the Post Office. Handwriting samples were duly requested from these two upright citizens, who proved innocent. And that was the end of the matter, at least judging from what remains in a thin folder in the archives of the Third Section entitled "On the anonymous letters sent to Pushkin."

But who originally reported the mysterious Tibeau's name? An agent? Another anonymous letter writer? Ruling out postal workers, officers of the General Staff, and, for obvious reasons, the bandit Pushkin's *Avaricious Knight* remembers as he contemplates his gold doubloons ("And this? It's Tibeau's, that fraud / that idler. Who could have given it to him? / Surely he stole it. Or else: / by night, in an ambush, in a wood . . ."), we have to wonder whether someone suspected the Thibaut who once taught history to the Karamzin brothers and continued to have contact with them and their family later. Cultured and well-informed, a regular at the hospitable residence on Mikhailovskaya Square, he would fit the profile of the anonymous perpetrator but for the fact that he was French. Or perhaps he was the son or grandson of a French expatriate (political refugee, tutor, tailor, actor), long since Russified for all intents and purposes, including use and knowledge of the language? We simply don't know, because Benckendorff's agents never got to him. As far as we can tell, they never got to anyone. We are amused and amazed at their incompetence. Granted, exposing the author of anonymous letters is never easy, but we're talking about the Third Section here, probably nineteenth-century Europe's largest and most powerful secret police apparatus.

Ekaterina Karamzina to her son Andrei, Petersburg, March 3, 1837:
You were right to think that Mrs. Pushkin would become an object
of solicitude for me, I have been to see her every day, at first with
a feeling of deep pity for her great pain, but then, alas, with the
conviction that although she is overwhelmed by it all for the
moment, it will be neither long nor deep. It is painful but true to
say so: The great, good Pushkin ought to have had a wife who
understood him better and was more in harmony with him. . . . She
is in the countryside with one of her brothers, passed through
Moscow, where her father-in-law, poor old man, has been living
since he lost his wife. Well, passed through without getting in
touch, without asking about him, without sending the children to
see him. . . . Poor, poor Pushkin, victim of the frivolity, rashness,
and thoughtless behavior of the young and beautiful wife who seems
to have risked his life for a few hours of flirting. Don't think I'm
exaggerating. I don't mean to blame her, you don't blame children
for the unwitting harm they do.

On March 2 the Dutch Foreign Minister informed Baron
Heeckeren that he could leave Petersburg immediately upon
the arrival of his replacement, Johan Gevers, the mission's
former secretary. Heeckeren was not offered a new posting,
a rebuff that might well have meant the end of his diplomatic
career. Moreover, it had been ascertained in The Hague that
at the time of the *chevalier garde*'s naturalization (and not
adoption, as everyone, including d'Anthès himself, believed),
his name had been entered in the rolls of the Dutch nobility;
he was therefore barred by Article 66 of the constitution from
serving in a foreign army without special permission from the
King. But even before this serious irregularity was unearthed,
an English courier had brought William of Orange the letter
that the Tsar feared would not withstand the curiosity of the
Russian postal service. The letter seems to have vanished, but
its tone and content can be guessed from the reply it elicited:
"I confess that the whole thing seems a wretched business to

me. . . . It seems to me that Heeckeren will be no loss from any point of view and that you and I were resoundingly wrong about him all these years. Most of all I hope that his replacement will be more truthful and will not invent things to fill his dispatches, as Heeckeren did."

To those unaware of what was going on in The Hague at the time – and what had happened the summer before – Heeckeren's recall, very like a dismissal without notice, seemed to confirm all the charges made against him in Pushkin's two letters, copies of which, patiently reproduced by hand, had been circulating in Petersburg for some time now. Many aristocratic houses had closed their doors to the Dutch ambassador, either in deference to the Tsar's now evident attitude or simply to settle old scores and grudges. Heeckeren felt increasingly beset by suspicion, ill will, and hostility. Since he, too, was unaware of the real reasons why Orange and Romanov were now dispensing with his fanciful, gossipmongering services, he thought of himself as a hostage to history, the victim of some dark political design. On March 5 he wrote to Verstolk van Soelen:

Great personal courage is one of the distinctive and most-noted aspects of the Emperor's character. . . . But few realize that this sovereign is at the same time under the influence of a faction he mistrusts, and not without reason, for it may be that this faction will soon hang its yoke on him. . . . The real head of this faction is Mr. Zhukovsky. . . . It is to him that the Emperor entrusted the task of examining Mr. Pushkin's papers . . . but nothing worthy of note was found in the papers of such an unruly man. Anyone who knows what's going on could have easily predicted that result. Like all those whose views are just beginning to be noticed, the Russian faction is still content merely to suggest reforms; it is winning them, but its demands will soon rise along with its strength, and the day may soon come when the Emperor, drawn into one concession after another, will no longer be able to resist and will yield in spite of himself to the will of a force that is in all respects following the trajectory of every revolution – hesitant at first, then demanding, and ultimately irresistible.

Poor Zhukovsky! Poor Nicholas I! But let us for once admire the disgraced ambassador, whose resentment afforded him prophetic foresight in a foreign land.

On March 11 the trial records, with the opinions of high-ranking military authorities, were forwarded to the Ministry of War, which one week later submitted the sentences for definitive review by Nicholas I: d'Anthès was to be demoted to private and posted to one of the Empire's remote garrisons; Danzas was given two months in prison. Nicholas I ruled: "Let the sentence be carried out, but since Private d'Anthès is not a Russian subject, let him be escorted across the border by the police after being stripped of his officer's insignia." At nine in the morning on March 21, the former officer of the Horse Guards was placed in the custody of Police Sergeant Novikov, who accompanied him to the Dutch Embassy to let him bid farewell to his wife and adoptive father. Shortly before two in the afternoon they got into the troika that was to take them to the Prussian border.

Catherine de Heeckeren to her husband, Petersburg [March 22, 1837]: I cannot resign myself to the idea of not seeing you for two weeks, I count the hours and minutes that I must remain in this cursed Petersburg, I wish I were already far away. It is so horrible to deprive me of my heart like this, poor dear, they make you trot along those horrible roads until your bones break, I hope that once you get to Tilsit you'll rest as you should. Please take care of your health and especially think of your arm. . . . Countess Stroganova stayed with us for a while after you left yesterday; always so good and attentive to me, she had me undress, take off my corset, and put on a robe, after which they had me lie down on the sofa and sent for Raukh, who gave me some vile stuff and told me to stay in bed again today to keep the little one safe, since, good respectful loving son that he is, he has been acting up since they took his most honored father away. . . . There's a servant woman (the Russian) who keeps raving about your intelligence and good looks, saying that she has never in her life seen the like of you and that she'll never forget the way you had her admire your slim little waist in your greatcoat.

Heeckeren was given the coup de grâce when the Tsar denied him the audience customarily granted to foreign ambassadors leaving Russia temporarily. And as if that were not enough, he also sent him a valuable diamond-studded gold snuffbox adorned with the Emperor's portrait – the usual gift for ambassadors leaving their post permanently. Ambassadors in Petersburg received Jacob van Heeckeren-Beverweerd's visiting card – with a hypocritical *"p.p.c."* (*pour prendre congé*, "to take leave") added in ink – only late in the morning of April 1, by which time the former ambassador and his daughter-in-law were already on their way to Königsberg, where d'Anthès was waiting for them. It was truly an ignominious flight.

Pushkin's revenge was complete, and everyone was talking about it. A string of triumphs for the poet unfolded between the afternoon of January 29 and the morning of April 1, 1837. He had worked it all out with maximum care, except for one unsatisfying detail. He had not yet breathed his last when the astute Dr. Arendt commented: "It's a pity he didn't die on the spot, for his suffering is ineffable; but it's a lucky thing for his wife's honor that he's still alive. None of us who saw him can have any doubt about his wife's innocence or about how much he loved her." The Vyazemskys, Zhukovsky, and Turgenev hastened to publicize the dying man's noble words of absolution: "You are not to blame." Vyazemsky wrote to Davydov: "Above all do not forget that he entrusted a sacred task to all of us, his friends, as faithful executors of his will:

protect his wife's name from slander." Vera Fyodorovna Vyazemskaya had a more touching argument: "In the wife's
defense I shall only remind you of something Father Bazh-
anov, who saw her every day after the catastrophe . . .
said to her aunt: 'For me it is a struggle to leave her with a
useful sense of her own guilt, since to me she is an angel of
purity.'"

Yet even the executors of Pushkin's last wishes couldn't
change the facts completely, nor manage wholly to silence
their own feelings about Natalya Nikolaevna. They insisted
that she'd been guilty of *no more than* thoughtlessness, frivolity,
and flirting – a rather lame defense which, while preventing
the deceased from acquiring a posthumous reputation as a
cuckold, did little to protect the wife from censure. And tor-
rents of condemnation duly poured down on the beautiful
Natalie, "shame and disgrace to Russian women." For
instance:

> *Drag yourself into the desolate desert,*
> *with a curse on your brow!*
> *For your bones in the cold tomb*
> *there is no place on earth*
> *. . . When in the tortures that precede death,*
> *the prayer welcomed by bitter tears*
> *with singing words*
> *descends on sinning lips,*
> *then to your bed of pain, in the depths of night,*
> *a silent shade will sneak,*
> *and the bloody hands*
> *will be raised against you in final judgment!*

And one night late in the winter of 1837 Pushkin's silent shade
did slip into a bedroom and, advancing in the darkness, its
expression terrifying, raised its bloody hand to pull the hair
of young Guber, author of this anathema in verse. Pushkin
was avenging not his dainty wife – he'd already done all he

could for her – but poetry, for even in death he raged against lame lines, bad taste, and bombast, and most of all against pathos, father of all poetic vices.

16

One Summer in Baden-Baden

Here they are, the protagonists and bit players in our story, reunited in Andrei Karamzin's letters to his family – as if in some banal dream sequence, like members of a wretched touring company whose handful of actors must play multiple parts, taking their curtain calls in whatever costume they happened to be wearing at their last appearance onstage. The Barons Heeckeren, the Smirnovs and the Borkhs, Countess Marya Grigorievna Razumovskaya, and even the grim and peevish Lady Censor, marring Pushkin's works even after his death and for a long time thereafter. All together, "happy and satisfied" in a famous Central European spa in the summer of 1837.

June 28
Yesterday I saw d'Anthès and his wife while I was out for a walk: both stared at me but didn't greet me, I went up to them *first*, whereupon d'Anthès literally threw himself at me and shook my hand. I can hardly express the jumble of feelings that filled my heart at the sight of these two representatives of the past who so vividly reminded me of what was and of what was not and will never be. After exchanging the customary civilities with them, I went off to join the others, my feelings as a Russian warring both with pity and with a voice inside me pleading on d'Anthès's behalf. I saw that he was waiting for me and indeed soon approached me anew, taking me by the arm and leading me along the empty streets.

Not two minutes passed before he began regaling me with his unhappy tale in all its particulars, heatedly defending himself against the charges I hurled at him, mincing no words. He showed me a copy of Pushkin's *appalling* letter and the minutes of his testimony at the military tribunal, swearing that he was utterly innocent. Most of all he forcefully denied having had the slightest relationship with Natalya Nikolaevna *after* his engagement to her sister and insisted that the second challenge *a été comme une tuile qui lui est tombée sur la tête.* He spoke of your attitude to him with tears in his eyes and said several times that he'd been deeply hurt by it. . . . He added: *"Ma justification complète ne peut venir que de Mme Pouschkine, dans quelques années, quand elle sera calme, elle dira peut-être, que j'ai tout fait pour les sauver et que si je n'y ai pas réussi, cela n'a pas été de ma faute, ecc."†* The conversation and walk lasted from eight in the evening until eleven. God will judge them, with him I will continue to maintain relations of acquaintance but not of friendship as before — *c'est tout ce que je peux faire.‡*

July 4:
Sunday there was a ball at Mrs. Polyektova's — the first since I've been abroad, and here I danced every dance *ex officio*: the mazurka with Countess Borkh and many waltzes and French quadrilles with the English ladies. . . . It was strange to see d'Anthès leading mazurkas and cotillions with that *chevalier garde* mien of his.

July 15:
Last Sunday, together with Countess Borkh, Mrs. Desloges, and other riders, we went on horseback to some ruins on a nearby mountaintop offering a splendid view, and there among the clouds the monastery of Strasbourg could be seen like a slender needle, fifty versts away. We were all happy and satisfied, only the poor,

* "was like a tile falling on his head."
† "My complete exoneration can come only from Mrs. Pushkin; years hence, when she has recovered her calm, perhaps she will say that I did all I could to save them and that it was not my fault if I did not succeed."
‡ "that's all I can do."

sweet countess was uneasy, since her husband, following us in a carriage, had been unable to go on because of the bad road and was forced to turn back – *elle s'attendait à une scène pour le retour, et cela ne lui a pas manqué.** The long face *de ce vilain avorton du mari*† plunged the entire company into melancholy (I was the only Russian). We dined merrily at an inn where d'Anthès, spurred by the champagne, *nous donnait des crampes à force de rire.*‡ Apropos d'Anthès: *Il m'a tout à fait désarmé en me prenant par mon faible: il m'a témoigné constamment tant d'intérêt pour toute la famille,*¶ speaking so often of you and especially of Sasha, mentioning him by name, that my last clouds of indignation dissolved, *et je dois faire un effort sur moi-même pour ne pas être avec lui aussi amical qu'autrefois.*§ Why should he play the hypocrite with me? He won't ever come back to Russia, here he's among his own and quite at home, and I'm nothing to him. Old Heeckeren returned here some days ago, the first time we met, at the roulette wheel, he sort of nodded in greeting, I pretended not to see him. Then he started talking to me on his own, I replied as to a stranger. I moved away from him, thereby avoiding having to treat him like a good acquaintance. D'Anthès has sufficient tact not to talk to me about him. This week Countess Razumovskaya arrived from Ems and was kind to me in memory of all of you. I went to see her several times. The other day we put Alexandra Osipovna and her husband in a carriage and went to Düsseldorf to see an exhibition, where he bought several paintings. The Smirnovs should be back within a week, and I await them impatiently. . . . I got *The Contemporary* from them and read *The Bronze Horseman* with pure delight; too bad the best parts were censored.

---

* "she expected a scene on our return, and that's just what she got."
† "of that mean little runt of a husband."
‡ "made us laugh so hard it hurt."
¶ "He disarmed me completely by hitting at my weak point, always showing such great interest in the whole family."
§ "and I have to force myself not to be as friendly to him as before."

Epilogue

Catherine de Heeckeren died in Soultz on October 15, 1843, sent prematurely to her grave by a violent attack of puerperal fever after giving birth to the male child she'd longed for with all her heart. She died thanking God for the happiness he'd granted her after her marriage. Georges d'Anthès's unmarried sister Adèle lovingly assumed care of the four little orphans (Mathilde, Berthe, Léonie, Louis).

In November 1838, after eighteen months at Polotnyany Zavod, Pushkin's widow, their children (Marya, Grigory, Alexander, Natalya), and her sister Alexandrine went back to live in Petersburg. Baron Korff noted in his diary on May 24, 1844: "Marie Louise profaned Napoleon's bed by marrying Neipperg. After seven years of widowhood, Pushkin's wife is to marry General Lanskoy. . . . Mrs. Pushkin belongs to that circle of privileged young women to whom the Tsar sometimes deigns to pay his respects. He went to see her just a month and a half ago, and whether as a result of that visit or by pure chance, Lanskoy was named commander of a Horse Guard regiment just afterward. . . . Lanskoy was formerly aide-de-camp in the regiment of the *chevaliers gardes*. . . . Gossip has it that he had very intimate relations with the wife of another *chevalier garde* commander, one Poletika [the name means "politics"]. Now they say he has left politics to devote himself to poetry."

On July 16, 1844, Natalya Nikolaevna Pushkina married General Pyotr Petrovich Lanskoy, with whom she had three more children. She was an exemplary wife and mother. She died in 1864.

In 1852 Alexandrine Nikolaevna Goncharova married Baron Gustav Vogel von Friesenhof, widower of the goddaughter of Xavier de Maistre and Sofya Ivanovna Zagryazhskaya, the Goncharova sisters' maternal aunt. She went to live with him on his estate of Brodany, in Hungary, where she died in 1891.

To the end of his days Baron Jacob van Heeckeren-Beverweerd showered his adoptive son and the latter's large family with his affectionate and generous attentions. Returning to the diplomatic corps in 1842, he served as ambassador to Austria for many years, retiring in 1875 for reasons of age. He then returned to Georges and his grandchildren in Paris. He died in 1884, at the age of ninety-three.

After Russia, everything seemed *"petit et mesquin"* to Georges de Heeckeren. But he eventually readjusted to his native land, embarking on a political career in the late 1840s. He was elected to the National Assembly in 1848 and to the Constituent Assembly the following year. Deserting the legitimist cause, he became a supporter of Prince Louis Napoleon Bonaparte, President of the French Republic. He was named a senator in 1852. In May of that year he was entrusted with a delicate secret mission, which he carried out brilliantly: sounding out Austrian, Prussian, and Russian reactions to Louis Napoleon's plans to proclaim himself Emperor of the French. To this end, on May 10, 1852, he held a private meeting in Berlin with Tsar Nicholas I, who declared himself satisfied with the new strong government in France, though somewhat puzzled at the resurrection of the Empire. Evidently smarting from his bad experience with the negotiator's adoptive father, Nicholas insisted that "the accuracy with which Baron Heeckeren relayed his words be ascertained."

"In the duel between Thiers and Bixio, d'Anthès was the latter's second."

Georges de Heeckeren remained on friendly terms with Russians vacationing in Baden-Baden, where he visited frequently. During his long stays in Paris, he was in regular contact with the capital's large Russian colony, often appearing at the salons of Count

Benckendorff's sister Princess Lieven or Chancellor Nesselrode's niece Marie Kalergis. In 1858 Marie Kalergis married Nikolai Alexeevich Orlov, the Russian ambassador to France. Alexander Herzen had this comment: "The *fine fleur* of our aristocracy celebrated this wedding in Paris! Princes descended from Rurik along with others of more recent vintage, counts, senators, men of letters . . . joined the Russian banquet in the ambassador's home; just one foreigner was invited as an honored exception: Heeckeren, the man who murdered Pushkin. Could there possibly be a Poshekhon, Iroquois, Lilliputian, or German with less tact than these Russians?"

According to Suvorin: "Sobolevsky reported that he saw d'Anthès and spoke to him at length, asking, 'Now that it's all water under the bridge, did you have intimate relations with Mrs. Pushkin?' D'Anthès replied, 'Of course.'"

On February 28, 1861, Prosper Mérimée wrote to Alberto Panizzi from the Senate, where a stormy session had just ended: "The next speaker after H. de la Rochejaquelein was Heeckeren, the one who killed Pushkin. He's an athletic-looking man with a German accent, a stern but refined mien, a very crafty sort. I don't know whether he'd prepared his speech, but he delivered it wonderfully, with an impressive restrained violence."

A Russian correspondent commented: "D'Anthès was wholly satisfied with his fate and said more than once that he owed his brilliant political career solely to his having had to leave Russia because of the duel, that had it not been for that unfortunate duel, his would have been an unenviable future as a regimental commander with a large family and meager resources in some small town in provincial Russia."

An able administrator under the Second Empire, Georges de Heeckeren augmented his wealth by investing in banks, insurance, railroads, shipping, and gas. He left politics in 1870, but remained personally concerned with what was going on in the world. On March 1, 1880, the Russian ambassador in Paris sent a coded telegram to Petersburg: "Baron Heeckeren-d'Anthès reports news from Geneva, from what he claims is a reliable source: the Geneva nihilists say that a heavy blow will be dealt next Monday." This information may perhaps have saved Tsar Alexander II (once the dangerous Zhukovsky's pupil) from yet another attempt on his life – but a year later the nihilists hit their target.

*

"Elle était si autre que le reste des femmes!" d'Anthès, now an old man, explained to his friends. Mentally reviewing a skein of distant memories, he admitted: *"J'ai eu toutes les femmes que j'ai voulues, sauf celle que le monde entier m'a prêté et qui, suprême dérision, a été mon unique amour."**

Senator Georges de Heeckeren died in Soultz on November 2, 1895, surrounded by his children, grandchildren, and great-grandchildren. He was eighty-three. Nothing is known of his love life after his wife's death. In his descendants' family archives there is a typed copy of a letter from one "Marie,"† dated Moscow, June 10, 1845. The copy is accompanied by a meticulous description of the size of the paper, the postmark, the stamp. A pity the original was lost: otherwise we could check whether the year was in fact 1844, as we strongly suspect. Here is what "Marie" had to say:

I am convinced that you are an honest man, Georges, so I don't have a moment's hesitation in asking a sacrifice of you. I am getting married, I wish to be a good and honest wife, the man I am marrying deserves to be happy – I beg you, burn all the letters you've received from me, destroy my portrait. Make this sacrifice for my security, my future. I ask this of you in the name of the few days of happiness I gave you. You have made me think about my life, about a woman's true vocation. You would not seek to destroy your work by making my return to goodness impossible – do not write to me anymore, I must not receive a single line that my husband could not read. Be happy, as I wish, with all the happiness I dreamed of for you and that fate would not let me give you. Now we are separated forever, you may be sure that I will never forget that you made me better, that to you I owe the good feelings and sensible ideas I lacked before I met you. . . . Once again, farewell, Georges.

* "She was so different from all other women! I had all the women I wanted, except for the one the whole world thought I had, and she, supreme mockery, was my only love."
† Possibly a pen name for Natalie, since Bulgakov, director of the postal service in Moscow, was ever lying in wait.

Sources

PERIODICALS

IsV: *Istorichesky Vestnik.*

PiS: *Pushkin i ego sovremenniki,* 1903–30, I–XXXIX.

RA: *Russky Arkhiv.* (The Roman numeral indicates the number of the volume, the Arabic numeral indicates the number of the monthly issue. Most of the volumes consist of three issues, but the review did not always follow the criterion of subdivision into four volumes and twelve issues annually, so the numbers vary, sometimes within a single year.)

RS: *Russkaya Starina.*

RV: *Russky Vestnik.*

(In the case of some periodicals, the page numbers refer to what are in fact columns.)

ARCHIVES

AR Bray: Archive of the Barons von Poschinger-Bray, Irlbach Castle, Bavaria.

AR Heeckeren: Archive of Baron Claude de Heeckeren, Paris, containing, among other things: letters from Georges d'Anthès, later de Heeckeren, to Jacob van Heeckeren, and to his fiancée and, later, wife, Catherine Goncharova; letters from the Goncharov family to Georges and Catherine de Heeckeren; letters from Jacob van Heeckeren to Catherine de Heeckeren; letters from friends and acquaintances to Georges and Catherine de Heeckeren. All these documents date from the 1830s and 1840s; another part of the Heeckeren archive (which presumably contains later documents) is today the property of another member of the

Heeckeren family, who has not given permission for it to be examined and studied.

AR Munich: Bayerisches Hauptstaatsarchiv, Munich.

AR Nantes: Ministère des Affaires Étrangères, Centre des Archives Diplomatiques, Nantes.

AR Naples: Archivio di Stato, Naples.

AR Stuttgart: Hauptstaatsarchiv, Stuttgart.

AR Vienna: Österreichisches Staatsarchiv Abt. Haus-Hof und Staatsarchiv, Vienna.

GARF: Gosudarstvenny Arkhiv Rossiskoy Federatsy (formerly CGADA: Centralny Gosudarstvennoy Arkhiv Oktyabrskoy Revolyutsy, vysshikh organov gosudarstvennoy vlasty i gosudarstvennogo upravlenya SSSR), Moscow.

RGADA: Rossisky (formerly Centralny) Gosudarstvenny Arkhiv Drevnikh Aktov, Moscow. In addition to the collections cited below, the papers of the following collections were consulted (for the relevant period; that is, the 1820s to the 1840s): Apraksin, Demidov, Gagarin, Golitsyn, Yusupov, Musin-Pushkin, Saltykov, Samoylov, Shcherbatov, Sheremetev, Stroganov, Shuvalov, Tolstoy, Vorontsov.

RGALI: Rossisky (formerly Centralny) Gosudarstvenny Arkhiv Literatury i Iskusstva, Moscow. The papers of the Karamzin and Vyazemsky collections, among others, were consulted.

RGVIA: Rossisky (formerly Centralny) Gosudarstvenny Voenno-Istorichesky Arkhiv, Moscow.

TEXTS

Arapova: Alexandra Petrovna Arapova, *Natalya Nikolaevna Pushkina-Lanskaya: K semeynoy khronike zheny A. S. Pushkina*, supplements to numbers 11406, 11409, 11413, 11416, 11421, 11425, 11432, 11435, 11442, 11446, and 11449 of *Novoe Vremya*. The number of the issue and the page of the supplement are cited.

Bartenev: P. I. Bartenev, *O Pushkine*, Moscow, 1992. (The recent edition provides an almost complete anthology of the numerous testimonials concerning Pushkin's life and art that the historian Pyotr Bartenev, the editor of *Russky Arkhiv*, collected between 1851 and 1912 and published, for the most part, in his review.)

Dal: *Zapiska Doktora V. I. Dalya*, in Shchegolev II (see below), pp. 178–83.

Danzas: *Poslednie dni i konchina A. S. Pushkina. So slov byushego tovarishcha i sekundanta K. K. Danzas.* St. Petersburg, 1863.

Delo: *Duel Pushkina s Dantesom-Gekkerenom (Podlinnoe voenno-sudnoe delo 1837 g.),* St. Petersburg, 1900.

Ficquelmont I: *Il Diario di Darya Fyodorovna Ficquelmont,* edited by N. Kauchtschischwili, Milan, 1968.

Ficquelmont II: Dolly Ficquelmont, Diary 1832–37, unpublished, Státní Archiv of Dechín, Czech Republic. A typewritten copy of the text was kindly made available by Nina Kauchtschischwili. Fragments of the diary (the long entry of January 29, 1837, in which she describes Pushkin's duel, other entries in which she reports on Pushkin, his wife, Heeckeren) have been published in periodicals, both in the original French and in Russian translation, starting in 1956.

Heeckeren: Letter from Jacob van Heeckeren to Karl Vasilievich Nesselrode, February 13, 1837, in Shchegolev I (see below), pp. 184–88.

Karamziny: *Pushkin v pismakh Karamzinykh 1836–37 godov,* Moscow-Leningrad, 1960.

Naschokiny: *Rasskazy P. V. i V. A. Nashchokinykh* [1881], in Bartenev, pp. 340–64.

NM: B. L. Modzalevsky, Y. G. Oksman, M. A. Tsavlovsky, *Novye materialy o dueli i smerti Pushkina,* Leningrad, 1924.

Polyakov: A. S. Polyakov, *O smerti Pushkina. Po novym dannym,* Petersburg, 1922.

PVS: *A. S. Pushkin v Vospominaniyakh Sovremennikov,* 2 vols., Moscow, 1985.

Rosset: *Iz Rasskazov A. O. Rosseta pro Pushkina,* in RA II, 1882, pp. 245–48.

Shchegolev I: *Duel i Smert Pushkina,* in PiS, XXV–XXVII, 1916. The work was reprinted many times, considerably revised and expanded. In the case of all non-Russian texts, the reference is to the first edition, which presented numerous unpublished documents in the original language. The citation Shchegolev II, however, refers to the most recent edition of the monograph: Moscow, 1987.

Smirnov: N. M. Smirnov, *Iz pamyatnykh zapisok,* in RA, I, 1882, pp. 227–44.

Sollogub I: *Nechto o Pushkine. Zapiska Solloguba junior* [written before 1854], in B. L. Modzalevsky, *Pushkin,* Leningrad, 1929, pp. 374–81.

Sollogub II: *I*ʒ *vospominany grafa V. A. Sologuba*, in RA, 5–6, 1865, pp. 736–72.

Sollogub III: V. A. Sollogub, *Vospominaniya*, St. Petersburg, 1887.

Spassky: *Zapiska Doktora Spasskogo*, in Shchegolev II, pp. 175–78.

SZK: P. A. Vyazemsky, *Polnoe sobranie sochineny*, St. Petersburg, vol. VIII, *Staraya Zapisnaya Kniʒhka*, 1883.

Trubetskoy: *Rasskaʒ ob otnoshenyakh Pushkina k Dantesu. Zapisan so slov A. V. Trubetskogo*, in Shchegolev II, pp. 351–56.

Veresaev: V. V. Veresaev, *Pushkin v ʒhiʒny*, 2 vols., Moscow, 1936.

Vyazemskie: *Iʒ rassdaʒov Petra Andreevicha i knyagini Very Fyodorovny Vyaʒemskikh*, in RA 7, 1888, pp. 305–12.

Vyazemsky: letter from P. A. Vyazemsky to Grand Duke Mikhail Pavlovich, February 14, 1837, in Shchegolev I, pp. 139–54.

Zhukovsky: V. A. Zhukovsky, *Konspektivnye ʒametki o gibeli Pushkina*, in PVS, vol. II, pp. 391–93. (This text follows the one established by I. Borichevsky in *Zametky Zhukovskogo o gibely Pushkina*, in *Pushkin: Vremennik Pushkinskoy Komissii* 3, 1937, pp. 371–92, which in some places corrects the text published originally in Shchegolev I.)

References to Pushkin's works are to the sixteen-volume edition, the so-called academic edition: A. S. Pushkin, *Polnoe sobranie sochineny*, 16 vols., Moscow-Leningrad, 1937–49 (PSS). Works in verse are cited with title, year of publication (or of composition in the case of works that were not published in Pushkin's lifetime), and line numbers; for *Eugene Onegin* the canto, stanza, and line numbers are given.

Notes

1. Dispatches from St Petersburg

1 All of Chapter 1 is excerpted from Shchegolev I, pp. 205–45 passim.

2. The Chouan

5 "Baron d'Anthès – may his name": Smirnov, p. 233.

5 "D'Anthès, Baron Georges Charles ... murderer": So, for example, one reads in Shchegolev II, p. 557. In all the Russian sources Heeckeren is called Louis, probably because he appears under this name in the biographical sketch *Georges Charles d'Anthès*, by L. Metman. It's unclear if this is an error of Metman's or if Heeckeren was in fact so called in French. The few letters I found in AR Heeckeren bear the signature "Baron de Heeckeren."

6 one of those "ultrafashionable" types: S. N. Karamzina to Andrei Karamzin, January 9, 1837, in Karamziny, p. 290.

7 called him a "stableboy": S. M. S[ukhoti]n, *Iz vospominany molodosti (O Pushkine)*, in RA 10, 1864, p. 1086.

7 "*Pasha à trois queues*": Smirnov, p. 233.

7 "D'Anthès," Count Apraksin once: RS 112, 1902, p. 602; "Apraksin" is the only possible interpretation of the abbreviation "A-n" which appears in A. Mörder's account; it seems to refer to Count Fyodor Stepanovich.

7 d'Anthès immortalized the event: S. A. Panchulidzev, ed., *Sbornik biografy kavalergardov, 1826–1908*, St. Petersburg, [IV], 1908, p. 77.

8 "that handsome, young, insolent d'Anthès": S. N. Karamzina to Andrei Karamzin, November 21, 1836, in Karamziny, p. 282.

9 "He never took the floor": *Dictionnaire de Biographie Française*, Paris, II, 1903, p. 1482.

9 "bourgeois king": Thus in many contemporary sources and in history textbooks (for example, Malet and Isaac, *L'Histoire: Les Révolutions: 1789–1848*, Paris, 1960); for his part, Pushkin wrote on January 21, 1831, to E. M. Khitrova: ". . . The French have almost ceased to interest me. . . . Their king, with his umbrella under his arm, is too bourgeois . . . ," in PSS, XIV, 1941, p. 148.

10 "On his way through Germany": Arapova, 11416, p. 6.

12 "with forty-two passengers on board": Arapova, 11406, p. 5.

12 "landowner, twenty-two years old": *Sanktpeterburgskya Vedomosti*, October 11, 1833.

12 notify the French Embassy: AR Nantes; the registration records 1830–40 have not yet been catalogued.

12 "The interest shown in various ways": L. Metman, *Georges Charles d'Anthès*, in Shchegolev I, pp. 294–95.

13 "I cannot adequately express": Ibid., pp. 262–63.

13 "Among other letters of recommendation": Danzas, pp. 5–7.

13 a later source: [P. A. Efremov], *Aleksandr Sergeyevich Pushkin, 1799–1837*, in RS 28, 1880.

14 "Here he is considered a spy": Ficquelmont I, pp. 87, 115, 146.

15 "that old snake": A. Y. Bulgakov to P. A. Vyazemsky, February 26, 1837, in *Krasny Arkhiv* 2, 1929, p. 230.

15 "a sly man, more calculating": P. P. Vyazemsky, *Aleksandr Pushkin, 1826–1837*, in *Sobranie sochineny. 1876–1887*, St. Petersburg, 1893, today in PVS, II, p. 197.

15 "an evil, selfish man": Smirnov, p. 234.

15 "an old scoundrel, always with a smile": Rosset, p. 246.

15 "an extraordinarily amoral man": Danzas, p. 8.

15 "famous for his depravity": Vyazemskie, p. 312.

15 "a tiny miniature, but a jewel": Ficquelmont I, pp. 118, 146.

15 "He told the most amusing stories": S. A. Bobrinskaya to her husband, A. A. Bobrinsky, July 20, 1832, RGADA, folio 1412, op. 1, ed. chr. 118, l. 50 verso.

15 "was ever assumed to contain": A.-G. de Barante, dispatch of October 8, 1836, in Henri Troyat, *Pouchkine*, Paris, 1946, II, p. 343.

15 "With the son it's all over": Sollogub II, p. 765.

16 his "providential" entry: D'Anthès to Heeckeren, May 18, 1835, AR Heeckeren. (Hereafter the source of quotations from letters written by d'Anthès to Heeckeren between May 1835 and the autumn of 1836 will not be given.)

16 the French *"bon enfant"*: N. Lerner, "Novoe o Pushkine" (which offered, in Russian translation, excerpts from the memoirs of Stanislaw Morawski, 1802–53, which had just appeared in Poland), in *Krasnaya Gazeta* 318, evening ed., November 18, 1928.

16 "Today General Sukhozanet told me": Shchegolev I, p. 262.

16 "And to think I've watered my horse": V. V. Nikolsky, *Idealy Pushkina*, St. Petersburg, 1899, p. 128, note.

17 "Baron d'Anthès and Marquis Pina": *Dnevnik 1833–35* (hereafter Diary).

17 "The Empress Alexandra Fyodorovna is writing": Diary, December 4, 1833; April 8, 1834.

17 "spoke of unhappiness as of a myth": Ficquelmont II, 10 November, 1833.

18 a "daughter of air": Ibid., July 27, 1832.

18 "February 28, 1834 . . . At 10:30 we repaired": GARF, folio 672, op. 1, d. 413, l. 58. This and other brief excerpts from the diaries of Alexandra Fyodorovna were published for the first time in Russian translation by E. Gershteyn, *Vokrug gibely Pushkina*, in *Novy Mir* 2, 1962, pp. 211–26.

18n "He started out a dentist": Baron F. Büler, *Zapiska A. S. Pushkin kavaleriste-device N. A. Durovoy*, in RA I, 1872, p. 203, note.

19 "a witty and quite amusing man": AR Bray, letters of April 26, May 23, May 15, October 24, 1834; May 19, 1835.

3. *Those Fateful Flannel Undershirts*

22 "Neither in his youth nor as an adult": Cited in Veresaev, II, p. 293.

25 accused him of being a spendthrift: Shchegolev I, p. 263.

27 "The Dutch ambassador's affectionate devotion": Metman, *Georges Charles d'Anthès*, op. cit., p. 296.

29 "Blazing young colt": E. Possenti, *Milano amorosa*, Milan, 1964, p. 174.

31 "He got up to all sorts of pranks": Trubetskoy, p. 352.

32 he condemned Balzac's *marivaudage*: A. S. Pushkin to E. M. Khitrova, between August and December 1832: (". . . How can it be that you are not ashamed to have spoken so slightingly of Karr.

His novel has some genius and is quite as good as the *marivaudage* of your Balzac . . .")

32 "certain deceitful declamations": Pushkin to Khitrova, June 9 (?), 1831. ("*The Red and the Black* is a good novel, in spite of several false declamations and some observations in bad taste . . .")

32 "a practical man who came to Russia": Vyazemsky, *Aleksandr Pushkin*, op. cit., p. 197.

34 "No one here can remember": G. Wilding di Butera e Radoli, dispatch of January 3, 1836, AR Naples, collection 1713: "Russia. Its Legation. 1836–1844," [fascio] 1837.

37 d'Anthès entered the poet's circle: What Alexandrine Goncharova wrote to her brother Dmitry on December 1, 1835, we already knew: ". . . We often go dancing, every Wednesday we go horseback riding at Bistrom; the day after tomorrow we will have a grand horse show: the most fashionable young men: . . . Valuev . . . d'Anthès . . . A. Golitsyn . . . A. Karamzin . . ."

38 "like the English *Quarterly Review*": Sollogub II, p. 751, note by P. B[artenev].

39 "My dearest friend, I feel": An excerpt from this letter (and from the one quoted on pp. 59–60) was published by Henri Troyat in *Pouchkine*, op. cit. II, pp. 356–57 and 359–60. Troyat's book contained several decipherment errors – among them "Broge" instead of "Bray" (for which Troyat also proposed the reading "Brage"), thus leading to farfetched guesswork about the mysterious person's identity.

Not all Russian scholars believed Georges d'Anthès. In *Vokrug Pushkina* (Moscow, 1978;s2), I. Obodovskaya and M. Dementev went so far as to suggest that the letters Troyat excerpted "may have been written by d'Anthès much later and left among his papers to 'justify himself' in his descendants' eyes." Obodovskaya and Dementev, who have done useful research on the Goncharov family and have published valuable archival material (though only in slipshod and even erroneous Russian translations), offer a thoroughly distorted and biased portrait of Natalya Nikolaevna, one that tallies perfectly with the image of the ideal wife hailed and fostered by Soviet propaganda (tireless worker, model mother and housewife, chaste angel of the hearth, invaluable collaborator with her husband, and so on). And the post-Soviet era is having trouble jettisoning this ossified stereotype, such that even in popular literature we find statements like: "Contemporary scholars have documented Natalya Nikolaevna's innocence and shed new light on the character of this extraordinary woman, a loving wife and devoted mother. It has been remarked that Natalya Nikolaevna had a rich, deep character." (Televidenie Radio Sankt-Peterburg, January 3 and 18, 1992.) A serious scholar, S. Abramovich, writes in *Pushkin v 1836 godu* (Leningrad, 1984; 2nd ed., Leningrad, 1989; 3rd ed. – with added materials previously issued by the author plus a review by M. Y. Lotman – St. Petersburg, 1994, under the title *Predystorya posledney dueli Pushkina*) that the passages from d'Anthès's letters published by Troyat "could clarify many things if they were viewed in the context of all the letters. . . . Outside this context . . . they give rise to highly subjective judgments." But after this philologically unexceptionable observation, her tone changes: "The January letter testifies primarily to the fact that d'Anthès was gripped by genuine passion. . . . But his statements about Natalya Nikolaevna must be viewed with great caution. His 'she loves me, too' reflects arrogant self-assurance more than the reality of the situation." But even if we were to agree with Abramovich, her method is awry: why believe d'Anthès when he talks about himself while denying him credibility when he talks about Natalya Nikolaevna or reports her words?

Another scholar, relying on a single sentence – ". . . she has the same name as the woman who was writing to you about me that she was sorry but plague and famine had ravaged her villages . . ." (in which all evidence suggests that d'Anthès was referring to the "Moscow aunt," Countess Charlotta Musina-Pushkina) – set off in search of any Russian woman of the day who might fit this description and from whom d'Anthès may have requested financial help but who was not named Pushkina or Musina-Pushkina: he just couldn't seem to swallow the notion that the wife of a great Russian like Pushkin could be in love or even infatuated with a Frenchman. Someone else, once again on the basis of the passages published by Troyat (who, we know for a fact, was given complete copies of both of the letters in question by Claude de Heeckeren), speculated that d'Anthès had invented the whole thing (his love for Natalie and Natalie's for him) in an effort to make Heeckeren jealous. In other words, his letters were part of a contest of erotic jousting between homosexuals (by definition sordid by the standards of Soviet prudery).

None of this is surprising: it's all part of the Russian distrust of every word and deed of Georges d'Anthès, who has been demonized for more than a century now. And also part of the posthumous beatification of Pushkin's wife over recent decades, explicable partly as a reaction to the antipathy to her that was so ill concealed during the nineteenth century and was openly displayed by the first true scholar of Pushkin's death, Pavel Shchegolev (1877–1931). Two great female poets of the twentieth century shared that antipathy: Anna Akhmatova (who was convinced that the stupid Mrs. Pushkin, blindly in love with d'Anthès, allowed herself to become an unwitting tool of Heeckeren, who chose her for the thankless task of reporting to her husband all the things that were meant to infuriate him and drive him to his death) and Marina Tsvetayeva (who wrote: "The pure embodiment of genius and the pure embodiment of beauty. Of beauty and emptiness, that is. . . . Natalya Goncharova was simply a femme fatale, the empty space upon which all forces and all passions focus and to which they flock. . . . A beautiful woman's whole being lies in her being seen. The salon and the ballroom were the Goncharova woman's native land. Only then did she exist").

In the autumn of 1994 a book called *Legendy i mify o Pushkine* was published in St. Petersburg. Among other essays demolishing the title's "Legends and Myths about Pushkin" (though not all of either of them, by any means) is one by L. Levkovich entitled "Zhena Poeta" ("The Poet's Wife"), in which the author, a woman, tries at last to approach Natalya Nikolaevna soberly, without biased distortions. May this book find a wide readership, though I fear it will be a long time indeed before all the platitudes and ideological accretions are scraped from the Pushkin monument.

40 "scratched each other's eyes": [V. V. Lents], *Priklyuchenya lifly-andtsa v Peterburge*, in RA 4, 1878, p. 454.

4. *Herring and Caviar*

42 "lovely wife": V. I. Tumansky to S. G. Tumanskaya, March 16, 1831, in V. I. Tumansky, *Stichotvorenya i pisma*, St. Petersburg, 1912, p. 310.

42 "most beautiful wife": F. J. Timiryazev, *Stranitsi proshlogo*, in RA I, 1884, p. 313.

42 "magnificent lady of the house": A. Y. Bulgakov to K. Y. Bulgakov, February 28, 1831, in RA I, 1902, p. 56.

42 "the beautiful Natalie": S. N. Karamzina to Andrei Karamzin, July 8, 1836, in Karaminy, p. 243.

42 "glorious woman": *Priklyuchenya liflyandtsa* . . . , op. cit., p. 454.

42 "most gracious creature": V. A. Zhukovsky to Vyazemsky and A. I. Turgenev, end of July–beginning of August 1831, *Pisma Zhukovskogo k A. I. Turgenevu,* Moscow, 1895, p. 256.

42 "supple as a palm tree": *Priklyuchenya liflyandtsa* . . . , op. cit., p. 442.

42 "like a lily on its stem": Sollogub III, p. 117.

42 "like a fine cameo": From the diary of A. P. Durnovo, in B. V. Kazansky, *"Novye materialy o dueli i smerti Pushkina,"* in *Pushkin: Vremenik,* 1, 1936, p. 237.

43 "a vagueness in her gaze": The testimony of E. A. Dolgorukova is cited in Veresaev, II, p. 130.

43 "The little Goncharova girl": A. Y. Bulgakov to K. Y. Bulgakov, December 7, 1836, December 29, 1829, in RA III, 1901, p. 382.

43 "Where does that woman": A. I. Turgenev to A. Y. Bulgakov, December 7, 1836, in *Pisma Aleksandra Turgeneva k Bulgakovym,* Moscow-Leningrad, 1939, p. 198.

43 "the high-necked black satin dress": *Priklyuchenya liflyandtsa* . . . , op. cit., p. 442.

43 "the fur-lined blue velvet cape": The recollections of the "Gypsy Tanya" (T. Demyanovna) are cited in Veresaev, II, p. 100.

43 "the white dress": Rosset, p. 245.

43 "the priestess of the sun": S. L. Pushkin and N. O. Pushkina to their daughter O. S. Pavlishcheva, March 16, 1833, in *Literaturnoe Nasledstvo,* 16–18, 1934, p. 782.

43 "the loose black gown": A. I. Turgenev to E. A. Sverbeeva, December 21, 1836, in *Moskovsky Pushkinist* 1, 1927, p. 25.

43 "the boa": A. P. Kern, *Delvig i Pushkin* [1859], in *Vospominanya o Pushkine,* Moscow, 1987, p. 116.

43 "elegant white dress": Cited in Veresaev, II, p. 299.

43 "Good Lord, how you bore me": O. N. Smirnova, *Zapisky A. O. Smirnovoy,* in A. O. Smirnova, *Zapisky: Iz zapisnykh knizhek 1826–45 godov,* St. Petersburg, 1895, I, p. 181.

43 "Be my guest, read": L. N. Pavlishchev, *Vospominanya ob A. S. Pushkine,* Moscow, 1890, p. 57.

44 "I am behaving myself": Letters of August 21, September 19, 1833, c. May 5, 1834.

45 "that very witty and intelligent little animal": E. E. Kashkina to P. A. Osipova, April 25, 1831, in PiS I, 1903, p. 65.

46 "that French laundress": Cited in I. Obodovskaya and M.

Dementev, *Natalya Nikolaevna Pushkina,* Moscow, 1987, p. 29.

46 "a shattered creature": N. A. Goncharov to his father, A. N. Goncharov, May 1, 1817, in *Letopisi Gosudarstvennogo Literaturnogo Muzeya* 1, 1936, p. 435.

47 "Our second *grand soirée*": Ficquelmont I, pp. 174–75.

47 "women found her a little strange": Sollogub III, p. 118.

48 "I was expecting an outburst": Letters of September 30 (c., not later), 1832; June 30, July 14, 1834.

48 "cross-eyed Madonna": Vyazemskie, p. 311.

48 the little girl from Moscow: Letter to his wife, October 30, 1833.

48 *petites femmes*: Ficquelmont II, June 23, 1832.

49 "You like it when the dogs": Letters of October 30, November 6, 1833.

49 "Mrs. Pushkin's poetic beauty": Ficquelmont I, p. 176.

50 "I don't know why": Letters of December 8, 1831; September 25, 1832; April 19, July 26 (c., not later), 1834.

51 "The wife of Pushkin": S. A. Bobrinskaya to A. A. Bobrinsky, RGADA, folio 1412, op. 1, ed. chr. 118, l. 76 verso.

51 "I'm not stopping you": Letters of October 21, 1833; April 5, 1830.

51 "Mrs. Pushkin, the poet's wife": Ficquelmont II.

52 "All the omens are evil": From the recollections of E. A. Dolgorukova, in Bartenev, p. 369.

52 "a faithful reproduction": *Eugene Onegin* (hereafter *EO*) 8, XIV, 12–13. *EO* 8, XV, 10–14.

52 "The most beautiful yesterday": Ficquelmont II.

53 "a nice new-style landau": N. N. Pushkina to her brother D. N. Goncharov, March 11, 1833, in Obodovskaya and Dementev, *Natalya Nikolaevna Pushkina,* p. 82.

53 "Natalya Nikolaevna stood leaning": *Ocherki i Vospominanya N. M. Kolmakova,* in RS 70, 1891, pp. 670–71.

53 "young woman standing at the tomb": Alexandra Fyodorovna to S. A. Bobrinskaya, January 30, 1837, GARF, folio 851, op. 1, d. 4, ll. 154–55.

53 "Only with great effort": Postscript to a letter from N. I. Goncharova to her son-in-law Pushkin, September 12, 1833, in PSS, XV, p. 148.

54 "*âme de dentelles*": Cited in P[yotr] B[artenev], *Eshche o Poslednikh dnyakh zhizny, poedinke i konchine Pushkina,* in RA 10, 1908, p. 295.

5. The Heights of Zion

56 describe his mood as "miserable": O. S. Pavlishcheva to her husband, N. I. Pavlishchev, January 31, 1836, in PiS XXIII–XXIV, 1916, p. 210.

56 "I lose my temper": S. S. Khlyustin to Pushkin, February 4, 1836, and Pushkin to Khlyustin, the same day, in PSS, XVI, p. 80.

57 "this never requested explanation": Draft of a letter to V. A. Sollogub (early February 1836).

57 "As a gentleman and a father": Letter of February 5, 1836.

58 "On the stairway stood rows": *Listki iż dnevika M. K. Merder,* in RS 103, 1900, pp. 383–84.

60 "in vain are your perfections": *EO* 4, XIV, 3–4. See also 7, XXIV, 14; 8, XLVII, 12–14.

61 "apotheosis of the Russian woman": Dostoevsky, *Pushkin* [1880], in *Polnoe sobranie sochineny,* 30 vols., Leningrad, XXVI, 1984, p. 140.

62 *à la Balżac:* Alexei Karamzin in Karamziny, p. 154.

63 "But look, don't these features": Sollogub II, p. 754.

65 *"Il l'a troublée":* Cited in Shchegolev I, p. 59.

65 "the sly spouse . . . Faublas's disciple": *EO* 1, XII, 9–14.

67 "with no worms, no dampness": Nashchokiny, p. 364.

67 "I have received Pushkin's *The Contemporary*": *Dnevnik K. N. Lebedeva,* in RA II, 7, 1910, pp. 356–57.

68 "And on your own account": Letter of May 6, 1836.

68 "one of the most beautiful eclipses": *Sanktpeterburgskya Vedomosti,* May 2, 1836.

69 "Baron Heeckeren . . . has found": AR Stuttgart, Ministerium der Auswärtigen Angelegenheiten. St. Petersburg Relationen, 1836.

70 "three countries and two surnames": E. N. Meshcherskaya to her sister-in-law M. I. Meshcherskaya [February 16, 1837], in PiS VI, p. 96.

70 "After receiving my respects": The dispatch was published by F. Suasso, *Poet Dame, Diplomaat: Het laatste jaar van Alexandre Poesjkin,* Leiden, 1988. The passage quoted here is on p. 143.

71 "The Princess of Butera": Karamziny, pp. 234–35, 236, 243.

73 ". . . *Lord of my days!*": *Otsy-pustynniki i żheny neporochny . . .* (The hermit fathers and the chaste women . . .), 1836, 10–16.

73 *"In vain I flee":* Naprasno ya begu k sionskim vysotam . . . (In vain I flee to the distant heights of Zion . . .), 1836.

74 "Novaya Derevnya was a fashionable place": Trubetskoy, pp. 352–53.

75 The two additional players: Shchegolev I, p. 50.

75 has been called "a broomstick": P. A. Vrevsky to his brother B. A. Vrevsky, December 23, 1836, in PiS XXI–XXII, p. 397.

76 became a go-between: Alexei Karamzin to Andrei Karamzin, March 13, 1837, in Karamziny, p. 309.

76 "I'm not popular anymore": L[oeve]-V[eimars], *Pouschkine*, in Shchegolev I, pp. 253–54.

77 "All at once, after a couple of balls": Danzas, p. 8.

78 "before the eyes of the entire": Ficquelmont II, January 29, 1837; all the quotations from Ficquelmont II that appear in the text from now on are taken from this long diary entry, and so the source will no longer be noted.

78 his "too unconstrained manner": Alexandra Fyodorovna to S. A. Bobrinskaya, September 15, 1836, GARF, folio 851, op. 1, d. 13, ll. 28.

78 his "abnormally flagrant" advances: G. Vogel von Friesenholf to A. P. Arapova, March 14, 1887, in L. Grossman, *Tsekh pera*, Moscow, 1930, p. 266.

79 "The dinner was excellent": S. N. Karamzina to Andrei Karamzin, September 19, 1836, in Karamziny, p. 266.

81 "There is something that goes beyond": The Russian translations of the "Philosophical Letters," beginning with that of the "First Letter," which appeared in *The Telescope*, have never done justice to the author's style; this citation is based on the most recent French edition: P. Tchaadaev, *Lettres Philosophiques*, Paris, 1970, pp. 53–54.

82 "We have resumed our city habits": Karamziny, p. 273.

82 "We alone in the world": P. Tchaadaev, op. cit., pp. 55–56.

82 "Having read the article": M. K. Lemke, *Nikolaevskie zhandarmy i literatura 1826–1855 godov*, St. Petersburg, 1908, pp. 413, 414.

6. *Pushkin's Button*

84 "*Il aurait pu se donner*": Diary, January 26, 1834.

84 "His Majesty has been so kind": Benckendorff to Pushkin, January 28, 1830, in PSS, XIV, p. 61.

84 "In the thirties a rich American": SZK, p. 182.

85 "He told me jokingly": From the diary of A. N. Vulf, in

L. Maykov, *Pushkin, biograficheskie materialy i istoriko-literaturne ocherki,* St. Petersburg, 1899, p. 177.

85 "Several indecent expressions": Cited in S. Abramovich, *Pushkin: posledny god,* Moscow, 1991, p. 103.

85 "Yusupov asked that Solntsev": SZK, p. 159.

86 "snot-nosed eighteen-year-olds": Diary, December 5, January 1, 1834.

86 that hated "striped caftan": Letter to his wife, June 28, 1834 (c.).

87 "One day during dinner": SZK, p. 119.

88 "I'm saying I'm ill": Letter of April 20 and 22, 1834.

89 "Bibikov told me of an episode": Vyazemsky, *Staraya Zapisnaya Knizhka,* 1813–52, in *Polnoe sobranie sochineny,* St. Petersburg, IX, 1884, p. 129.

89 "policing, sedative effect": Nashchokiny, p. 364.

89 "Stratford [Lord Canning] came to Russia": SZK, p. 75.

90 "protect the oppressed": Lemke, op. cit., p. 11.

90 "Benckendorff [Count Alexander's father]": SZK, pp. 90–91.

91 "The whole business": Diary, May 10, 1834.

91 *"Ce n'est pas tout"*: SZK, p. 86.

92 "On a cold winter day": SZK, p. 246.

93 "pimping for his own daughters": *D.M.* [for M.D.] *Delaryu i A. S. Pushkin,* in RS 29, 1880, p. 219.

93 "To live without political freedom": Letters of June 3, June 11, May 29 (c., not later), 1834.

93 "For you Russia": SZK, p. 51.

93 "After all, there are set rules": Diary, April 16, 1834.

94 *"le bien-être générale"*: SZK, p. 242.

94 "My humble thanks": Diary, January 7, 1834.

94 "The dependency of family life": Letter of June 8, 1834.

94 "I stand in no one's way": Zhukovsky to Pushkin, July 3, 1834, in PSS, XV, p. 173.

94 "I forgive him": Tsar Nicholas I to Benckendorff, undated, in *Starina i Novizna* 6, 1903, pp. 10–11.

95 "I would rather be taken for inconsistent": Pushkin to Benckendorff, July 3, 1834.

95 "At a court reception": SZK, pp. 118–119.

95 "Now my ideal is a fine wife": *Otryvki iz Puteshestvya Onegina* (Fragments from Onegin's Journey), in PSS, VI, p. 201.

96 *"Il n'est pas de bonheur"*: Pushkin to N. I. Krivtsov, February 10, 1831.

96 "I am bourgeois": The testimony of Pavel Petrovich Vyazemsky is quoted in Veresaev, II, p. 81.

96 *"Le fait est que":* Pushkin to E. M. Khitrova, May 19–24, 1830.

97 a placid middle-class life: Pushkin to P. A. Pletnev, February 16, 1831 (c., not later).

97 "When cholera first appeared": SZK, pp. 121–22.

97 "teacher surpassed by his pupil": Thus Zhukovsky described himself, giving Pushkin a portrait of himself when he published the poem *Ruslan and Lyudmila.*

98 "Despite our friendship": Draft of the letter from Vyazemsky to Grand Duke Mikhail Pavlovich, February 14, 1837, in Shchegolev I, p. 158.

98 *"It's time, my friend, it's time":* Pora ... moy drug, pora ... (It's time, my dear, it's time . . .), 1834.

98 *"Bonjour,* Pouchkine!": S. M. S[ukhoti]n, op. cit., p. 981.

98 "He draped his famous almaviva": *Perebelennye stranitsy vospominanii grafa V. A. Solloguba,* St. Petersburg, 1893, p. 251.

98 "March 11, 1831. Decree": *Polnoe Sobranie Zakonov Rossiskoy Imperii,* collection II, VI, first section, St. Petersburg, 1832, pp. 224–30.

99 *couplets sceptiques*: Pushkin to Khitrova, first half of January 1830.

100 "Yes indeed, marvelous": *Severnaya Pchela,* June 18, 1836, p. 645.

100 "Why not? There are some good lines": A. V. Nikitenko, *Dnevnik,* 3 vols. [Leningrad], I, 1955, p. 178.

100 "We can picture many a poet": SZK, p. 18.

100 "poets of the Pushkin era": The notion of a "Pushkin era" in Russian culture is a twentieth-century one. *Poety Pushkinskoy Pory,* the title of an anthology published in Moscow in 1919, edited by Y. N. Vierkhovsky, was reprinted many times, establishing itself in the critical literature.

100n Zhukovsky was then living: *Ostafevsky Archiv knyazey Vyazemskikh,* St. Petersburg, III, 1903, p. 281.

101 "Some are no more": *EO* 8, LI, 3.

101 "aristocratic," "high society" wing: V. G. Belinsky, *Vtoraya knizhka Sovremennika,* [1836], in *Sobranie sochineny,* 9 vols., Moscow, I, 1976, p. 517.

101 "art for art's sake": Much nineteenth-century criticism rebelled against "art for art's sake" ("pure" art, as Belinsky defined it), beginning in the 1840s (see, for example, N. A. Nekrasov, "Zametki o Zhurnalakh," 1855, in *Polnoe sobranie sochinenii i pisem*, Moscow, IX, 1950, p. 296).

101 "knights of gentle Pegasus": *D. V. Davydovu* (*To D. V. Davedov*), 1836, 5–7.

101 *le prince-chimiste*: E. N. Meshcherskaya to her brother Andrei Karamzin, May 28, 1836, in Karamziny, p. 235.

102 "miserable anachronisms striving": These are the words Belinsky (in *Vtoraya knizhka Sovremennika*, p. 518) used disparagingly of contributors to "worldly" reviews like Pushkin's *Contemporary*.

102 "he seemed to pour out his guts": Rosset, p. 246.

103 "Countess Tolstaya used to say": SZK, p. 126.

103 "in a place where things boil": Vyazemsky, *Polnoe sobranie sochineny*, op. cit., II, 1893, p. 109.

104 "I never did understand": SZK, p. 119.

104 "historic grace": Ibid., p. 185.

104 "Orloff was a regicide": *Table Talk*, in PSS, XII, p. 177.

104 *"le néant du passé"*: Vyazemsky, *Zapisney knizhki* (1813–48), Moscow, 1963, p. 274.

104 "Many things in our past": SZK, p. 68.

104 "Pushkin's carriage": Sollogub II, p. 755.

105 *"I don't care much"*: *Iz Pindemonte*, 1836.

106 "Orderlies, choristers, scullery boys": *Gosti s'ezhalis na Dachu* . . . (The guests arrived at the dacha . . .), 1828–30, in PSS, VIII, first part, 1948;52, p. 42.

106 "The late N. N. Raevsky": *Table Talk*, p. 171.

106 "Wednesday I was at the Khitrovos'": Diary, December 22, 1834.

107 a kind of mini-encyclopedia: Belinsky, *Sochinenya Aleksandra Pushkina: Statya devyataya*, op. cit., VI, 1881, p. 425.

107 "Suvorov always observed the fast days": *Table Talk*, p. 156.

108 *"And they tell me"*: Na eto skazhut mne s ulybkoyu nevernoy . . . , 1835.

108 poetic inspiration *dryan*: *Egipetskie noci* (Egyptian Nights).

108 *". . . Vrai démon pour l' espièglerie"*: *Mon Portrait*, 1814, 1–4.

108 the "negro monstrosity": Letter to his wife, May 14 and 16, 1836.

109 "wide and very red": *Pushkin na literaturnom vechere u grecha*, in RA II, 1902, p. 253.

109 "How sad I am": Smirnov, p. 233.

110 "memory of the heart": *Otryvok iz vospominany S. A. Sobolevskogo o Pushkine*, in NM, p. 123.

110 "He was an enigmatic man": *Vospominanya Valeryana Ivano-vicha Safonovicha*, in RA 4, 1903, p. 493.

110 *"No hands have wrought"*: *Ya pamyatnik sebe vozdvig nerukotvorny* . . . , 1836.

111 "I met Nadezhdin at Pogodin's": *Table Talk*, p. 159.

111 "The chill of calm pride": *EO* 8, VII, 3.

112 "Count Kochubey was buried": *Table Talk*, p. 164.

112 "In this connection . . ." and following quotations from *Eugene Onegin*: *EO* 1, LVII, 1; 4, XVIII, 12–13; 4, VII, 1–2; 1, XLVI, 1–2; 4, XXI, 8; 4, XX, 2–13; 6, XLIV, 9–12; 7, XXIV, 8.

114 "Delwig did not like mystical poetry": *Table Talk*, p. 159.

115 "Where's Pushkin, What's he up to?": Pushkin to Delwig, mid-November 1828.

116 "At a German spa": SZK, pp. 431–32.

116 "During the Ochakov campaign": *Table Talk*, p. 173.

116 "Old K***, a tender and loving husband": SZK, p. 329.

117 *"Our tumultuous celebration"*: *Byla pora: nash prazdnik molodoy* . . . , 1836, 9–12.

117 "As for our historical insignificance": PSS, XVI, p. 172; when Pushkin learned of the repressive measures taken against Chaadaev, he did not send the letter; only the draft survives.

117 "How low we have fallen": Vyazemsky, *Zapisney knizhki*, op. cit., p. 203.

118 "Posterity will tax me": *Ocherki i vospominanya N. M. Kol-makova*, op. cit., p. 665.

118 *"L'exactitude est la politesse"*: *Zametki i aforismy raznykh godov*, in PSS, XII, p. 180.

119 *"Mў vsyé ŭchílis' pŏnemnógu"*: *EO* 1, V, 1–2.

7. The Anonymous Letters

120 *"Liza was here in the city"*: *Moe znakmostvo s Pushkinym (Iz Vospominani Aleksandry Mikhailovny Karatiginoy)*, in RS 28, 1888, p. 572.

120 the daughter's soirées: Pushkin to Khitrova, end of January 1832.

120 "had no need to read": SZK, p. 493.

121 "No, not there, that's Pushkin's": Sollogub III, p. 133.

121 "Is it not high time": Vyazemsky to A. O. Smirnova, March 2, 1837, in RA 2, 1888, p. 300.

121 "and with every fresh winter": From *Filida s kazhdoyu zimoyu*

... 1838, in E. A. Boratynsky, *Polnoe Sobranie Stikhotvoreny,* Leningrad, 1989, p. 190.

121 "She covered it like an alabaster vase": Vyazemsky to V. F. Vyazemskaya, June 3, 1830, in *Zvenya* 6, 1936, p. 264.

122 "How singular my fate": Vyazemsky to Smirnova, March 2, 1837, op. cit., p. 299.

122 "Now he, too, can say": Vyazemsky, *Zapisny knizhki,* p. 211.

122 "Christian" ... "pagan": Vyazemsky to Turgenev, April 25, 1830, in *Ostafevsky Arkhiv knyazey Vyazemskikh,* III, p. 193.

122 The "old fanatic's" ardor: Khitrova to Pushkin, August 10, 1830, in T. G. Tsyavlovskaya, *Neizvestnye pisma k Pushkinu − ot E. M. Khitrova,* in *Prometey* 10, 1974, p. 252.

122 Ermina's enraptured heart: Vyazemsky to Vyazemskaya, May 30, 1830, in *Literaturnoe Nasledstvo* 16−18, 1934, p. 806.

122 "That's what you're like": Pushkin to Khitrova, early August to mid-October 1830.

123 manifesting her "burning tenderness": Khitrova to Pushkin, March 18, 20, 21, 1830, in PSS, XIV, p. 71; May 1830, ibid., p. 92.

123 "Dear Friend," she wrote: PSS, XVI, pp. 180−81.

125 "Isn't this odd?": Sollogub II, pp. 756−57.

125 "the titan of national poetry": A. F. Voekov to A. J. Storozhenko, February 4, 1837, in PiS VI, 1908, p. 107.

125 "My little boy −": Sollogub III, pp. 116, 115, 117.

125 "Have you been married long?": Sollogub II, p. 749.

126 "The first issue was too good": Ibid., p. 752.

126 "Do you think I enjoy fighting": Sollogub I, p. 375.

128 "I've seen it already": Ibid., p. 377, and Sollogub II, p. 757.

128 "THE SUPREME COMMANDERS AND KNIGHTS": PSS, XVI, p. 180.

129 "The wife is sleeping": Shchegolev II, p. 378.

129 "Troubling the serenity of families": C. von Hohenlohe-Kirchberg, dispatch of December 17, 1836, AR Stuttgart, Ministerium der Auswärtigen Angelegenheiten, St. Petersburg Relationen, 1836.

130 "I owe the treasury": PSS, XVI, pp. 182−83.

131 "placed in an open sleigh": Shchegolev I, p. 203.

132 "Monsieur le Comte": Aimable-Guillaume de Barante, draft of a dispatch of February 4, 1837, AR Nantes, "Ambassade de France à St. Pétersbourg, Inventaire des volumes reliés de la correspondance politique, 1802−1907, 48: 1837 (Arrivée et départ)." In a rather incorrect Russian translation this letter was published as a note to the translation of Barante's dispatch in *Iʒ depeshey Barona Baranta: 1836–37*, in RA I, 1896, pp. 444–45; here the dispatch is dated February 2, 1837, and no element, internal or external, connects it to the one dated November 4.

132 *"le roi citoyen"*: See Malet and Isaac, op. cit., p. 249.

133 a "conflict between Slavs": *Klevetnikam Rossii (To the Calumniators of Russia)*, 1831, 4–5.

133 *"delenda est Varsovia"*: Pushkin to Khitrova (not later than February 1831).

133 "They shoot at our poetry": Vyazemsky, *Polnoe obranie ochineny*, prev. cit., IX, p. 200.

134 "You can't imagine how much": *Iʒ moey stariny: Vospominanya knyazya A. V. Meshcherskago*, in RA I, 1901, p. 101.

134 "anonymous letters": Sollogub II, p. 758.

135 "Notice sur Pouschkin": AR Stuttgart, Ministerium der Auswärtigen Angelegenheiten, St. Petersburg Relationen, 1837; the original, from which this is translated, presents minimal variations with respect to the text published in Shchegolev I, pp. 227–31.

136 to be an "impartial summary": N. Y. Eydelman, *Sekretnoe donesnie Geversa o Pushkine*, in *Vremennik Pushkinskoy Komissii 1971*, 1973, p. 10.

136 "Many letters even came": Ibid., p. 14. Eydelman hypothesizes that Gevers was the true author of the "Notice," which Hohenlohe would have drawn on. Glasse ("Duel i smert Pushkina po materialam arkhiva Vyurtembergskogo posolstva," in *Vremennik Pushkinskoy Komissii 1977*, 1980) claims, on the other hand, that the "Notice" should be attributed to the ambassador from Baden-Württemberg: he had lived for a long time in Petersburg and had been able to get to know Pushkin and appreciate his work, and certainly he was better informed than Gevers. This second hypothesis seems more likely, although one cannot exclude the possibility that both diplomats drew on a single source by an unknown author.

137 "a number of printed forms": Sollogub II, p. 766.

138 the "lackey's slanting handwriting": Ibid., p. 757.

139 "They say, among other things": A. N. Vulf to E. N. Vrevskaya, December 22, 1836, in PiS XXI–XXII, 1915, p. 347.

139 "a head with horns": *Pushkin i Dantes-Gekeren*, in RV 3, 1893, p. 299.

139 "One lady, in love": Voekov to Storozhenko, February 4, 1837, op. cit., p. 108.

139 "began to receive anonymous letters": I. T. Kalashnikov to P. A. Slovtsov, February 12, 1837, in PiS VI, p. 105.

139 "He was informed of the plot": Y. K. Berkgeym (Berkheim) to Raevsky, February 1837, in PiS II, 1904, p. 20.

139 "He began to receive anonymous letters": *Pushkin v vospominaniyakh i dnevnike N. I. Ivanitsogo*, in PiS XIII, 1910, p. 32.

139 "true murderer": Sollogub II, p. 768.

139 his "moral assassin": Modzalevsky, *Kto byl avtorom anonimnykh paskviley na Pushkina?*, in NM, p. 14.

139 "without those letters": Danzas, p. 10, note.

140 "To me it is truly a disgrace": The letter was published (in French and in Russian translation) by Tsyavlovskaya, *Neizvestnye pisma k Pushkinu – ot E. M. Khitrovo*, op. cit., pp. 254–55.

140 "the whispered snickering of fools": *EO* 7, XLVIII, 14; 6, XI, 11.

8. *Suspects*

142 "nameless little river": K. Gorbachevich and E. Khablo, *Pochemu tak nazvany?*, 1962, p. 159.

143 nasty case of "scarlet fever": Vyazemsky to Turgenev, October 5, 1835, in *Ostafevsky Arkhiv knyazey Vyazemskikh*, op. cit., III, p. 277.

143 "Orthodoxy, Autocracy, National Spirit": The citation here is from Y. Gordin, *Pravo na poedinok*, Leningrad, 1989, pp. 157, 159.

145 "haughty and insufficiently servile": N. I. Grech, *Zapiski o moey zhizny*, Moscow-Leningrad, 1930, p. 702.

146 "Uvarov is a scoundrel": Diary, February 1835.

146 "This is a bleak year": Pushkin to I. I. Dmitriev, April 26, 1835.

146 *"Vice-president of the Academy"*: *Na Akademii nauk . . .*, 1835.

147 *"You were dying"*: *Na vyzdorovlenie Lukulla: Podrazhanie latinskomu*, 1835, 1, 17–20, 25–26, 30–32.

147 "My compliments to the translator": Turgenev to Vyazemsky, March 9, 1836, in *Literaturnoe Nasledstvo* 58, 1955, p. 120.

147 "You don't believe it?": Y. A. Grot, *Pushkin, ego litseyskie tovarishchi i nastavniki*, St. Petersburg, 1887, p. 314.

148 "All I ask is that": Draft of a letter to Benckendorff, late January or early February 1835, in PSS, XVI (where A. N. Mordvinov is indicated. as the recipient), p. 79; it is not known whether Pushkin sent the letter, of which only the draft survives.

148 "Let not one, but two": N[ikolay] N[ikolaevich] T[erpigorev], *Rasskazy iz proshlogo,* IsV 41, 1890, p. 337.

148 "Evening at Bravura's": Shchegolev II, p. 253; in the translation the abbreviations that appear in the text are spelled out.

148 "Tsar Alexander Nikolaevich": *Moskovsky Pushkinist* 1, 1927, p. 17.

149 "ripe and even somewhat faded": *Zapiski F. F. Vigelya,* Moscow, Part 5, 1892, pp. 61–62.

149 "weakness of character": *Imperator Nikolay I i ego spodvizhniki (Vospominanya grafa Ottona de Bre. 1849–52),* in RS 109, 1909, p. 124.

149 "an extortionist, a gossip": Dolgorukov's words are cited in Shchegolev II, p. 389.

150 it was "serious": *Iz zapisok barona (vposledstvii grafa) M. A. Korfa,* in RS 102, 1900, p. 49.

150 "While Golitsyn was indoctrinating": Shchegolev II, p. 389, note.

150 "I don't want my wife": Nashchokiny, p. 358.

151 "suspected a woman": Sollogub II, p. 758.

151 "the officer Lermontov": M. D. Nesselrode to her son D. K. Nesselrode, February 28, 1840, in RA 5, 1910, p. 128.

151 "the Austrian Minister": These are also Dolgorukov's words, cited in Shchegolev I, p. 388.

152 "There is no excess": K. V. Nesselrode to I. N. Inzov, May 4, 1820, in RS 53, 1887, p. 239.

153 "My mother always believed": NM, pp. 128–29.

153 the nickname *le bancal*: Danzas, p. 9, note.

154 "Zanfteleben building, on the left": Sollogub I, p. 377.

155 "Lunch with Mrs. Karamzin": Shchegolev II, p. 249.

155 "devastated by some secret": Smirnov, p. 235.

155 "on the basis of the account": Danzas, pp. 9–10.

155 "for bad behavior and laziness": Shchegolev II, p. 412.

156 "Wallenstein in disgrace": Y. F. Samarin to D. A. Obolensky, 1844, in RA II, 1880, p. 329.

157 "hope for a post as physician": M. Zhikharev, *Pyotr Yakovlevich Chaadaev (Iz vospominany sovremennika),* in *Vestnik Evropy* 9, 1871, p. 48.

157 "His Highness has a *guaranteed* method": Shchegolev II, p. 448 (there is a photograph of the anonymous letter).

158 "In his youth he lived": Cited in Shchegolev II, pp. 425–26.

158 "Until now the ignorant gentleman": Cited in Shchegolev II, pp. 427–28; the text's enigmatic *perenos podmetnykh pisem* (lit., "transport of anonymous letters"), recopied by a scribe and corrected by Odoevsky, has been translated as "spread of anonymous letters"; in the autograph draft of the same text one reads: ". . . in the field of literature this man has practiced solely in the *writing* [italics mine] of anonymous letters" (Shchegolev II, p. 428, note); Odoevsky, copying in his diary Dolgorukov's article, in which Pushkin was also mentioned, added in parentheses: "the very man to whom Dolgorukov himself *wrote* [italics mine] the anonymous letters that were the cause of the duel" (Shchegolev II, p. 426).

158 "I have just learned": NM, pp. 20–22.

159 "On March 2, 1856": Ibid., pp. 41–42, 43.

159 "From Petersburg we hear": Cited in Shchegolev II, p. 432.

159 "Dolgorukov merrily tells of another": NM, p. 39, note.

159 "In the winter of 1836–37": *Iz zapisnoy, knizhki Russkogo Arkhiva*, in RA 8, 1892, p. 489.

160 "At one of Prince V. F. Odoevsky's": Büler, *Zapiska A. S. Pushkina . . .* , op. cit., p. 204.

160 "The thing is still not proved": Cited in Shchegolev II, p. 407.

161 "I have too much respect for Gagarin": NM, p. 21.

161 "extreme caution in speculating": Cited in Shchegolev II, p. 407.

161 "Peto": A. I. Herzen to N. P. Ogarev, May 8, 1868, in Herzen, *Sobranie sochineny*, 30 vols., Moscow, XXIX, 1963, I, p. 342.

161 "Prince Hippopotamus": Herzen to M. Meyzenburg and O. A. Herzen, June 15, 1868, ibid., p. 376.

161 "It would suffice for experts": Sollogub II, p. 768.

163 "unintelligent, arrogant, and rude": K. L. von Ficquelmont, dispatch of December 16, 1835, AR Vienna, Staatenabteilungen "Russland," III, Karton 105, 1835.

163 "You know, sir,": Pavlishcheva to Pavlishchev, December 20, 1835, in PiS XVII–XVIII, 1913, p. 203.

164 ". . . *My grandfather wasn't a pancake seller*": *Moya rodoslovnaya*, 1830, 17–24.

164 "Asiatic vice": The expression is Dolgorukov's, cited in Shchegolev II, p. 413.

164 "In those days a number": Trubetskoy, p. 356.

165 "friend" of Decembrists: Shchegolev II, p. 356.

165 "In 1836 I. S. Gagarin returns": L. Vishnevsky, *Eshche raz o* *vinovnikakh pushkinskoy tragedii,* in *Oktyabr* 3, 1973, pp. 207–15. Vishnevsky was obsessed by the idea of a Jesuit plot. Back in 1962 (in *Sibirskie Ogni,* No. 11) the "lecturer in historical sciences" published an essay ("Pyotr Dolgorukov i paskvil na Pushkina") in which he said, among other things: "We hold that the direct murderers of Pushkin, closely linked to Nicholas I's immediate entourage, were no less closely linked to the order of the Jesuits. We are convinced of this by, if nothing else, the fact that some years after Pushkin's tragedy Baron Heeckeren conducted negotiations on the Concordat with Pope Gregory XVI. . . . Negotiations of this kind were being undertaken by the Pope with various governments with the aim of freely consigning public education to Jesuit hands. Only a person considered absolutely trustworthy, a representative of militant Catholicism, a secret Jesuit devoted to bolstering the Pope's power, could have acted as mediator in this shrewd and complex maneuver. D'Anthès, too, was a fanatical Catholic." V. Pigalev, on the other hand, writes (in *Pushkin i masony,* in *Literaturnaya Rossiya,* February 9, 1979) of a Masonic plot (what else?): in May 1821, it seems, Pushkin joined the "Ovid" lodge in Kishinev (closed seven months later); a powerful foreign Masonic center, later seeking his death on charges of apostasy, chose d'Anthès as the instrument of its revenge.

But the prize for inventive nonsense in the pseudo-scientific literature on Pushkin's death goes to one E. B. Fyodorova, who in *Vestnik Moskovskogo Universiteta* 3, 1991, proposed yet another scenario for Pushkin's duel and death: "(1) Heeckeren is an intriguer and a businessman, perhaps a member of a secret society whose leaders are in Holland. (2) The secret society and Heeckeren personally have a lucrative plan which they need money to finance. (3) The publication in Europe of the memoirs of Catherine II (written in French) can generate vast profits. (4) To implement this plan it is necessary: (a) to obtain the text of the memoirs; (b) to prepare the groundwork for publication by sowing dissension between Nicholas I and the Dutch ruler, William of Orange; (c) to find a 'scapegoat' to take the blame. Heeckeren was able to pick Pushkin for the thankless and deadly dangerous role of 'scapegoat' because: – he has Catherine's memoirs . . . – he is a nobleman, but poor and saddled with debt . . . – he is under close police surveillance because of his past and does not have the right to go abroad . . . – he may have documents or know something ugly about Heeckeren and so could damage him. It was inevitable that Pushkin would enter into mortal conflict with such an enemy. . . . Heeckeren began to insinuate himself into Pushkin's home through d'Anthès, who set about courting Natalya Nikolaevna in full view of everyone. . . . The most likely hypothesis is that the serious clash between Heeckeren and Pushkin occurred in late October or early November 1836. It is possible that Heeckeren resorted to threats, and when Pushkin received the anonymous letter on November 4, he immediately realized whose work it was. . . . The blow inflicted by Heeckeren was meant to completely demoralize its victim. . . . Hence the main conclusion: Pushkin's premature demise was not the death of a poet but the tragic end of a historian in mysterious circumstances."

This "essay" has all the earmarks of the ideological police films that were long the sole entertainment offered viewers by grim state television in the Soviet era: greedy Western businessmen, juicy documents smuggled out of Russia, publishing scoops. One wonders what horrible crime Pushkin committed to deserve all this.

9. *Twelve Sleepless Nights*

167 "the ignorance of the men": *Kniga prikazov kavaliergardskogo polka*, RGVIA, folio 124, op. 1, d. 79, l. 198.
168 "Touched by the father's distress": Vyazemsky, p. 142.
169 "Stupidity! Lamentable, selfish": Zhukovsky to Pushkin, July 3, 1834, in PSS, vol. XV, pp. 172–73, 175.
170 "evening of November 6": The date proposed here is based on the contents of the letter (it seems clear that the "story" between d'Anthès and Pushkin has barely begun) and takes into consideration the days when d'Anthès was on guard duty in November 1836 (otherwise the *chevalier garde* would have had no reason to communicate with his adoptive father in writing). The letter was published, with mistakes in decipherment and the impossible date "February ?, 1837," in E. Ternovsky, *Pouschkine et la tribu Gontcharoff*, Paris, 1993, p. 182.
170 "led to demands for explanations": Vyazemsky, p. 141.
174 *"cartel verbale"*: Shchegolev I, p. 178.
175 treated him to new "revelations": Zhukovsky, p. 391. Following are Zhukovsky's notes on the events of November 4–17: *"4 novembre. Les lettres anonymes. 6 novembre.* Goncharov at my house. My trip to Petersburg. To Pushkin's. Arrival of Heeckeren. The rest of the day at Vielgorsky's and Vyazemsky's. In the evening a letter

from Zagryazhskaya. *7 novembre.* In the morning to Zagryazhskaya's. From there to Heeckeren's. (*Mes antécédents.* Utter ignorance of what had happened earlier.) Heeckeren's revelations. About
the love of his son for Katerina (my mistake about the name).
Revelation about the relationship; about the planned marriage. –
My word. – Idea of stopping everything. – Return to Pushkin's.
Les révélations. His fury. Meeting with Heeckeren. Vielgorsky
brought him up to date. Young Heeckeren at Vielgorsky's. *8. Pour-
parlers.* Heeckeren at Zagryazhskaya's. I to Pushkin. Great tranquil-
lity. His tears. What I said to him about his flirtations. *9. Les
révélations de Heeckeren.* My offer to mediate. Three-way quarrel
with father and son. I propose a meeting. *10.* Young Heeckeren to
me. I withdraw the proposal for a meeting. My letter to Heeckeren.
His reply. My meeting with Pushkin. Afterward I was rejected.
E[katerina] I[vanovna] sends me to call. What Pushk. said to Alexandrine. My visit to Heeckeren. His demand for a letter. Pushkin's
refusal. Letter in which he refers to the marriage. Meeting between
Pushkin and Heeckeren at E[katerina] I[vanovna]'s. Letter from
d'Anthès to Pushkin and the latter's rage. Again a duel. The second.
Letter from Pushkin. Note from N[atalya] N[ikolaevna] to me and
my advice. It happened at the Ficquelmonts' rout. Engagement.
Arrival of the brothers."

176 "As you know, sir,": Shchegolev II, p. 172.

177 "I am happy to know": RGADA, folio 1265, op. 1, ed. chr.
3252, ll. 126; the Russian translation of this letter is in Obodovskaya
and Dementev, *Vokrug Pushkina,* op. cit., pp. 247–49.

177 "father and son had the audacity": Vyazemsky, p. 143.

178 "stating that he renounced": Heeckeren, p. 185.

178 "It is still possible to call": PSS, vol. XVI, p. 183.

179 "I don't want you to get": Ibid., pp. 184–85, where it is dated
only *"10 novembre."*

181 "If you need a second": Sollogub II, p. 758.

181 "more scrupulously and strictly": M. von Lerchenfeld-
Köfering, dispatch of November 18, 1836, AR Munich, Bayerische
Gesandtschaft in St. Petersburg, 40, 1836.

182 "Baron Heeckeren did me the honor": PSS, vol. XVI, pp.
232–33, with the wrong recipient ("V. A. Sollogub") and the wrong
date ("November 17, 1836"). I believe that Pushkin delivered to
Zhukovsky the draft of the letter to Heeckeren on November 13,
because in his notes Zhukovsky speaks of the letter in question
before Pushkin and Heeckeren met in Mme. Zagryazhskaya's house.

182 "You are treating me": PSS vol. XVI, pp. 185–86, where it is dated "November 11–12." The new date (of both this letter and the one given on pp. 164–65) was proposed by S. Abramovich in *Pushkin v 1836 godu,* op. cit., and justified by her in *Perepiska Zhukovskogo s Pushkinyim v Noyabre 1836 g. (Utochnenie datirovki)*, in *Zhukovsky i russkaya kultura*, Leningrad 1987. This is not the only occasion on which I have agreed with Stella Abramovich in dating and interpreting documents and events. Abramovich's works are now considered the most reliable and in many respects definitive reconstructions of Pushkin's last duel. But they are not definitive in regard to some decisive documents. This is not because of ignorance (a fault of which she is completely innocent): as I mentioned earlier, this scholar's philological scrupulousness and undoubted critical intelligence are marred by preconceptions and received ideas. Most damaging is her Manichaean view, with its consequent division of the world into victims (Pushkin and his wife) and persecutors (d'Anthès and Heeckeren, of course, but also the Tsar and Tsarina, the aristocracy, etc.).

183 ". . . having become convinced by chance": Shchegolev I, pp. 175, 174.

184 "an enchanting fairy": GARF, folio 851, d. 13, l. 34.

184 "Last night I went to Vyazemsky's": PSS, XVI, pp. 186–87, where the letter is dated November 14–15.

186 "Baron Heeckeren tells me that": Shchegolev I, p. 174, where Zhukovsky's name is missing; in the original of the draft letter, preserved in AR Heeckeren, one reads, instead, "M.J.," which evidently stands for "Monsieur Joukowsky."

187 "Come to my place tomorrow": Sollogub I, pp. 378–79, and II, pp. 759–63, from which the quotations hereafter are taken, up to (p. 190, line 14).

190 "The young man": Vyazemsky, p. 144.

190 "As you wished, I have gone": PSS, vol. XVI, p. 188.

191 "to the Moyka, where": Sollogub II, p. 763.

191 *"Deeply shaken by what he read"*: PSS, XVI, p. 188.

192 "I shall not hesitate": Ibid.

193 "This may be enough": Sollogub II, p. 764 (from which the following quotations in this anecdote are also taken).

193 "My congratulations. D'Anthès": Rosset, p. 247.

194 "My dear, good Catherine": AR Heeckeren; I have dated the letter November 21, based on the reference to guard duty at the Winter Palace.

10. *Remembrance*

195 "When for mortal men": *Vospominanie*, 1828.

11. *The Deleted Lines*

196 "I'm going to read you": Sollogub II, p. 765.

197 "Dear Baron,": The two drafts of the letter to Heeckeren are in PSS, XVI, pp. 262–66; in the same volume, pp. 189–91, is the text reconstructed on the basis of the first draft. The two drafts and the reconstruction of the first published in N. Izmaylov, *Istorya teksta pisem Pushkina k Gekkerenu*, in *Letopisi Gosudarstvennogo Literaturnogo Muzeya* 1, 1936, pp. 339–48, are more nearly complete and correct. Photographic reproductions of them are in [P. A. Efremov], *Aleksandr Sergeevich Pushkin: 1799–1837*, in RS 29, 1880.

200 "How was I to react": Sollogub II, p. 765.

201 "Dear Count,": PSS, XVI, pp. 191–92; the text is the one published for the first time in Danzas. The original of the letter did not reappear until the 1970s, among the papers of Miller's descendants; today, along with other Pushkin autographs from the same collection, it is housed in the manuscript section of the Russian State Library of Moscow. As a result of this fortuitous find, N. Y. Eydelman was able to establish with almost complete certainty (*Desyat avtografov iz arkhiva P. I. Millera*, in *Zapiski Otdela rukopisey*, GBL 33, 1972, pp. 280–320) that on November 21, 1836, Pushkin did not send the letter to Benckendorff. This translation is based on the autograph text, which contains minor variations with respect to the one previously known.

203 "Yes, it was certainly society": RA 7, 1888, p. 296.

203 "perverse and still obscure": Vyazemsky to Davydov, in RA 6, 1879 (where the letter was erroneously published among those addressed to Bulgakov), p. 253.

203 "The more you think about": Vyazemsky to Bulgakov, in RA 6, 1879, pp. 253–54.

203 "Pushkin and his wife": Vyazemsky to E. K. Musina-Pushkina, in RA 3, 1900, p. 391.

203 "the unfortunate victim": Draft of a letter written by Vyazemskaya in early February 1837, in *Novy Mir*, 12, 1931 (where it was hypothesized that the recipient was E. N. Orlova; more likely it was addressed to N. F. Chetvertinskaya), p. 193.

204 "The sending of the infamous certificates": Arapova, 11416, pp. 6–7.

205 "of old man Heeckeren": Vyazemsky, p. 141.

205 "ceased receiving d'Anthès": Danzas, p. 9.

205 "I have fun with him": Vyazemsky, p. 309.

205 *"Il m'amuse, mais voilà tout"*: Diary of Marya Ivanovna Baryatinskaya, RGADA, folio 1337, op. 1, ed. chr. 8, 1. 64 verso. (This and other short passages from Baryatinskaya's diary were published for the first time in *Novy Mir* 8, 1956.)

205 "So, has your cousin's engagement": Ibid., 1. 64.

206 *"Maman* found out from Trubetskoy": Ibid, 1. 64 verso.

206 "staying at Idalie's": Letter to his wife of c. September 30 (not later), 1830.

206 "At d'Anthès's insistence": Vyazemskie, p. 310.

207 "He saw your mother": Friesenhof to Arapova, March 14, 1887, op. cit., p. 267.

208 "I am said to have encouraged": Heeckeren, p. 185.

211 One may therefore surmise: I have been unable to find confirmation of this supposition. In no contemporary source, published or unpublished, is there mention of any reception given by Maximilian von Lerchenfeld-Köfering and his wife, Bella, in the autumn of 1836 – not even among the extremely interesting Lerchenfeld papers: a few years of them are preserved in the Staatsarchiv in Hamburg. (The records of the Bavarian Embassy in Petersburg, which might have provided useful information, were lost in the wreck of the ship that was bringing them back to Germany after the outbreak of the First World War.) Nor have the available sources allowed us to date the evening gathering at the Vyazemskys' at which the "only man," d'Anthès, was present. Although I have been led to believe that d'Anthès's letter was written shortly before the illness on account of which he was granted leave from October 19 to 27, I would note the other dates when Georges d'Anthès was on guard duty (each duty lasted twenty-four hours, from noon one day until noon the next) that month: 2/3, 6/7, 10/11, 12/13, 29/30.

213 "had never *completely* forgotten": Heeckeren, p. 186.

213 "a fundamental innocence": Vyazemsky, p. 141.

214 "Pushkin suspected that Heeckeren": Ibid., pp. 141–42.

214 "Eager to separate d'Anthès": A. Akhmatova, *Gibel Pushkina* [1958], in *Sochinenya*, Moscow, 1986, vol. II, p. 98.

215 "My name has been linked": Heeckeren, p. 186.

216 "If you mean the anonymous letter": Polyakov (the French text is followed by a translation that is filled with mistakes), p. 17. A photograph of the original is in Shchegolev II, p. 438.

216 "copy of the insulting letter": Sollogub II, p. 760.

217 "... à cacheter ...": PSS, XVI, p. 266.

217 "because of the similarity": Danzas, p. 9.

217 "The paper and the seal": Akhmatova, op. cit., pp. 95–96. The first to suspect that behind that "fraudulent document" were secret aims, "comprehensible only to the recipient," was Shchegolev (see Shchegolev II, p. 227).

218 "the identical content": Danzas, p. 9.

219n "hailstorm" of them: Countess Merenberg recalled the "hailstorm" of anonymous letters, on the basis of her mother's stories, in NM, p. 127.

220 "Furious at Natalya Nikolaevna's": Arapova, 11421, p. 5.

220 "They say that the young man": AR Bray, letter of January 14, 1837.

221 "One morning d'Anthès saw Pushkin": *Mémoires d'un Royaliste par le Comte de Falloux,* Paris, 1888, I, pp. 136–37.

221 "D'Anthès was suffering from consumption": Karamziny, p. 309.

223 "He told you that I suspected": "That I suspected the truth" (*"que je soupçonnois la vérité"*) was proposed by B. V. Kazansky in "Razorvannye pisma," in *Zvezda* 3, 1934, p. 145. Izmaylov, in *Istoriya teksta pisem Pushkina k Gekkerenu,* op. cit., p. 347, note 60, also proposed *"que je comprenois," "que je concevois la vérité."*

224 "Morality in Petersburg is plummeting": Rosset, p. 248.

227 "Obviously, Natalya Nikolaevna could not": Akhmatova, op. cit., pp. 96–97.

227 "D'Anthès was a nobody": Karamziny, p. 309.

230 "with almost supernatural": Sollogub III, p. 133.

230 "What would you have done": L. Maykov, *Pushkin v izobrazhenii M.A. Korfa,* in RS 99, 1899.

230 "Today I had a long talk": Note from Bartenev to [M. P. Pogodin], *Iz vospominany o Pushkine,* in RA 1, 1865, p. 96.

231 "not to fight a duel": E. A. Karamzina to her son Andrey Karamzin, February 2, 1837, in Karamziny, p. 300.

231 "if the issue flared again": Vyazemskie, p. 308.

12. *The Bold Pedicurist*

232 "I have another remarkable bit": Karamziny, pp. 282–83.

233 "sense of moral rectitude": Heeckeren, p. 186.

233 "I love you . . . and want": Undated letter, Shchegolev I, p. 266; ibid., p. 268.

234 "Never since the world began": RGADA, folio 1412, op. 1, ed. chr. 121, ll. 10–11. The letter was published in Russian translation in *Prometey*, 10, pp. 266–69.

235 "concerned about a family matter": A. I. Turgenev to N. I. Turgenev, Shchegolev II, p. 255.

236 "What in the world": Alexei Karamzin to his brother Andrei, March 13, 1837, Karamziny, p. 309.

236 "Either the marriage is in good faith": A. P. Dolgorukova to her mother, S. G. Volkonskaya, January 30, 1837, in Kazansky, *Novye materialy . . .* , op. cit., p. 241.

236 "Devotion or sacrifice?": Alexandra Fyodorovna to E. F. Thiesenhausen, in *Pisma Pushkina k E. M. Khitrova*, Leningrad, 1927, p. 200.

236 "What the hell is this": Andrei Karamzin to his mother, December 3, 1836, in *Pisma Andreya Nikolaevicha Karamzina k svoey materi Ekaterine Andreevne*, Moscow, 1914, p. 4.

236 "My sister-in-law isn't sure": Danzas, p. 13.

236 "You're the fellow": Vyazemsky, p. 144.

237 "This bearish climate of ours": *Vospominanya V. P. Burnashova*, in RA 1, 1872, p. 1790.

237 "The baron wants me to ask": AR Heeckeren, undated letter. I have dated it December 22, 1836, because in it a ball is mentioned which d'Anthès could not have attended (because he was sick, it would seem) and at which the court would have been present and that would be the ball at the house of Princess Baryatinskaya, which took place on that day.

238 "Coming back to the gossip": Karamziny, pp. 288–89.

239 "Full of hatred for his enemy": Alexei Karamzin to his brother Andrei, March 13, 1837, Karamziny, p. 309.

239 "He was disturbed, upset": Vyazemsky, p. 145.

240 "My God, I'd be afraid": Vyazemsky, p. 310.

241 "At least take a quick look": SZK, p. 168.

242 "Count and Countess Stroganov": Heeckeren to J. Verstolk van Soelen, January 30, 1837, in Shchegolev I, p. 189.

243 "You'll take it, scoundrel": Danzas, p. 15.

244 ". . . in Mrs. Valueva's presence": Polyakov, pp. 53–54.

245 "in her relations with d'Anthès": Vyazemsky, p. 145.

245 "She has gained in composure": Alexandrine Goncharova to her brother Dmitry, [January 20–24, 1837], is in Obodovskaya and Dementev, p. 255.

246 *"histoire du lit"*: Zhukovsky, p. 392.

247 "We call ourselves writers": P. Melnikov, *Vospominanya o Vladimire Ivanoviche Dale*, in RV 104, 1873, pp. 301–2.

247 "Glory to God in the highest": *Perepiska Y. K. Grota s P. A. Plenevym*, St. Petersburg, 1896, II, p. 731.

247 "I managed to see Pushkin": I. S. Turgenev, *Sobranie sochineny*, 12 vols., Moscow XI, 1983, p. 13.

248 "I went to Pushkin's house": The testimony of G. P. Nebolsin is cited in Veresaev, II, p. 363.

248 "Shortly before his death": P. V. Annenkov, *Materially dlya biografi A. S. Pushkina*, St. Petersburg, 1873², p. 307.

249 "for a crust of bread": [*O Miltone i shatobrianskom perevoke "Poterjannogo raya" Miltona*], in PSS, XII, p. 144.

249 "D'Anthès spent part of the evening": *Listki iʒ dnevnika M. K. Merder*, op. cit., p. 384.

250 "P. suspected that his wife": *Les Mystères de la Russie*. Tableau politique et moral de l'Empire Russe . . . Rédigé d'après les manuscrits d'un dyplomate et d'un voyageur par M. Frédéric Lacroix, 1845, p. 126.

251 "Returning from the city": Trubetskoy, p. 354.

251 "At one ball Mrs. Pushkin": *Pushkin v vospominaniyakh . . . Ivanitskogo*, op. cit., pp. 31–32.

252 "It wasn't d'Anthès's bullet": Alexander Blok, *O naʒnachenii poeta* [1921], in *Sobranie sochineny*, 8 vols., Moscow-Leningrad, VI, 1962, p. 167.

252 "Could you have expected anything": *Iʒ ʒapisok . . M. A. Korfa*, op. cit., p. 574.

252 *"C'est pour ma légitime"*: Vogel von Friesenhof to Arapova, March 14, 1887, op. cit., p. 266.

252 "He claims," d'Anthès added: Sollogub II, pp. 766–67.

253 "Insane as I may be,": Chaadaev, *Sochinenya i pisma*, Moscow, 1913, I, p. 200.

253 "I suppose you've already been": Rosset, p. 247.

253 "Sunday there was a big": Karamziny, p. 297.

254 "continued to stand as a third": Vyazemsky, p. 144.

254 "Monday. Heeckeren arrives": Zhukovsky, p. 393.

255 "Allow me to summarize": PSS, XVI, pp. 221–22, where it is dated "January 26, 1837," on the basis of the copy of the letter made at the trial of d'Anthès and Danzas and published in 1900 in Delo, p. 113. The original should have been in AR Heeckeren; according to Claude and Janine de Heeckeren, that's where it was for many years, but there is apparently no sign of it today. The copy Pushkin made for himself is undated. D'Anthès, Danzas, Turgenev, and Heeckeren maintained that the letter was written on January 26, and the "26 janvier" in Delo seems to speak unequivocally for that date. But this may have been a slip of the pen by Pushkin or the copyist, since Vyazemskaya's detailed testimony immediately after Pushkin's death (see below in the text) argues clearly for the twenty-fifth, as does that of S. N. Karamzina, M. A. Gorchakova, Baron von Liebermann, and Vyazemsky. It is hard to imagine why Vyazemskaya would have confected her conversation with Pushkin on the evening of January 25 out of whole cloth ("... he has no idea what's waiting for him at home," "did you write to him?" and so on), especially since, according to her own account, she and her husband did nothing to try to prevent the duel and therefore might be regarded by their correspondents as guilty of failing to help and of tacitly abetting a crime. It is therefore impossible that Vyazemskaya was lying out of vanity. We must also decisively rule out the hypothesis that Pushkin, fearing that someone might interfere in his "family matter" by preventing the duel, told Vyazemskaya that he had already done what he was in fact only preparing to do the next day. In other words, to this day it is impossible to establish with certainty exactly when Pushkin wrote and sent the letter to Heeckeren. I personally believe Princess Vyazemskaya, but if Pushkin wrote the letter on the morning of January 26 and had it delivered to Heeckeren by messenger, the consequences would have been exactly the same.

257 "What amuses me is to see": Letter from Vyazemskaya [to Chetvertinskaya], early February 1837, op. cit., p. 189.

257 "Could I let it go": Heeckeren, p. 187.

257 "Challenge the author": Heeckeren to Verstolk van Soelen, op. cit., p. 190.

258 "Not being familiar": PSS, XVI, p. 223.

258 "merry, full of life": Turgenev to his cousin A. I. Nefedeva, January 28, 1837, in PiS VI, 1908, p. 48.

259 "The Tsar knows all about it": M. I. Semevsky, *K biografi*

Pushkina, in RV 11, 1869, p. 90. According to Vrevskaya, Pushkin said: ". . . the Emperor, who is acquainted with all my affairs, has promised to take them [his children] under his protection." I have slightly modified this testimony, which was obviously influenced by the recollection of what the Tsar did after his death, to make it coherent: the Tsar would never have promised Pushkin to take care of his future orphans, implicitly authorizing, almost pushing him toward, the duel.

259 "a long and interesting chat": I. T. Lisenkov to P. A. Efremov, April 25, 1874, in *Russkaya Literatura* 2, 1971, p. 111.

259 "The undersigned informs Mr. Pushkin": PSS, XVI, p. 224.

259 the "sick parrot": Rosset, p. 248.

260 "He awoke cheerful at eight": Zhukovsky, p. 392. Here are the notes on the first half of January 27: "He awoke cheerful at 8. – After tea he wrote a great deal – until 11. At 11 lunch. – He walked back and forth in the room, unusually cheerful. Then he saw Danzas from the window and welcomed him eagerly at the door. A few minutes later he sent him to get the pistols. – After Danzas left, he began to dress; he washed, put on all clean linen; ordered the bekesh to be brought; went out on the steps. He went back in, – ordered the long fur coat to be brought to his study, and went on foot to get a carriage. – It was exactly one o'clock. – He didn't come home until after dark." My reconstruction is based on these notes, which Zhukovsky wrote very soon after the events, evidently gathering testimony from Pushkin's family and servants. Subsequently everyone claimed, including Pushkin himself, that he and Danzas had run into each other by chance on the street; this was clearly an effort to mitigate Danzas's legal culpability. Some details of the available testimony confirm it, but I seriously doubt that Pushkin, however ice-cold and impassive he may have been in the face of death, would have been standing by a window just a few hours before a duel for which he had yet to find a second and just happened to notice Danzas, who just happened to be coming to see him. Since it seems obvious that he was waiting for him, we must assume that he'd written to him asking him to come. As for "He didn't come home until after dark," this is probably what Zhukovsky heard from Natalya Nikolaevna and Kozlov just after Pushkin's death or even during his death agony, when many things were still unclear. We know for a fact that Natalya Nikolaevna wasn't home in the early afternoon of January 27, and Kozlov was presumably nowhere near the master's rooms (some of the Pushkins' servants lived in tavern basements) when Pushkin came back and wrote to Ishimova. Our certainty that he returned home after going to the French Embassy with Danzas arises from the fact that the letter to Ishimova was posted soon after three in the afternoon (she recalled: "He sent a servant with the letter and the book just before setting out to meet death"). Zhukovsky himself would later write to Pushkin's father: "He left the arrangements to Danzas and d'Archiac and went home. . . . An hour before going out to the duel he wrote to Ishimova."

260 "It is indispensable that I meet": PSS, XVI, p. 225.

260 "Viscount, I haven't the slightest intention": Ibid., pp. 225–26.

262 "I would have stood": S. Sobolevsky, *Tainstvennya primety v zhizny Pushkina*, in RA, 1870, p. 1387.

263 "*weisser Ross, weisser Kopf*": M. P. Pogodin, *Prostaya rech o mudrenykh veshchakh*, Moscow, 1875³, p. 23.

263 "There are two kinds": Vyazemsky, p. 1435.

263 "This is my second": Danzas, p. 19.

264 "Dear Madam, I am truly sorry": PSS, XVI, pp. 226–27.

264 "The two adversaries will stand": Shchegolev I, pp. 176–77.

13. *Table Talk*

266 "Pavel Isaakovich Hannibal": Pavlishchev, *Vospominanya . . .* , op. cit., p. 22.

266 "Pushkin loved his friend": Bartenev (based on the recollections of V. I. Dal), *Pushkin v yuzhnoy Rossii*, Moscow, 1914, pp. 101–2, note 68.

267 "Pushkin and Korff were living": Pavlishchev, *Vospominanya . . .* , p. 33.

267 "One morning at exactly 7:45": From I. I. Lazhechnikov, *Znakomstvo moe s Pushkinym*, cited in Veresaev, II, pp. 130–32.

268 "In late October 1820": *Iz dnevnika i vospominany I. P. Liprandi* in RA, 1866, pp. 1413–16.

269 "Pushkin and Lyudmila were taking": V. A. Yakovlev, editor, *Otzyvy o Pushkine s yuga Rossii*, Odessa, 1887, pp. 90–91.

270 "Once he was talking": *Iz dnevnika i vospominany I. P. Liprandi*, p. 1245, note 22.

270 "Usually we played *stoss*,": Bartenev, *Pushkin v yuzhnoy Rossii*, pp. 101–3.

270 "One evening at the casino": Ibid., pp. 106–8.

271 "There was a rumor": *Iz dnevnika praporshchika F. N. Luginina*, in *Literaturnoe Nasledstvo* 16–18, p. 674; Luginin's diary entry is from June 15, 1822.

271 "Once, in Moldovia": Kalashnikov to Slovtsov, February 12, 1837, op. cit., pp. 105–6.

271 "I don't recall the details": Dal, *Zapiski o Pushkine*, [1907], in PVS, vol. II, p. 265.

271 "Pushkin used to carry": M. N. Longinov, *Pushkin v Odesse*, in *Bibliograficheskie Zapiski* 18, 1859, p. 553.

272 "An old friend of the poet": Bartenev, *Zametka o Pushkine*, in RA, 1865, pp. 390–91.

272 *"Now they have stepped"*: EO 6, XXX, 9–12; XXXI, 1–6.

14. *The Man for Whom We Were Silent*

273 "but Pushkin's wife was nearsighted": Danzas, p. 22.

273 "You're late": The testimony of Augusta von Hablenz (née Lützerode) is in *Literaturnoe Nasledstvo*, 58, p. 138.

273 "Where are you going": Danzas, p. 23.

273 "whom to turn to": M. N. Longinov, *Poslednie dni zhizni i konchina A. S. Pushkina* [1863], in PVS, II, p. 382.

274 *"Voilà deux ménages"*: Shchegolev II, p. 378.

274 "It makes no difference to me": Danzas, pp. 24–25.

275 "It doesn't matter anyway": Vyazemsky to Davydov, op. cit., pp. 249–50.

275 "It's still not over": Annenkov, *Materialy dlya biografi...*, op. cit., p. 420.

275 "It was only a heavy contusion": *Pismo V. A. Zhukovskogo k S. L. Pushkinu v pervonachalnoy redaktsii*, in Shchegolev II, p. 155, with the draft of a long, detailed letter about the duel and the death of Pushkin, dated February 15, 1837, which Zhukovsky wrote to the poet's father (who was living in Moscow at the time). Under the title *Poslednie minuty Pushkina*, the letter, whose reliability is often undermined by the desire to idealize the poet's end, was published in a mutilated version (due to self-censorship) in the fifth issue of *The Contemporary*, the first to come out after Pushkin's death.

275 "The bullet passed through his arm": S. N. Karamzina to her brother Andrei, January 30, 1837, Karamziny, p. 298.

276 "ricochet like a Ping-Pong ball": M. Komar, *Pochemu pulya Pushkina ne ubila Dantesa*, in *Sibirskie Ogni* 1, 1938, pp. 135, 137, 136.

277 "Duel or homicide?": V. Safronov, *Poedinok ili ubiystvo?* in *Neva* 2, 1963, pp. 200, 202, 203.

277 "Last winter the mystery": A. Vaksberg, *Prestupnik budet nayden*, Moscow, 1963, pp. 97–98.

277n "absolutely the same": Danzas, p. 21.

278 "one thing he couldn't do": Cited in M. Yashin, *Istorya giveli Pushkina*, 5, in *Neva* 12, 1969, p. 188.

278 "For the moment": Yashin, op. cit.

279 "Pushkin did not conceal": Vyazemsky, p. 310.

279 "I'm afraid it's like Shcherbachev's": Danzas, p. 27.

279 "You must be sorry": Zhukovsky, p. 393.

280 "*N'entrez pas*": Zhukovsky. Following are the notes relevant to the afternoon and evening of January 27: "Danzas comes in, asks: Is the lady at home? – The servants got him out of the carriage. – The manservant took him in his arms. Are you sorry you have to carry me? – he asked. He met his wife in the hall – fainting – *n'entrez pas*. They laid him on the sofa. Chamber pot. He undressed, and put on clean linen. He ordered everything himself; then he went to bed. Danzas was beside him. His wife came in when he was dressed and they had already sent for Arendt. – Zadler – Arendt around nine."

280 "Calm down, none of this": Turgenev to Nefedeva, January 28, 1837, op. cit., p. 50.

280 "What do you think": *Zapiska doktora Sholka*, in Shchegolev II, pp. 174–75 (from which the following quotations are taken, up to p. 290, line 7).

281 the testimony of Spassky: Spassky's testimony, written on February 2, seems very precise: "At the patient's house I found Arendt and Zadler. . . . On leaving, the doctors turned the patient over to me. At his friends' and relatives' wish, I spoke to him of his Christian duties. He immediately agreed. . . . Dr. Arendt returned at eight. They left him alone with the patient. In the presence of Dr. Arendt the priest arrived, too." On the other hand, the testimony of the Vyazemskys and especially of Zhukovsky clearly strives to emphasize the Tsar's beneficent role in Pushkin's dying a Christian, so our version could be closer to the truth. But it's hard to understand why Turgenev would have written at nine in the morning on January 28: "The sovereign sent Arendt to tell him that he would be very pleased and would pardon him if he confessed and took communion. Pushkin cheered up, had them send for the priest." Turgenev – who incidentally mentions only an oral message and was still unaware of any note from the Tsar – arrived at Pushkin's at about eleven (he'd been at a soirée at the Shcherbatovs', where Grigory Skaryatin told him of the duel, and he stopped by the Meshcherskys' on his way) and stayed until midnight. He then returned to the Meshcherskys', where he stayed until two, then went back to Pushkin's until four. He was therefore probably not a direct witness to the events in question and could report them only because he'd heard from people who'd spent continuous hours with the dying poet. Perhaps the Vyazemskys and Zhukovsky deliberately decided to modify reality for the better, thinking of the future of the widow and orphans, for whom the Tsar's protection would be indispensable. As for Zhukovsky's notes on Pushkin's death, they read: "Spassky. Wife and Grech. He asks forgiveness. They go away. Suffering at night. Return of Arendt. The courier. Arrival of Arendt. The note [from the Tsar]. Confession and communion." He had originally written "Suffering at night. Return of Arendt" at the end of this section of his notes, but later moved the two short sentences to their present position. That would seem to demonstrate that he was at least uncertain as to the actual sequence of events.

281 "We managed to convince him": Turgenev to Nefedeva, February 1, 1837, in PiS VI, p. 66.

282 "Yes, it's bad": Spassky, p. 176 (from which the following quotations are taken, up to line 23).

282 "Poor girl, poor girl": Vyazemsky to Bulgakov, February 5, 1837, in RA 6, 1879, p. 244.

282 "Ask the Tsar to pardon me": *Pismo V. A. Zhukovskogo . . .*, op. cit., p. 158.

283 "The patient's exceptional presence": Spassky, p. 177.

283 "If God wills that we": Turgenev to Bulgakov, January 28, 1837, in PiS VI (where the recipient is said to be unknown and the letter is erroneously dated January 29), p. 53.

283 "Everything goes to my wife": Spassky, p. 176.

283 "He's not going to die": Turgenev to Bulgakov, January 28, 1837, op. cit., p. 53.

283 "His misfortune began in 1836": Longinov, op. cit., p. 382.

284 "Why such torture?": Spassky, p. 176.

284 "Go to the country": Vyazemskie, p. 311.

284 "If I see the Tsar": *Pismo V. A. Zhukovskogo* . . . , pp. 162–63.

284 "Tell him I'm sorry": Vyazemsky to Bulgakov, February 5, 1837, p. 244.

284 "*Quelque chose me dit*": Turgenev to Bulgakov, January 28, 1837, p. 53.

285 "The first half of the night": Modzalevsky, *Byulleteni o sostoyanii zdorovya Pushkina 28 i 29 Janvarya 1837 goda*, in *Pushkin: Vremennik Pushkinskoy Komissii* 3, 1937, p. 395.

285 "to die in peace": Spassky, p. 177.

285 "Things are bad, friend": Dal, pp. 178, 179.

286 "How long do I have to go on": Ibid., p. 179.

286 "It's here," he said: Vyazemsky to Bulgakov, February 5, 1837, p. 245.

286 "That's fine, it's perfect": Dal, pp. 179, 180.

287 "The patient's condition": Modzalevsky, *Byulleteni* . . . , p. 395.

287 "I think I will": Turgenev to Nefedeva, January 28, 1837, pp. 51, 52, 53.

287 "*Moroshki, moroshki*": *Pismo V. A. Zhukovskogo* . . . , p. 168, note 9.

287 "Don't worry," he said: Dal, p. 181.

287 "You'll see," she said to Spassky: *Pismo V. A. Zhukovskogo* . . . , p. 169.

287 "He's going.": Dal, p. 181.

288 "That's good": Spassky, p. 177.

288 "I'm having trouble breathing": Dal, p. 181.

288 "His wife still doesn't believe": Turgenev to Bulgakov, January 29, 1837, p. 56.

15. *The Ambassador's Snuffbox*

289 "When the abdominal cavity": Dal, pp. 181–82.

289 "How light he is!": *Iz zapisnykh knizhek, Russkogo Arkhiva*, in RA 6, 1889, p. 356.

289 "Frightful, frightful": Turgenev to Nefedeva, January 28, 1837, op. cit., p. 52.

291 "kept sprinkling the deceased's head": The recollections of V. N. Davydov are cited in Veresaev, II, p. 440.

291 "women, the elderly, children": E. I. Meshcherskaya to her sister-in-law M. I. Meshcherskaya, February 16, 1837, in PiS VI, p. 96.

291 "officials, officers, merchants": S. N. Karamzina to Andrei Karamzin, February 2, 1837, Karamziny, p. 300.

292 "Poor Pushkin" wrote the grieving censor: Nikitenko, *Dnevnik*, prev. cit., I, pp. 194, 178, 196.

294 "Turgenev or Prince Vyazemsky": A. I. Turgenev to his brother N. I. Turgenev, February 28, 1837, in PiS VI, p. 92.

294 "He departed this vale of tears": *Severnaya Pchela* 24, 1837, January 30.

294 "The sun of our poetry": *Literaturnye pribavlenya k Russkomu Invalidu* 5, 1837.

294 "What was the meaning": [P. A. Efremov], *Aleksander Sergeyevich Pushkin: 1799–1837*, in RS 28, 1880, p. 537.

295 "Afflicted by the deepest pain": *Severnaya Pchela* 24, 1837, January 30.

296 "Look at them, will you": *Moe znakomstvos A. S. Pushkinym . . .* , op. cit., p. 572.

296 "*One in the afternoon*": PiS VI, pp. 67–68.

297 "After this event": Polyakov, pp. 36–37, 39, 41.

298 "a devastating condemnation": E. S. Uvarova to Zhukovsky, January 31, 1837, in PiS VI, p. 64.

298 "In general this second society": Karamziny, p. 301.

299 "*wie ein grosser Kerl*": GARF, folio 672, d. 415, l. 15.

299 "I've heard two conflicting versions": *Pushkin i Dantes-Gekeren*, op. cit., pp. 299–303.

300 "few lines exonerating his personal behavior": Shchegolev I, p. 183.

300 "If I might be permitted": Ibid., p. 193.

300 "of Baron d'Anthès, Kamerger Pushkin": Delo, p. 14.

301 "tragic event that ended": Shchegolev I, p. 170.

301 "The event has stirred countless rumors": RS 110, 1902, p. 226.

301 "chamber pot": A. O. Smirnova, *Avtobiografya*, Moscow, 1931, p. 182.

302 "too enthralled by military ideas": M. von Lerchenfeld-Köfering, dispatch of May 28, 1836, AR Munich, Bayerische Gesandtschaft in St. Petersburg 40, 1836.

302 "*trop célèbre Poushkin*": Nicholas I to his sister Anna Pavlovna, February 3, 1837, in Shchegolev I, p. 170.

302 "I feel sorry for the poet": Cited in Veresaev, vol. II, p. 464.

302 "an old friend of the deceased": Benckendorff to Stroganov, February 2, 1837, in PiS VI, p. 69.

303 "Winter! The peasant celebrating": *EO* 5, II, 1.

303 "Most esteemed Alexei Nikitich": A. N. Mordvinov to A. N. Peshchurov, February 2, 1837, in PiS VI, pp. 109–10.

304 "Moscow society is quite concerned": RGADA, folio 1278, op. 1, ed. chr. 148, ll. 35, verso 36.

305 "Those papers that could damage": Shchegolev II, p. 198.

305 "Many saw it as a chance": Smirnov, p. 237.

306 "Just after the duel": AR Stuttgart, Württembergische Gesandt-schaft St. Petersburg 1808–93, 1837; it is the draft of the dispatch, which differs significantly from the text sent to Stuttgart and published in part in Shchegolev II.

306 "Of what expressions did the letters" and all further citations from the court records: Delo, pp. 61–78, 107.

311 "I heard from General Dubelt": Shchegolev II, pp. 210–13, 217; this second draft of a letter to Benckendorff, written between February and March 1837, survived among Zhukovsky's papers; it is unknown whether or not the letter was actually sent.

311 "What can you have to fear": Vyazemsky, pp. 151–52.

312 "Natalya Nikolaevna left": PiS I, 1903, pp. 57–58.

312 "Wasn't it one Tibeau": Polyakov, p. 26.

312 address of one "Viskovskov": Ibid., p. 29.

313 "And this? It's Tibeau's": *Skupoy Rytsar (The Avaricious Knight)*, 1830, scene ii, 52–53.

314 "You were right to think": Karamziny, p. 306.

314 "I confess that the whole thing": William of Orange to Nicholas I, March 8, 1837, *Zapiski Otdela rukopisey*, GBL 35, 1975, p. 202, note.

315 "Great personal courage is one": Ibid., pp. 227–28.

316 "Let the sentence be carried out": Delo, p. 140.

316 "I cannot resign myself": Shchegolev I, pp. 270–71.

317 with a hypocritical *"p.p.c."*: Luigi Simonetti, dispatch of April 3, 1837, Shchegolev I, p. 217.

317 "It's a pity he didn't die": Vyazemsky to Davydov, Feb. 5, 1837, op. cit., p. 245.

318 "In the wife's defense": Vyazemskaya [to N. F. Chetvertin-skaya], early February 1837, op. cit., p. 193.

318 "shame and disgrace to Russian women": From a lyric by an unknown author found in the Vrevsky Archive, in PiS XXI–XXII, 1915, p. 401.

318 *"Drag yourself into the desolate desert"*: The lyric, published in *Moskovskie Vedomosti*, 136, 1857, was republished in Kazansky, *Gibel*

Pushkina: Obzor literatury za 1837–1937, in *Pushkin: Vremennik Pushkinskoy Komissii* 3, p. 450.

16. One Summer in Baden-Baden

320 "June 28 . . .", "July 4 . . .", "July 15": *Pisma Andreya Nikolaevicha Karamzina k svoey materi* . . . , op. cit., pp. 86–87, 88, 89–90.

Epilogue

323 "Marie Louise profaned Napoleon's bed": From the unpublished diary of M. A. Korf, cited in E. Gershteyn, *Vokrug gibeli Pushkina*, op. cit., p. 226.

324 *"petit et mesquin"*: Mikhail Pavlovich to his brother Nicholas I, June 2, 1837, in RS 110, 1902, p. 230.

324 "the accuracy with which Baron Heeckeren": Cited in L. Grossman, *Karera d'Antesa* [1935], in *Zapiski Darshiaka: Pushkin v teatralnykh kreslakh*, Moscow, 1990, p. 441.

324 "In the duel between Thiers": S. A. Panchulidzev, editor, *Sbornik Biografy Kavalergardov* . . . , op. cit., [vol. IV], p. 89.

325 "The *fine fleur* of our aristocracy": A. I. Herzen, *Sobranie sochinenii*, 30 vols., Moscow, XIII, 1958, p. 349.

325 "Sobolevsky reported that he": The passage from the diary of A. S. Suvorin, who recorded what P. A. Efremov told him, is cited in Veresaev, II, p. 476.

325 "The next speaker": *Lettres de Prosper Mérimée à Panizzi*, vol. I, Paris, 1881, pp. 178–80.

325 "D'Anthès was wholly satisfied": *Poslednie novosti* 3340, 1930.

325 "Baron Heeckeren-d'Anthès communicates": Cited in Grossman, *Karera d'Anthès*, op. cit., p. 450.

326 *"Elle était"*: Arapova, 11416, p. 6.

326 "I am convinced": As I say, only the postmark would be convincing, since experience has taught me to be suspicious of dates written at the beginning of letters. On the basis of a letter dated May 15, 1837, from Natalya Ivanovna Goncharova to her daughter Catherine in Soultz (". . . you write me about your trip to Paris; who will take care of the child while you're away?"), L. P. Grossman concludes that Mathilde-Eugénie de Heeckeren was born not on October 19, 1837 (by the Western calendar, of course), as her parents stated at the town hall in Soultz, but long before. Not everyone believed that this was a slip of the pen on Natalya Ivanovna's part, and the evidence of Catherine Goncharova's pre-marital pregnancy seemed to cast telling new light on the background of her unexpected marriage to d'Anthès. But Stella Abramovich recently cleared the matter up: in the same letter the mother of the Goncharov sisters speaks of the marriage of her son Ivan, and this wedding took place on April 27, 1838. The error in the date on the letter was therefore obvious. I, too, on the basis of the quite visible date (January 30, 1838, new style) on a letter that Anastasie Khlustina de Circourt, a childhood friend of Catherine Goncharova, wrote to her from Paris, believed for some time that I had come up with documentary evidence of my suspicion that the Heeckerens lied when they declared that their first child was born on October 19. In her letter Anastasie de Circourt recalled "little Mathilde," whom she'd seen in Plombières-les-Bains, alive, blooming, and utterly charming, last August — in other words, August 1837. Only after managing to read other parts of the letter that were far more difficult to decipher did I realize that it had to date from January 1839, not 1838 (though many other details and circumstances still incline me to believe that Catherine Goncharova was in a family way when she married d'Anthès). I am also convinced that ladies of the era, or at least the Goncharov sisters and their friends, had a penchant for mixing up years, however disastrous the practice may have been for scholars. We therefore have every right to be suspicious. As for the postmark, in transcribing the date Claude de Heeckeren could have been influenced by what he read (or thought he read) more clearly in "Marie's" letter. Moreover, as I can attest having read other documents of the same era held in the Heeckeren archive, postmarks are often faded and illegible.

Index of Names

from 1835 extraordinary ambassador from the Kingdom of Naples and the Two Sicilies to Petersburg, 2, 34, 58, 242

Butera e Radoli, Varvara Petrovna (Barbara, 1796–1870), Princess of; née Princess Shakhovskaya; in her first marriage Countess Shuvalova, in the second Countess Polier, 58, 71–2, 242

Byron, George Gordon (1788–1824), Lord, 206, 302

Canning, Stratford (1786–1880), British diplomat, 89

Catherine II (Catherine the Great, 1729–1796); from 1762 Empress, 91, 95, 104, 117, 143, 241

Cavour, Camillo Benso, Count (1810–61)

Chaadaev, Pyotr Yakovlevich (1794–1856); joined the military, fought in the Battle of Borodino; from 1816 ensign in the Hussar Guards stationed at Tsarskoe Selo, resigned as captain in 1821; member of the Union of the North, the secret Decembrist organization; Freemason; left Russia in 1823, he returned in 1826 and settled in Moscow, where in 1836, after the publication of the "First Philosophical Letter," he was placed under medical and police surveillance; political journalist, philosopher, 81, 82, 117, 123, 154, 157, 253

Charles X (1757–1836), King of France, 1824–30, 9, 70, 181, 187, 234

Chateaubriand, François-René de (1768–1848), 96, 129, 249

Cherkassky, Mikhail Borisovich (1813–18?), Prince; lieutenant in the Horse Guards; on

October 27, 1835, he was transferred to the Glukhovskoy Cuirassiers, 31

Cornwall, Barry (pseudonym of Bryan Wallar Procter, 1784–1874); English poet, 264

Dal, Vladimir Ivanovich (1801–72); doctor, writer, lexicographer, author of a valuable *Dictionary of the Living Language of Greater Russia*, undertaken at Pushkin's suggestion, 247, 285–8, 292

Danzas, Konstantin Karlovich (1801–70); from 1827 staff captain in the detached company in the Caucasus, from 1836 lieutenant colonel in the 3rd Reserve Battalion of Engineers, later major general; decorated many times for valor in combat; Pushkin's classmate at the Tsarskoe Selo lyceum and his second in the duel with d'Anthès, 13, 14, 17, 77, 128–9, 139, 155, 160, 174, 205, 217, 218, 236, 260, 261, 263, 264, 273–6, 277nn, 279–85, 287, 288, 300, 302, 307–10, 312, 316

Davydov, Denis Vasilievich (1784–1839); Hussar; fought against Napoleon in 1812; lieutenant general, retired 1832; poet, military writer, member of Arzamas, 100, 317

Delavigne, Jean-Casimir (1806–88); French dramatist, 235n

Delwig (Delvig), Anton Antonovich (1798–1831), Baron; Pushkin's classmate at the Tsarskoe Selo lyceum; a government official, after 1824 he devoted himself to literary activity; poet, editor of literary almanacs, 101n